REEL LIFE

An autobiocinememoir

by

TONY SLOMAN

Published by
QUOIT MEDIA LIMITED
www.quoitmedia.co.uk

QUOIT

This paperback edition first published in 2021 by Quoit Media Limited, Brynmawr, Llanfair Caereinion, Powys, SY21 0DG. This first reprint published 2022.

For more copies of this book, please email quoit@quoitmedia.co.uk

ISBN 978-1-911537-15-1

A CIP catalogue record for this book is available from the British Library.

Design: Rick Davy. Cover design: Alan Hayes. Proofreading: Mary Dockwrey. All photos © the author apart from: Page 151 © Rick Davy, pages 157, 162 © QML, page 261 © Globe.

Printed and bound in Great Britain by Clays Ltd, Elcograf S.p.A.

FSC
www.fsc.org
MIX
Paper from responsible sources
FSC® C018072

For my sons -
Jonathan and David
and also for
Rick Davy, without whom...

"They say...What say they?...Let them say!"

---- Julian Sloman (1913 - 1977)

(Quotation attributed to both George Reith, 1638 - 1716, 5th Marshal of Aberdeen College, Scotland, and also to Bishop George Berkeley, 1685 - 1763).

REEL ONE

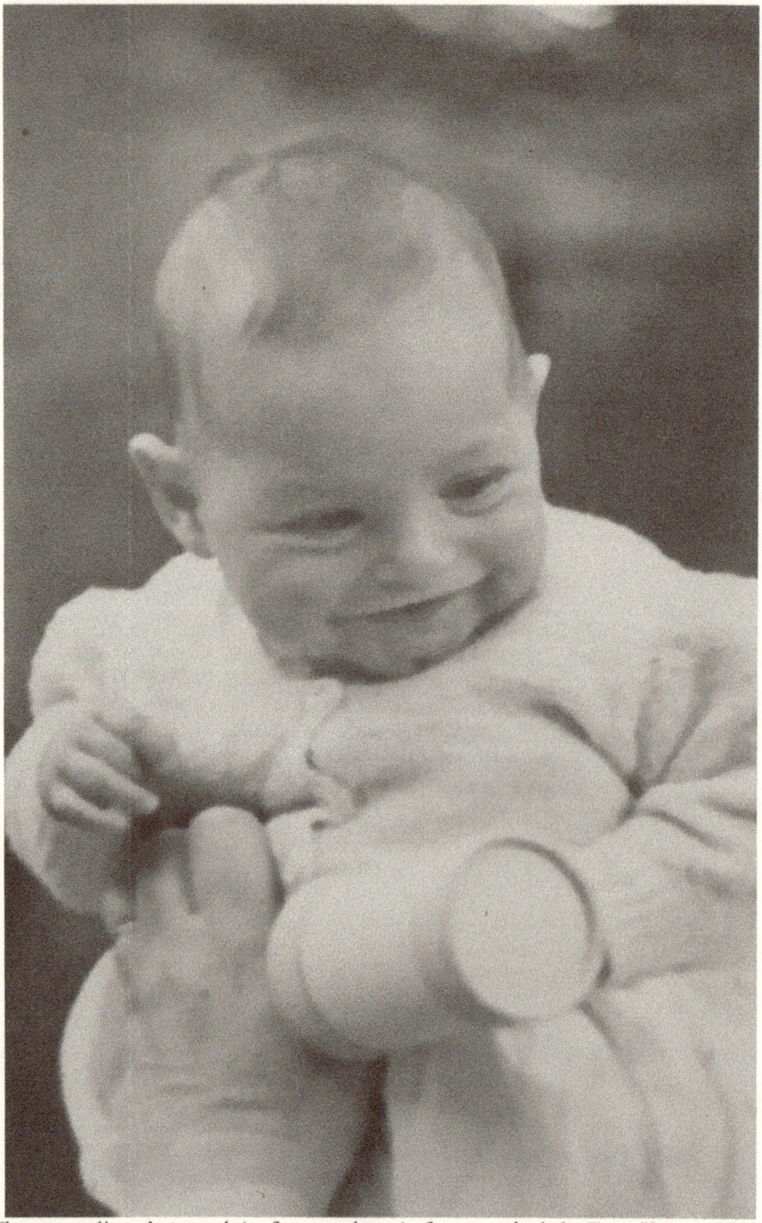

The very earliest photograph (as far as we know) of yours truly, baby Tony Sloman, 1945.
Note the trademark dimple on chin: it never went away!

To begin my life with the beginning of my life… No, hang on. Wait. I think that somebody else has begun their book that way. Let's try this…

D-Day; Me-Day; V-Day…

That's a little better. That's the historical lineage of the 20th century that, as a youngster, I used to tell to anyone who'd listen to me what I considered to be the greatest events of a great decade:--

D-Day: the Allied attack on occupied Europe, on June 6th, 1944.

Me-Day: the birth date of yours truly, Anthony Barney Sloman, May 6th, 1945.

V-Day (or VE-Day, as it is now more popularly known): The date of victory in Europe, the end of World War II, May 8th, 1945, a day and a bit after I left maternity hospital.

History indeed!

I was born at 8.20p.m., on Sunday, the sixth day of May 1945, at the "Sun-Trap" Maternity Home, High Beech, Essex.

The doctor's name was Warner (Was that possibly an omen? It couldn't have been MGM, Universal, Fox, or Paramount), and the nurse was named Tribble. The place was Epping, a sub-district of Chingford, Essex, and my birth was recorded by registrar Frank Jackson, and the official ceremony of welcoming the new baby boy into the Jewish faith, the bris, took place on May 13th, the Reverend Davidson presiding. The forty-nine guests attending brought young little me a grand total of forty-three gifts. How do I know all this? You may well ask…

My wonderful Mother, Eve Sloman, born Eva Zidman, had bought a tome called "The Progress Book" (especially printed for Mellins Food Limited, London) by one W.M. Pilley, which, according to the introduction on page 7, "provides a simple means of keeping an accurate account of an infant's development, and of the interesting events that occur during early infancy and childhood." My Mother, God bless her, kept it up in detail until the end of my fourth year. I myself continued it until the eighth year, and somewhat randomly thereafter, until my Bar Mitzvah year. Very, very randomly... But, for now, to return to the very beginning…

In the personal column (page 15) of *The Bulletin*, the magazine of the Union of Young Israel Societies of Great Britain and Ireland, dated July 1942, issue Number 7, listed under "Engagements" in the personal column, appears the line:--

Julian Sloman (Finsbury Park) and Eve Morris.

My very own parents (although not quite yet). The Young Israel Union's congratulations were duly extended. Eve Morris was using her father's – my Grandfather's – first name as her surname. His real surname was Zidman, and her name was Eva Zidman.

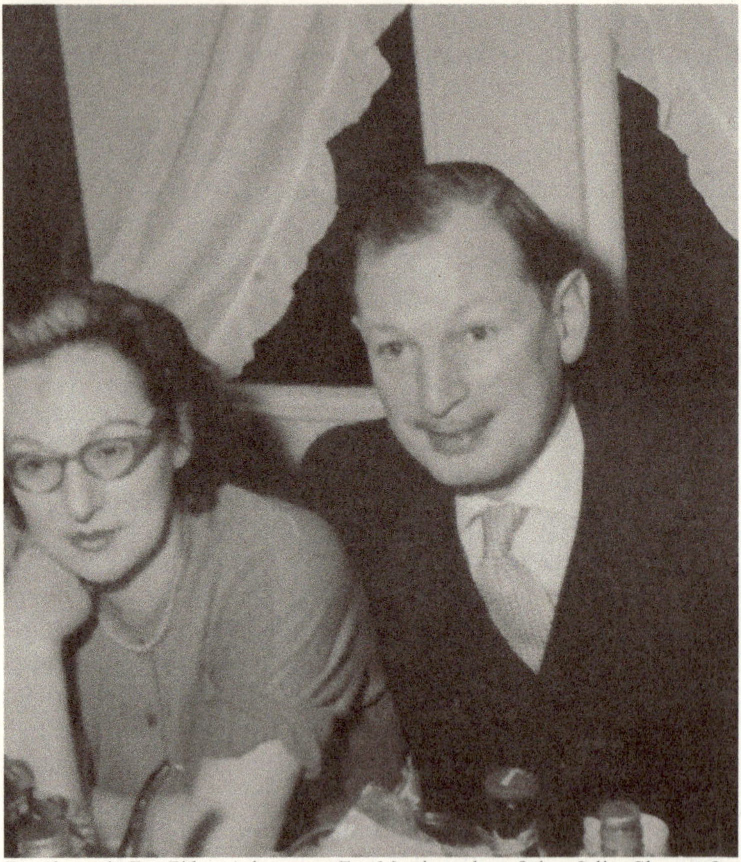

My mother Eve (formerly Eva Zidman), known as Eve Morris, and my father, Julian Sloman, January, 1960. From the look of the table, I'm guessing New Year's Eve in Streatham.

Grandad had fled Kiev and crossed Europe on foot to escape Russian anti-Semitism, courageously making his way as far as London, where he met and married Annie Levenstein, who I knew as my beloved Nanna, one of five sisters, which seemed appropriate since Grandad was one of six brothers, of which he was the youngest, I believe. He never, ever, spoke of the Russian pogroms, and, as far as I know, never saw his brothers again, and only one browning ancient photograph, originally labelled “Cabinet Portrait”, exists of all of them together. Grandad’s original name was Moishe Zidman, anglicised to Morris Zidman: my very own Grandad Morris, who met and married Annie Levenstein, the parents of my beloved Mother, Eva, forever anglicized as Eve. They had two other children: my lovely Auntie Doris, known as “Dol”, and a son, Simon, now no more than a legend, if remembered at all.

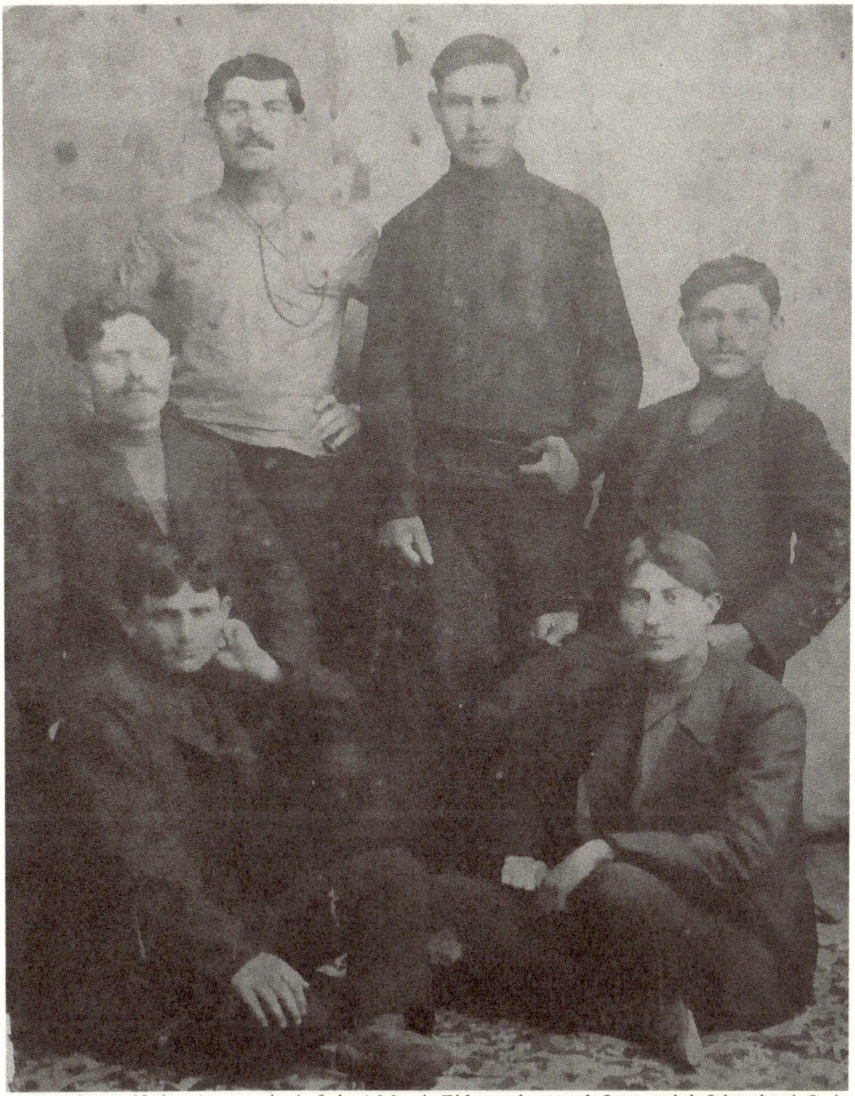

My maternal grandfather (my mother's father) Morris Zidman, bottom left, seated, left hand to left cheek, with his brothers, a studio portrait taken in a Moscow studio around the turn of the century before he left Russia forever to avoid the pogroms. I don't know what happened to the rest of the Zidman family, and, very probably, nether did Morris, although we do have some distant relatives over in Israel.

Simon Zidman was nicknamed "Sonny", after the hit song "Sonny Boy", introduced by Al Jolson in the 1928 film *The Singing Fool*, and Sonny just loved those moving pictures. Nanna and Grandad were also great fans of the cinema. Grandad once told me, in his Russian accent, that one of his favourite films was the Western movie, *Cimarron*, starring Richard Dix, and it was Grandad who would invariably take me to what we then called "The Pictures" when I was young and growing up. But it was Sonny, who, of course, I never knew, who really loved the cinema. The only memoir of Sonny that remained after he died so tragically and suddenly of an illness (I could never find out the details) just before his Bar Mitzvah, was a page torn out of his diary, which reads "Saw *Mutiny on the Bounty* at the Tivoli." That would have been a very special trip to The Pictures. The Tivoli cinema was in the Strand, and was an MGM pre-release cinema, showing films often concurrent with their West End debuts, invariably immediately prior to their general circuit release. Oh, Sonny Boy..."You made a heaven right here on earth," sang Al Jolson. Did I inherit a part of young Sonny's being, that all-pervading, almost to the exclusion of all else in life, sheer love of cinema? The understanding that films were matchless, as both art and entertainment, an understanding that was to become both obsession and driving force in my own life.

I knew, eventually, that somehow I had to be involved in the making of cinema films, some feeling inside that I couldn't quite put into words: to make films, yes, but also, and I could hardly understand it myself, to live film, and virtually almost <u>be</u> film. Was that because of Sonny? Was he, in some divine way, a part of my own soul?

The war was over. Julian, my Father, returned to civvy street to marry my Mother, turning in his Royal Air Force uniform (he taught new recruits how to fly, based at R.A.F.'s Chipping Norton), and Eve's sister, Doris, married Don Gilbert (neé Kulikofsky), newly returned from capture as a soldier in an Italian prisoner-of-war camp. With Nanna and Grandad Morris also in residence, the family home at Forest Lodge, Chigwell, was about to become very crowded, and I, as a growing baby, had developed a very unusual habit:-- whenever I heard an aeroplane flying overhead I dived straight under the kitchen table, which, of course, is what my Mother would've done when she was pregnant with me, fearing enemy attack. Apparently, I soon grew out of it. Grandad Morris was beginning to establish himself as a fishmonger, and had bought a fried fish shop in London's Barking Road, on the fringes of the East End, that hub of immigrants (largely Jewish, then) and marketeers, centred on Petticoat Lane. Both Julian and Don were skilled tailors, the former Savile Row-trained. Now that both had wives, a new family home was sought, closer to the fish and chip shop, but large enough to contain the whole family: Nanna and Grandad, Eve and Julian (plus me!), Doris and Don (soon to give birth to my cousin David), and now with the addition of Nanna's mother, my Great-Grandma Deborah Levenstein, who was so Orthodox Jewish that she wore the traditional sheitel, a hair wig. (Yes, I can still barely remember her, a tiny, tiny woman, in contrast to the other Levenstein sisters, my great-aunts). We called her "Booba", Yiddish for grandmother, affectionately, and, for a very long time, I believed that she was, in fact, Grandad Morris' own mother, and that he had brought her over to live here from Russia. Would that I had read my own "Progress Book" much earlier!

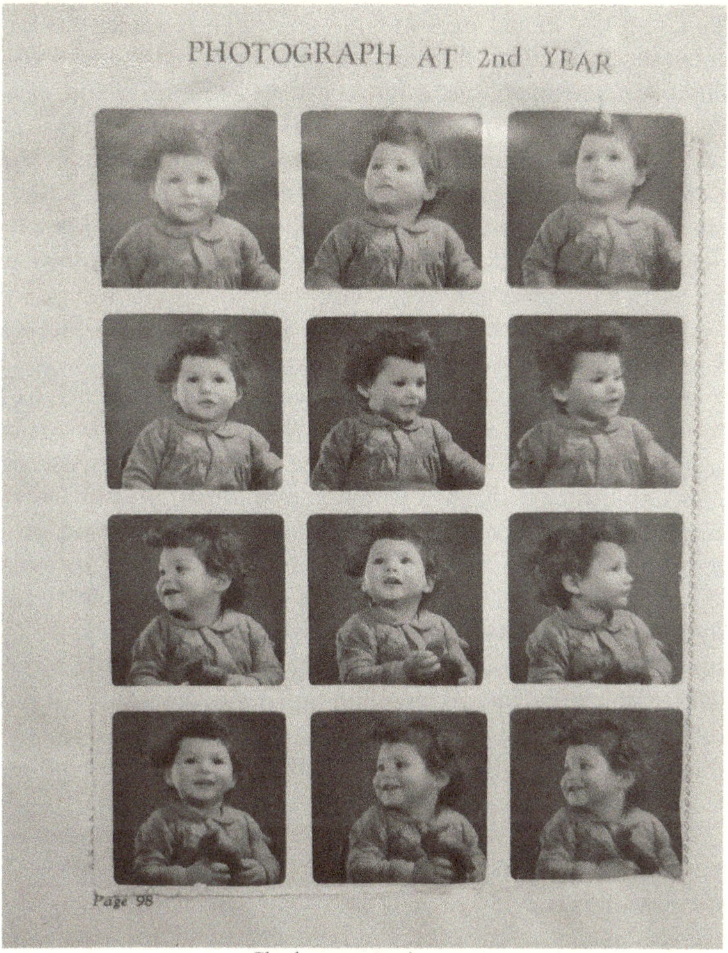

Cheeky me at two!

We all moved from Chigwell on June 21st, 1945, to 38, Claremont Road in Forest Gate, an East London suburb, convenient enough for the East End, and easy enough for Grandad Morris to go to Billingsgate Fish Market well before dawn to purchase product for his fish and chip shop in the Barking Road, not surprisingly named "Morris" (but always referred to as "Morris's") rather than "Zidman's". (When I eventually interviewed East End local lad Terence Stamp at the National Film Theatre, he remembered "Morris's" with great affection.)

It was at 38, Claremont Road, that absolutely huge Edwardian house (at least, to me), where my earliest memories really begin. I don't really remember Chigwell at all, not even riding in Grandad's fabled pony-and-trap, which apparently I loved, but which, alas, he had to part with when we moved. I well remember my own Father, Julian (who, of course, I called "Daddy") bending over my cot in our upstairs bedroom at Forest Gate, attired in his Royal Air Force uniform, and moustachioed in the then-current style of film stars like Clark Gable and Ronald Colman. I clearly remember one day when he attempted to pick me up from my cot, and he had shaved off his moustache. I screamed and screamed, and Mummy kissed and cuddled me and said that Daddy would grow it again, and that he did, never removing it as long as he lived, as far as I can remember. From my upstairs bedroom (and, I recall, actually from my cot) I could see wartime barrage balloons high in the sky, above the streets and houses, hovering high over Wanstead Flats. I don't know when they were dismantled, but they seemed to be always present throughout all of my early childhood in Forest Gate.

My other very early memory of 38, Claremont Road was the death and subsequent funeral of Booba, who had lived with us. We and the Gilberts shared the upstairs, but Booba and Nanna and Grandad had bedrooms downstairs. I was truly too young (three? four?) to really understand what was actually happening, but I was driven to the funeral with my parents, in a very, very posh limousine, perhaps a Rolls or a Humber. To placate me, Mummy had brought along a Rupert Bear comic book for me to read on the journey, but, sitting in the back of the limo, I had dropped it down the front of the seat backing onto the driver's compartment, a seat that I couldn't manage to pull down in order to extricate my Rupert book, when suddenly we arrived at the cemetery and had to get out. I tried to explain how I had lost Rupert, but other things were happening and no one paid much attention to me. I never saw that particular Rupert book again (although promises were made to buy me another one, which I think actually happened), and that's all I remember of Booba's funeral.

38, Claremont Road was fun, but crowded. Grandad had bought a new-fangled device called a television, and we were amongst Britain's first TV audiences. I was allowed to watch the BBC introductory demonstration film that was shown every morning, and did so often, learning such choice items by heart as Nelson's speech before Trafalgar, and Lupino Lane's *The Lambeth Walk*, excerpts of which were prominently featured to show off the abilities of the new TV in action. Everything on it, of course, was in black-and-white.

And there were other treats too: one especial treat was being taken to Regent's Park Zoo to see Brumas, the brand-new baby polar bear, born in 1949, the first baby polar bear to be successfully reared in the U.K. I well remember our visit to this day. Indeed, I wonder if we as visitors were partially and helpfully responsible for the 1950 attendance annual record figure at the Zoo of around three million admissions, which was roughly one million more than was usual in those days, a figure never exceeded previously or since. But even at such an early age – I was barely five – I knew that Brumas was no substitute for what was rapidly becoming my true passion, although I didn't know it yet, and that sheerest of pleasures was what became known as "Going to The Pictures".

It all started when a visit to the Cameo cinema either in Great Windmill Street or The Strand became part of a Sunday trip "up West", a weekend treat wherein Mummy and Daddy, on a pretty regular basis, took me out to visit, in no particular order, the Horse Guards in Whitehall (and to feed sugar lumps to the horses, then allowed), a trip to Trafalgar Square to feed the pigeons (cost a penny a bag for pigeon food), plus a cartoon show at a Cameo cinema, all invariably topped off by tea at a Lyons' Corner House, I think more often than not the one in The Strand, but I seem to remember other Corner Houses as well: I was well on the way to being well and truly spoiled rotten.

In "The Progress Book", Mummy's entry, under the "Recreations and Amusements" heading, dated June 1949, reads: "Likes to go to 'Cameo' and see coloured cartoons, very fond of river trips on the Thames". All of which I can still remember vividly. The war was over, and I was indeed being spoiled, but, of course, I never knew it. I well remember being taken to see the Danish animated feature of Hans Christian Andersen's *The Tinder Box* at one of the Cameo cinemas, and being very impressed by it. I also visited the circus annually, alternating between Bertram Mills Circus at Olympia, where I saw the great Coco the Clown and the wonderful white-faced bejewelled elegant clown Percy Huxter, and also the Tom Arnold Circus at Harringay, where one wonderful year I saw the great Tex Ritter on his horse singing his hit record *High Noon* (of course, I hadn't yet seen the film) at the "Texas Western Spectacle". I was really privileged to be taken, usually by my Dad, to such wonderful treats.

I had also already visited local cinemas even before those regular, and magical, trips "up West". At the very far end of Claremont Road there loomed the Odeon, Forest Gate, just beyond the bombed site at the end of our road, where I played with motley playmates. There were also occasional huge film posters on display near the Odeon, and I recall seeing the vivid poster for *Jolson Sings Again*, and being told that Jolson had died that very day.

On that bomb site at the end of our road, there was kept a horse, and my friend and neighbour Brian and I used to go and visit it, often unaccompanied by an adult. One day Brian couldn't come with me, and I later learned that he had been kicked in the head by that horse. I never saw Brian again, and eventually, much later on, I overheard that he had died from his injury. Of course, nobody would have told me that then, at my age.

The first feature films I remember seeing were at our local cinemas: MGM's *Easter Parade* at the ABC in Green Street, just up from the Romford Road, and *Samson and Delilah* (we went "up West" for that, I think), plus *David and Bathsheba* at the Forest Gate Odeon, the one that was at the far end of our street in the Romford Road. I was so scared during the storm sequence in that particular film that I can remember getting off of my seat and hiding on the floor until it ended. My parents coaxed me back up: "It's only a film." But it was very real, and very frightening to me, and of course I loved it even more for so being. I was also taken to see the eminently suitable *The Greatest Show on Earth*, also at the Forest Gate Odeon, and, following that and *Samson and*

Delilah, I therefore knew, and was aware of, a man called Cecil B. DeMille, who actually made films. So, they didn't just "happen"...

Obviously, *David and Bathsheba* and *Samson and Delilah* were excellent movies to take a young Jewish boy to see, but there were others too that I saw in those earliest of my years, mainly also at the Odeon, Forest Gate: John Mills as *Scott of the Antarctic*, Walt Disney's *Treasure Island*, Errol Flynn in *Kim* (unusual, then, I later learned, for an MGM film to play the Odeon circuit), John Ford's wonderfully Technicolored cavalry Western *She Wore a Yellow Ribbon* (an exciting trip to a Stratford cinema, I seem to recall), and also Ford's extremely suitable *3 Godfathers*, both starring John Wayne, plus Disney's animated feature *Melody Time*, James Mason as *Rommel – Desert Fox*, Joel McCrea in *Saddle Tramp*, Danny Kaye in *On the Riviera*, and Bob Hope in *Son of Paleface* (or could it have been the actual original *The Paleface*?). These were largely Technicolor features, so, of course, I thought every film was in colour (except James Mason as Rommel, but, of course, he was a German), until Grandad took me to see a special "Sunday for one day only" presentation of *The Treasure of the Sierra Madre* because he liked Humphrey Bogart. In black-and-white, and I loved it.

But there were far greater cinematic treats in store for this increasingly very spoilt youngster. For very special films – all three of them MGM Technicolor musicals – I was taken as a treat to the West End cinema that termed itself in its advertising as "The Showplace of the Nation", after New York's famed Radio City Music Hall, MGM's London home, the vast Empire Leicester Square, where all films were accompanied by a live stage show production by one Nat Karson (I remembered his name because it was so like Kit Carson, whose cowboy comics I used to read), and I can well remember the garishly-costumed dancers and the full orchestra and chorus, directed, I think, by George Melachrino, backed up by colourful acrobats and jugglers, at every single performance.

The first such treat was *On the Town*, in 1949 (or maybe 1950), followed by *Show Boat* and *Annie Get Your Gun*, all films, as I would later discover, produced by the great Arthur Freed for MGM. I couldn't contain my pleasure and my excitement:-- singing, dancing, colour, and live music! What more could anybody ever want? So, belated thanks, Metro-Goldwyn-Mayer, who owned the Empire and produced all three films, you set a pattern for life. But most especially "Thank you" to my parents; I think they knew exactly what they were doing, introducing me to such classy pleasures, even way back then, although they couldn't ever have possibly guessed what it would lead to...

Of course, other post-war events and activities impinged, but I was fast growing into a spoilt, selfish little lad. I can still just about remember, but now with appropriate shame, the one time that I threw one of my baby cousin David's socks on to our hearth fire, just to see it burn. When my Auntie Doris, David's mother, accused me of so doing, I immediately lied and denied all knowledge. It never occurred to little me that a pair of socks would therefore be ruined, and that baby socks cost real money in a post-war world. What a little shit I was becoming! I was also never particularly healthy either. In "The Progress Book" there are constant references to my health:

Until 1947 still suffering from bronchitis and colds.
June 26th 1948 age 13 months, asthma and bronchitis.
December 20th 1948 bronchitis, age 18 months.
Christmas 1948 still suffering from cough and cold.
Still attending Great Ormond Street Hospital,
but much better than previous winter.
November 1948 discharged from hospital.

But I still had to go regularly to Great Ormond Street to have my nasal passages cleaned, even after we moved to Streatham. Of course, I hated such visits, but there was always relief in sight. Yes, you've guessed it. The bribe was to go to The Pictures – a new film of my own choosing – after every hospital visit! My Mother, to placate me afterwards, offered to take me to a suitable programme of my own choice, and I was very specific about the selection of films, and thus I saw the CinemaScope spectacle *Prince Valiant* at the Granada, Kennington, and the Martin and Lewis VistaVisioned *3 Ring Circus* at the New Victoria, amongst others. Spoiled? You betcha!

But before we actually leave Forest Gate altogether, perhaps it's worth recounting some other – now very faded – memories: after all, it wasn't quite all about "going to the Pictures". It never occurred to me then, or to, I suspect, anyone else, that perhaps my persistent asthmatic conditions were aggravated, if not incited, by the simple fact that everybody, absolutely everybody, smoked. Grandad smoked "Craven A", and occasionally I would be sent to buy a packet. I'm not sure if Mummy and Daddy had favourites, but I vaguely recall Woodbines and Players cigarette packets around, mainly of twenties. In the cinemas we visited, a veil of cigarette smoke always hung in the air, between us and the actual screen: it wasn't unusual to have difficulty peering through the smoke to actually view the screen. Everybody smoked – on buses, in the streets, in the shops, at home, and, as far as I know, nobody made any connection at all between smoking and my own health conditions, which miraculously cleared up eventually when we moved to Streatham, where our house in Downton Avenue was up a steepish hill off the Streatham High Road, on far higher ground than the Claremont Road house in Forest Gate.

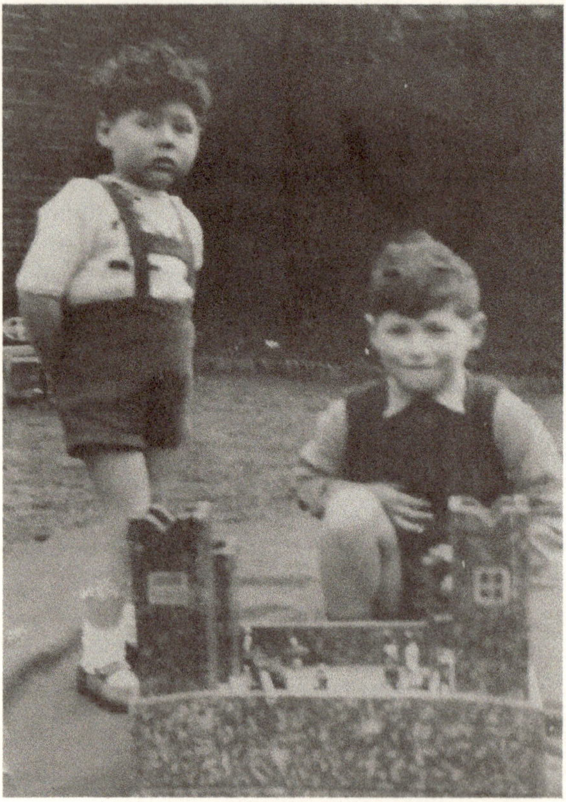

Me at age 4, with a new present of a toy fort, years before I had ever heard of (or, for that matter, seen) *Ivanhoe*. That's my 2-year old cousin David, left, staring at the camera, playing in our garden with me at 38, Claremont Road, Forest Gate, where our two families lived together with our maternal Grandparents.

We also had a pet in Claremont Road, a black cat called Peter. I had almost forgotten Peter, until one day, much, much later, when I was introduced to a country clairvoyant by a girl that I had met in Cannes, and I took time off from work to visit this fortune-telling lady, who duly informed me that I once had a black cat called Peter, and that Peter was now all right. She then made some prophesies which, once they were interpreted, seemed to have all come true.

But there were other aspects of post-war life that I subsequently learned about, things that I suspect were deliberately kept from me, things that perhaps a young Jewish child should not know. I can just about still recall being held aloft by Grandad Morris above the crowd in Trafalgar Square to witness the unveiling of a brand-new flag, the blue-and-white of the newly-created State of Israel, and how proud Grandad seemed to be on that day in May in 1948, and especially how very proud he was for me to be there to herald the birth of a new nation, our nation. It would be a long, long time before I learned of the unbearable horrors of the German concentration camps, and of Hitler's attempts to erase the Jews, our people, from history for ever. When such mentions were made, I was usually gently removed from the room, or signs were made amongst the adults: "Not now". It was many years before I realised that we had lost friends and relatives to the Nazis.

During the war, the underground tube stations served as air raid shelters, and my own family used regular ones every night. But family legend has it that one particular night Grandad Morris suggested another shelter: he had a "feeling". And they all followed his unusual advice. Just as well for, that very evening, a German bomb destroyed their regular shelter, killing nearly everybody there. Such a tale marked my childhood.

There was one more aspect of Forest Gate life (and also continued into Streatham, of course) that I recalled with unalloyed pleasure, and that was our regular visits to family and friends in Southend-on-Sea on the Thames Estuary, and its adjacent seaside complex Westcliff-on-Sea, both resorts virtually festooned with friends and relatives, as I was to discover extremely early in my life. As early as July 1945, when I was taken on holiday to spend a week with my Father's mother, my Grandma Miriam Fine, who had married one Harry Fine after Barney Sloman (hence my middle name) had died suddenly. "The Progress Book" says I spent a week in Southend with them, and in 1948, in June, I spent "a month at Westcliff with Grandma Fine", an entry followed by "Aug. 1951 week at Westcliff with Grandma Miri".

I have very vague memories of those early holidays, unsurprisingly, but I have nothing but affectionate and strong memories of staying on the Essex coast, particularly my two weeks in Westcliff with my maternal grandmother, Nanna Annie Morris, and a week at the "Queen's" Hotel, a posh palace in Westcliff with my parents, close to Grandma Miri's, both in 1950. In 1952 I was actually allowed to spend three whole weeks with Grandma Miri in Westcliff. Those were the days!

For me, Southend (and Westcliff) were sheer delights. The Southend pier was, allegedly, the longest pier in the world, and was certainly the Pride of Essex, which also happened to be the name of a motor launch which travelled along the Essex coast, and a photograph exists of a very young me alongside the Captain of "The Pride of Essex", standing proudly on the very ship itself. Southend-on-Sea would also forever be remembered as the home of the Kursaal, a major amusement part on the English coast, but I was a little too young for early visits. Instead, I enjoyed immensely the Peter Pan's Playground, just adjacent to the famous Southend Pier, which, as its choice of name suggests, was eminently suitable for post-war youngsters of my own age. I was always accompanied by an elder, and vividly remember the site itself, distinguished by a big wheel and an open-air roller coaster (the latter of which I loved!) and a very real Crooked House, in which there was, amongst other things, a very crooked bench on which you could sit, or try to sit, and make a wish. I can remember my wish: it was always the same. Not health, nor wealth, but… I always truly wished to meet our Queen one day, and, ideally, to have tea with her!

Roughly between Southend Pier and the Peter Pan's Playground was moored a scale replica of Sir Francis Drake's great ship "The Golden Hind", and many a time I enjoyed visiting her, negotiating my way past all sorts of waxworks of various mariners, visiting a life-size torture chamber (sometimes with my eyes closed), and many other naval trophies. I especially liked the guns, and thought that they were real (they may have been!). And guess what? One Christmas, my parents gave me a replica model of "The Golden Hind". Eventually, I managed to break off and destroy every single mast. Was I destructive? Was I spoiled? Alas, most certainly. I was also an ingrate, and never, ever realised how privileged I was, nor how very very fortunate I was allowed to be.

It wasn't only my Grandmothers (both of them) who endeared me to Southend-on-Sea: I had other friends and relations there, too. My Auntie Julie, Nanna's cousin, and her husband, Uncle Dave, also lived in Southend, and their son, my second cousin Gerald, whose real surname was Althasen, though everyone called his father "Dave Davis", grew up to come to town and live with us for a short period in Streatham in 1958, on leave from his National Service in the Army, a period in which he took me to see the highly controversial (and, frankly, probably quite unsuitable for me at the time in content) film of the infamous novel *Peyton Place* at the Odeon, Streatham, a trip in his then highly fashionable red "bubble" car that I will never forget, sandwiched as we were between two buses in Streatham High Road, dwarfing us on our way to "The Pictures". (Gerald eventually became a high finance "gunser-macher", ending up for a while as an actual part-owner of the Southend Kursaal itself, where *The Prisoner* episode "The Girl Who Was Death" was largely filmed on location.)

But it was with Grandma Miri, my father's mother, that I was allowed to stay most often, first in her house in Southend proper, and then later on when she and "Grandad" Harry moved to be nearer to the Westcliff railway station. I only knew Grandad Harry as a very, very deaf old man, but he actually managed to outlive virtually all of my relatives, and I eventually discovered that his real surname was Eisenstein and, of course, he was Russian, as well. (I wondered if my two Russian grandads ever spoke Russian together, but I suspect it was only Yiddish.) No, I never did ask, couldn't ask, and probably suspected that the answer would be "No", if he was related to one of the greatest, most innovative film directors who ever lived, the great Soviet film-maker Sergei M. Eisenstein, director of *Battleship Potemkin*, of which, of course, I'd never have heard in those early young days in Southend-on-Sea.

Nanna Morris had formed a relationship with a hotelier who I only knew as "Bessie" in Westcliff-on-Sea, the adjacent seaside to Southend, and I was allowed to stay with Nanna quite often at "Auntie Bessie's" on several occasions. The boarding house was but a short walk downhill to the sea front, and I walked clad only in my swimming trunks and sandals, quite often. But nearby there were two other outlets for me in Westcliff-on-Sea that veritably warmed my youthful heart and soul…

Along the cliff-side promenade that ran parallel to the actual sea front, there was a parade of shops and cafes, many local restaurants, and in the centre of this parade was a Penny Arcade, with genuine pre-war artefacts lining its interior. For 1d. you could watch scenes of torture (not real!), or have your fortune told (a fake Swami model would "hand" you an archaic pre-printed card), or flick a metal switch which would shoot a ball into a hole, invariably a non-winning one, as I regularly discovered. Paradise! And only 1d. a go! I begged Nanna to give me a shilling (which the man in the arcade would split into twelve bronze pennies), and this she did, and I would join her after my spend on a bench or in a deckchair afterwards on many, many occasions. (I don't think I ever won anything at all on those machines).

The other aspect of Southend that mostly enchanted the young me came as a total surprise that will surprise no-one who has already read thus far. In Southend's High Street there was a bakery called "Garon's", and to my surprise, and delight, it actually housed a cinema on its upper floor: an actual, proper cinema, showing release films on (I discovered later) real 35 millimetre, in fact a proper, thorough "Picture Palace", albeit slightly smaller and more cosy than those that I had previously enjoyed. I couldn't wait to see a film there. Taken first, I think, by my parents, to the black-and-white Kirk Douglas western *Along the Great Divide*, was an especial treat for me as I had never previously heard of it. It may well have been the first black-and-white feature film I had ever seen; I can't remember if it pre-dated *Rommel – Desert Fox* or *The Treasure of the Sierra Madre*. No point in looking up actual dates: Garon's played to their own booking schedules, unavailable today for reference. Ergo, for me Garon's tea room, a bakery shop and café with a cinema upstairs, became a "must-see" on all my visits to Southend. Though still far too young to go on my own, I would nag my parents and my grandparents, and any other likely suspects around, to take me to Garon's as often as possible, although, of course, they all wondered why I wouldn't rather go and play on the beach. After all, we were at the seaside! But, as far as I can remember, we only actually went to the pictures at Garon's three or four times. I remember seeing Tyrone Power in the Cold War black-and-white thriller *Diplomatic Courier*, which, of course, I didn't really understand, and two eminently suitable special Technicolored treats: Burt Lancaster as *The Crimson Pirate* and Danny Kaye as *Hans Christian Andersen*. My tastes were beginning to be shaped for life!

But I can also remember another cinema visit in Southend that wasn't so propitious. I think it was Nanna who let somebody that she knew from a hotel who had a daughter to take us (me and the daughter) to "The Pictures". No cause to worry, the lady seemed eminently trustworthy. But I do remember that occasion vividly, because that woman did something that I thought so horrendous that I never, ever, did it again. Now, it was customary in those days of the 'fifties (and the decades earlier) to enter a cinema at any time during a performance, and leave when the film reached the point of entry. Indeed, the expression "This is where we came in" had become an indelible part of the regular picturegoer's vocabulary, including mine.

But at the double-bill of *Hansel and Gretel* and *The Scarlet Spear* on that particular occasion, the daughter and I were ushered out early, not waiting until the "This is where we came in" point. The friend said we had to get back, and, of course, I protested vehemently (I was such a horror!), arguing that we had to stay to see the film up to where we actually came in. The lady would have none of it, saying we had to leave now, and we left accordingly. I never saw her and her daughter ever again, to the best of my knowledge, nor did I ever again knowingly miss a part of a feature film. It became a matter of self-honour to see <u>every</u> film complete (if not always exactly in the right order) from the very beginning to the very end. But Southend and Westcliff were great fun, nevertheless, and the visits were plenty and often, but, unbeknownst to me, major life moves were afoot.

We moved to 35, Downton Avenue, Streatham Hill, on March 7th, 1951. I don't remember the actual move, or the circumstances of the move at all. Selfish as ever, I only noted that I had a bedroom to myself, and a huge top-story room which began as a playroom, and ended up as a "Disc Den" in my teens.

Interestingly, with hindsight, I never went to school in Forest Gate. Obviously I should have done so, and I have memories of Mummy opening the front door of 38, Claremont Road, to a man who enquired "Why isn't your son going to school?" and was told that we were moving imminently and that I would start school when we moved. I do recall that he called again, so I never knew if he was placated or not. All I knew was, I liked not going to school quite yet. (But what I didn't anticipate, of course, would be the fact that the later I started school meant that I would always be a bit behind my contemporaries, and I never, ever, caught up in maths.)

Streatham was very different. South London as opposed to East London, and it wasn't too long before I discovered its very many pleasures for a small boy. I started missing those especial pleasures of East London, mainly those found around London's East End, but my visits to the East End still continued nonetheless. One of the reasons, if not the main reason, that we moved to Streatham was because Daddy had found a suitable shop location in which to set himself up as "Julian Sloman, Exclusive Tailor", running his own business at last at 62, Streatham Hill, now his very own boss after a long Savile Row apprenticeship. He took all the orders and measured up the customers himself, certainly, but he also had several "outside workmen", specialists all, and they all seemed to be in the East End, where he had built up business associates, trouser-and-waistcoat-makers, and also many good friends.

And so it was, on Sunday mornings, Dad would go and visit these East End piece-work tailors, and sometimes, if I was very lucky, he would take me with him in the car. Waistcoat makers, shirt-makers, heaven knows who else, it didn't really matter to me, for I just looked greatly forward to diving into a barrel for a pickled cucumber (a "wally") from the outside wooden barrels at Rogg's famous delicatessen, or eating blintzes – the Russian, proper variety, not the American "blinis" – and smoked salmon on brown bread at Dubovsky's Jewish restaurant with my own gourmet Daddy. (But I never shared Dad's taste for jellied eels, even if they came from the most famous stall in the East End, if not the world, Tubby Isaacs himself.)

Sometimes, Dad would drop me off at my Auntie Becky's (Nanna's sister) in Vallance Road, and then, accompanied by her son, my cousin Michael, we'd go down Petticoat Lane, the world-famous thoroughfare which, on a Sunday morning, was a veritable pleasure garden of delights. If we were lucky, we'd see the famed racing tipster, the garishly bedecked Prince Monolulu, calling out his catchphrase to all and sundry: "I've gotta horse! I've gotta horse!". We'd find colourful American comics (British ones were still all black and white) invariably left behind by U.K.-based G.I.'s (and that's not all they left behind…) on many stalls, cheap at thruppence each, far better (i.e. more gory and violent) than our own homegrown *Beano* and *Dandy*, and far more exciting than our own rather staid *Eagle*, *Topper*, or the then-new *Swift*.

It was in the Petticoat Lane markets that I discovered something else: back issues of magazines that would colour my young life forever:-- older copies of British film magazines, the weeklies *Picture Show* and *Picturegoer*, both of which I was eventually to subscribe to, until their respective demises in the 'sixties.

I began with *Picture Show* which listed and reviewed all new films, and graded them zero to three stars, and boasted a very rigid, but nevertheless enjoyable, format, and then I graduated to the more topical and glamorous *Picturegoer*, which also graded new films, but with more leeway than *Picture Show*, awarding nought to four stars, and blessing very, very special films with the *Picturegoer* Seal of Merit, and those very special films were few and far between. I preferred *Picturegoer*, but collected them both avidly, buying earlier copies when I could find them down "The Lane", and subscribing (with my parents' help, of course) to both of them, their weekly arrivals by post among the highlights of my week. Alas, they both collapsed almost simultaneously under the incoming change of the "Swinging Sixties", when they, quite simply, began to look old-fashioned. *Picturegoer* clumsily tried to re-vamp as *Date*, but its day was soon over.

Picturegoer had a letters page, and, young though I was, I managed to have as many as five letters printed. Don't believe me? Check out *Picturegoer* for the 10th June 1958, 29th October 1958, 21st May 1959, 13th October 1959, and 14th January 1960: if they weren't the dates of the issues, they were certainly the dates on the cheques, because when I received the cheques in the post, I gave them to my Dad to cash, and he gave me the seven shillings and sixpence on encashment. Except that he never cashed them: he gave me the money and kept the *Picturegoer* cheques for history. I only discovered that fact when he died, and I found the five uncashed cheques amongst his papers.

What I learnt from *Picture Show*, and, to a greater extent from *Picturegoer*, was to similarly grade the films that I saw myself. Yes, every single one: shorts, cartoons, features, documentaries, and I still continue to do so to this very day, having filled exercise books and, latterly, diaries, with movies and my ratings, and hope to continue to do so as long as I am divinely allowed. (Although instead of *Picturegoer*'s rarely-awarded Seal of Merit, I grade from zero to five stars, the latter representing in my own mind that much-lamented Seal of Merit, and believe me, there are very, very few of the latter, very few indeed.)

The time arrived when I could no longer avoid going to school:---

I don't know exactly how my first school came to be chosen, but it was a converted church building on the border where Streatham and Brixton converge, not too far from our new home. It was called the Richard Atkins School, and my start date was the 12th of March, 1951, and I remember that I really, really did not want to go to school. At all.

I truly cannot remember exactly what happened on those first few days at that school in New Park Road. I vaguely recall that, as a newcomer in mid-term, I was seated with a few other new pupils, on the floor, cross-legged, and was given various picture books to peruse, whilst the rest of the pupils were being taught a lesson in another part of the same area, with a teacher and a blackboard in front of them. I wasn't happy. I wanted to be part of the main group, I recall. Eventually, and it seemed like a forever, Mummy came and fetched me, and we went home, whether I stayed for the full day or only half-a-day, I can't remember, but I well remember what followed.

On the second day I flatly refused to go in. I screamed and screamed, and Mummy didn't know what to do. All I selfishly knew was that I really didn't want to leave my Mother and all the comforts of home to go into that awful Gothic monolith called school. There seemed to be no alternative. A strappingly-built female teacher called Miss Reid picked me up bodily, and carried me into the building, completely disregarding all my struggling, kicking, and screaming. I just, quite simply, did not want to go inside that school. I was being totally selfish, and just generally utterly appalling – I clearly didn't care how this looked to my beloved Mother, nor do I remember what she actually did, but I'm pretty sure she left me there, being carried in aloft, me screaming at Miss Reid. In "The Progress Book" Mummy wrote:-- "Started school at New Park Rd. Streatham on 12th March 1951. Wasn't very keen at first but soon began to like it." What an understatement! "Soon began to like it." Hah! News to me! (Although I did participate in the Richard Atkins School Christmas play in 1951, amazingly. No, I don't recall the part I played.) Apparently, I had already started revealing what "The Progress Book" referred to as an "amazing memory": after all, I did know my alphabet at two-and-a-half, and was apparently learning poems by a year and eight months. Under "Poems and Recreation" in "The Progress Book" Mummy wrote: "First recitation and first poem learnt: 1 year 8 months. Poems and recitations learnt too numerous to mention. Songs, poems, nursery rhymes, amazing memory." And to cap it all, I took my first dancing lesson in April, 1948, when I was almost three! Nevertheless, I absolutely hated that Richard Atkins school in New Park Road. Although I did manage to settle down there after a fashion, I never liked going there at all. But there was to be a new school for me on the horizon, a very brand new school indeed.

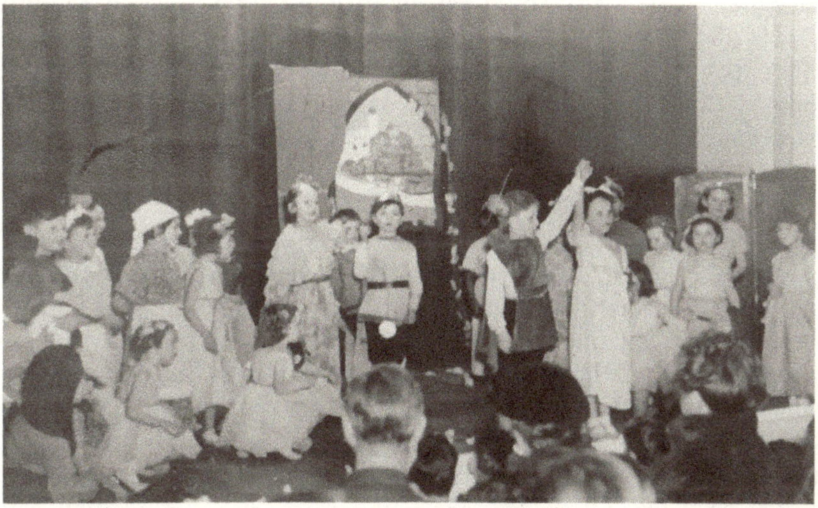

The Richard Atkins School Christmas play *The Sleeping Beauty* (with my school friend the lovely Geraldine Johnson in the title role). I'm on the extreme left of frame, a high collar halving my right ear, holding what looks like a home-made cardboard trumpet. Ever one to blow my own! I'm six years old, and already in the show biz!

My beloved Mummy was already looking around for other schools nearby, and she found out that a new school was about to open in Upper Tulse Hill. It was an infants and juniors establishment, to be called Fenstanton Junior Mixed, and was to begin classes, most conveniently for us, in 1952, on the site of a converted totally rebuilt old fifteen-bedroom mansion. The local word was that Fenstanton was to be a prototypical model of modern school design, with each classroom possessing a "wall of window" overlooking the school playgrounds. Mummy and Daddy decided that Fenstanton sounded much better for me. And so it came to be. We were all school newcomers to Fenstanton, and the large classes were exceptionally well-balanced. Boys and girls together, of course, and a few children from the local West Norwood Jewish Orphanage who had lost their parents to the war were in my class, and we bonded instantly.

I began at Fenstanton J.M. (Junior Mixed) on September 2nd, 1952. My headmistress was one Miss Yeomans, who appeared to me to be very stern, but was actually (though heaven forfend that you should guess) kindness itself, and I suspect that it is to her that I owe eternal, everlasting gratitude for selecting me to be a pupil at Fenstanton, where both reading, not to mention visits to the cinema, were encouraged. I was still no good at maths. Once behind, always behind.

I was also very fortunate to be at Fenstanton in a very great day in South London history. After the Coronation, in 1953, when Elizabeth II was enthroned as the nation's Queen, the Royal Couple, the Queen and her husband Prince Philip, the Duke of Edinburgh, departed for a tour of Great Britain, and, as luck would have it, Christchurch Road was on their South London itinerary, so we all stood outside of Fenstanton to catch a glimpse of the Queen and Philip in their open limousine passing my school, and I remember feeling both proud and glad simultaneously. I'd eventually get to see a lot of famous film stars in my time, but this happened to be the only time that I ever saw our own gracious Queen.

Also, I was now discovering Streatham. "Julian Sloman, Exclusive Tailor" was based at 62, Streatham Hill, near the Bus Garage. You could walk there from where we lived: straight down Downton Avenue towards Streatham High Road, turn right, cross over the road, and there you were. So you couldn't very well miss on your journey that huge building at the foot of Downton Avenue, on the other side of Streatham High Road. It was the newly-renovated Streatham Hill Theatre, a historic artifice bombed by the Germans in 1944 and now restored to its former glory in 1950, just in time for yours truly, who wasn't actually around in those days when it opened in 1929, until that war damage caused it to close.

I'd been taken to a few West End shows by then:-- John Mills in *Charley's Aunt* at the New Theatre in the Strand, and the *Billy Cotton Band Show Christmas Party* at the Prince of Wales, featuring ventriloquist and radio star Peter Brough, and his inimitable dummy Archie Andrews, and also, more locally, the great ventriloquist Dennis Spicer as *Dick Whittington* at the Granada, East Ham, but I'd never, ever dreamed of having a real live proper working full-scale theatre such as the Streatham Hill Theatre virtually on my own doorstep. All right, so I knew that it wasn't exactly a "Picture Palace", as we all used to call cinemas, but I eventually grew up to realise that there never really was anything quite like watching a real live show unfolding before your very eyes, with costumes, scenery, music, and actors, all in glorious reality, was there?

Daddy had a brilliant idea by way of showmanship. He booked an advertisement for his new shop in the centre pages of the Streatham Hill Theatre's weekly programme, initially on the primary page wherein that week's show title would appear, and eventually in the middle double-page spread, underneath the cast and scene listings. Not only was this a classy advertising deal for the dapper show business tailor that my father was, or wanted to become known as, because it did indeed attract the kind of local show business custom that he sought, but it also resulted in him being given two complimentary tickets for the first Monday night of every show taking place in the theatre. So I, who loved the cinema above all else, was also able to see an awful lot of very good live theatre, usually shows just prior to their

West End run, or commencing their nationwide tours just afterwards, on every Monday evening when there was a show considered age-appropriate, which there was virtually nearly every week it seemed to me as I grew up. What an education!

The very first theatre trip to the Streatham Hill Theatre that I can remember was to see the then-popular singing star Jill Day (very glamorous!) in a revival of the musical *The Belle of New York*. I also remember seeing Billie Worth (who took over from Ethel Merman on Broadway) and her husband Donald Burr in Irving Berlin's wonderful *Call Me Madam* after its London Coliseum run. What treats! I was also taken to see the Ballet Rambert as well, but I wasn't so keen on that.

On the opposite corner to the Streatham Hill Theatre was the newly-opened Moo-Cow Milk Bar, which was exactly what its name suggested: An American-style drugstore, serving sandwich snacks, teas and milkshakes. We didn't really frequent it (we didn't need to), but it looked just so glamorous, what with its pure post-war kitschy semi-art deco design. Directly opposite the Moo-Cow, on the very corner of Downton Avenue itself, was Fisher's Music Salon, selling not only pianos and gramophones, but actually having a record department, with the sleeves of that then brand-new invention the Long-Playing record displayed in the shop's windows. I had discovered records at Forest Gate, but the gramophone there was Grandad's and his records were mainly Yiddish or Al Jolson. Remember, it was 1950, and very soon the whole world was to have brashly revealed to it the music that would change almost everybody's life, including, and especially, mine.

On the corner opposite to Fisher's was L.Shulman, the kosher butcher. Very convenient for us, as we kept a kosher house, as indeed we had done in Forest Gate. Further down the High Road, on the opposite side of the road, was a cinema under repair: the Gaumont had been bombed during the war, and was soon to re-open as part of the Rank circuit. In the meantime, there was the ABC Streatham, the Regal, just off Leigham Court Road, and the very grand Streatham Astoria, soon to be renamed the Odeon, further down. Opposite the Gaumont there was a brand-new Wimpy Bar, and this was to eventually feature a new and potentially exciting device: a video jukebox called a Scopitone, in which you inserted half-a-crown and could see an artist perform. It was not only expensive, but had few major artistes on display: it largely featured second-raters like Al Saxon, Vince Hill or Mr. Acker Bilk. I tried it out by paying to watch rock'n'roller Vince Taylor perform his "Brand New Cadillac", but I thought that he wasn't really value for what was then half of my weekly pocket money, and never went back. Eventually the Scopitone was removed, and I learned much later that the American film star Debbie Reynolds had lost a small fortune on this soon-to-go-bankrupt foreign investment.

Two repertory cinemas existed on Brixton Hill: the Clifton, near my old school Richard Atkins, and further down, opposite the Lambeth Town Hall, was a Pullman, a sister flickhouse to the one I would later discover in Herne

Hill. Further along towards Tooting Broadway, there was an Essoldo, and in Tooting itself the repertory houses the Vogue and the Classic were mere blocks apart, in addition to the magnificent bejewelled picture palace that was the Granada, Tooting. I could not have been happier!

I also swiftly learned to discover what was playing. Although we probably had access to a local newspaper in Forest Gate, I never knew of its existence. But now we had *The Streatham News* – the local paper – delivered to our front door every Friday, and that contained a full page of the following week's film and theatre listings. Bliss! (Of course, I wasn't yet old enough to go anywhere on my own, and films still had to be considered "suitable" for me, but, with a little nagging I seem to have managed to see most of what I selfishly wanted to see, providing that it was suitably certificated, in those early, far-off days.)

I think that the first feature film that I was taken to see in Streatham was at the ABC Regal cinema, and it was the MGM Technicolor remake of *King Solomon's Mines*, which, frankly, could be said to have informed my cinematic taste for the rest of my life. And, significantly, it granted me a favourite film star. The English actor Stewart Granger portrayed the hero, romantic explorer and all-round action man Allan Quartermain, and, frankly, I desperately wanted to be him! I had never encountered such a dynamically virile handsome (and well-spoken) Technicolored hero before, and I had already seen a lot of films and plays for my age. I knew that I wanted to see every Stewart Granger film thereafter. I'd discovered a favourite film star, and one film, quite soon, would cement that celluloid relationship for ever. (I was not exactly alone, either, I later discovered. A young cinema usher in Memphis, Tennessee, had to be hauled out of his seat after viewing multiple screenings of that same particular MGM African epic to dash to a radio station that was playing his first newly-cut recording on the air. His name was Elvis Presley).

At that performance of *King Solomon's Mines* at the Regal, my Mother bought me a copy of the *ABC Film Review*, a monthly publication produced to publicise Associated British Cinemas, and eventually I built up a collection of the magazines, which I read and re-read regularly. That Christmas season, Dad received an invitation for the family to attend a children's party at the nearby Stork Club, and Mummy had the brilliant idea of cutting up all my *ABC Film Reviews*, attaching them to my clothes, and folding up one issue for me to hold as a "fan" (pun intended), and subsequently entering me in the Stork Club fancy dress competition as a "Film Fan", replete with a cocked hat made from the colourful covers. Well, I won a prize, but alas for all my magazines!

Other films followed:- also at the Regal, Streatham: Robert Taylor and Elizabeth Taylor in MGM's *Ivanhoe*, the first non-Biblical film I had ever seen featuring prominent Jewish characters identified as such in the story (no Fagins or Shylocks here!), Alastair Sim and a cast of British stalwarts in *Laughter in Paradise*, and Douglas Fairbanks Jr. and the lovely Yolande Donlan in *Mr. Drake's Duck*. Little could I ever possibly foresee that one day in my distant future I would be escorting the very same Yolande Donlan to meet her director husband Val Guest, and actually sharing a seat with her in James Leasor's extremely rare 1937 American Cord open sports car, on our way to the set of MGM's *Where the Spies Are*, on which I was working as the second assistant editor.

Two weeks after seeing *Ivanhoe* at the Regal I was taken by Gladys, who was the lady at the time who came in and "did" for us (the housekeeping, that is) at Downton Avenue, to see a film that may not exactly be deemed the best motion picture ever made, but immediately became my own personal favourite film of all time, and still is. Always was, still is, and probably forever will be, and I saw it first on its original release, at the ABC Regal, Streatham. I could not believe how simply wonderful *Scaramouche* was. As a movie, as a spectacle, as a romance, as sheer fun. Nor how magnificent, or just how perfectly cast, was Stewart Granger in the title role. When I first saw the film, that time in Streatham, I quite literally basked in its Technicolored qualities, and, much later on, on subsequent re-viewings, I began to appreciate its true values, notably how well made it was by director George Sidney.

Besides containing the longest-ever sword fencing match (Granger and Mel Ferrer – no doubles!), its design in Technicolor is exquisite, and Janet Leigh's stylish close-up introduction is, for me, the very best ever in screen history. I can never thank MGM enough. Of course, there may well be better, more worthy, more important, more innovative, and more humane films, but *Scaramouche* remains my own personal all-time favourite, and, I suspect, will always remain such. (I couldn't contain my childish delight at discovering that Stewart Granger and I shared the same May 6th birthday!).

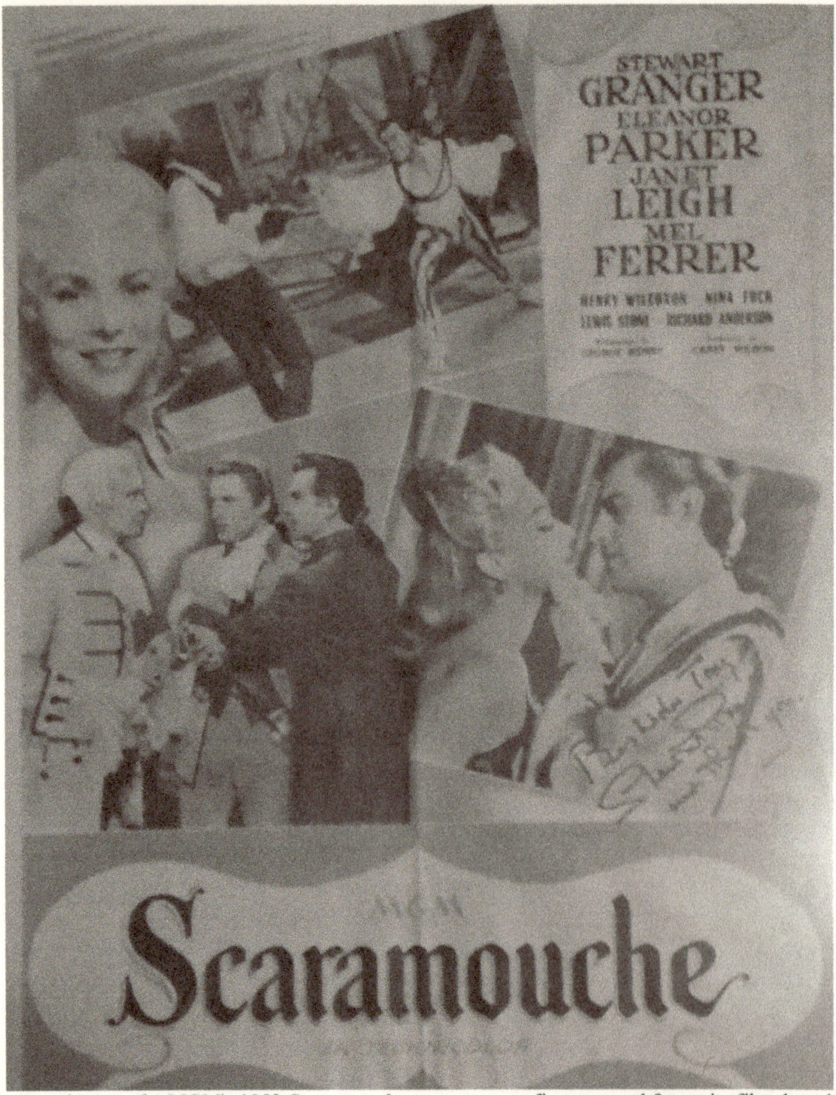

The French poster for MGM's 1952 *Scaramouche*, my own very first personal favourite film, bought in Paris, and, as you can see on the bottom right, personally autographed by Stewart Granger when I met him at his book-signing at Liberty's in London. The "and thank you" was nice. We met a few times later, notably when he asked me to sit in the front row at his NFT lecture to be there for him if he needed any help! (And also in Hollywood, when he invited me to a home-cooked Sunday lunch, but, alas, I had to leave Los Angeles the prior Saturday).

And there were other films at other cinemas. A weekend trip back to Forest Gate resulted in being taken to the Gaumont, Stratford, to see Walt Disney's *The Story of Robin Hood and his Merrie Men* (supported by a very poor British "B" crime film entitled *Hammer the Toff*). This was a screening that nearly drove my parents insane at my behaviour in the cinema. We were seated in the circle (considered the better or "posh" seats, although I eventually always preferred the stalls: closer to the screen), when my parents looked around for me and I was nowhere to be seen. The very young me had decided to try out almost every circle seat vacant, for the best possible view. We were seated about three or four rows back, and my young self clearly thought I could do better. I vaguely remember being "rescued" by my father from a seat at the side of the circle, and I clearly eventually decided that the seats in the very middle of the front row was where I preferred to sit. Not a care for the fact that my parents thought I had been kidnapped, or, worse, lost. What a terribly thoughtless and selfish brat I had now become. A cine-brat, indeed. Although I did stay put for all of *Robin Hood*; I only moved around during the second feature. Selfish as ever, little me never realised at the time how upset my parents must have been when they first noticed that I was missing in the dark.

Of course, I begged to see all the next available Stewart Granger films, and, although no *Scaramouche* (what could ever better it?), *The Prisoner of Zenda* and MGM's Coronation treat *Young Bess* were both deeply satisfying. I also liked Robert Taylor too, and, thanks to Granger turning down several roles that were already actually being prepared for him (Granger apparently didn't want to do any more costume pictures! – Actors!! They just don't know what's good for them!), I enjoyed very much both *Knights of the Round Table* and *The Adventures of Quentin Durward* and, eventually, its once-forbidding "X" certificate reverted to an "A" with cuts, *Quo Vadis?*, all eminently most suitable for my age-group.

But television was starting to take hold all over the land. Although I watched Annette Mills (John's sister) and *Muffin the Mule*, and Humphrey Lestocq with Mr. Turnip on *Whirligig*, not to mention *Andy Pandy* and *The Flowerpot Men*, I felt that television didn't fit my over-sophisticated needs. But, of course, everything was soon to change, when the music itself transformed, and, in England, that particular previously shut-down television slot between the closing of the children's hour and the start of adult-oriented television gave birth to the well-named, and much loved, *6.5 Special*, albeit still in black-and-white. But in the meantime, there was Streatham High Road, where my beloved Mother took me to see Gregory Peck in *The Million Pound Note* (called *Man with a Million* in the U.S.), and Alec Guinness as *Father Brown*, which was supported, I well remember, by Mickey Rooney in *Drive a Crooked Road*, all at the Astoria Streatham (later rechristened as an Odeon), and – an absolute major treat for me – the wonderful Ray Bolger in *Where's Charley?* at the ABC Regal, a Technicolored musical version of *Charley's Aunt*, which I already knew from having seen it on stage with John Mills, and was later to see at the Streatham Hill Theatre with the fabulous Frankie Howerd. And sometimes we would catch a suitable programme in the East End while visiting with relatives: I remember a terrific (to me at the time) Warner Bros. release double bill of the musical *About Face* and the Randolph Scott Western *Carson City* at the ABC, Stratford.

Monday nights at the Streatham Hill Theatre continued aplenty: Joan Rice (Walt Disney's Maid Marian) in *Rebecca*, Ralph Richardson in Robert Bolt's *Flowering Cherry*, Margaret Lockwood in Agatha Christie's *Spider's*

Web, major stars all, in those far-off days. But one evening, later on, I was very annoyed when the West End star of *The Long and the Short and the Tall*, one Peter O'Toole, didn't tour with the play. Alongside the other two featured players, Robert Shaw and Frank Finlay, I was disappointed to find O'Toole's touring understudy in the leading role of Private Bamforth, a then totally unknown actor called Michael Caine, who turned out to be, quite simply, absolutely bloody brilliant.

I took it all for granted, not to mention the special Christmas treats of seeing comedy stage and music hall stars such as Tommy Trinder (who was actually born in Streatham), Arthur Askey, and Jimmy Wheeler in pantomime at Streatham Hill, and also Laurie Lupino Lane and George Truzzi doing their "wallpaper" sketch, later immortalised on television by Norman Wisdom and Bruce Forsyth, plus the likes of Hughie Green, Shani Wallis (both in *Aladdin*), and Dick Emery and also especially not to mention that most wonderful long-legged panto principal "boy", Patricia Burke. I certainly never knew that, with the sole exception of the London Palladium, the traditional panto was on its last knockings, largely thanks to the proliferation of television sets. Cinemas, too, were taking a beating – the motion picture industry had to come up with something new, and that it did, twice.

I first heard about 3-D with the opening of *Bwana Devil*, a film obviously quite unsuitable for my young viewing, and one evening I was baby-sat while my parents went off to the Regal to see a film in 3-Dimension, called *Metroscopix* (in actual fact a joined-up collection of vintage MGM 3-D shorts) which supported Clark Gable in *Never Let Me Go*. I'd been baby-sat before, when Mummy and Daddy went off to see such popular adult hits as *The Snows of Kilimanjaro* or *La Ronde*, but this time I was really jealous: they were seeing 3-Dimension before I could, albeit being a black-and-white collection of 3-D shorts, viewed through supplied red-and-green glasses.

I could hardly wait to see this newly-revived movie process enlisted to fight the coming of television, but those early 3-D features turned out to be most unsuitable for me: it was well over fifty years later that I finally saw *Bwana Devil* in full 3-D at the Stereoscopic Festival in Hollywood at Grauman's Chinese Theatre, not to mention *House of Wax* and *Dial M for Murder*, also both caught up with many years later in Polaroid 3-D. However, the actual arrival of "suitable" 3-D features was swift, and in quick succession I saw MGM's wonderful *Kiss Me, Kate*, and then *Arena* (which was double-billed with the non-3-D *Latin Lovers*), plus the Warner Bros. westerns *The Charge at Feather River* and the marvellous *Hondo*, which began with John Wayne seeming to walk right past me in my very seat in the cinema. Wow! My young self was convinced that Third Dimensional cinema was here to stay. But unbeknownst to me at the time, 20th Century-Fox had something else quite special up its corporate sleeve…

Fox were experimenting with a wide-screen anamorphic (squeezed image) process that they called CinemaScope, which was to quite literally change the shape of picture-going forever. Coupled with magnetic stereophonic sound, it intended to be Hollywood's method of defeating its young upstart rival television once and for all, and at the time, before television went into colour, it very nearly succeeded. The cinema circuits had to completely re-equip their cinemas, and originally weren't keen to do so, but public demand initially for *The Robe*, Fox's first film in CinemaScope, forced their hand. Well, of course, I was desperate to see (or be taken to see) *The Robe*, but it remained in the West End, and was deprived of the usual commercial release because the main circuits weren't eager to change their screen sizes, so wisely Fox established a new circuit of their own, as gradually all Granada cinemas were newly converted to CinemaScope. I, of course, pestered Mummy and Daddy to take me to see 'Scope, but *The Robe* didn't initially play locally, and besides, was this tale of the Crucifixion really suitable for a young Jewish lad?

I must have pestered my parents badly enough (I really was a terror!) for Dad to take me "up West" to see what was to be my first film in 'Scope, and obviously considered suitable was the feature film of the Queen's Royal Tour, *Flight of the White Heron* at the newly-converted Carlton in the Haymarket. I was immediately converted myself despite the frankly rather unexciting subject and the newsreel approach to the subject matter. What a pain I must have been! (But eventually, Dad did take me to see *The Robe* at the Davis Cinema, Croydon: an adventure indeed!) But life wasn't only about the pictures. We'd acquired a Scottie dog who we called Judy, who was most affectionate, and we also had two kittens, who grew into two very independent cats, and my father and sister Linda named them (to my horror) Prudence Sue and White Apron Front. They co-existed with Judy (let alone us) beautifully, and, as far as I knew, happily.

Of course, I did know that the world wasn't entirely all about 3-D and CinemaScope, although they seemed important to me at the time, indicative, perhaps, of what a false sense of proportion I was already developing. After all, I was starting at a new school, and about to meet some new neighbours and make new school friends. And Mummy was pregnant again.

Once settled into our new home in Downton Avenue, we began to get to know our own neighbours. Next door, on the right, lived the Iveys, a family with three daughters: June, who was a few years older than me, Jilly (for Gillian), a shade younger than I, and Caroline, alliteratively known as Jo-Jo, who was much, much younger. All three girls were my playmates as I grew up into my teenage, and from all three did I gradually discover, in one way or another, what were then termed "the facts of life". I was closest to June, whose breasts were just beginning to bud, but both Jill and Jo-Jo were the first ever girls that I saw completely naked, and that's something you never forget. In their back garden, adjacent to ours, they had a pond in the centre, and a sand pit out the back. We just had a rather ordinary lawn, rather like the one I was used to at Forest Gate, though not quite as big. When Mummy and Daddy saw how much I enjoyed playing with the girls, unbeknownst to me Dad asked Bill Ivey if he minded if we copied his pool-and-sandpit combination in our own garden, and could he supply the name of the contractor? And that's exactly what happened. I played with the girls on their side, and they played with me on our slightly larger side, now converted to match theirs.

I was in heaven in the summer of course, and how I was spoiled! I discovered (in many ways) that girls were very different from boys, and how I liked it, especially when Jill and Jo-Jo often didn't bother with bathing costumes! But I developed a different kind of relationship with June Ivey. She seemed to recognise my love of film and theatre, and suggested that we put on a show for our parents, and that, somewhat amazingly, we did, upstairs in our top-of-the-house playroom. I was all of age six when we first performed these shows, and all of seven before we stopped. Programmes still exist for three of them, and I can't recollect how many shows we actually did eventually. The earliest programme I kept reads (in June's writing):--

1 Tight rope walking.

2 Clowns.

3 Juggling and Balance.

4 Funny Speeches.

5 Climbing.

6 Sing.

Apparently, I only featured on acts 2 and 4, and the finale, Act 6, has an "X" written beside it, so I assume, for whatever reason, it didn't happen. On all three existing programmes, I had written who the performers were, and it is quite clear to me now that June was the star, although I vaguely recall setting up all the necessary props and doing the stage introductions. One of these shows was actually (according to the programme) fiction. Called *Murder for Two*, it featured four characters, three played by June, and one (Peterson) by yours truly. I have no memory whatsoever of this particular event, but I do recall climbing awkwardly over the red-painted wooden shelves that served as our "stage". Our audience of respective parents applauded our activities, and, indeed, encouraged them. I guess I realised then that I did not want to ever perform in public, rather to be on the other side of the spotlights, in one way or another, for life, no Stewart Granger, me.

But there was another side to playing games with June and her various contemporary girlfriends. I hadn't yet learned the word "sex", but I knew – indeed we both knew – that the games that we played revolved around our respective sexual status. For instance, we played a game of forfeit around our sandpit, wherein I asked June to do something outlandish, usually athletic, and she asked me to do something similar, like name a comic character or a screen star. The penalties for failure were very interesting. It was summer, so questions that couldn't be answered or antics that couldn't be pursued were interestingly punished. June "punished" me by holding the waist of my swimming trunks and pouring sand over my genitals, at which she took a very good look and occasionally brushed against them slightly with her hand. I pretended embarrassment but I secretly loved it, and often, deliberately, gave a totally wrong answer. She, bright as a button, invariably got all her questions right. I don't remember her paying any forfeits, but I do remember and will never forget, me barging into her bedroom once afterwards when she and her girlfriend were taking off their swimming costumes and were about to get dressed. Ah, sweet memories of youth!

But it was June's younger sister Gillian who kind of really initiated me into the wonders of sex. You see, we were often left alone in the newly re-titled playroom, the Disc Den, to play, but we were of an age when the rules of "play" were changing, and so were we. We began by kissing, and then by feeling up each other's bodies, gradually growing more and more daring. It was exciting and wonderful, and very, very nice, but somehow contemporary conditioning told me it was "wrong", or, at the very least, "naughty". Eventually, I sent her home one afternoon around teatime, but she returned later that very evening. I scooted her out before my parents knew, and promised we would carry on another day. But we never did.

We had other neighbours on Downton Avenue as well, and they had daughters too. Over the road Mummy got pally with Dora Dormer, "Scatty Dora" Dad called her, but, of course, never to her face, and she had a daughter called Pauline, who had a friend called Christine, who also lived nearby, and they were of my age. They were, individually, my first ever real "dates". Christine was a great Anthony Newley fan, and we shared together listening experiences to his very first L.P. in her bedroom, and I eventually took Pauline to see Jimmy "Handy Man" Jones at the Elephant and Castle Trocadero, supported by a then-unknown Mark Wynter. Later on, in my teens, I discovered that Pauline's father had been a film cameraman, and worked with a British shorts-maker called Widgey Newman. I didn't believe such a name at first, and thought he said "Ritchie" Newman, but no, when I eventually found out, I wished that I had quizzed him more. He also had a 16mm. projector, the first I'd ever seen, and he showed me one evening in the early sixties a black-and-while excerpt from MGM's *Plymouth Adventure*. But it was getting late, so afterwards I dashed home to be greeted by Mummy, who told me that President Kennedy had been shot. Incredible. We immediately switched on the television to find the BBC tastelessly showing a Harry Worth sitcom, which, of course, they should have cancelled, after which we heard the unbelievably tragic news from Dallas: that the President was dead.

Further down Downton lived the Evans family, Joan and Di (that's male: I never actually found out what "Di" was short for, but he was Welsh, so I guessed that it was Dafydd). Di embarrassed me much later on by smoking a cigarette in synagogue at my Bar Mitzvah. The Rabbi stopped preaching and stared at him. All eyes followed his gaze, and, realising what he had done, Di put out the cigarette, and the Rabbi resumed. Joan and Di had three sons: David (my age), Stephen (younger), and – I forget. One day Di was collecting me and David from Fenstanton when his back car door opened suddenly and Stephen fell out on to the road. I didn't know what to do. Di stopped the car, got out, picked Stephen up, and drove off swiftly to the nearest hospital. Stephen was badly scratched and frightened, but eventually okay, thank goodness. Our other neighbours included May and Nat Freedman, and their son Martin, and, as far as I knew, they were the only other Jews in Downton Avenue. What a difference from Forest Gate and the East End!

Other major changes were on the horizon as well. My Mother seemed not to be very well, and the state of her health was always kept a secret from me by Daddy, who always seemed to hate disruptions to his life-style. For instance, I never knew until much, much later on, that, when I was taken to see *Easter Parade* at Forest Gate, it was because Mummy was having all her teeth removed at once at that very moment. Were they all diseased? I never knew, never found out. I just knew that at night she took them all out – upper and lower – and they lived in a glass at her bedside. Daddy, too, also had false teeth, and at night his teeth resided in a similar glass at his side of the bed. At the time, I assumed it was natural, and happened to everybody. What did I know?

And now, in the autumn and winter of 1951, my Mummy was very pregnant, and the baby was due in February. Except no-one actually told me. Linda Susan Deborah Sloman was born on February 17th, 1952, at the Lambeth Hospital. Daddy wanted to call her "Lindy Sue", hence the two first names, but that American-style teeny bop name never really suited her, and she has never, ever, used it to my knowledge, even to this day. "Deborah" for Nanna Morris' mother, who I knew only as "Booba", and then barely. Mummy was in hospital for quite a while, and Nanna came to look after me and stay with us at home. It seemed a long time to me before Mummy came home with Linda.

Suddenly, I was no longer the centre of family attraction. Well, I did have "The Pictures". No-one told me that Mummy would need so much time to recover from the birth, and I'm pretty sure I didn't really understand what had actually happened, nor what changes to my own life would be incurred. (All I really can remember of Mummy being in hospital was a visit from Auntie Doris and Uncle Don wherein Auntie Doris went off to visit Mummy and Uncle Don took me and my cousin David to the Brixton Pullman cinema to see a revival of *The Cruel Sea*. As per custom, we entered whenever convenient to us, during a scene where Stanley Baker referred to his pork sausages as "snorkers". David and I were quite baffled, hearing language never previously witnessed. But soon the word was translated in on-screen dialogue, and we then knew exactly where to see the film round to again before we left the cinema: our cue was "snorkers".)

One new fact I was sure of. The presence in our home of Linda meant that my visits to the cinema with my parents would be severely curtailed: she was far too young to leave with a baby-sitter. But I was wrong. I'd underestimated my parents, whose worry, I found out later, for me that was my love of cinema would indeed be curtailed, and so I found myself being taken to "The Pictures" by a whole new batch of people, of which more later.

In the meantime, how to get myself to the Pictures? A new British film was making the chat circuit. People were talking about *Doctor in the House*, which had a "U" certificate, and I was very anxious to see it. But Mummy was nursing Linda, and Daddy was working during the day. Now, I can't be sure whose idea it was – Mummy's or mine – but I ended up actually in the street outside our house, holding a hat with a motley collection of small "lucky dip" items in it, begging strangers to buy something for a penny, to take a chance, in order to raise the ninepenny price of child admission to go to the Odeon. I remember that for one of the objects, I had raided a pack of Dad's cards for the Ace of Diamonds (I don't think he ever found out), and the other items included some disposable Dinky toys, and a few then-new Matchbox toys. I really needed that child admission price of 9d.! And I managed it! It took a while, but a few good-natured passers-by took pity on this child, and paid a penny each for a good luck charm. In about an hour, I had secured my price of admission ticket and rushed inside to tell Mummy, who, I think, then advanced me threepence for my bus fare to the Odeon and back. And off I went to the pictures…

Now, of course, this meant that I would now break my newly self-made rule of not going in during the film, but I really couldn't wait (it had already been a minor heartache waiting to see if I could actually raise the financial "readies" in the first place), so when I actually arrived I paid and went in immediately, to be greeted on screen by a row of Technicolored babies' bottoms. To me, then, this was both daring, funny and appropriate, since I had just left Mummy doing something very similar to Linda's behind! But much more importantly, it made it very, very easy for me to remember where I came in. So, disregarding any promise I may have made to myself after *The Cruel Sea* "snorkers" viewing, I stayed around until the bottoms appeared again, and just a smidgeon longer to make absolutely certain it was the right place to leave, and then I got up and I vacated the Odeon. My first visit to a cinema on my own! (But "This is where we came in" – a much-used and popular line of dialogue amongst cinemagoers in those days –was never really quite part of my own vocabulary, for obviously purist reasons).

My Dad was a keen poker player, and once a week he played cards with a very sophisticated and interesting group of people – interesting to me, that is. The game circulated, and we played host roughly once a month before Linda was born, and about once every six weeks afterwards. I found them all exotic and extraordinarily interesting, to say the least, and I well remember my embarrassment at having to kiss my father "Goodnight" in front of them before I went to bed:-

Gary and Louise. Gary was a very distinguished-looking Russian Jew, with a pronounced accent, and his wife Louise was, I thought, ravishingly lovely, as beautiful and as sophisticated as she was cool. I adored her.

Freddie and Barbara Sparks. Freddie Sparks had been one half of a comic duo, and had played the music halls. A close friend of theirs was the comedian Max Wall, whose then-current off-stage antics involving his wife and various mistresses, including 1955's Miss Great Britain, virtually caused the collapse of his career at the time, but he made a splendid recovery in the 'seventies. Freddie was still a very funny man.

Pamela and Gerry Hart were also extremely sophisticated friends of Dad's, and were extraordinarily kind to me later on in my life, offering me accommodation after Mummy died.

Ron – well, he was just "Ron". I thought him grumpy, and he never said "Goodnight" to me when I had to say "Goodnight" to everybody before I went to bed.

"Uncle" Laurie, who was a genuine uncle from my father's London side, the Morrises. One day, Uncle Laurie would help me get to Paris for the first time; I'll never forget that, but that would be in the future for now. He was related to Alf and Lily Morris, who we used to visit sometimes in the East End of a Sunday morning, and to Uncle Roy Morris, the Morris of the Rose-Morris music instrument store in Denmark Street, Tin Pan Alley itself, the home of British pop music, birthplace of English rock'n'roll.

So you see, while Mummy was nursing Linda there were card games going on. We lived in a gambling house!! But the stakes were very small: pennies, shillings and even maybe half-crowns. These games were strictly for the players' enjoyment only, and when I popped in to kiss Daddy goodnight, I could sense a feeling of annoyance that the poker game actually had to stop for a family "Goodnight". But that was just fine with me. I didn't linger long for two reasons. The first was the sheer embarrassment of having to kiss my father goodnight in public, and the second was the smoke: I couldn't stand the atmosphere – I could barely see my father, let alone the door to leave them all alone in their pleasure! Everybody there – but everybody – smoked, Uncle Laurie the worst of all with his cigars. Later, neither I nor my sister Linda ever smoked, ever, nor did we either find card-playing attractive.

How did I enjoy Fenstanton school? Well, at first, that September 1952, I quite liked it. I truly don't remember starting there, but by September 1953 I had graduated from the infants to the juniors, and in January 1954 from Class 3A to Class 3. I had a Swiss lady teacher called Miss Leitschi (or close) for a while, and we got on famously. On discovering that I actually liked to read, she encouraged me to bring some books of my own to school to add to the class library temporarily, and she was surprised that I was so well-read in both children's literature (I'd already read, and loved *Orlando, the Marmalade Cat* by November 1948, according to "The Progress Book"), and also most of the children's classics that were recommended in "The Progress Book" itself. I'd already ruined that Book's pages by crudely indicating with an ink blob those that I had read: forty-seven blobs, no less, and some fifteen other titles added in ink by 1952. Miss Leitschi suggested I loan some of my books that I had particularly enjoyed to the form library for others to read. That I did, regretting it later because the books were invariably returned damaged in some way or another. It put me off lending books for life.

I have a strange memory of Miss Leitschi. One day, we were reading a nautical book out loud, and the expression "broad beam", referring to a ship, occurred, and someone laughed. Miss Leitschi picked up on the expression, and asked us nine-year-olds if we knew another meaning for "broad beam". We all looked blank, and she, chuckling, blithely informed us it also meant "big bottom". We laughed at her rudeness, and then she asked us all – would you believe? – if anyone with a "broad beam" would put up their hands. Well, to my surprise, a few children did so, mainly girls. Then, to my extreme horror, she then suggested that I, and another quite chubby boy called Alan Jones, who was the class misfit clown, put our hands up as well. Mortified, we duly did so. More laughter, but his time at my expense. Unsurprisingly, that's all I remember.

It was at playtime at Fenstanton that I really got to know people. I was useless at sports, and desperately uninterested in them, so I got talking to others, and discovered a mutual interest. Jane Dunn told me she had seen a film called *The Lavender Hill Mob* that her parents had taken her to see, and she described it to me. I remember feeling jealous. Peter Westlake and I discussed our favourite film stars. Mine were Stewart Granger and Robert Taylor, and his were Alan Ladd and Audie Murphy, neither of whom at that time I had ever seen; but when I told other children what I <u>had</u> seen, no-one ever recognised the titles, and I vaguely remember feeling jealous of someone who had been taken to see *Where the River Bends* (U.S. title *Bend of the River*). I really had no need to be jealous – after all, I had virtually seen <u>everything</u> considered "suitable", which *Where the River Bends* clearly was not.

The headmistress, Miss Yeomans, grew aware of my extraordinary propensities for both film and literature, and was about to play an extremely important role in my life. The nearby distinguished public school Dulwich College was about to establish a new entry method for parents who couldn't pay the fees demanded by the school. It was called the Gilkes (after a celebrated Dulwich headmaster) Experiment, and the London County Council would contribute to the cost of chosen pupils. Miss Yeomans asked my parents if it would be allowable, if my school marks continued to be acceptable, to recommend me for entrance to Dulwich College for my further education, which, usefully, would then lead to a major university. Although it would not be until January of 1956 that I would be taking the Common Entrance Examination, it was something to contemplate earlier, in order to propose it, and she was also recommending a friend of mine from Fenstanton, Peter Chappell, for the same examinations.

Now Peter had a really unique and utterly fascinating (though singularly disgusting) playground trick: I have no medical training at all, so I do hope that you'll forgive the following lay description:-- At will, Peter could produce streams of green snot from either of his nostrils, or even both simultaneously, and could manage to control their descent. These streams could, either together or individually, reach as far as his knees, or even be made to halt before reaching his shoes, and then, at a sniff, could be recalled instantly back into his nose. Amazing, no? Well, this unique procedure simultaneously revolted and fascinated me. After all, I had visited both Tom Arnold's and Bertram Mills' circuses at Harringay and Olympia respectively, and had never, ever seen anything like this, not even ever suggested, and nor, I suspected, had anyone else. That I found the whole business utterly revolting left me in a minority. It clearly made Peter Chappell the most famous person in the whole playground, and it was interesting to me that his biggest audience seemed to be the girls, the boys preferring sporting activities. Me, I used to watch the girls watching Peter. I liked watching the girls – I liked watching them tuck their skirts into their underwear just before they played netball. I especially remember pretty Valerie Carter (whose best, inseparable friend was sweet Angela Groombridge) one day, in front of me, deliberately dropping her panties down to her ankles, and then bringing them back up, over her skirt, instead of just tucking the skirt into the pants. Did I catch a glimpse of anything naughty? No, but the action itself was – at least to me, then – so sexy that I can remember it to this day!

I invited both Valerie and Angela to my 11th birthday party (or was it my 10th?) but neither came. Neither did another invitee, the pert and pretty Caroline Williams, who used to walk home with me. She lived in an adjacent road, and her father had a stamp collection, and that, ostensibly, was the reason to invite me home one day. I was an avid stamp collector at the time (British Empire only), and Caroline and I were close enough then for her to make the offer. I met her father, and we talked stamps, ignoring Caroline completely. We were never as close again after that. In fact, at my 11th (or was it 10th?) birthday party, I had only one guest who was a girl, a nice Jewish girl whose name was Gail Richman, and the rest were all boys. You know, it never ever occurred to selfish me just how Gail must have felt as the only girl present.

Peter Chappell, like my cousin Michael and certain other boys that I had got to know, was fatherless, the war having taken a heavy toll, and we became very close friends at Fenstanton, despite my extreme distaste for his nasal displays. When he found out that I loved "The Pictures" (no-one British called them "movies" in those days, and "Cinema" was far too posh a word for the likes of us), he mentioned me to his mother, and also the fact that I must have shared with him my regular on-going complaint, that with Mummy looking after baby Linda all the time, and with Daddy working all hours, I therefore had nobody to take me to the Pictures. (Of course, a complaint which, like all the "facts" I told people about myself at the time, wasn't quite strictly true.) Anyway, Peter Chappell's mum was pleased that her son had found a seemingly close friend, and so she duly took us to the Pictures. A particular treat for me was the Audie Murphy biopic *To Hell and Back*, since it was "A" certified, but we also saw "U" programmes as well: the Humphrey Bogart comedy *We're No Angels*, and a Universal double bill (60-40 split) of Jeff Chandler in *The Spoilers* together with the series flick *The Kettles in the Ozarks*, all programmes seen from my favourite seats, the front stalls at either the Astoria or the newly-refurbished Gaumont, Streatham.

But eventually I behaved very, very badly to Peter Chappell, and I deeply regret it, even until this day. Both Peter and I took that same entry examination to Dulwich College. I got in, but he didn't, and he went to Dulwich's sister school, Alleyn's. When we met again after having been close friends for several years, with much in common, I'm afraid that I behaved like an absolute shit. He came round one day to listen to some records and have a chat, and I – and I don't know why – behaved appallingly and snobbishly. At Dulwich, it was drilled into us that we Alleynians were far superior to those less fortunate who had to go to Alleyn's, or indeed any other schools, and I began to talk down to Peter. I really don't know why. I don't even know if I did it consciously, but I know I made him uncomfortable. We played a few then-popular records, and chatted, but he left, and I never saw him again. Why did I do it? I really can't remember at all what I said to Peter that day – it was just my condescending manner, my whole general attitude, a Public School snob in the making, I'm ashamed to admit, but I remember, and I have regrets....

My father's card-playing cronies also began to grow close to me. "Auntie" Barbara Sparks took me all the way to Tooting to see *There's No Business Like Show Business* at the extremely lavish Granada cinema, part of 20th Century-Fox's new unofficial CinemaScope circuit, which, amongst other pleasures, afforded me my first cinema sighting of that soon-to-be icon of the nineteen-fifties, Miss Marilyn Monroe herself. But for me, the real novelty of that film was seeing the then-current singing sensation Johnnie ("Cry") Ray playing a man of the faith, of course both Marilyn and Johnnie Ray being much more interesting to me at that time than the film's actual stars, Ethel Merman, Dan Dailey and Mitzi Gaynor. (I would learn much better, later on.)

I came late to Marilyn. Via the cinema advertisements page in our local paper *The Streatham News*, I discovered that a Fox CinemaScope feature that had done badly on its West End opening, called *On the Threshold of Space*, was being supported on its release by a revival of the very film that propelled Marilyn Monroe to international stardom, *Gentlemen Prefer Blondes*. But that film (despite censor cuts in its day) bore the dreaded (to me) "A" certificate, which meant that I couldn't go without an accompanying adult. What to do? Well, obviously, ask my Dad to take me (but, of course, not on a card night). But he didn't want to. Well, that just wasn't acceptable to selfish little me. Not at all. With hindsight, I think that he just wasn't interested in seeing that particular programme, or he probably didn't want to leave Mummy on her own for an evening. Whatever. I didn't care. I did the only thing that my spoilt little self thought possible: I threw myself onto the floor of my bedroom in tantrum mode, and screamed. I wouldn't go to bed, wouldn't even undress, let alone think of putting on my pyjamas, until Dad promised to take me to see that revival of *Gentlemen Prefer Blondes*. How else could I see it? Waah! Waah! (My goodness, what a little shit I was!) Waah! Waah! Waah! And it worked! Dad did take me to the Granada Tooting, and I did get to see Marilyn Monroe in all her Technicolored glory. In my opinion, she never ever looked quite as gorgeous again as she did when immortally performing "Diamonds are a Girl's Best Friend" (with George Chakiris in her backing chorus, although, of course, I didn't know who he was at the time).Was I ashamed of my wicked methodology, of how I raised hell to get to be taken to "The Pictures"? Was I heck!!

Oddly, Daddy didn't seem to hold it against me. In fact, he seemed to enjoy it as much as he did when taking me regularly on a Monday night to the Streatham Hill Theatre on his freebies, whereby I saw, and was duly educated by, those pre- or post-West End theatre runs. And then Dad managed to do something special for me at that theatre, something unutterably wonderful. Dad had gotten to know the stage door keeper at the Streatham Hill Theatre, and knowing that I wanted to collect autographs, had come to an agreement with him wherein he would leave my autograph book with this gentleman, who would then acquire the signature of the players for me. And he did. Peter Cushing in *The Sound of Murder*, George Baker in *Towards Zero*, and several other major British talents, and then only in the shows that I was allowed to see, that is, those shows that were considered "suitable", which, by the way, *West Side Story*, a show of which I had never previously heard at the time, playing two weeks instead of the usual mere one at Streatham Hill prior to its West End opening, was absolutely not!

But there was a moment when a very real, very famous American movie star did appear at the Streatham Hill Theatre. I had seen Tyrone Power in *Diplomatic Courier* and in two CinemaScope specials *The Long Gray Line* and *The Eddie Duchin Story* and knew of his background at 20th Century-Fox and all about his love scandals (no, not the gay ones – we were at least a decade --or more-- away from all of those particular revelations) and his current relationship with Linda Christian, everything detailed in my regular weeklies *Picturegoer* and *Picture Show*, of course. Well, Dad left my autograph book with the Streatham Hill Theatre stage door keeper. And when I received it back – what a glorious surprise! Tyrone Power had actually signed a photograph of himself for me! Actually!! A real Hollywood film star! Life could surely get no better!!

But I wasn't really paying attention to real life, nor did I wonder why I was having such a wide variety of baby-sitters to look after me. Mummy seemed to take a long while to recover from giving birth to Linda, and I recall that over that period Nanna Morris came to stay with us for quite a while, but of course I was far too selfishly obsessed with "The Pictures", and also in newly discovering South London, most notably Streatham Hill and all its environs. Daddy took me as a special treat to see Judy Garland in *A Star is Born* at the Streatham Regal, and I was also taken to see *Guys and Dolls* there. Suddenly, CinemaScope and Magnetic Stereophonic Sound seemed a very necessary part of my pre-teen existence. A life pattern was beginning to form.

Further down Streatham High Road, at number 158, Streatham Hill to be precise, was situated the dance hall palace run by Mecca called The Locarno, glamorously, garishly illuminated at night and clearly immensely popular. I was, of course, far too young (and, frankly, disinterested) at the time to visit the Streatham Loc. as it was colloquially termed, but I well knew that my own parents actually met each other at a dance hall, legendarily when Dad was on R.A.F. leave and when Mummy and Auntie Doris were regularly visiting the famed Astoria Ballroom on London's Charing Cross Road (later to become the Astoria cinema, home of 70mm. presentations) on Sundays to dance, usually, to the Joe Loss Orchestra, invariably playing American dance band hits. My Dad, attractively moustachioed and in his smart R.A.F. uniform, picked up Eve, and the rest is history. My history in fact, so I knew quite a bit about what went on in dance halls.

Above the Locarno itself was situated a genuine night club, unusual outside the spurious glamour of London's West End, called the Stork Club, which featured evening dancing regularly, and was a venue for classy, usually local, show business customers, which invariably included my parents Eve and Julian, and their friends, and I was then left with the baby-sitter, indeed quite a variety of differing baby-sitters.

I was beginning to learn quite a bit about life from my baby-sitters, who were often accompanied by their various current boy friends from whom I also learned a lot, mainly about new usages in current slang, at least until it was time to put me to bed. There was one special time that I recall when a baby-sitter's boyfriend brought along his portable record player and a collection of records, which were all singles on 45 r.p.m. At that time I only had a few 78 r.p.m. singles, blue label Philips titles like "The Deadwood Stage" doubled up with "Secret Love" by Doris Day, Frankie Laine's "Moby Dick", and Johnnie Ray's "Just Walkin' in the Rain". But I knew, we all did, that something new and exciting was happening in the air in the world of popular music, and I recall first hearing some of that newly-minted rock'n'roll sound in the records that my baby-sitter's boyfriend brought along that special night (before, of course, I was sent to bed). He brought over a batch of utterly spellbinding 45s, all of them by (to me) new American artistes, most of which whose names I can't remember now, but one artiste stood out like none other, and his name was Carl Perkins, and his record label was London-American which, the boyfriend explained to me, was the collective label name used by English Decca for their U.K. release of various independent American record labels. I was in a new and exciting world, and eager to learn. (My domestic music education had previously consisted of having had pointed out to me the English musical acts who happened to be Jewish, which seemed to be almost everybody I liked: Frankie Vaughan, who was my mother's favourite of favourites, Anne ("Lay Down Your Arms") Shelton, Lita Roza, *Melody Maker* magazine's Number 1 male vocalist Benny Lee, plus Marion Ryan from T.V.'s *Spot the Tune*, and heaven knows who else...). But there and then, on that particular turntable, that evening I was introduced to Carl Perkins, Arthur Alexander, Ronnie Hawkins, Johnny Burnette, and some absolutely wonderful doo-wop groups, including The Platters and Frankie Lymon and the Teenagers. I simply couldn't believe those sounds! For someone brought up on the likes of Dickie Valentine and David Whitfield on television, this music I was hearing was not only exciting but also exotic, and somehow extraordinarily relatable. I made a major mental note to save my pocket money in order to buy such discs. The boyfriend also mentioned that a someone called Elvis Presley had recorded a cover version of a Carl Perkins song called "Blue Suede Shoes", and to listen out for it on the radio. Well, the rest is history, not just mine, for the whole wide world was about to start rockin' and rollin', if they hadn't already. "You should hear 'Hound Dog,'" the boyfriend said.

And so I did, and purchased it immediately. It cost five shillings – a whole week's pocket money – for that particular HMV 78. I saved up to buy it, hurried to bring it home, and played it over and over again. And then I played the "B" side "Don't Be Cruel", and it was even better than "Hound Dog"! I couldn't stop playing it! What on this whole planet could possibly be better than American rock'n'roll? Nothing!! (Still true, although at that time I hadn't yet discovered 70mm., gourmet cooking, lots of money, or even sex!).

I mentioned my new-found love of rock'n'roll to my parents, but it seemed to come as no great surprise to them, and to my utter astonishment Dad revealed that he had been asked to work with The Platters on their upcoming British tour, to supply them with frilly shirts and matching ties, and that he had already made suits for a couple of well-known British band outfits: Locarno regulars Bob Miller and his Millermen, who famously played an engagement at the Locarno on the Queen's Coronation Day, and also Chris Barber and his Jazz Band, which at that time featured future skiffle star Lonnie Donegan. I was suitably (no pun intended) impressed. Not only that, but through his contacts with Bob Miller, Dad was able to get ticket passes to Bob Miller's weekly radio show *Easy Beat*, and he took me a couple of times to their live transmissions during the school holidays.

Now, *Easy Beat* featured a regular *Juke Box Jury*-type panel show, with panellists chosen from that day's audience, and I was selected on two occasions (I suspect Dad had a hand in my selection, but that never occurred to me until well after it had happened). The second show was notable for the instant, and loud, audience rapprochement that I earned when, after having been subjected to deep-throated Helen Shapiro's then-new release "Don't Treat Me Like a Child" I said to the packed audience (and, of course, the radio listeners), "I'll buy a Helen Shapiro record when she starts sounding like a girl!" Uproar in the house!!

I was far too young to see the notorious *Blackboard Jungle* when it was first released in 1955. Although initially truncated by the British film censor, it always bore the "X" certificate which forbade it to us under-sixteens. Nevertheless, the Bill Haley track of "Rock Around the Clock" used in the film had an unsurpassed effect which changed the whole world's listening habits forever, including mine when I finally caught up with it on the occasion when Dad took both myself and my cousin Michael to see *Blackboard Jungle* in an MGM reissue programme, double-billed with a revival of *Rogue Cop*, co-starring for me Robert Taylor from *Ivanhoe* together with Janet Leigh from *Scaramouche*, just across Streatham High Road at the new Gaumont. Well, I might have been a little late in actually buying that Brunswick 78 of "Rock Around the Clock", but I did get to see on release (also playing at the very same Streatham Gaumont) the then-notorious "U"-certified film follow-up which was actually entitled *Rock Around the Clock*, a film now famous for rock'n'rollers rioting in the aisles (at certain screenings only, infamously allegedly possibly aided by some dubious financial bribery from *The Daily Mirror*). To be able to purchase Elvis Presley and Bill Haley 78s then with my own pocket money was a clear indication of my musical tastes, then as now, and, to quote Wordsworth in another context, "Bliss was it in that dawn to be alive, but to be young was very heaven…"

Southend wasn't our only holiday resort visited. When Mummy was better we had two caravan holidays en famille in Bognor Regis, in both 1956 and 1957, on a caravan site in Shripney. We all took off, all four of us, in Daddy's car, and drove to the South East resort. I don't remember very much about the first caravan holiday, but we must have liked it or we wouldn't have gone back the following year. All I can remember – surprise, surprise – were the pre-release films we saw which had opened, I guess, concurrently with London's West End, only in Bognor, where we saw them, they invariably played with a supporting film, which wouldn't have happened in London. I recall being impressed by Jack Hawkins in the CinemaScoped *Land of the Pharaohs*, supported by a Clint "Cheyenne" Walker hour-long TV film, either *Border Showdown* or *Mountain Fortress* (I saw them both, but I can't remember with which), and – a real highlight – my first Alfred Hitchcock film:-- *The Man Who Knew Too Much* in Technicolor and VistaVision, after which I, as did most of the known world, bought Doris Day singing "Que Sera, Sera", on that famous Philips blue label 78. Daddy also took me to a couple of "Sunday for One Day Only" screenings on those holidays: *Joe Macbeth*, a British gangster version of Shakespeare, starring America's Paul Douglas and Ruth Roman, and then Walt Disney's much more suitable *The Littlest Outlaw*.

Meanwhile, when back home and generally throughout the school holidays, I was finally actually allowed to go to "The Pictures" on my own at last, when the programmes being screened were both "U" (for "Universal") certificated by the British Film Censors Board. I recall seeing such eminently suitable double bills as *Yankee Pasha* and *Rails into Laramie*, *Dangerous*

Mission and *The Sea Around Us*, *Khyber Patrol* and *The Golden Mistress*, *Four Guns to the Border* and *Abbott and Costello Meet the Keystone Kops*, *Glory* and *The Treasure of Pancho Villa*, and *Malaga* and *Why Men Leave Home*. Titles all virtually totally forgotten today, and with good reason in general, but *Why Men Leave Home* especially interested me, for it introduced me to the world of Hollywood make-up, featuring as it did Ern Westmore, of the groundbreaking Westmore film and cosmetics make-up family. As for that newcomer, that box in the corner: Television, eat your heart out!

Also, some rare weeks, if I saw a programme that I particularly enjoyed on the Sunday it reached my local, I would go again to see it on the following Saturday, which would be the very last day of the London circuit release. I recall doing this at least twice. Once was with the splendid Doris Day Warner Bros. CinemaScope musical *Lucky Me*, which I absolutely loved, and again with the pleasurable MGM double bill of Stewart Granger as *Beau Brummell* together with a rather slight but nevertheless very enjoyable Jane Powell and Debbie Reynolds musical about body-building called *Athena*, although the latter co-feature, seen again some fifty years later surprisingly programmed in a National Film Theatre lesbian and gay season, turned out to be quite disappointing when re-viewed, the MGM gloss notwithstanding. "Never go back" is the lesson learned there! But perhaps that more recent memory of seeing "Athena" again was somewhat soured by the circumstances of my attempting to leave the NFT quickly afterwards in order to catch a bus home from Waterloo Bridge when my walk up the steps to the bridge was deliberately halted by two largish butch lesbians in front of me who attempted to block my pathway, and duly addressed me with "Oh, does the little man want to get past, then?" After I didn't reply, the two of them formed a barrier, and continued to attempt to stop my progress. I muttered something like "Would you please excuse me?", and managed, thank goodness, to roughly force my way past them. Who needs that?

It was to be a particularly singular co-feature that originally played with Victor Mature's *Dangerous Mission* on release that was to loom very large in my later career. When I was working as second assistant editor on *One Million Years B.C.* for Hammer Films at Elstree Studios, I remembered the opening sequences of *The Sea Around Us*, which I had seen in that original release double bill back in 1954 at the Odeon Streatham, when Hammer said that they needed a Creation of the Earth montage sequence, and I mentioned that specific film to producer Michael Carreras, and so Hammer, on my recommendation, subsequently sought the footage, and eventually used it for the opening of their film. Director Don Chaffey remembered this, and his memory of it played a major part, I believe, in my being hired as the Film Librarian on that legendary ITC television series *The Prisoner* in 1966, but much, much more of that later on…

Speaking of *The Prisoner*, the first time that I encountered the name of Patrick McGoohan occurred around this time. My mother took me to the Streatham Odeon (at my urging, I suspect), to see a film programme in which I was really interested. Older pundits were forever seeking an end to rock'n'roll, and Columbia studios and producer Sam Katzman, the makers of both *Rock Around the Clock* and *Don't Knock the Rock*, thought that they had come up with the answer; the cha-cha, and so they made *Cha-Cha-Cha Boom*, featuring Perez Prado, which bombed worldwide, and I was interested to see it. In the U.K. that particular film went out on Odeon circuit release supporting *Zarak*, a CinemaScope Northwest Frontier adventure also starring Victor Mature, and I persuaded Mummy to take me, which she gratefully did. Although Mature and Michael Wilding were the real male stars of *Zarak*, their scenes were stolen by the actor playing Wilding's military adjutant, who opened the film in a dynamic plot explanatory scene set in the barracks billiard room, and then appeared regularly throughout the movie. The end credits roll revealed that the actor playing the character called Moor Larkin was one Patrick McGoohan, and his *Zarak* impact resulted, I was to discover, in a "Talent Spot" article by the ever-perceptive film critic Margaret Hinxman in a then-recent issue of my current *Picturegoer* magazine, replete with a photograph from *Zarak*. Little could I possibly imagine that a mutuality of certain futures would be forever interlinked.

I took my Common Entrance examination in January, 1956, and the Entrance Examination to Dulwich College in April, 1956. According to "The Progress Book", in my own juvenile writing, the result of the former was "Excellent", and of the latter "V. Good". I won three book prizes whilst at Fenstanton, which seemed to indicate to me that my teachers either really understood my interests in life, or actually thoroughly misunderstood them. I was awarded three books over three years: *Through London's Highways*, *Coronation Scrapbook: Our Young Queen*, and *Radar Looks Like This*, this particular latter further awarded for "Conduct, Effort and Hobby".

Being awarded the Coronation book had an irony that only I appreciated. Whilst I was incredibly loyal to the throne and deeply respected the British Royal Family (what English Jew didn't?), I was really annoyed, rather than upset, when the King died. I had been allowed by my parents to take a day off from school because Daddy had matinee tickets for *Peter Pan* at the Streatham Hill Theatre, with Jean Forbes-Robertson repeating once again her famous title performance, and we had already set out to see the show when we ran into someone on our way down Downton Avenue who informed us that the King, George VI, had passed away that very morning, 6th February 1952, and all theatres were suddenly closed. Selfish as ever, was I pissed off!

(However, I did eventually get to see many Peter Pans:-- firstly, eventually, Jean Forbes-Robertson, then Joan Greenwood – in whose programme and under whose photograph appeared Daddy's shop advertisement – then Margaret Lockwood and Sarah Churchill, all at the Streatham Hill Theatre, then latterly Mia Farrow at the Shaw, and, most recently, Cathy Rigby in New York, who was then nearing her 30th year of playing Peter Pan.)

I had found a new friend in Streatham, a girl called Angela Smith, a cute brunette who lived with her mother in Downton Avenue. We quite literally met on the street, opposite our house on a bombed-out site, where a group of us boys used to play war games and suchlike, with plastic toy machine guns, and tinny toy Colt-45s. I'm guessing that I was not yet eleven, and just out of Fenstanton. Angela Smith and I bonded immediately over – guess what? Yup, going to The Pictures. We actually never went to the cinema together, at least not then, her mother invariably taking her, and me being taken by my parents, or various friends of my parents, or by those "ladies who did" for us, who I always seemed to call "Auntie". (It was, after all, "Auntie" Gladys who took me to see *Scaramouche*.) Independently, however, both Angela and I had seen *Marty* on separate occasions, the Academy Award-winning "little" film that turned out to be the surprise hit of its year, and she and I discussed its merits in relative depth (at least, for pre-teens), and we discovered a deep common interest. Angela Smith was about three or four years older than I was, and our two lives would cross certain paths, in many more way than I could possibly imagine, as we both grew much older, but not necessarily much wiser.

Before we finally leave Fenstanton School behind us, let me just make a mention of the only sport that I almost enjoyed. Once a week in my last year at Fenstanton we went swimming. Fenstanton itself had no swimming pool of its own, so my classes trooped across the wilds of Brixton from our base in Tulse Hill to fetch up at the swimming pool at Dick Sheppard's Girls School, just past the Lambeth Town Hall, an interesting walk for me in particular because we passed the Brixton Pullman repertory cinema (three different shows a week: Sunday for one day only, Monday to Wednesday, then Thursday to Saturday. It's now the Brixton Ritzy) and I could enjoy looking at the film stills outside as we passed by. No-one else seemed at all interested: they were all probably watching out for themselves and their safety as we all crossed over Brixton Road, sensibly avoiding traffic at the intersection with great care.

But opposite the Pullman, directly over the Brixton roundabout, and therefore directly in our path, was the reconstructed old ABC Cinema Brixton, about to re-open as a brand-new Regal after war damage, and, tantalising to me, every week on its outside hoarding a new letter of the alphabet would be added to indicate what the title of the new opening feature film would be called. When we started initially to go swimming that hoarding bore only one letter on the extreme left-hand side: Y. Well, I was certainly intrigued, but I don't think anyone else cared, nor even noticed.

I didn't get too much in the way of enjoyment out of swimming, but I soon began to realise that it was possibly the least offensive of sports. I found the pool quite chilly, but our swimming teacher, a large lady called Miss Varndell, instructed us to get our shoulders under the water and we would feel warmer, and she was right. I have done so ever since. Mr. Sills, our form teacher, was in charge. He was a nice man, and somehow I discovered his first name was Maurice. This was a novelty to me, because I had a few relatives, to say the least, with the same name, both as first name and surname, but they all spelt it "Morris". I was concerned, but didn't quite know how to broach the subject with Mr. Sills. When I finally did, he said, "I shouldn't worry about it. You can still call me 'Sir'."

Mr. Sills did say something else to me that I will forever remember. I was a chubby child, with fatty tissue on my chest. Mr. Sills, who should've known better, suggested – I think as a joke – one day, as we were coming out of the changing room, that perhaps I should wear a "chest protector". I didn't realise that it was his little joke, until I understood that he meant a brassiere. I never thought it was funny, and I've never forgotten it. But he was a nice man.

Oh, that sign outside the Regal? Gradually it revealed itself: "Y" "I" "E" "L" "D" "T""O" "T" "H" "E" "N" "I" "G" "H" "T", the brand new Diana Dors film, which hadn't then opened anywhere, tantalisingly and sensationally based on the story of Ruth Ellis, the last woman to hang. It was "X"-certified, so I never got to see it. (At least, not until very many years later.).

I commenced Dulwich College on a September day in 1956, in class 1F, the lowest entry class of all. (The classes assigned were based on the result of the Entrance Examination taken in April of that year.) And, although proud of being chosen, and happy for my parents, I began to feel, on the very first day, that perhaps it might not be the best school for little me (although, of course, eventually, it certainly was, in many, many, ways that my eleven-year-old self couldn't have possibly imagined). It wasn't long before I soon realised that my cinema visits, amongst other domestic pleasures, were to be severely curtailed. But to begin at the beginning…

First of all, there were no girls. I knew that in advance, of course, but I wasn't quite ready for it: I'd always enjoyed feminine company, and a totally all-male establishment seemed quite anomalous to me (although I'm sure it improved study and exam results). Oh, well.

Dad had acquired, as far as I knew, three cars throughout his working life to date. I was never really aware of cars (although I did collect Dinky toys), and frankly regarded them as what they actually were, just vehicles. My early memory is a little shaky here, but I think the first family car was a Ford Popular. I am, however, certain that our second car, in Streatham, was a smart sleek-backed black Standard Vanguard, one of the classiest of all British vehicles, and it was that car which got us to Bognor on holiday and was Dad's stylish, if showy, daily vehicle. And then he acquired a black Humber Super Snipe, a posh limousine if ever there was one, not what you'd call a family car, but, by thunder, it was smooth and classy (Freudians out there, you well know what to make of all of this).

And so it was that Daddy dropped me off at Dulwich College that first day in that polished black Humber Super Snipe. Everyone else, I'm certain, arrived by foot, so, of course, I felt embarrassed, but Dad was unperturbed, and drove off. My other source of embarrassment was my jacket. It was bad enough having to wear long trousers for the very first time, but what I wasn't aware of was that for whatever reason (probably financial) my beloved parents thought that they could get away with me wearing my navy Fenstanton blazer with a Dulwich College badge sewn onto the top pocket where the Fenstanton one used to be. It might have worked on its own alone, but my navy blazer stood out against a sea of new black jackets: black jackets and long grey trousers, the official Dulwich College uniform.

I was beyond embarrassment. It was bad enough not knowing anybody else there, and it gradually dawned on me that there were distinct murmurings afoot about my navy blue jacket. I didn't really know what to do, other than to fall-in with the rest of my new class, 1F. To tell the absolute truth, I really just wanted to cry and go home. It wasn't a good start. But it only lasted that one first day. Daddy reacted immediately. I didn't know how he knew, or if he even found out, or perhaps he had a black jacket arriving, and it didn't quite get there in time, but the next day I had a proper brand-new black jacket to wear, which didn't quite totally fit, but which, for me, was absolutely perfect.

Going to Dulwich College certainly curtailed my cinemagoing. School was six days a week, inclusive of Saturday mornings, plus compulsory additional so-called minor games activities on two after-school evenings per week, plus, of course, homework. In fact, so concerned were my parents of my attending school on Shabbat, that they asked my elderly and sensible Grandad Morris if I should actually undertake schooling on a Saturday morning, when I was originally accepted for Dulwich College. Grandad wisely replied that acceptance at Dulwich was a great honour for a Jewish boy to win an entrance to a British Public School, and that, yes, of course I should attend school on Shabbat, and be the very much the wiser for it, and it would not alter my eternal Jewishness at all. As it so happened, Dulwich College actually had a Jewish prayer service each day as a simultaneous alternative to the morning school prayer assembly, which I duly regularly attended. (I certainly wouldn't have said prayers every day at home).

In my very first week at Dulwich at the commencement of the winter term, I managed to convince my mother that I was capable of going to The Pictures immediately after school, and still be able to complete my homework. She agreed to try it, and so I went to see *The Long Arm*, supported by *Edge of Hell*, at the Gaumont, Streatham, one evening after school, perversely preferring the grubby supporting feature to the Jack Hawkins Ealing police drama. But Mummy was right: it didn't leave enough time to do my homework properly, and I had absolutely no idea of how arduous that homework would be. Or would become. There would be no more evening trips to "The Pictures".

I didn't manage to make really close friends in that first year at Dulwich College in form 1F, nor did I particularly like any of the masters teaching me. And I absolutely hated the sport, which seemed relentless. The school holidays, though, more than made up for it. They seemed to be much longer than those at Fenstanton, as indeed they were. They needed to be, for there suddenly was much of interest for me going on in the world, not least the dynamic rise of rock'n'roll, particularly on television (still in black-and-white), where BBC's *6.5 Special* and the tremendously exciting *Oh Boy!* vied for audiences early on Saturday evenings. Not to mention veteran disc jockey Jack Jackson's own show (called *The Jack Jackson Show*, no less), and the new and exciting *Cool for Cats*, wherein choreographed would-be 'hip' dancers grooved to brand-new rock'n'roll records, smartly introduced by Canadian (with an accent I thought that was really cool) Kent Walton, later famed for his Saturday afternoon wrestling commentaries, who I later happily met up with when he was producing *Can You Keep It Up for a Week?*, a British sex comedy on which I worked as assistant editor, which Kent pseudonymously produced in tandem with the equally pseudonymous veteran writer Hazel Adair, perhaps better known as the creator of two of British television's most famous soap operas, *Compact* and *Crossroads*. Their joint nom-de-film was Elton Hawke.

I really had little in common with my early Dulwich school fellows. In class, we were seated alphabetically, and I never really ever got used to addressing my classmates only by their surnames (and I don't think that I ever really got used to an all-boys only school, either). In general, my conversations with my contemporaries seemed not to be successful (it, of course, never occurred to selfish little me that they wouldn't even want to talk to me, or that maybe that they thought I was always talking rubbish, which may well have been true.) My experiences outside of school didn't seem of interest to anyone. I remember telling a classmate about the time Dad took me to the Festival of Britain, a really exciting outing for the young me, and how I was scared on entering the Dome of Discovery, and how I had to be swiftly taken outside again, an event which to me was absolutely major, but there was total disinterest from my new school acquaintances.

Seated as we were alphabetically in 1F, my newest new possible friend was Sullivan, M. who actually invited me to his (11th? 12th?) birthday party in Croydon. Mummy accompanied me, and took tea with Martin's mother, and it was one evening after school. All I can recall of it was that there were no girls there, and we boys chased each other around Martin's garden. One of the boys was called Nigel Bennett, and I was to meet up with him again much later in life, first of all on the train to Shepperton when I was working on *Othello*, and he was on his way to train as a lawyer, and latterly when he became one of the major U.K. movie legal beagles, and most notably represented Albert Finney, and we used to meet up at various film festivals, once most memorably in Los Angeles after a minor earthquake (my quite terrifying and only experience of such, when, in my Los Angeles hotel bed I felt that my legs were being pulled away from my body, and that my head was being pulled in another direction, onto my pillow), when we met up at a

Hollywood cafe for breakfast and I discovered that my experience was exactly that as I have so described, and not just a very realistic bad dream, and the talk was indeed of earthquakes and not at all of the film industry. I last saw Nigel when I introduced him to a singularly attractive female film director. Nigel paid for the lunch. (By the way, I never met, nor associated with, Martin Sullivan at all again after 1F.).

Outside of school, there was some release. I desperately wanted to see a brand-new West End musical play called *Expresso Bongo*, written by the Jewish writer Wolf Mankowitz, the film of whose novel *A Kid for Two Farthings* was both set and shot in the East End that I knew only too well, and to which I made Mummy take me to see at the Essoldo cinema in Tooting. (Ever awkward, I insisted that we went to see it at the Essoldo rather than at the much nearer Astoria Streatham because it was playing with a different support feature that I would rather have seen than the British "B" film that was its general release support. It never occurred to me at the time that it might've been easier on my Mother to go more locally.) *Expresso Bongo* was seminal for me. It was the first ever British rock'n'roll theatrical musical, with a subject close to my teenage heart, the discovery and success of a young bongo-drumming sensation, played on stage by James Kenney, the cinema's "Cosh Boy" himself. The manipulating agent was essayed by Paul Scofield, and Millicent Martin and Hy Hazell headed up the female cast, which also included a young Susan Hampshire. The veteran Yiddish actor from the East End's Grand Palais Meier Tzelniker also made the cast especially interesting for me.

To my great surprise, Dad agreed to take me to see it as a treat! Wow! We were actually going to buy – as in "pay for" – West End theatre front-row stalls seats, at the Saville Theatre, in London's Shaftesbury Avenue, and it was to be my first proper "grown-up" visit to the very heart of London's theatreland, as opposed to complimentary tickets at the Streatham Hill Theatre, or Christmas shows, or even to the "suitable" *Charley's Aunt* at the New Theatre. And so we went...

Well, I just <u>loved</u> *Expresso Bongo*. I saved up my pocket money to buy the show cast L.P. (rare for an original British musical to have a long-playing album), and then guess what? Yup, I begged Dad to buy me some bongo drums. I'd forgotten that Dad's cousins were Derek and Roy Morris, of Rose-Morris, the leading musical instrument suppliers in England's very own Tin Pan Alley, at Number 10, Denmark Street, and, to my surprise and excitement, either at Christmas or for a birthday (I can't remember which) I received a pair of authentic bongo drums as a present. Talk about hip! Since my violin lessons were turning out to be catastrophic, and I couldn't be bothered to learn to play a then-fashionable guitar, I was in seventh heaven. (But, typical me, I never even learned how to play those bongos really properly.) I had photographs taken of me "playing" the bongos, and sent them to the musical paper *New Musical Express*, but they were never printed. I did, however, stick the bongos in a place of honour in my converted playroom upstairs, now newly-renamed my "Disc Den". (Eventually, *Expresso Bongo* was filmed in beautiful black-and-white Dyaliscope, the French CinemaScope process, and I would be fortunate enough to work on my first studio feature film as an assistant editor, *Where the Spies Are*, with the actual director and also the editor of *Expresso Bongo*, the convivial and talented Val Guest, and his regular cutter, Bill Lenny, respectively. In the film, one of my British rock'n'roll heroes, Cliff Richard, played James Kenney's role, and the topical satire was, necessarily, slightly diluted. I saw it on its first release at the ABC Regal, Brixton, and now am happy to have my very own 16mm. copy of it.)

Looming in the near future, of course, as with any Orthodox Jewish boy, was my Bar Mitzvah, and the time was arriving when I was to start studying for it, because, ideally, the newly mature 13-year-old should be able to read the portion of the Old Testament in synagogue on the Sabbath of his birthday perfectly, with ease, in Hebrew, together with the associated benedictions. It was more than merely expected, it was ordained: Bar Mitzvah means, quite literally, Son of the Commandment, and indicates the life point at which a boy becomes a man. Traditionally, and when affordable, it is accompanied by a massive family celebration.

Meanwhile, there was school work to contend with, plus compulsory sport four times a week (Mondays and Thursdays after school, Wednesday and Saturday afternoons), and Hebrew classes Sunday mornings. At Dulwich, a so-called minor sport was expected. And since I had no interest whatsoever in the likes of boxing, tennis, or gymnastics, I chose, yup, fencing. But it took a very short while to discover that I was no Scaramouche, and after a round with one David Penn, who had become a friend, in which I very nearly took his eye out, I gave up, or, in actual fact was recommended to give it up, by the gym instructor, one Mr. Cromey, who clearly knew better. David forgave me, and we went off one afternoon "up West" to see *The Alamo* in 70mm. together at the newly-converted Astoria, Charing Cross Road. Interestingly, David was another fatherless boy (cf. Peter Chappell) that I bonded with at school, although when we met up years later at an Old Alleynian gathering we discovered, after a rather forlorn supper, that, sadly, we had nothing in common whatsoever. I never saw him again. Meantime, in my second year at Dulwich I was upgraded from 1F to 2E. Not much better, but better, nevertheless.

I knew what was expected from me at my Bar Mitzvah. I just was never sure if I was quite up to it. When we moved to Streatham, we went to the Orthodox Jewish synagogue in Brixton, a huge, forbidding building, which I well remember mainly because it was directly over the road from the new Regal Brixton and right along the road from the Pullman. But nearer to us in Streatham was, in fact, the Orthodox Streatham synagogue in Mitcham Lane, and that we joined in order to hold my Bar Mitzvah there, and the Rabbi in charge, Reverend Schneider, would actually take the Bar Mitzvah service, and had agreed to tutor me (for a fee, of course). So I started Hebrew classes on Sunday mornings at the Streatham shul.

Well, that really only left the school holidays on which to go to The Pictures. But there were other things for a young teenage boy to think about, mainly girls. Difficult on pocket money, but possible, well, just about, maybe. Rock'n'roll shows were starting to happen, but of course, I couldn't afford them. However, my Dad wanted to keep up with the latest fashions, and so I persuaded him to take me to the first great British rock show at the Royal Albert Hall, featuring Marty Wilde and the *Oh Boy!* cast, the whole second half an on-stage re-creation of *Oh Boy!* itself. What a show!! The sensation of the evening was Billy Fury's appearance – I didn't actually, to be truthful, fully realise what he was up to, at least not until I read the *Daily Mirror* next day, but it seems that he was simulating masturbation with the microphone. All I knew it was bloody great rock'n'roll, and – it was British!! "Maybe Tomorrow", "Margo, Don't Go," "That's Love" – all self-penned by a British Elvis. Of course, I realised that Billy Fury might be just a copycat, but the chances of seeing Elvis himself were non-existent, and Billy turned out eventually, in his short life, to be our best ever true British rock'n'roll star. In actuality, I preferred Marty Wilde, who had more of a sense of humour, and used it, but Billy was quintessential rock'n'roll, and I was privileged to witness him in his prime, thanks to my Dad.

Mummy and Daddy used to visit the Stork Club in Streatham of an evening when Mummy was well enough, and Dad had befriended Charles Chaperlin, the manager and chief compere. One evening my parents were seated next to, and introduced to by Charles, pop stars Terry Dene, the Elvis lookalike who became infamous for flunking out of his National Service and marrying pop chick Edna Savage ("A White Sports Coat and a Pink Carnation" was his only really significant hit), and Ricky Valance, who went to number one in the U.K. charts with his cover of Ray Peterson's U.S. hit "Tell Laura I Love Her", a much reviled (by adults) "Death Disc", which, of course, I bought with my pocket money. Dad, God bless him, asked them for their autographs for his son, me. I couldn't thank him enough the following morning, and I still cherish them to this very day. Dad also took me to the Stork Club to see *Oh Boy!* stars Neville Taylor and the Cutters perform, for whom Dad had provided some tailoring work. They weren't exactly The Coasters, but they were bloody good, nevertheless.

I started to want to see more live rock stars, and the Granada, Tooting obliged in great style. The American rocker Gene Vincent was the very first imported artiste I saw there, making his U.K. debut as guest star in the Marty Wilde show. I went alone, and was blown away. Black-garbed, his damaged leg adjacent to the microphone, he "Be-Bop-a-Lula'd" like nobody else. I felt very privileged to be in that audience, and I sensed that we all felt that Gene was not long for this world, so bloody dynamic was he, it couldn't last. But it did, and I was privileged to see him again on several occasions, once double-billed with his female equivalent, Brenda Lee. In actual fact, Gene outlived most of his contemporaries, such as Buddy Holly and Eddie Cochran, both of whom predeceased the great Gene Vincent.

But it eventually dawned on me, shouldn't I, a budding teenager, be taking dates, i.e. girls, to see these rock'n'rollers?? Or indeed, shouldn't I be going out with girls anyway by now? I certainly thought so. After all, I'd seen enough movies to know how it works, and those girls over the road were also growing up. I really fancied Christine, who had the hots for Tony Newley, but there was also Pauline, and besides I wanted to speak to her Dad about his work in film.

I thought Jimmy Jones's two MGM record hits "Handy Man" and "Good Timin'", were great records, so I bought two tickets to see him at the Trocadero, Elephant and Castle, and asked Pauline if she'd like to come with me. She did. I collected her that night – would you believe I wore a packamac (they were new then, and I thought fashionable), and we walked down Downton Avenue to get a bus to the Elephant and Castle (a 133, I think). We didn't speak too much. We saw the show. Jimmy Jones was in good voice, but didn't really have a stage act; his moves were clumsy, as were his attempted acrobatics. We left, and got a 133 bus back to Streatham Hill, and I walked Pauline home. We still didn't talk much. That, as far as I can remember, was my first actual "date". (It seemed quite different to those I'd seen in all those movies, particularly the American ones.) I didn't like to admit it, not even to myself, but I think I preferred going to The Pictures on my own to this, although I didn't discuss it with anyone, especially not with my parents; after all Mummy was friends with Pauline's mother Dora.

Meantime, Daddy, recognising my passion for The Pictures, had regaled me with tales of three of his favourite films, and had promised to take me to see them should they ever be reissued anywhere, and those three were *A Matter of Life and Death* (easy to see how that would resonate with the handsome moustachioed devil of an R.A.F pilot that Dad was), *The Secret Life of Walter Mitty* (Daddy himself was also a secret fantasiser, sometimes not so very secret), and *Gone with the Wind*, which, like so many others, he considered to be the best film ever made. And now, surprisingly, *Gone with the Wind* was about to enjoy a reissue. I had heard of it for years, first of all when it was revived in the 1950s, and we were passing the ABC in Stratford when I asked Mummy what was that Technicolor Civil War film on there, and she replied something like that it was the best film ever made, and that I was far too young to see it.

Well, it seemed that now my time had come. It was school holiday time, and *G.W.T.W.* was revived for an exclusive showing at the Gaumont, Haymarket, in London's West End. We, Dad and me, drove "up West" in the Humber Super Snipe. Dad prided himself on knowing all the "back doubles", as he called them, and where to park at night in the West End, and I believed him. But when we got near the Haymarket, it seemed to me that something was going on: there were a lot of policemen around. Dad told me not to worry, and he managed to find a parking space off of the Haymarket itself. We went up to the Gaumont only to find out that *Gone with the Wind* was full up. (In those days booking seats, even in the West End, was not common in cinemas. You came and went as you pleased.) Well, we weren't happy, especially not yours truly. What to do? What to see? We were already in a secure parking space, we might as well see a movie. But what? I didn't want to see anything that I could see locally, and also wanted to take advantage of Dad's presence to take me in to anything that didn't have a "U" certificate. We walked around a bit, and there at the Cameo-Royal Charing Cross Road, a cinema that specialised in "naughty" French X-certificated features, was playing the film version of the French comedian and music hall star Robert Dhéry's Paris show, originally entitled *Ah! Les Belles Bacchantes!*, but re-titled, for U.K. consumption, the more slightly understandable (and utterly translatable) *Femmes de Paris*. I knew a) that it was "naughty", and b) it would never play anywhere else, let alone locally, because it had been given an "A" (London) certificate by the censor. In other words, it had been banned, but London, and London only, had passed it with an "A" (for adults, and children under 16 who were accompanied by an adult) certificate, so my chances of ever seeing it anywhere else were virtually nil. I knew that it would be "saucy", and maybe not "suitable", but almost certainly Dad would like it (he loved smut), and, equally almost certainly, I would be extremely embarrassed to see it with him.

So, of course, I suggested we see *Femmes de Paris* instead. And we did, and we both enjoyed it very much. Coming out of the cinema, we headed to where Daddy had parked the car, and, lo and behold! – it wasn't there! What was going on? Had it been stolen? It couldn't have been towed away because it was in a valid parking bay. Dad was aghast and, for a moment, transfixed. I didn't understand either, but had no idea whatsoever of what questions to ask, and it was now dark, and getting very late. Daddy, very sensibly, looked around for a policeman. He found one, and with me in hand, explained to the cop what had happened, and the policeman then subsequently took us to a police box and called into his local police station (no mobile phones back then). We stood outside the box, waiting. The policeman then emerged, deeply apologetic. It seems that just down the road there had been a major film Royal Premiere at the Carlton cinema in the Haymarket (I discovered later that it was Rock Hudson and Jennifer Jones in *A Farewell to Arms*) and it was in the presence of Her Royal Highness Princess Margaret. Police were under instruction to clear all cars from the area, and Dad's big Humber Super Snipe had been duly impounded, and he could collect it at the nearby Savile Row police station. That's exactly what we did, and returned to Streatham to regale Mummy with our experience, and explain why we were so late, and, of course, we had to tell her what the film was that we ended up seeing. I have a feeling to this day that she felt that the whole missing car incident was some divine intervention or retribution for Dad having taken me to see a "naughty" picture.

It was about this time that I started attending Saturday Morning Pictures, the Minors' Matinees at the ABC Regal, Streatham, only sixpence on Saturday mornings. I first went because the Regal had advertised a very special guest appearing on Saturday next: Robby the Robot, the metallic "star" of MGM's *Forbidden Planet*, would appear, prior to the film's opening on the following week, and indeed, turn up he did, in a large truck outside the actual cinema, and, to my utter amazement, "answered" questions from the very young crowd, including showing some knowledge about local football teams. That's when I realised that he himself may well have been the real Robby, but the voice was definitely a fake. Nevertheless, I did go to a few more Saturday morning matinees, but swiftly gave up. Even at only sixpence a show, it was becoming a chore to me, singing the "Minors' Matinee" theme song every week, and watching rubbishy "B" movies like *The Golden Gloves Story* and old Rod Cameron westerns. However, when I finally did get to see *Forbidden Planet* itself, I thought it a minor masterpiece, and the passing of time has confirmed my taste.

After form 2E it became time to contemplate what "side" I wanted to enter at Dulwich College, and what would be the most appropriate. I wasn't at all interested in the then-newish courses of the sciences, so that rather limited me. My best subjects were English and History, and that's what I chose, not expecting to secure them, merely to be pushed into the stream referred to as "General". However, much to my surprise, my exam results were acceptable, and I was chosen for form 3A, the prime third year class. Pleased as I was, I knew that it meant work, work, work, together with my out-of-school Hebrew classes and the Bar Mitzvah preparations, but at least (I hoped) I would make my parents proud of me. The Bar Mitzvah itself was booked to take place at the Streatham synagogue, 15a, Mitcham Lane, S.W.16, on Saturday, 17th May, 1958, when, as it said on the invitation, "Anthony Barney will read a Portion of the Law". And to my absolute delight, where do you think it said the reception would be? Yup, to quote the invitation again, "And on Sunday, May 18th, 1958 Reception 4p.m. Dinner 6p.m., Buffet and Ball 8p.m., at the Stork Club, Streatham Hill, S.W.2" Hooray! (But I had my work cut out: responsibilities!!).

Now, I'd been to quite a few parties already -- according to "The Progress Book", the first wedding that I'd attended was that of Mummy's friend Renee Pliskin on 11th August 1946, and, at age 15 months, I also went to Brenda Phillips' 11th birthday party. Both of those entries were written by, and duly signed in Brenda Phillips's own handwriting. "I went to Auntie Doris' wedding (to Uncle Don), on September 15th, 1946," added my Mummy, "I was a very good baby, and stayed up until 12 o'clock at night, I played and ran about all the time. I wore a white satin suit and white fur coat for "shool" (synagogue), and a biscuit trouser suit in the evening." But those were only the beginnings of the festivities: "Went to cousin Harold's Bar Mitzvah March 25th. I danced the 'Hokey-Pokey'." "June 15th went to Uncle Derek's wedding at 'Gunters' Park Lane, and Mummy said I behaved very nicely." These last entries in 1947.

Eventually, I attended cousin Michael's Bar Mitzvah, and cousin Gerald's, and cousin Harold's Bar Mitzvah too, none of which I have any recollection. I do, however, recall Harold's engagement party, at which I behaved very badly. I had already started collecting film advertisements from the newspapers by then, cutting them out and keeping them in a box that previously had contained my Junior Crime Investigation Detective equipment, and I was building up quite a vigorous collection, but, of course, I could only acquire current and recent adverts. At Harold's party, wandering at leisure around Harold's house (which must have been that of his parents, my Auntie Fanny and Uncle Hymie) I snooped, and found in a cupboard a pile of old *Melody Maker*s, well pre-dating my own stashes of *Record Mirror* and *New Musical Express*. Out of curiosity, I opened one to check out the pop charts before my time, as it were, when I spotted a film advertisement, a half-page for *The Birth of the Blues*. Well, this clearly pre-dated my own collection of film ads, so evil little me carefully tore it out and put it in my pocket. (No, I didn't even think to ask permission, so sure was I anyway that I wanted it, regardless.) It then occurred to me that there might be others, and so I ruffled through the collection, and did, indeed, find other ads which I tore out and stuffed in my pockets. Rummaging complete, I then returned "innocently" back to the party, dreading being found out. Well, I never was, and put the ripped-out ads in my collection at home. There were never any repercussions: I wonder if Harold ever checked – I wasn't too tidy putting them back, after all.

So, you'd gather from the above, perhaps I wasn't the best, most well-behaved kid to have around. I don't remember Gerald's or Michael's Bar Mitzvahs at all, but I do remember very clearly Anthony Morris's one, because it was held at the famous and wonderful Café Royal in Piccadilly, and the Bar Mitzvah band was that of Bob Azzam, who had just released a cover version of the then-popular hit "Mustapha". I pestered them : "We mustafa chance to hear 'Mustapha'". I punned (badly) to all and sundry. Amongst the guests were dancers that I recognised from *Expresso Bongo* (and who I later also recognised from Cliff Richard's earlier film *Serious Charge* on a subsequent viewing), and also among the celebrants was Tony's sister Judith, who I immediately developed a crush on. It seemed mutual, and we left the Café Royal together and went for a long intimate walk down Regent Street, with not a thought that our respective parents might be missing us: we had rock'n'roll, and each other, in common. We eventually returned to the Bar Mitzvah party and, as far as I can remember, we never saw each other again, alas. So I knew parties…

Dad had booked the Streatham Stork Club for my own Bar Mitzvah party, and Mummy had organised the guest list and the food, as far as I knew. Reverend Schneider, who would take the service on Saturday, couldn't do the bruchas – the blessings over the food – on the Sunday, so I suggested instead the one and only Jewish master at Dulwich, who actually also took me for my French in 3A, Mr. H. I. Alexander, and fortunately he agreed, and so he and his wife became an incongruous, but necessary, couple seated at our own top table on the night. (I guess Daddy reimbursed him, but I never knew, nor gave it a second thought.)

The event turned out to be utterly spectacular, but I, as usual, behaved badly, again, as usual, hoping nobody would notice. I was under strict instructions from my parents that if anybody gave me an envelope at the party at our house after synagogue on the Saturday, to turn it immediately over to Dad, unopened, for it would almost certainly contain money. And that I did for all envelopes but two. I guess I couldn't resist, and I was by then such a pesky ungrateful little shit, anyway.

I managed to get through the service on the Saturday morning, so all those extra religious lessons paid off. Afterwards, back at Downton Avenue, I'd never seen so many people, friends and relatives, all congratulating me. And yes, I was given a few envelopes. The first ones I didn't open as per instruction, and passed them on to Daddy. But then I got an idea, probably a very bad one, but it seemed like a good idea at the time. There were two film record soundtrack albums that I desperately desired of recent films that I had just seen and loved, and their sleeves were both on display in Fisher's Music Salon window at the foot of our road. What if I was given an envelope, opened it, and discovered it contained enough to buy them, or at least one? I knew that they both cost 32/6 each. Could I make this work?

And so, I opened the next envelope I was given. It contained two pounds. I swiftly left my own party, dashed down the road to Fishers on the corner, and bought *The Pajama Game* film soundtrack. I pocketed the change, rushed back to the party, and took the record upstairs to my bedroom and secreted it away. Hmm, I thought, this does seem to work, and, would you believe, at that very moment I was greeted and given another envelope. Well, guess what? Yup, I opened it, and discovered that this envelope also contained £2, as did the first. Well, well… So I actually did it again: I left my own party and dashed down to Fishers on the corner. Selected the brand-new *Pal Joey* film soundtrack album, parted with the money, and dashed back to the party. Again, my absence hadn't been noticed, and I secreted *Pal Joey* next to *The Pajama Game*. Missions accomplished, although I did, barely, give a thought to what would or might happen if my parents discovered what I had just done. They never did.

The next day, the Sunday, was the best Bar Mitzvah party anyone ever had: a real smasheroonie! Everybody looked so smart at the Stork Club in their evening dress, and the band – Nat Temple and his Orchestra, from the Locarno – were terrific. The speeches went well, and it was the first (and would turn out to be the last) time that all my (and, of course, my parents') friends and relatives would be all well, healthy, and together, and thank goodness, we have a photographic album (now in my possession) of the whole wonderful event: the two Grandads playing cards together, the five Levenstein sisters (my Nanna Annie Morris and my four great-aunts) in one photograph posed standing together side-by-side, my father dancing, as only he could, the traditional Russian gazutska --- oh, what pictures!! Thank goodness for such an excellent cameraman, and a great band. Oh, and I guess I didn't do so badly myself after all.

What did it all cost a tailor from Streatham Hill? I never gave it a second thought, selfish as ever, it never, ever, occurred to me that real hard-earned money must have been spent on my Bar Mitzvah. Was it an investment? Was it for show? Was it just to show off? I never, ever, thought about that at all. Could we, in actual fact, afford it? Did we even break even, money and presents-wise? I never knew, never found out, didn't even care: "Today, I am a man". But I was growing up as a selfish little shit: I just didn't know it yet. Were they inherited genes? Time alone would tell.

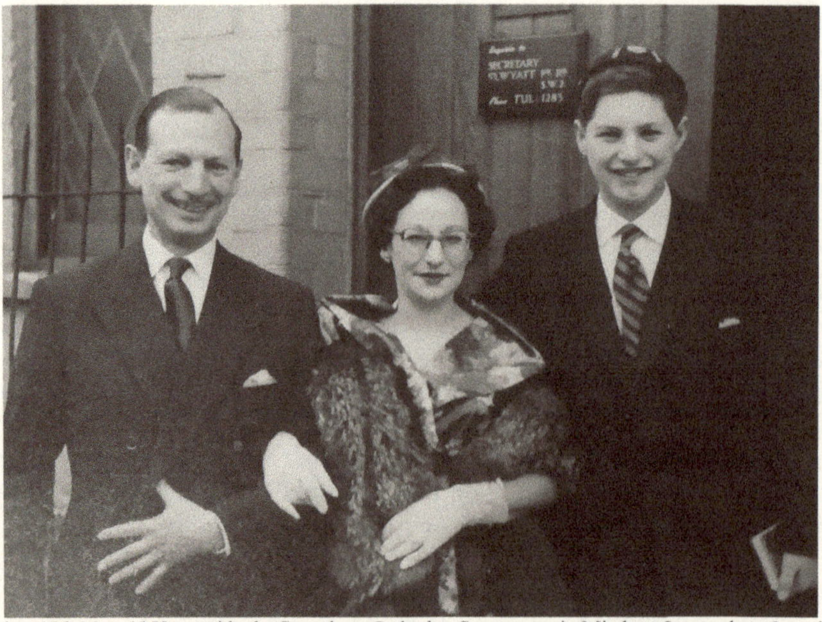

Saturday, 17th May, 1958, outside the Streatham Orthodox Synagogue in Mitcham Lane where I read my portion of The Law (in Hebrew), flanked by my proud parents. Note that I'm in my Dulwich College school uniform, replete with school cap.

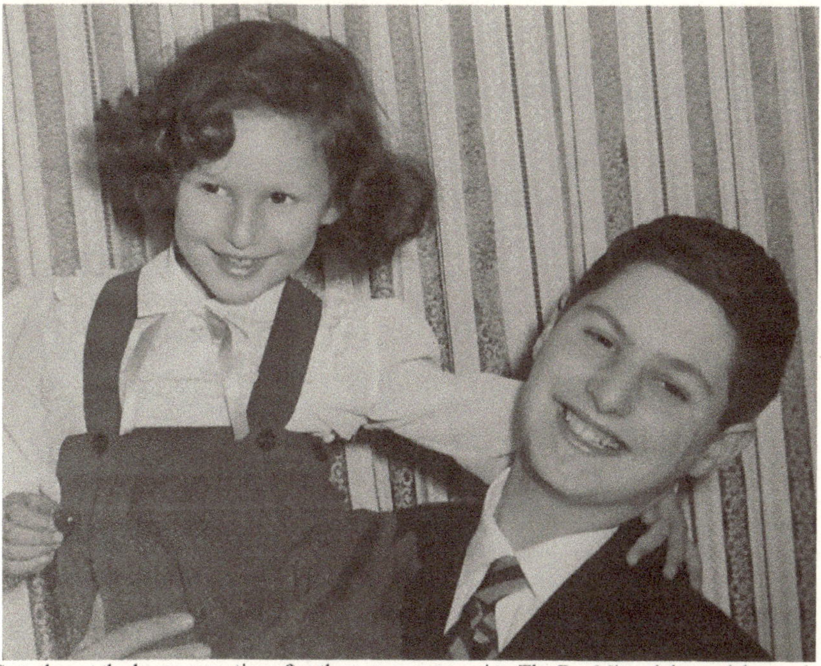

Also Saturday, at the home reception after the synagogue service. The Bar Mitzvah boy celebrates by holding his young sister Linda aloft: note the naughty look in her eye: she wasn't about to let me be the only star that day in the Sloman household.

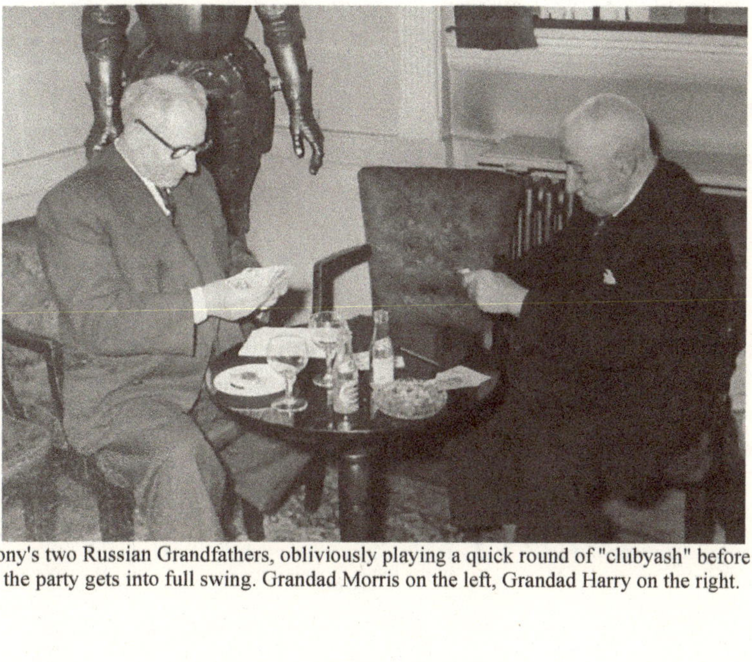

Tony's two Russian Grandfathers, obliviously playing a quick round of "clubyash" before the party gets into full swing. Grandad Morris on the left, Grandad Harry on the right.

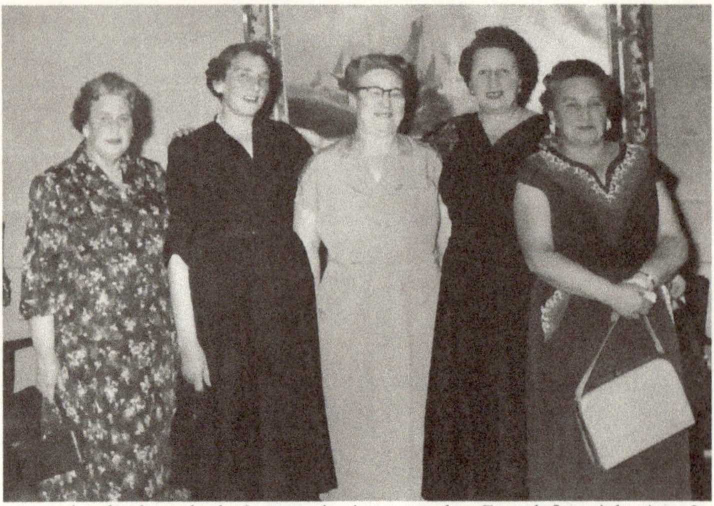

It was a rare occasion that brought the Levenstein sisters together. From left to right: Aunt Leah (Fink); Aunt Pet (Levenstein, she never married); my beloved maternal Grandmother Annie Morris (Zidman), in the centre, and rightly so; Aunt Becky (Michael's mother Rebecca Mantus), and Auntie Fanny Harris.

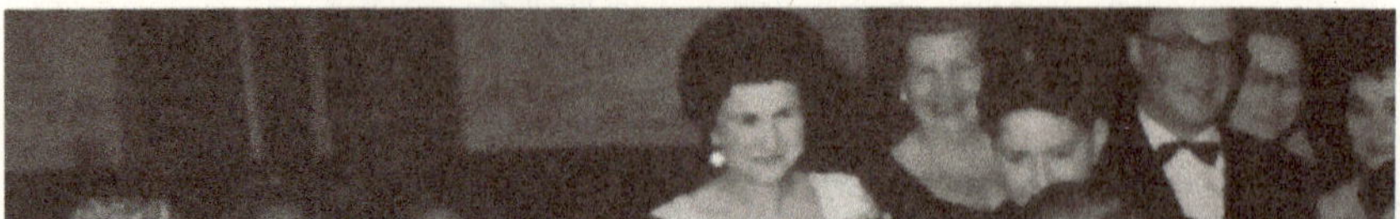

My father Julian dances his speciality, the Russian "gazutska" at my Bar Mitzvah. That's me clapping along on the left of the photo.

-----END OF REEL ONE-----

REEL TWO

Form 3A at Dulwich College would turn out to be the most academically influential year of my young life, leading to Geography Fourth, where I managed to make friends for life, and finally settling on thoughts of a possible career in the film industry. In the meantime, that first term in my third year at Dulwich commenced with a serious parental threat:-- that if my school marks and general reports were as poor as they had been the previous school year, then, quite simply, I would not be allowed to go to The Pictures in term time at all. To me, the worst kind of punishment ever. So, what to do? Respect my parents' wishes, and hopefully achieve better school results, or behave badly and skive and hope that they never find out? Of course, it should never have been a dilemma: I should have acquiesced to my parents' demands immediately. Besides, I was pretty certain that it was my Father's idea alone, and not my Mother's. But nevertheless…

The new term commenced. I waited for an opportune moment to defy my ban. In the wintertime, when the weather was bad, sometimes the grounds were unfit for rugger, and the school games houses (mine was Grenville) held what were termed "House Meetings", taking place on Wednesday afternoons when there was no sport owing to the inclement weather. Incidentally, when there actually was sport, I was so awful at it that I was always relegated to a lower, if not the lowest house team, which always started later, and finished around normal school finishing time. The "House Meetings" held instead also finished at around the same time, allowing us to reach our respective homes at roughly normal school leaving times.

So, what did I think up? Banned for a term, I decided to try to go to The Pictures on a Wednesday when I actually wasn't chosen for a team, i.e. worst than the worst; unplayable. I'd noticed, on my bus route, that the Pullman cinema in Brixton was playing a double-bill of *What Lola Wants* (the U.K. title for the baseball musical *Damn Yankees*) which I'd already seen, with a must-see (for me – because it was a film that pre-dated my "going to the Pictures" regularly) Technicolor western called *Arrowhead*, starring Charlton Heston, both "U" certified. But there was a big problem: the double-bill programme was too long for me to see between leaving Dulwich at lunchtime and arriving home at the normal time. Nevertheless, I – very naughtily and feeling very guilty – went into the Pullman at the only time I could, which was well into *Arrowhead*, but then realised I couldn't sit the programme around and see the rest of the film without severely compromising myself, so I saw what I could of what was left of *Arrowhead*, then as much as I could of *What Lola Wants* (all but the last twenty minutes, but I'd seen it before) and left for home. I knew my mother would know I hadn't worn my rugger kit (which, of course, she would normally have flung immediately into our washing machine), so I lied. I said we had had a House Meeting. I don't know if she knew I was lying (House Meetings didn't usually last long, or at least not that long), or if she believed me, or if she actually thought I'd done that dastardly thing and gone to The Pictures. Would she tell Dad? What hadn't I counted upon, dear reader? Yup. Guilt. In spades. So I never did it again, and bore the whole term without a trip to the cinema. (Thank the Lord for surrounding me with enough repertory cinemas enabling me to catch up.) No, and as far as I can remember, Monday nights at the Streatham Hill Theatre were out, also: I had homework to do.

But my school work still suffered. I just wasn't any good at all at maths, and that would eventually lead to private (paid) coaching after school with a master called Mr. Wilkinson, which led to even more longer hours spent at school. Whether maths would ever play a major part in my life I never considered, but I knew Oxford and Cambridge entrance certainly demanded a good maths pass mark. We did have a careers master, "Spud" McKinley (who, by the way, turned out to have a very attractive daughter, far too classy and too old – by about two years-- for the likes of me), who, not unnaturally, wanted to know what we all wanted to do with our lives after we had left university, and his main purpose was to secure such types as legal beagles and would-be educationalists as early as possible in their correct placement, not to mention those who wanted serious careers in the armed forces, Dulwich having a distinguished military corps record. I, of course, wanted nothing to do with that deplorable business of the school corps, and, though I was ridiculed at the time, I'm pleased today to state that I never served in an organisation that taught young boys how to handle weaponry, and how to march and ultimately how to kill, and it's also worth recalling that National Service itself was just about to be abolished, so what indeed was the point? Anyhow, "Spud" asked me what did I want to do for a living, when I left school? I had spent long and hard times thinking over this dilemma, and had finally come to a conclusion, which I revealed to nobody, especially not to my parents, and I wasn't sure if I should even tell McKinley, but eventually I did:--"Sir, I want to be the head of the British Board of Film Censors."

He said nothing. I didn't tell him that I had figured out – eventually – that, not only was it a way to see uncut films for free (and be paid for so doing), but it would also give me some kind of authority to make sure films were not (in my opinion, at least) unnecessarily censored. In the U.K., where was Jane Russell's song "Ain't There Anybody Here for Love?", cut from *Gentlemen Prefer Blondes* allegedly because of the transparent bathing costumes on the male chorus? Why was my acting hero Marlon Brando's *The Wild One* totally banned in the U.K.? Why were all horror films "X"-certified, and cut, to boot? No, I didn't throw any of those questions at "Spud". He just nodded, clearly very surprised, and said something like "Well, we'll see what we can do." But I never believed him.

My main concern was to try to get good grades. I never wanted to be banned from "going to The Pictures" ever again. Not ever. Although there was quite a considerable amount of homework to do in the school holidays, I had gradually begun to return to my East End roots, well, sort of…

Nanna thought it would be nice if I would like to spend a day or two with her in "Morris's", their fish-and-chip shop in the Barking Road in the school holidays. Well, this seemed to me to be a sheer trip to Paradise:

fish'n'chips for lunch, and then, a special treat indeed, Nanna would let me spend the afternoon in the little independent cinema a few doors down from her shop. Wow, certainly sounded like heaven, if Mummy would only let me…

And let me she did. Nanna bribed the cinema manager with free fish'n'chips to let me in, so it cost nothing, and I could see anything, even "A" films, on my own, which was strictly against licensing laws (under 16s had to be accompanied by an adult for an "A":-- "A" for Adult). Of course, Nanna made sure the programmes were suitable, sort of, and so off I went.

It was also about this time that I was still collecting film advertisements from the newspapers, so what on earth could be better for young me than a fish-and-chip shop, where all the sales product was wrapped in, yup, newspapers?? I was in seventh heaven, ploughing through the newspapers as soon as I arrived, providing I didn't take them from that day's ready-to-use wrappings, adding to my film advertisements collection, then lunching on the most wonderful fried fish'n'chips (and "wallies" – local slang for pickled cucumbers) in the whole wide world, and finally seeing a double-feature film programme in a proper cinema next door, and then eventually going home with Nanna and Grandad. What glorious days they truly were!

And what I saw at that little cinema next door in the Barking Road was utterly revelatory, although I could never have predicted at the time what its forever effect would be on me. The first programme I saw there was Bogey and Katie Hepburn in *The African Queen*, plus in support the little Italian masterpiece *Never Take No for an Answer*. I was spoiled for life. Sometimes I had already seen the programme, when Dad, or, say, Mrs. Chappell, might have already taken me, but this didn't stop me seeing James Cagney in *Tribute to a Bad Man* again, plus the costumer *The Scarlet Coat* for the second time, and thus enjoying this MGM double bill twice as much. Or indeed, seeing *Forbidden Planet* yet again. What a pleasure that was! And there was once a real genuine cinematic revelation to me:-- on with Robert Mitchum in *Foreign Intrigue*, a colour thriller, was a new crime release in black-and-white starring Sterling Hayden called *The Killing*. It was astoundingly good, and I duly responded to it as to no other film, recognising the sheer originality of its characterisations, the tightness of the clever story-telling, the tragic desperation of its conclusion. For the first time that I can remember, I made a note of the director's name: Stanley Kubrick. In my childish heart, I was glad that he might be Jewish. But who could I tell? No-one.

Sometimes, when I stayed overnight at Forest Gate, Grandad Morris would take me with him to go greyhound racing at West Ham Stadium. I don't know how he chose which dogs to bet on, because he couldn't read English (he could barely speak it) in order to study form, so he must have bet on the look of the greyhound itself or because he liked the name of the dog, or maybe he just bet on "lucky" numbers, or tips. I never knew. Anyway, I found it all very exciting. The actual races were so swift that they barely registered. But the shouting of the gathered crowd was loud enough. And sometimes

Grandad won – I think he gave me a sixpence or so a couple of times from his winnings, and once, as a treat, he took me with him to his beloved Turkish baths, which I absolutely hated. Eventually, when I was old enough to bet, I would place a few bob on the National or the Derby, and one day I won, which resulted in a surprising repercussion involving me rendering a major Hollywood star helpless as a result of my win on the horses, but more on that strange occurrence later on...

I don't really remember very much about life in form 3A, to be honest. My "going to The Pictures" ban was lifted, and I toiled as much as any third year public schoolboy, or so I thought. But come year's end, and examination results, my next year was duly one of demotion. It seemed quite clear to all in charge of my learning that I would never be a classical scholar, linguist, historian, or scientist, so there seemed to be only one path for me: Geography Fourth. "Geography" was a polite Dulwich College term for "General": it certainly seemed less offensive when the "G" for General was termed "G" for Geography, but it was indeed the lowest fourth grade form of all, nevertheless. But it was absolutely right for me, because it was in Geography Fourth that I met those fellows who would become friends for life (and still are!), although I could never have known it at the time. Seemingly, our common interests turned out to be roughly in this order: rock'n'roll, (later feebly termed pop music), girls, going to The Pictures, and then at the very last, and for me not at all, sports. And it was in this year events happened at school that led me to an eventually fateful career decision...

I was still in love with the cinema, and the actual product itself was undergoing a mammoth change. Television had made massive inroads into theatrical viewing figures, and the big screen was at last growing up, and responding to the challenge. The gigantic wide screens worked for a while, but the content was just still pure entertainment, largely without challenge, and films were generally reviewed by journalists and show business writers, and not taken really seriously by the public, at least not in England. But in France, in Paris, a group of young men and women were challenging the very modes of French cinema. All of this is documented better elsewhere, but, to summarise, the French New Wave (the Nouvelle Vague) was about to break: Truffaut, Godard, Chabrol, and Agnes Varda were amongst the new talents on show – people who knew and loved film, often former film critics, to whom film was life. In America, exciting new directors were arriving from television: Sidney Lumet, Martin Ritt, John Frankenheimer, Arthur Penn, plus others whose concerns were not necessarily purely financial, nor merely to entertain, such as the likes of John Cassavetes, or Stanley Kramer..

So what was happening in Britain? Plenty: – director Jack Clayton's *Room at the Top* was a revelation. "X" certificated, but I sneaked in, as also were *Saturday Night and Sunday Morning*, *A Taste of Honey*, and *This Sporting Life*. Britain had discovered its own new wave, directed by former film critics and people from documentaries, and shorts, and the theatre. To me, and others, these films were revelatory: we were living in exciting times. I was beginning to feel that, somehow, I wanted to be part of this. I just didn't know how.

But first of all, you may well be wondering how did I get to see those above-mentioned titles, since they all have that oh-so-forbidding "X" certificate, barring viewing for under 16s? Well, when I arrived in 3A, it became time to acquire a bus pass, allowing schoolchildren of 14-plus to obtain reduced fares on public transport, on proof of identity and age suitability. This pass, of course, had to be produced on every London bus, and it commenced on the third year of secondary schooling. One's age had to be written on the pass, and authorised by a schoolteacher's signature. Well, my own form master, a terribly nice man called Mr. Howlings – "Norm" to us – was signing a row of bus cards, and I was in the queue. I left the age blank, and proffered it to "Norm" to sign, with my thumb over the age space, and he duly signed it without so much as a glimpse at the "age" section, and, when I returned to my desk, I filled it in myself: 16. Proof of identity if requested at any cinema. I didn't give a thought as to what would happen to me if ever I was found out. But I was found out over something else, and the shame of my behaviour still lingers in my thoughts today…

Dad used to take me "up West" for a birthday treat of my own choosing, and that year I wanted to see *Raintree County*, the only other MGM film after *Ben-Hur* to be shot in the 70mm. process called MGM Camera 65. It opened at the Empire, Leicester Square, but did poorly, and was swiftly transferred to the next-door Ritz, where, on a previous birthday treat, Dad had taken me to see *The Last Hunt* (after I had seen *Richard III* in the afternoon, on my own), which was heavily censor-cut (unbeknownst to me) wherein the U.K. censor board (of which I still wanted to be chief) had removed all the material of the buffaloes being killed, the raison d'être of the plot. Anyway, we saw *Raintree County* at the Ritz, and very impressive it was, too. Indeed, so impressive that I really wanted to read the book it was based on. And so, with my pocket money, after school I set out to go to the W.H.Smith's bookstall in Streatham Hill station, where I had seen it on display.

Now, I had developed a rather disquietingly bad habit. On sale at Woolworth's were plastic viewers that could take film frames, all trimmed ever-so-slightly to fit the shape of the viewer itself, about ten at a time, all different. So if you wanted more, you couldn't purchase them separately, you'd have to buy another viewer to get an extra packet of frames. Not only could I not afford to do this, I didn't need an extra viewer. So I stole additional packets of film frames. It became a habit. I nicked a packet from the counter whenever the salesperson turned away. I was swift, and very, very bad. I managed this dastardly feat about five or six times. So I had already become a criminal, with no thought of being caught.

Back to W.H. Smith's: *Raintree County* by Ross Lockridge, Jr. was still on display at the station bookstall, and I had enough money (3/6, I think) to pay for it. But I also saw another book I wanted, but couldn't afford. Sneakily I tucked the other book under *Raintree County* so it couldn't be seen

– or so I thought – and went to pay for *Raintree County*. The salesman took my money, and then said something like "What about the other one?" "What other one?" I replied, trying to stuff the other paperback in my pocket. "That one," he said, pointing. I didn't know what to do. He came around the counter, and took it out of my jacket pocket. It was quite obvious to him what I was doing, or at least attempting to do: I was stealing a book. He asked me what my name was and where did I live? I replied, "Anthony Sloman, 35, Downton Avenue". I was too intimidated and far too frightened to lie. "Sloman?" he said. "Is your Dad the tailor up the road?" I thought, he thinks I've lied about the address. "I'll go and see him now, with this." And he took the other book in his hand. "You've paid for that," he said, indicating. "Now take that and get out of here."

And so I did, and went home, shaken. Mummy had tea ready, as always, and I simply couldn't speak, I didn't know what to say. Dad arrived and told me to go straight to my room while he told Mummy what had happened – the book seller had gone to Daddy's shop, and told him what his son had done, and said he was lucky that he didn't go to the police. Well, Mummy stayed downstairs and Dad came up and confronted me. The rest is a memory blank. I cried and cried, Mummy cried and cried. I was punished, but I can't remember how, and I never, never, ever stole anything again.

But, in truth, I well knew what I had gone and done. I could have been arrested. I could have been chucked out of Dulwich. I could have… Well, it just doesn't bear thinking about. What a foolish, stupid idiotic boy I was! Spoiled beyond measure, with not-so-hidden criminal tendencies to boot. The matter was never brought up again, and I had learned a heavy lesson, but years and years later I wondered to myself if it could have been possibly in my own paternal genes.

Geography Fourth was almost a joy – well, for Dulwich, that is. As I mentioned earlier, I found myself in excellent company. And made friends for life. It was the pleasure of going to The Pictures that bonded us, and I was genuinely pleased to find that there were others who shared my filmic tastes, although love of sports also seemed to loom large in their lives as well.

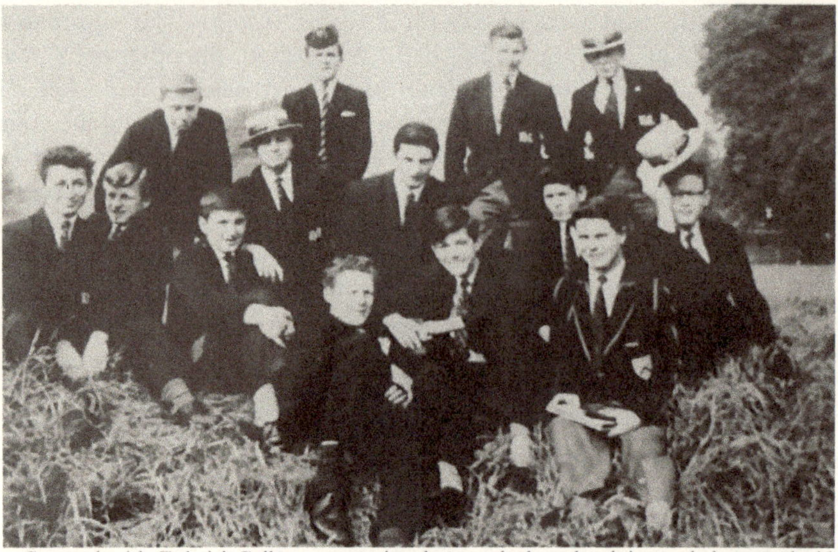

Class Geography 4th, Dulwich College, an exterior photographed one lunchtime and photographed by a classmate (I forget who) using my new camera (hence me in the middle with the class surrounding me!) on "The Mound", a small promontory on the playing fields. The line-up,then, left-to-right: Colin Turner, Gerald Powell, "Charlie" Chase, Alan May, Lee Curtis, Alan Chambers, Dave Lythell, Tony Sloman (dead centre!), Paul Rusling, Rodney Peters, Johnnie Walker, and Paddy Clarke, with Tony Thomas and Andrew Izod standing to the left of me, behind Peters. Amazing that I remembered all those first names, because in those days surnames only were generally used at Dulwich.

There was also one other thing that my Father had encouraged me to do, and that was to enter every single competition around that dealt with my two specific interests, films and rock music, and this proved to be more fortunate than I could ever imagine…

TV's Saturday evening *Jack Jackson Show* had a win-an-L.P. competition every week, and I regularly entered it, and eventually won, to Mummy's delight (for he was her favourite), an album of Frankie Vaughan's Greatest Hits, most of which I had already bought previously as singles. When the Gaumont cinema in Streatham was eventually turned into a Top Rank Bowl, it was Frankie Vaughan himself who was invited along to chuck the first ball on opening day, and then to sign autographs. I took along my L.P. prize, but my pen wouldn't write on the laminated record sleeve, so I only got a rough "Frankie" before he gave up with an apology. But I'd tried, and what a gentleman Frankie Vaughan had turned out to be.

Another prize win was entering an *Our Man in Havana* contest at the Regal, West Norwood, the prize being a brand-new Hoover Constellation vacuum cleaner as featured in the film. I won, and, to my delight, I was invited to the Odeon, Leicester Square premiere of Columbia's new film *Strangers When We Meet* starring Kirk Douglas and Kim Novak, to collect my prize. I asked if I could bring my parents, and to my surprise, the reply was affirmative. And so we three went, front row circle. The film was sexually quite strong and adult for its day, and was I embarrassed?!!

I was also quite anxious to see any American rock'n'rollers when they came over, but, in truth, it was often too expensive, and not always easy to get to where they were performing, and my parents frowned on me going to evening shows that far away, even as far as the Elephant and Castle, where London's largest cinema (and therefore largest show venue) was located. But here Daddy came to my rescue. He may not have necessarily known the work of the artistes I wanted to see, but he sure as heck wanted to know what they were wearing nowadays, and so he took me to one of the greatest, most unforgettable, rock gigs ever, and yup, it was at the Trocadero, Elephant and Castle itself. Emile Ford opened for Duane Eddy and his Rebels, and the near-riot that Eddy caused with his "twangy" guitar made him a hard act to follow. But after the interval Clyde McPhatter was simply terrific, and he preceded bill-topper Bobby Darin, in sub-Sinatra swinging style, who could not be bettered – by anybody! "Mack the Knife", "Beyond the Sea", "Things" – what a repertoire! What class! Truly, the best I'd ever seen. Dad said, would I like to go backstage afterwards and try to get his autograph? Would I?? So Dad, using all his natural native charm plus, convinced the stage door manager to let us in, and so I met Bobby Darin personally, who signed my autograph book "To Tony"! I kept the pen he wrote it with for several years on display in my bedroom. (And years later, in Hollywood, I met the onetime Mrs. Darin herself, Sandra Dee, and their son, who both autographed her then-new memoir for me).

Now, at Dulwich, we had quite a series of distinguished lecturers who would visit us and who were invited to speak to the classes, who would gather in the Science Block en masse to hear the speakers. We had all three heads of our political parties down to talk (James Cameron's son was already a Dulwich pupil), plus various scientists, statesmen, and famous teachers. And one very, very memorable day, we had somebody it seemed that, among my contemporaries, only I had heard of: Dr. Roger Manvell, known well to me (though not, of course, in person), as the author of the *Pelican Cinema Film Review* series and its companion publication *Film and the Public*, not to mention such tomes as *A Seat in the Cinema*, *The Technique of Film Music* and *History of the British Film*. He also edited *The Penguin Film Review* from 1946 to 1949. I was excited to hear him speak in person.

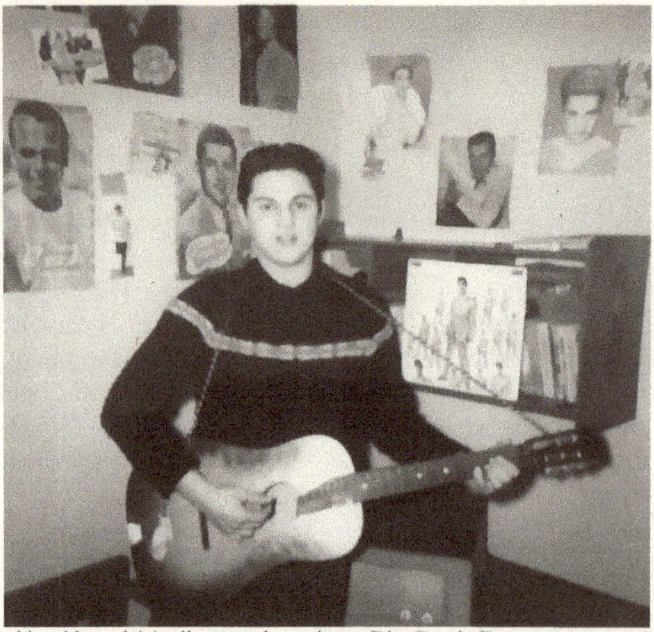

Adopting a then-fashionable rock 'n' roll pose at home in my Disc Den in Downton Avenue, Streatham. No, I never learned to play that guitar, but it made a great prop! Just dig the period surround! (That's the then-new Elvis L.P. in the background, above my record-player just behind me, and centrefolds from "Valentine" and "Photoplay" adorn the walls).

His lecture was excellent and appropriate, but to me seemed terribly out of date. He praised the studio system, particularly the way any scene could be recreated in a fashion that made it possible to facilitate drama: David Lean's work in both *Great Expectations* and *Oliver Twist*, for example. He discussed screen acting, with no mention of the relatively then-new "Method" or screen naturalism (he mentioned neither Brando nor James Dean), and he pointed out how audiences were manipulated, whereas in the theatre they merely watched the play unfurl naturally, and he didn't seem to recognise, not mentioning by default, all of those major new changes in cinema that were currently transforming the medium, virtually on a weekly basis: widescreen, location shooting, fractured narrative story-telling, adult themes, and naturalistic performances (i.e. you can't see the "acting"), matters I have previously alluded to in this text, and of course, had learned to respect, if not to love.

At the end, he took questions. I listened to a couple, and thought them immature and irrelevant. I had seen Andrew Stone's *The Last Voyage* over that prior weekend, and I put up my hand. I pointed out, not rudely I hope, to Dr. Manvell, just how this basically average studio picture worked so well, and why, virtually in violation of all his theories, by being shot totally on the location of the story, i.e. a real ship, not a studio mock-up, by featuring a cast of well-known screen actors, not necessarily stage stars in make-up (i.e. Robert Stack versus Alec Guinness; naturalism versus "acting"), who totally convinced in character, and at a pace and speed generally more rapid than that found in the so-called top British movies. I also pointed out to him his non-recognition of the burgeoning European New Waves, including ours, here in Britain. Well. There was a shocked silence in the hall, and then a burst of prolonged applause from the audience, applause for me, not for Dr. Manvell. I was, of course, embarrassed, but inwardly secretly pleased. When the applause died down, Manvell attempted to address my comments. I don't remember what he said, apart from the fact that he hadn't yet seen *The Last Voyage*, but it appeared to me that he was hopelessly out-of-touch, and, worse, patronising towards me. There were no more questions. He was thanked by the Masters present, and, as far as I was concerned, vanished into the night.

But something big had happened. Boys, including senior prefects, came up and congratulated me. Pupils I hardly knew came over and spoke to me. Even my form master, Mr. Howlings, who barely gave me the time of day, took time out to chat to me. What had exactly happened? I didn't understand it. All I knew was I didn't intend to steal Dr. Manvell's thunder in any way, I was just asking a question that I felt needed to be asked. The result was another meeting with the Careers Master, who finally said, "Perhaps you ought to go into the film industry." Presumably this was a reference to my previous wish to become chief film censor, but maybe, just maybe, he was right. We never discussed just how, exactly, but it was certainly food for thought. Unsurprisingly though, "Spud" McKinley's main concern was to make sure that I achieved decent GCEs at "O" and "A" level first.

Mummy seemed to be often unwell, and didn't seem to be improving in health. Visits to our local doctor, Dr. Hiley, and various medical recommendations of his didn't seem to be helping, either. She went for a session in hospital, and Nanna Morris came to look after us for a while, but Mummy came back, seemingly much better. At the time, selfish as ever, I wasn't overly worried. Mummy seemed fine to me.

My new school pals used to come over in the holidays, or I would go to their places, or we'd go to The Pictures together, and, in actual fact, we bonded for life, and really, it is for this to which I owe deference to Dulwich College. Friends are rare indeed, but friends the nature of mine are gold dust, and it is Dulwich, and Geography Fourth, to which I owe the lifelong fellowships of David, Nick, Tim, Rod, Alan, Mart, and Gerald, and Paul, who left us far too early.

Something very strange happened when Mummy was in hospital that first time, something very strange indeed, and it's still hard and awkward for me to put it into words to this very day. I came home from school early one sports day, mercifully not having been chosen for any team, to find my father, seemingly naked, in bed in our main bedroom, and my old girlfriend, Angela Smith, administering to him in a way that I could not comprehend. Angela was fully dressed, but blushing, and my presence seemed to unnerve them – they were speechless. I hadn't seen Angela for some, maybe five, years, and we just looked at each other. Suddenly the doorbell rang, and Daddy said to me, "You'd better get that, son." Which I did, barely thinking "What's Daddy doing home at this hour?" or even "So how does he know Angela, and since when?" I opened the door to reveal Pauline's mother, Mummy's friend "Scatty" Dora, and she said she was just looking in to hear how Mummy was. But more questions were in my mind: she couldn't have known that I would be home, let alone Dad. I, playing devil's advocate, asked her if she wanted to speak to Dad, who was upstairs. She said, "Yes," and I started to show her up. At the bedroom door entrance, Angela was just leaving and Dad was clearly finishing dressing very quickly. Dora just said "Hello," and that she'd popped in to see if we were all all right, and how was Mummy? Dad's reply was brief, and Dora left, saying to me that if there's anything she could do, just to let her know. And then Angela came downstairs, passed me on her way out, and said, "Give me a phone call. It's the same old number," and left.

Just me and Dad in the house. Nanna had gone to pick up Linda from school. What to do? Well, Dad behaved, as I recall, as though nothing untoward had happened (maybe it hadn't, I wanted to believe), and I didn't know what to say. I just went to my room…

And that's all that I remember of that particular day. Like a bad film, it has stayed in my memory for ever. And then I began to grow up. If I was ever truly innocent, I wasn't from that day on.

"O" levels flew by, then Geography Remove "B", and finally Geography Sixth. And then what? It was quite obvious to everybody that I wasn't Oxford and Cambridge material, and I really didn't want any further education. I wanted to go into the film industry. I had no contacts, none whatsoever, and I didn't really know what I wanted to do in film, only that I was certain I wanted to be in film production, not distribution nor theatrical, and certainly not anything in that fiendish newcomer television, which clearly, to me, was only intended for children, idiots, and stay-at-homes.

There was, however, a surprising respite from worry. I had established a friendship – which I'm happy to say turned into a lifelong one – with Nicolas Nacht, another Taurean soul, a schoolmate who sported a most sophisticated upbringing, at least to me: As I understood it, Nick's mother was French and his father was a Romanian Jew. They were moderately wealthy, owning what seemed to be a cattle ranch in Argentina, and they seemed to me to live in France, and one school holiday actually Nick asked me if I would like to visit him in Paris. Would I??

But how to afford it? Dad had a brilliant idea. He would ask his cousin, my Uncle Laurie (of the card evenings), if I could work for J. Lyons for a fortnight, to earn the money for Paris, and so I did, sweating and washing dishes in the kitchens at the Lyons Corner House where Uncle Laurie was a manager, the one in the Strand where I used to be taken as a child for tea and sandwiches. Of course I didn't like it, but it was a real revelation to me, nevertheless. I remember once some greens fell off a plate onto the floor of the kitchen, and the instruction was to scoop them up, wipe 'em down, and serve. I was horrified! But the two weeks paid off, and I fetched up in a small Left Bank hotel that Nick knew. Nick's mother, a most wonderful, sophisticated and elegant ersatz Parisienne, showed me around Paris, with Nick accompanying. We had wonderful, magical unforgettable moments...

Taken out to lunch with Nick and his mother to a most sophisticated (to me) underground diner, his mother treated me to a wonderful meal: I still remember how the waiter most carefully unwrapped the transparent tissue paper that my veal (Nick's mother's choice for me) had been cooked in, when I looked up to see no less than Simone Signoret, the great French-Jewish actress Oscared for *Room at the Top*, sitting only two tables away. I happened to have with me a newly-purchased copy of *Une Semaine de Paris*, the French equivalent of our own *What's On in London*, which featured La Signoret on the cover, because her new film *Le Jour et L'heure* was opening in Paris that week. Dare I ask her to autograph it for me? Nick's mum insisted that I did, assuring me that Signoret spoke English. Well, I took it across to her, and she did indeed autograph it for me. What more could I possibly wish for? (And yes, the food was superb.)

Well, there was more, much more, all of it magical. Folk singing was all the rage. In London, Nick had seen that newcomer Bob Dylan (on the very same day that I had seen Roy Orbison), and the coolest folk place in Paris was L'Abbaye, where the American duo of Gordon Heath and Lee Payant played regularly. I vaguely knew of Gordon Heath, who had been the narrator of the Halas and Batchelor animated feature film of *Animal Farm* (which I had seen at the Clifton cinema, Brixton Hill), and who was famous for starring in Elia Kazan's stage production of *Deep Are the Roots* (in which, incidentally, the supporting cast in both the London production and the touring versions included both Patrick McGoohan and Earl Cameron), but I knew nothing of his Communist past, nor of his longterm relationship with his partner Lee Payant (homosexuality was still illegal in Britain). Nor did I know how famous L'Abbaye was, or would indeed become, as a Parisian folk venue. The audience, excepting me and Nick, consisted almost entirely of what would soon be called hipsters (cf. the *Funny Face* film's French underground club sequence), and the duo were superb. I bought their current 10" record album there, and they both signed it for me.

And then I discovered the Rue Champillon, Paris's street of cinemas. I couldn't thank Nick enough, and I could barely believe the programming! Vintage and new, fashionable and cult, all in a row. Nick and I saw Lubitsch's *To Be or Not to Be* with Jack Benny and Carole Lombard, Roger Vadim's new sex and vampires film *Et Mourir de Plaisir* (unsubtitled of course, a first for me) starring Catherine Deneuve, and, at last, one of the most famous, and best, film noirs ever, Otto Preminger's superb *Laura*.

Left on my own one day, I decided to try to see *Johnny Guitar*, the Nicholas Ray baroque Western, having located it in *Une Semaine de Paris* at a cinema called La Pagode, which Nick knew about, a famous cinema built on the lines of a Chinese pagoda. Shouldn't be hard to find. But I got hopelessly lost, despite the street map of Paris I carried with me. I managed to find a policeman near Raspail, and made an attempt to ask him, in schoolboy French, where was the cinema, La Pagode, that I was looking for? To my surprise, he replied in broken English, and his reply both enhanced and endeared Paris to me forever: "La Pagode? Ah! "*Johnny Guitar*", he said, "Mais oui, certainment…Choan Crawford… Stirleeng 'Ayden...Oh, et Nicholas Ray." And he then pointed me in the right direction. And so I loved Paris for ever more.

School was coming to an end. I vaguely knew that, whatever my examination results, I didn't want to go to university. I wanted to work in the British film industry. I had no contacts, and the careers master at Dulwich couldn't help. He was sympathetic, but he truly couldn't help. But Dulwich did help in one way, inadvertently. One quite renowned Old Alleynian was jazz saxophonist Bruce Turner, and a documentary film featuring him was being presented at London's National Film Theatre on the South Bank, which I had up until then never previously visited. I purchased a ticket and went along, arguably to one of the most momentous discoveries of my life. No-one had ever mentioned to me that we had a repertory cinema of this type on site of the old Festival of Britain, and when I eventually saw the NFT programme and checked out future seasons I was in my own seventh heaven. I joined immediately, and thus the British Film Institute and the National Film Theatre began to prove a vital injection into my suburban life. Amazingly, although I had taken over the running of the Dulwich College Film Society from one David Thomson (who would go on to become, arguably, the world's greatest and most prolific film writer ever), I knew nothing of the NFT at all. Well, that was Dulwich for you: all sports. Movies?-- Never, at least not then. I could never get anybody at Dulwich College, neither mates nor masters, to understand my attitude to sport: I just didn't see any point in compulsory participation in activities wherein someone, or some whole side, would end up as losers. Life wasn't about winning or losing, but about sharing, creating, loving, and achieving personal satisfaction, at least in my book. It certainly wasn't about hitting a ball across a net or at three sticks in the ground, or even kicking or thrusting one into another kind of net: it was about sharing many other pleasures on offer: good company, food and drink, music, literature, theatre, cinema, dance, and, hopefully, sex. I hadn't learned the word "anathema" yet, but that certainly was what sport would become to me.

I soon began to make a lot of enquiries: common sense suggested going to a film school, and there actually, amazingly, was one quite nearby, in Acre Lane, Brixton, called "The London School of Film Technique", but it was fee-paying (no grants) and highly expensive, and guaranteed no entry into the industry itself. (It was later to move to Covent Garden, where it is now, and to have several distinguished graduates, and to fill many vacant film and television technician slots around the world.) I also wrote letters to a few key people in the film industry. My reply from film producer Harold Hecht was pretty typical: "I'm sorry but there just isn't anything I could do for you." At least he replied; most didn't.

The day I left Dulwich seemed to be kind of symbolic in the choice of film programme that Nick Nacht and I selected to see together that one last afternoon, a double bill (60/40) of two brand-new MGM films: *It Happened at the World's Fair*, starring The King, Elvis Presley, already beginning his cinematic decline into family-orientated trivia, coupled with my idol (and also co-incidentally Elvis's) Stewart Granger, swashbuckling away in what was to be his last costume outing, the Italian-made colourful *Swordsman of Siena.* The times they were indeed a-changing. What would have been the school holidays were upon us. Except it was no longer a school holiday: it was life. I was out of school permanently, at last. I couldn't carry on writing unanswered letters forever. I had to earn some money: it was time for pocket money to end.

Angela Smith had come back into my life. I ran into her, I think, in Streatham High Road, and we started dating, of sorts. I took her to see *Top Hat* at the NFT, and then to *West Side Story* in its premiere 70mm. run at the Astoria, Charing Cross Road, yes, "up West", which to me was a major date, but you'd be quite right, it wasn't a wise thing to do, with hindsight.

In my last terms at Dulwich, running the school film society was what I liked doing best, and I made many mistakes, mainly, not to book only films that I liked, but to book movies that young teenagers may not have had heard of. My first booking was Stanley Kubrick's *Paths of Glory*, which I had seen on release, a sheer masterpiece from a director that I felt I had personally discovered with *The Killing*, but I was very disconcerted when a hand-made poster that I had created, and pinned up in the North Block loo, was disfigured and the film re-titled, in large black ink, *Tin Baths of Glory.* I bet my predecessor David Thomson didn't have to put up with such nonsense. (I eventually met, and became friendly with David via our varied social circles, and told him that story. He replied, quite rightly I guess, that you should never have put a screening poster up in the toilets. Who could argue? My cock-eyed reasoning was that everybody goes there.) I then booked the colourful, but poorly-released, musical film *L'il Abner*, which I had liked very much, but I learned an important life lesson from it. I always liked to sit through the films shown at school with the audience, and to be available for questions afterwards, but I had made a date with Angela that day, and promised to meet her at the Streatham High Road toy shop in which she worked on that very evening, which meant leaving *L'il Abner* about twenty minutes in. (I've never had a great sense of priorities.) And so I did, but there was hardly any audience there in the first place: I had badly underestimated a boys' school interest in a comic strip musical. Well, I left when I had to. The next day I was asked by a Master not only why did I leave, but why did the slim remaining audience follow me out? Of course, I had no idea they did, and was in a spot. The master-in-charge decided that, perhaps, he should be responsible for booking the next, and what would be the last, film under my directorship of the Dulwich College Film Society. And so he did, and played the all-time classic *All Quiet on the Western Front* to a packed house.

Angela and I were seeing each other. Mum didn't actually disapprove, and Dad kept well away. But our relationship was strange. One evening I was waiting for her at the bus stop outside the Streatham Hill Theatre, at the foot of our road, to meet her as previously arranged, to go and see *Spartacus* at the Granada Brixton. (I had already seen it properly, taken by Dad to the premiere 70mm. presentation at the Metropole, Victoria, and had written a review, which was commended by my English master Mr. Jagger. Films didn't get much better than *Spartacus*, in my book.) It was a day when my Aunts Becky and Petsy were visiting us, and their bus stop was the same one at which I was expecting Angela, at the bottom of our road. To my chagrin (and shame) they saw me as they were leaving Streatham while I was still waiting for Angela at that very bus stop. I had no alternative but to put up with their joshing before they got on their own bus home. I waved goodbye, embarrassed but furious. I waited and waited, but Angela didn't show. I then did what I never, ever, did again. I got on a bus and went to the cinema, missing the first twenty minutes or so of the feature film. I phoned Angela the next day.

I should have broken up with her there and then, but I was weak. Angela said that she just couldn't come, but didn't say why. I didn't press her. When we next met, she told me that her own brother-in-law had sexually assaulted her. I didn't know what to think, or what to say. There was a party coming up in Dulwich, with us school leavers celebrating, and I asked her along. She said, "Yes", and I eventually picked her up, and took her to the party. I can't remember whose house it was, but the parents were away, and the single bedroom was empty and available. Unsurprisingly, the ever-sophisticated (to me, anyway) Gerry Powell was first in, with his girl friend, and he eventually emerged, lipsticked and tieless, (probably just for show, I realised much, much later), and then Tim Block went in with his regular girl friend Cathy. I was a little embarrassed, because it seemed that Angela and I were next expected to make that particular visit to the bedroom, which we indeed did after Tim emerged with the widest smile adorning his face. We went into the bedroom, and then wordlessly kissed, embraced, and undressed. I'd never seen her naked before, and was surprised to find that she had a single, very long black hair growing out of one breast. We discussed it. I lost all sexual feeling (I knew from somewhere that a hairy tit was a mark of a witch). She said no-one had ever seen it before, except her brother-in-law. Whaaat? Still a technical virgin, I discovered that I didn't want to know any more, to say the least. We dressed, exited the bedroom, and left the party. I never saw her again. Ever.

But then I remembered that Angela was, I think, an executive of the Jimmy Young fan club, the British singer whose hit parade hits were massive, pre-rock'n'roll, and included "Unchained Melody" and "The Man from Laramie". I always loathed him, and, in fact, I bought Canadian vocalist Edmund Hockridge's cover version of "The Man from Laramie" on a

Parlophone 78 at the time. This singular fact afforded me a very peculiar degree of youthful satisfaction with regard to dropping Angela. What a schmuck I had been!

I remained close, well, close-ish, to my old school buddies for the rest of my life, happily, except perhaps for Howard Rogg, who seemed to disappear after I attended his first wedding, but he was a good mate in those far-off times. My closest friend remained, and remains, Nick Nacht, and in those days he was, I think, pursuing a theatrical career, and appeared as a tango dancer (type-casting!) in a Royal Court play, and sundry other semi-professional appearances. He shared a flat, or was it his girl friend's, with a young playwright called David Hare. Wonder what became of him?

I was no closer to any kind of work, and Mummy's health didn't seem to be getting any better. She could no longer manage the stairs at 35, Downton, and it seemed that we would have to move to a new one-level home. Which we did. Daddy found a marvellous single-level flat at 38, Leigham Hall, on the very corner of Streatham High Road between the Regal and the Astoria, now renamed the Odeon, and it suited us all fine. But now when I think about it, I wonder what happened to our cats and Judy the Scottie dog, because when we moved we eventually got new pets: Bruno, a black dog of good nature and no distinctive breed, and a cat that my sister named Stripey, for what were obvious reasons. I wonder what little joke Sigmund Freud swung to make me forget the demise of my early former pets? Selfish as ever, that's what I remember most about the move, but I'm sure that it was definitely much better for Mummy. And we had access to a swimming pool in the grounds of Leigham Hall. And it was summer time.—

My school friends came over to bathe and lark about in the pool, only disturbed by the fact that Dad occasionally wanted me to pick up something for him from an outside workman in Soho or the East End, a waistcoat or invariably a pair of trousers which were ready, of course, immediately. So sometimes I, resentfully, had to leave my mates in what I regarded as "my" pool. Selfish, selfish, selfish – of course, I should have been delighted to be able to help my Father with his business: after all, he was only paying my way while I wasn't working.

There was one instance when I helped him, though, or so I thought. The Leigham Hall friends and neighbours decided to throw a summer party, and Dad offered to organise it, which he did. It was to be called a "Barbi-Q-Splash", and there would be dancing. My old mate from 3A, Pete Snowden, was getting together a new rock band (about the same time as four blokes from Liverpool were doing a similar thing), and so I suggested "Pete Snowden and the Blue Stars" play for us, and Dad hired them. As I recall, it was all a great success, but the Blue Stars didn't realise how much they would have to perform, and played all of their repertoire twice over. (I don't think anybody there noticed!) Also, I remember Dad M.C.-ing with one arm in a sling; I have absolutely no idea why. Nevertheless, the evening was considered a success, and we met other residents of Leigham Hall, one of whom was one Brian

Sommerville, who, Dad told me, had some show business connections, and who would be pleased to talk to me about future career possibilities. I truly had no idea who he was at the time. (Brian was, of course, press agent in those heady days for that extremely exciting new Liverpudlian rock'n'roll band that called themselves The Beatles.) So I agreed to see him.

It was a strange meeting. His Leigham Hall flat was utterly unlike any other I had ever seen: dark burnished wood, dark green curtains, a large desk, and virtually no furniture. I thought that it resembled what I believe a formal man's club would've looked like. Brian asked me what I wanted to do in my life, and I told him: "The film industry". Strangely, I thought, he didn't ask me as what, but he did ask me what I was doing about it. I told him the truth: that I'd enquired at the film union, who told me that I couldn't get a job without being a member, and can't get a job without a union card, and wouldn't get a union card without first having a job. He thought this over, and then gave me some very wise advice: get a job, any kind of job, that will free you up to take interviews, and see everybody that you can. Use every contact, and try to find more contacts, but earn some money, because money buys freedom, and then he told me about the industry "bible", the *Kinematograph Yearbook*, in which I would find all the addresses and contact numbers that I would need, and he reached into his desk, took out his own copy of the *Kine Yearbook*, and put it in my hand, loaning me his copy. But he held it a little too long in my hand, and then I, an ex-public schoolboy, remember, realised that he was "queer". The drapes, the colours, the furniture, no sign of a partner, let alone a woman. O.K. then, time to go, and fast.

Dad put me in touch with another local film-maker, Laurence Knight, whose latest celluloid masterpiece was a little epic called *My Bare Lady*, playing in a sex cinema in the West End (on which he stole as his credit the Christian name of the distinguished American film writer, Arthur, of the same surname. It was a somewhat tasteless gag that seems to have endured in perpetuity: check out the IMDB). I went over to his flat, which he shared with his mother and a friend. He helped me by suggesting that I write a lot of letters asking for any job in the film industry. We drank a little wine, and then I noticed that his male friend was putting his arm around Laurence, and giggling. Laurence said he could arrange an introduction to the producer of *My Bare Lady* (to be fair, he did that) and would I like to stay for coffee, his mother chuckling in the background. It didn't take me too long to realise that Laurence and his male friend both lived together with Laurence's mum, so I made my goodbyes and said thanks as quickly as possible, and left.

But Laurence was as good as his word, and I duly met up with Morton Lewis, his credit on *My Bare Lady* being his name backwards, Notrom Siwel, and discovered to my utter amazement that he had been, or so he said, the clapper boy on *Citizen Kane*. He was, after all, American, and grew up in the studios, and I believed him. However, he was brutally honest: "There just isn't anything I can do for you" was his parting remark.

So, what to do? I couldn't keep living off my parents. I had to earn some money, somehow. And I seemingly had to join the A.C.T.T., by any means possible. Not only could I not find work, but even if I was, by some divine chance, offered a job, I wouldn't be able to accept it if I wasn't in that union. Besides which, I didn't even know what I wanted to do in film, except I was becoming pretty sure I that wanted to become a film director, nothing less. I went to the library, found another *Kine Yearbook*, and wrote to everybody, about a hundred letters. I got three replies, all negative, but at least I had some addresses. I also scoured the "Wanted" ads in the daily and evening newspapers, looking for – I didn't exactly know what… I needed income. I was getting too old for pocket money. And Mummy still wasn't well, and I didn't want to be a burden to my parents.

Dad suggested a couple of temporary solutions, the main one of which was that, perhaps, I ought to go to evening classes in film, if there were any, to learn how to work in the medium. Very wise. So I checked out all the local evening classes, and the Brixton Film School, but we clearly couldn't afford the latter. While I was doing all this research, and helping Dad out with various pick-ups from his outworkers, we met some nice friendly Jewish people in our new flats, Stanley and Irene Millar, who had opened a dry cleaning business, impressively called "Matisse", right next door to the Regal cinema, Streatham.

Stanley asked Dad if he wouldn't mind if I could help them out in their shop. It would be for a pittance, but he would allow me to take time off for interviews, should there be any. After all, autumn was drawing in and people would need a fair amount of dry cleaning before Christmas, Stanley reasoned. Dad put this to me. And I had to think about it a lot. Was this what I'd got my "A" and "O" levels for? And then, what if my mates saw me in the shop? But, again, what were the chances? Dad also said I could go to film evening classes if we could find something suitable, and that was an idea I hadn't even thought about. And that's what happened, with life-enhancing and life-changing consequences that I could not even imagine in those far-off days of 1963…

Mummy still wasn't well. After another spell in hospital (over which Nanna came and stayed and looked after my sister and me again) there was a final diagnosis: an illness we had never heard of before called Hodgkin's disease, and what we weren't told (although I suspect Dad might have been informed) was that it had invariably fatal consequences. Dad blamed Dr. Hiley for not spotting the symptoms earlier, but it was too late for blame. Mummy didn't know how ill she was, and, as far as I know, nobody ever told her. Or me either, then. The summer was drawing to a close. Poolside gatherings were growing fewer. There were a few more parties at friends' houses, and jobs and university entrances began to loom large, but not, so far, for me.

My parents were anxious for me to get a job, any job. Dad had known noted actor-writer-film director Bryan Forbes from Forest Gate, where Forbes used to live, and contacted him to ask his advice as to how I could get into the film industry. Forbes was helpful, although he himself couldn't help at the time. He had just begun directing, and achieved great critical success with both *Whistle Down the Wind* and *The L-Shaped Room*, and was in a production partnership with Richard Attenborough. However, he did suggest that I speak to the Boulting Brothers, and see what they could suggest. Would we like him to call them? Dad, of course, said "Yes" (without asking me, but that was O.K.) and, sure enough, I got a call from a Boulting brother to arrange a meeting at their offices in Broadwick House, Soho. (By the way, years later when I ran into Bryan Forbes at Pinewood where he was making *The Madwoman of Chaillot*, I accosted him in the restaurant and thanked him for making that connection. He was pleased, and flattered, and said that he remembered Dad, but, I thought, perhaps wrongly, that he clearly didn't remember him at all. Why on earth should he?).

I took the meeting with either John or Roy Boulting. Twins, you couldn't tell them apart, and I really don't remember which one I met. However, whoever it was, was really chatty and friendly, and said, although they weren't at present in production and had no opportunity to take on a trainee, he (John or Roy) would introduce me to a man who had offices just across the corridor, and who was regularly making films for the Children's Film Foundation, and perhaps he could help. And he literally ushered me across the way to meet Bill Luckwell, and departed after the introduction. Bill said he was busy right now, and we made a date to meet up in the very near future. In the meantime, I went back to the Streatham Library and took out every single book they had on film production: yes, both of them:-- *The Technique of Film Editing* by Karel Reisz and Gavin Millar, and a Focus handbook on 16mm. filmmaking. I tried to memorise the key content of both books by heart, and, thanks to reading Karel Reisz, determined for myself exactly what area of film production I wanted to enter: Film Editing.

Film Editing because, it seemed to me, that it was the only true area of motion picture making that was utterly unique to that particular industry. Every other aspect occurred in other industries; lighting and camerawork in photography; acting in theatre and in television; art direction ditto, also construction and costume; music in concert halls and recordings; production and direction in both theatre and television. Editing seemed to me to be utterly unique to film, which indeed it was, and the more I learned about its capabilities, the more I wanted in. I also noted that many of my own favourite director discoveries had prior editing credits: Robert Wise (*Citizen Kane*, no less), David Lean (*Pygmalion*), Mark Robson, John Sturges, Charles Crichton, Edward Dmytryk – the list grew longer with every visit to the NFT.

I turned up, worried and excited simultaneously, for my eventual interview with Bill Luckwell. Bill first made it clear that he couldn't exactly offer me a job, but he'd see what he could do. I knew that he was making features for the Children's Film Foundation, so I (foolishly) thought that I was in with a good chance. The interview was terse, and short. He said, quite simply, that he was going to test me by asking three simple technical questions, and then "We'll take it from there." "All right," I thought to myself. The first question would've been easy enough to answer, but not, of course, for me. "Which side of the film is the cel side, and which is the emulsion?"

I didn't know. I actually felt myself looking blank. I was mortified. Then…"How does film go through a camera, or through a projector?" "Oh, smoothly," I replied, sure of myself. He just stared at me. Of course, I had never heard then of the "Maltese Cross" system of intermittent motion, whereby each single frame is exposed at one twenty-fourth of a second, in order that the photographed image would appear seamless when properly projected, providing a constantly moving image to a viewing spectator. Mr. Luckwell just nodded solemnly, and proceeded with third, and last, question:- "What do you do when your recorded dialogue on a shoot is unusable?"

Ah! I remembered the answer to this from that 16mm. handbook I'd taken out of Streatham Library. Confident and cocksure, I replied strongly, but, of course, I'd only read about the technique, I'd never heard it said out loud, so I pronounced it completely incorrectly. "Why, you post-synch, of course." That's how it was written in the book. I'd never heard it called, correctly, "post-syncing". No "h". No "ch". Mr. Luckwell said, "Post-synch?" "Yes, sir." "Well, Mr. Sloman," he went on, "it seems to me that all your film experience is from books. It seems to me that you have never spoken to anyone who works in film, nor have you ever visited a film-making studio or location. Come back and see me when you have acquired some experience. Try film school, or evening classes in cinematography – the L.C.C. have some excellent ones. Goodbye, Mr. Sloman." And he got up, we shook hands, and that was that.

I phoned Stanley Millar at "Matisse", and started working in his dry cleaners the following Monday, vowing to myself to check the job columns in the evening newspapers every day, and to look into the availability of evening classes in cinematography. And so I signed on at the Streatham and Tooting Institute for cinematography classes on Monday evenings. My old school friends were gradually starting their future apprenticeships: David Trace into accounting, Howard Rogg into law, Nick Nacht to Cambridge. I was busy, but I was also lonely. Only now, I buried myself in film: I went to the National Film Theatre whenever I could afford it, and met, over the years, a whole new crowd of people, including notable British film historians and film critics who befriended me, amongst them John Gillett, David Shipman, Derek Malcolm, and Allan Eyles, and also active film practitioners, most notably the editor Derek York, and his friends Lindsay Anderson and Leslie Hardcastle, who was then the actual manager of the National Film Theatre, all gentlemen generations older than me at the time. I wanted to learn everything.

The evening classes in cinematography turned out to be soul-enriching and life-enhancing, in many ways that I couldn't possibly have conceived, and for which I shall be forever eternally grateful. But in the meantime, dry cleaning assistant by day, would-be cineaste by night, and forever learning –

via viewing, primarily – everything, but absolutely everything, about motion pictures: their history, their techniques, their future… And Mummy wasn't getting any better. Leigham Hall was a happy home, nevertheless. My sister was bright and clever, and the pets were certainly fun. If Dad had financial trouble with the shop, I never saw signs of it, but I had a feeling that business wasn't getting better, as Dad began to talk about merging, or even selling up and moving in, perhaps, with other tailoring associates. This didn't sound like Dad at all, and, ever only self-interested, I didn't give it a second thought. But Dad was, indeed, thinking of giving up 62, Streatham Hill, and offering his services elsewhere, for whatever reasons then I never knew, so concerned was I about my own parlous future: I didn't want to be an assistant in a dry cleaning shop in Streatham forever, that was certain.

Suddenly, I became jealous of my old school pal Tim Block. He had, I think, with the aid of his brother Giles, managed to secure a role with Michael Croft's newly-established National Youth Theatre, and was then the only person I knew who was actually working in the show business. I contacted him to see if he had any advice. He didn't, but he did invite me to see him play a tiny part in the new Old Vic National Youth Theatre production of *Troilus and Cressida*, and to meet him backstage afterwards. Well, this was certainly exciting for me: I had never been backstage before. So I went along, and saw the show, and met Tim afterwards, and his brother Giles. Giles introduced me to the two leads, neither famous then. Simon Ward was Troilus, and Helen Mirren played Cressida. I was so struck by Miss Mirren that I actually asked her if she'd like to go out with me. She declined. I persisted, she declined more firmly. Abashed, I retired, hurt. Today, I am absolutely sure that Dame Helen Mirren has absolutely no recollection whatsoever of that insolent young ex-schoolboy's over-persistent, unrequited, request for a date! (Tim Block was horrified and embarrassed at my behaviour, he later told me).

It seemed that dry-cleaning and evening classes would be the immediate future. But I still kept looking in the evening papers, and also the Kinematograph Weekly, newly discovered, for any kind of job in the film industry. Dad had a Streatham friend, a heavily-built (and to me, slightly overwhelming) Jewish tailor called Leonard Starr, whose gaze, through his glasses, seemed, I thought, omnipotent, and whose manner was, to me, very bossy, but he knew of someone who worked on the fringes of the film industry, who exploited young men by paying them a pittance to work for him in his cutting rooms in Soho. Cutting rooms in Soho! I was all ears. Leonard told Dad he'd make some enquiries, but in the meantime, I'd better try to acquire some sort of experience in handling film. Not to mention trying to get out of the business of dry cleaning!

There were some bright moments at "Matisse", but not many. TV singer Jackie Rae, then married to Janette Scott (I think before she went off with Anthony Newley, or was it the other way around?) popped in one day, and we had a brief chat about contemporary music. I can't remember any of the conversation, but he said he'd be in touch. He never was, of course. None of the other Streatham show biz "celebrities" – Benny Lee, Harry Dawson, Shaw Taylor, David Jacobs – ever appeared. It was dull, dull, dull.

And then it all started to happen. I spied an advertisement in the Evening Standard classified column that I read regularly that said, and I'll never forget the magic words, "Boy Wanted. Film Company", and listed a telephone number and application address in the Strand. I phoned up immediately and made an appointment. Stanley Millar understood, and so I fetched up at the Film Producers' Guild in Exchange Court, just off the Strand, being interviewed for a job as a dispatch boy, i.e. a deliverer and collector of films, for the documentary and advertising company called The Film Producers' Guild. I answered all the right questions, and when I was asked would I work for £4. 10 shillings a week, I said "Yes", but my true answer should have been "Not 'alf, matey, I can't wait!" They said they were seeing others, and they'd contact me. Oh well, back to "Matisse"...

But I did get a letter, asking me when could I start? I checked with both Dad and Stanley Millar, and Dad was pleased, although he did realise that, after all of my Dulwich education, I was ending up as just a dispatch boy, but I think Stanley was genuinely sorry to see me go. So it was definitely time to leave "Matisse". Two weeks' notice was the solution, and the Film Producers Guild accepted that (and later on I was told my honesty was applauded, since they seemed to realise I wouldn't leave them in a similar lurch if I received a better offer later, which, only four weeks later, I actually did).

And so two life-changing things happened, almost simultaneously, in 1965, I enrolled in the Streatham and Tooting Evening Classes in Cinematography, and also commenced work in London's West End, just off The Strand, at the Film Producers' Guild as a dispatch boy. It was a start, and if Leonard Starr, Dad's friend, ever came up with anything else, well, I thought that would indeed be a miracle.

I wore a brown suit in my new day job, one that one of Dad's customers had ordered but never collected (nor paid for, either). It fit where it touched, but of the three dispatch boys, I was the only one in a suit. The Film Producers' Guild was largely involved in sponsored documentaries and commercials, but they had a small studio and some projection facilities at Exchange Court, plus cutting rooms, so I was actually in a fine place to learn film craft, despite the constant schlepping. Two rather senior ex-army buddies were in charge of dispatch, and I remember one of them, Frank Smethurst, with affection: he could see how ambitious I was, and he helped me immeasurably by introducing me to the people (all men) in the cutting rooms, some of whom I would meet eventually later on in the studios (notably kindly Len Tremble), and he also introduced me to the senior editor, who also usefully happened to be the Guild's shop steward, a film buff (although they weren't called that then) called Roy Galloway, a genuinely nice chap, who seemed to be the only person there who was actually interested in films, that is to say, the cinema, as opposed to the commercials and "docos" that everybody there seemed to be working on, and he eventually ended up owning and programming the newly independent Curzon Cinema, Eastbourne, which closed in 2020, by which time Roy was well into his eighties.

I can't truly say that I actually enjoyed working at Guild, but I don't have any bad memories of the relatively short time – only four months – that I was in fact working there, largely because, perhaps, of my simultaneous enrolment in the evening cinematography classes at the Streatham and Tooting Institute taught by Ray Selfe, a film practitioner himself (he worked daytime at ATV), a film lover and a man who was to play a deeply significant, most influential, and most profoundly effective part in my future life. However, as I gradually progressed through the film industry itself, I did meet again, and was able to renew friendships with, several of the folk that I met for the very first time at the Film Producers' Guild. Not just Roy Galloway, who I would meet often at the National Film Theatre, but also in the cutting rooms there I ran across Len Tremble, Tony Morris and his brother Jonathan, who became Ken Loach's editor, and also fellow-runner Kevin Albrecht, and his elder brother Andy, who recognised me well over forty years later, when I began lecturing on cinema on cruise ships.

Eventually, Dad's friend Leonard Starr really came up trumps. Turned out that an acquaintance of his, one Robert R. Bucknell, ran a suite of editing rooms at 22, Greek Street in Soho, and permanently employed two young lads to help him run it, i.e. to do the dirty work for him, and one was about to leave. He was looking for a new replacement, but, Leonard added, the pay would be very bad indeed, barely a living wage, if that. Was I interested? Was I?? And so Dad arranged an interview for me at Caledonian Films, 22, Greek Street in the daytime, so that I could go when I was making deliveries for Guild. No-one would notice.

And that's what happened. Robert R. "Bob". Bucknell was a man of many talents, although, it transpired, utterly without any real creative ability himself, although he once produced and directed a British quota cheap film called *More Deadly than the Male* (not to be confused with the Bulldog Drummond thriller *Deadlier than the Male*). He was primarily a thorough Wardour Street hustler, who owned and let out an editing suite of several cutting rooms in a Soho building situated between a negative cutting service downstairs (very useful) and the offices of the famed (and then very new) satirical magazine *Private Eye* on the floor above, where is where, at 22, Greek Street, I would be based. Bob Bucknell actually ran the business side, and two trainees (although perhaps "trainee" was not exactly an accurate definition) did the work. These trainees, "Bob's boys", as I found out we were so termed, were actually glorified runners, although the job involved everything from laying soundtracks, both effects and music, to cleaning out the mutually-shared lavatories on all floors.

The "boy" leaving was Jim Elderton, who had the opportunity to work on the first series of a new television programme called *Doctor Who*, and who later went on to a successful production career in Canada, and the boy staying, alongside whom I was supposed to work, turned out to be a rude and ignorant clod named Colin, whose only connection, or even interest in film, was that he was a relative of someone high up who worked at Kay's Film Laboratories on nearby Soho Square. I had never met such a creature before. We began by his not acknowledging my "'Morning, Colin" greeting on the very first day, and continued similarly throughout my whole time at Caledonian. (I did realise, however, that he would indeed have had to take his breakfast sandwich out of his mouth in order to greet me.) To say he was jealous of what film knowledge I possessed at the time would be an understatement. Nevertheless…

There was a fair bit of work going on at Caledonian when I arrived. Bob was completing the filmed series *The Telegoons*, a puppet version of BBC radio's famous *Goon Show*, directed by feature director (*My Death is a Mockery*) Tony Young, a smartly-dressed man with a throaty voice, which would turn out to be symptomatic of the cancer that ended his life. Also, regularly coming in on virtually a weekly basis were a series of three film Central Office of Information magazine programmes: *British Calendar*, *Commonwealth Review*, and *African Panorama*. These were actually edited at the C.O.I. itself, and sent to Caledonian for track-laying and music-placement. In fact, full delivery.

The Telegoons were just finishing up, and I got to meet one of my heroes, Spike Milligan, who came in to check the final married prints. Bob put me in charge of the sound effects library, and to help Spike select effects from the lists that he provided, but one day I couldn't find a particular required effect from the Caledonian sound library. Spike had written "Footsteps entering gas oven" on his list of requests. Pretty specific, eh? At the time, I didn't know anything about creating sound effects in a studio, and Spike said something like, if you can't find it, we'll record it. And so we did, with me holding a microphone as Spike walked across a manhole cover, and that's how I learned about shooting sound fx "wild", and then cutting them to fit. I bought a copy of Spike's then-new first published book *A Dustbin of Milligan*, and asked him to autograph it for me which he kindly did, dedicating it "To Tony". I kept it and cherish it to this day. What a lovely man! (But I have since learned never to ask autographs of people you are working with. It's just not professional: we're all in it together. But I broke my own rule twice: Laurence Olivier signed his RCA album of speeches from *Hamlet* and *Henry V* to me, when asked, and Sam Peckinpah was pleased to dedicate a poster of his *Pat Garrett and Billy the Kid* for me when I worked on *Cross of Iron*. Can you blame me for asking?).

Days at Caledonian dragged on. We found material for the C.O.I.'s tracks, and sometimes I took the sound effects over to the actual C.O.I. itself, where I met the editor Cliff Boote, who had worked on such classic features as *Journey Together* and *Thunder Rock*, and was now churning out the C.O.I.'s regular propaganda documentaries. I noticed that he seemed to be missing either a thumb or a finger, I can't remember exactly which, and he caught my glance, and told me I was lucky I didn't have to use cement joiners anymore, because with tape joins, the so-called "safety joiners", there was no risk of injury such as his. That old-fashioned foot joiner took his appendage clean off. It was a salutary lesson, and he showed me one of the last foot joiners in existence, in a C.O.I. cutting room, and showed me how it happened. A grim reminder of what I had missed working with, thankfully. Also at the C.O.I. I met the delightful Jenny Holt, director Seth Holt's (*Taste of Fear*, *The Nanny*) former wife, who regaled me with the tales of the cutting rooms at Ealing, where Seth edited, amongst others, *The Lavender Hill Mob* and *The Titfield Thunderbolt*, and associate produced *The Ladykillers*. Jenny and I had much to talk about, and she often came up to Caledonian for coffee with me. Her sister, Joan Holt, by the way, was married to Ealing director Robert Hamer (*Kind Hearts and Coronets*, and editor of Hitchcock's *Jamaica Inn*, amongst others). I felt that I was in the right place at last.

One day at Caledonian, Peter Cook and Dudley Moore, the creators of *Beyond the Fringe*, then a major West End show, descended from their floor above us to tell us that they had to re-record a tune for *Private Eye*'s first-ever giveaway flexi-disc, and it had to be done very quickly since it was to be in that week's issue. Could we help? The problem was interesting. To the tune of the then-fashionable and also brand-new "Hello, Dolly!" the Private Eyesters had recorded new lyrics about a long-running story, itself based on a then-current comic misunderstanding. Apparently, a photograph of the Prime Minister, then Sir Alec Douglas-Home, had been printed in a daily newspaper incorrectly captioned "Baillie Vass". Well, *Private Eye* ran with this gag for quite a while, deliberately mis-captioning the current Prime Minister as Baillie Vass at every possible opportunity. Now Rupert Murdoch had launched a new daily newspaper, appropriately called *The New Daily*, and the *Beyond the Fringe* team had written a new lyric to "Hello, Dolly!" which they called "Hello, Baillie!" to be on the first *Private Eye* complimentary record, released with every copy sold. Only they had made one, rather serious, mistake: they had recorded it to the tune of "Hello, Dolly!" but had neglected to clear, or even suggest to pay for, the use of the copyright. Peter Cook explained the solution to us. Could they re-record the lyrics, which they themselves had written, in verse, this time without music, to avoid having to pay for the music rights? Apparently, their lawyers said that would be permissible. And also could they do it here, and now, at Caledonian, because it has to be delivered with every copy of *Private Eye* this coming Friday, and today is Tuesday? And could we all, me, Bob, Colin, and Tony Young who was finishing *Telegoons*, recite the lyric alongside Peter himself and Dudley Moore?

Bob said "Yes", and only Colin wanted nothing whatsoever to do with it. Fine. And so we did, and now it's a collector's item. If you can find it, you'll hear me, Peter Cook, Dudley Moore, Jonathan Miller, plus Tony Young, reciting – emphatically <u>not</u> singing – the following verse, which begins, as recorded in the Caledonian office by Mr. Bob Bucknell: "Well, Hello, Baillie!, This is 'The New Daily', It's so nice to have you back where you belong..."

I still have a copy of that flexi-disc somewhere. I never recited with such distinguished company again!

In the meantime, whilst at Caledonian, I realised that, if I were to have a serious future in film, I would have to be accepted by the union, the Association of Cinematograph and Television Technicians, in point of fact, an un-admitted "closed shop", virtually denying every applicant admission on submission of a signed form. I visited their headquarters in Soho Square, and got a form, saying that my current employer would sign it. After all, I knew that I couldn't get another job without a union ticket, and couldn't, by the way, get a ticket without a job. But Bob Bucknell refused point blank to sign it, and suggested I just completely forget about it for now. Of course, I hadn't realised then that I would be placing Bob in jeopardy. After all, the hiring of non-union "Bob's boys" and paying us such a low pittance would not have been good, to say the least, for Bob and Caledonian, should the union ever find out.

But life at Caledonian was not so bad for me, except for one thing, which I thought was rather serious, but which taught me resolve, if nothing else. One of our functions at Caledonian was to track-lay the chosen music (invariably chosen by Bob, until I got so familiar with the De Wolfe film music library that he let me do it myself. No, no increase in salary) for the C.O.I. magazine films, and to take the laid tracks along to Cyril Brown at Kay's, Soho Square, for final mixing. Bob showed me how to do it, both track-laying and dubbing charting, and took me with him to my first sound mix. Well and good.

Until I met the mixer Cyril Brown, who let forth with such a fury of anti-Jewish sentiment that I was nearly forced to tears. It wasn't personally directed at me, it was just "out there", impersonal anti-Semitism. I'd never heard such remarks before, uttered so casually, and so unnecessarily. It was only a C.O.I. "doco", after all. (No, of course I can't remember what he said. I've psychologically blocked it out forever.) I mentally made a vow that Colin would attend all of Cyril's mixes in future, and so it came to be. (Bob either didn't notice, or didn't mind. I didn't care.)

I'd come across anti-Semitism before at Dulwich, but in a more subtle manner. When I began at Dulwich, after the blue blazer incident the first day, Dad offered me a lift to school on some days, to make things a little easier and for me to avoid that two-bus route, when he himself had to be in his shop earlier. His car in those days was the Humber Super Snipe, a flash black limousine in anybody's book, and when he gave me a lift, he drove right through the school gates, all the way past the main buildings to the new junior school block where my classroom, 1F, was situated, dropped me in the playground just outside the classroom, and presumably drove back the way he came, right through the school and out into Dulwich itself. This happened with irregularity, but quite often in my first month at Dulwich. Well, one day, at the end of morning assembly, the head of the Junior School, a Mr. Starr (known to us boys by the nickname "Tweaky", for his habit of tweaking the boys' hair sideburns as punishment) called me out to see him at the end of the assembly, which I did. He told me that he'd been told that I was the boy who was delivered to my classroom by a limousine. Could this stop? I replied that since it was my father driving, I didn't know. He asked me to ask Dad to drop me at the school gates in future, if it continues to happen. I didn't ask why, I just acquiesced, thinking that he didn't want our Humber Super Snipe to set a bad example. So that evening, I related this tale to Dad, who said something like perhaps he'd better not take me to school, at all, because it would set a bad example to other boys, sorry. So that's what happened, but over the years at school I began to hear various comments about Jews and their cars, and couldn't but wonder.

Another time, at a gathering of me and my friends at, I think, David Trace's house, I wore, for the first time to show it off, a sweater my mother had newly knitted for me (she was always knitting) to my specifications: it was bright yellow, with "Elvis" on the front and "Bill Haley" embroidered on the back, in black, both on music staves, surrounded by single notes, a pattern found in one of her women's magazines. Yup, a real rock'n'roll sweater, both fashionable and cool. Nobody at the party said anything about it (why should they?) which was perfectly fine by me, until I overheard a comment by Dulwich boarder Mick Golder, to one of my other friends, either Gerry or Tim, I think. Golder, indicating me in my new yellow sweater, observed "Typical flashy Jew". That hurt. Why? Who ever knows "Why"? Where on earth did that come from? From his parents? From boarding at Dulwich College? It was Rodgers and Hammerstein who wrote, in *South Pacific*, that oh-so-wise song about racial prejudice, "You've got to be Carefully Taught…" As you can tell, I never forgot it. And years and years later, when I received a letter from a very despondent, possibly dying, Mick Golder, forty years on, I never replied. There are some things you just don't forget.

Meanwhile, it was Caledonian in the day, and evening classes twice a week: Cinematography in Tooting on Monday evenings, and Film Appreciation classes in Tulse Hill Friday nights, when I could make it, both classes run by Ray Selfe. It was to be a very busy 1965. (And 1965 itself really began with me seeing The Beatles' 1964 Christmas Show live at the Odeon Hammersmith. What a great way to welcome in the New Year!)

Christmas at Caledonian was kind of interesting. There was no real celebration as such, but Bob Bucknell, I'd like to think finally recognising how much (or, more pertinently, how little) he paid his staff of two, gave us an unexpected Christmas bonus, and also a financial gift. Let me deal with the latter first. Colin and I were regularly paid our weekly salary in pay packets by Bob's wife, Jean, usually in £1 notes. This particular Christmas we both opened our packets to find an extra five pounds in one-pound notes. Except I didn't. On counting, I discovered that I had been paid a £6 bonus. I thought (stupidly!) that this couldn't be right, since we were both told we'd get a five quid Christmas bonus, so I told Jean there was one pound more in my pay packet and gave her the £1 back. She was surprised, and called Bob in to tell him of my honesty. Bob duly took back the extra pound. Jean kissed me for so doing, and Colin called me a four letter word beginning with "c" and ending with "t", prefaced by "silly". An extra pound would've gone quite far in those days, so maybe honesty doesn't always pay, and Colin was right: they never would've known if I hadn't told them.

The other Christmas surprise from Caledonian was a present from Jimmy DeWolfe. Now, Caledonian (i.e. Bob, Colin and me) had been using DeWolfe recorded music virtually throughout all of the C.O.I. series episodes sent in to Caledonian for dubbing, with occasional, but rare, dips into the Southern or Francis Day and Hunter catalogues, usually after Bob Bucknell had been wined and dined by their representatives. Jimmy DeWolfe had asked Bob if he could reward Colin and myself with a Christmas gift of records of our own choosing. Not recognising a bribe, I thought it was a very charming gesture, and an opportunity to acquire discs that I wouldn't usually buy, or perhaps couldn't afford. I'd always wanted the only complete film soundtrack on disc that I knew of, which was Laurence Olivier's *Richard III* on three L.P.s, perhaps as a reminder of the first time I went to the cinema twice in one day, *Richard III* at the Odeon, Streatham, Saturday matinee, and then "up West" with Dad to see *The Last Hunt* at the Ritz, Leicester Square, for my birthday treat, May 6th 1956. But I had left it too late, by nearly ten years. There were no copies of the original soundtrack three-disc set of *Richard III* available anywhere, Jimmy De Wolfe, ever smiling, told me, and then asked me what else would I like instead? It didn't take me too long to think: I wanted the two-disc set of the soundtrack of Harold Pinter's *The Caretaker* film starring Donald Pleasence, on the Oriole label. And so, that became my Christmas present from De Wolfe. I could never afford a two-disc set on Caledonian's salary, let alone afford a search for the three-disc *Richard III* soundtrack set. I was very happy, happier still much later on when I went to a recital by Harold Pinter himself in a Dulwich Village pub and, on request, Pinter signed both of my then new "The Caretaker" L.P. sleeves "To Tony".

Not too surprisingly, eventually the C.O.I. became fed up and extremely annoyed, to say the very least, with Bob Bucknell using the same old De Wolfe music over and over again on their three film series (Bob was particularly fond of a piece called, I think, "Brighton Roundabout", or something very similar, and certainly over-used it: it saved him the bother of listening to anything else, or trying to find something new), and they decided to cancel their relationship with Caledonian eventually, but this happened after I had left. Caledonian, though, was to feature in my career, and personal life, pretty strongly much later on, but Bob Bucknell was long gone by then: the Thompson group had taken over Caledonian themselves, and were dismayed by their loss of the C.O.I. contract, and Bob subsequently departed with his wife to Mauritius, I guess for good.

Mummy's health continued to deteriorate, and she was in and out of hospital over this period. Nanna Morris came and stayed to look after Linda primarily, but it was, with hindsight, clear that something was going on that I wasn't being told about. Selfish as ever, I carried on with my very busy life,

Soho by day, and occasionally by night, as I had now discovered the Flamingo club, and saw such terrific visiting American greats as Wilson Pickett, Arthur Alexander, and Lou ("Take a Message to Martha") Johnson, all backed by Georgie Fame and his Blue Flames on Wednesday nights, after work, all invariably supported by either John Mayall's Bluesbreakers (whose guitarist was the young Eric Clapton) or Zoot Money's Big Roll Band. I went alone: this was not "date" material. The only time that I took a girl, which was to see the visiting American act The Soul Sisters, she was bored stiff, thought it all too loud, and we left after the Sisters' first set. No, unsurprisingly, I can't remember her name.

Evening cinematography classes were the highlight of the week. Ray Selfe was extremely amiable, and sure enough knew his movies, and conveyed great affection for them, which, outside of the NFT and the wonderful constant film repertory of the Starlight Club in the Mayfair Hotel, was revelatory to me, although I had struck up a firm friendship with film editor Derek York at Caledonian, and he had regular Sunday screening evenings at his flat (one of which was very exciting for me: he showed Howard Hawks' *I Was a Male War Bride* – U.K. title *You Can't Sleep Here* -- in the presence of its U.K. line producer Ronald Kinnoch, and did we get some great Cary Grant stories!).

In Ray's class were several serious film buffs (although they weren't called that yet) and a few others who not only took films seriously, but actually worked in the film industry itself. I mean the film industry proper: the studios, not merely just in and around Soho. I became friendly with a girl called Christine Lenham, whose brand-new husband David was a real-life clapper loader, working at MGM's British studios (sadly, he died young at 37 in 1980, his credits including *A Clockwork Orange* and *Superman*). I wanted desperately to meet him, and eventually she brought him to classes, when he could make it. Also in the class was a strange, reclusive, oddly silent at first, boffin-style gentleman, a year older than me, called Martyn Green, and my friendship with him would change the course of my life forever.

When I first met Martyn at the Streatham and Tooting Institute in Ray Selfe's class he initially seemed to be withdrawn and unfriendly. Ray Selfe called him "strange", but that would be an understatement. "Intense" might have been a more accurate appreciation. It just seemed to me that Martyn didn't particularly want to be liked, or even friendly. However, we got to chatting regularly about films, and eventually (after about a month or so) he told me that he was currently working at the MGM British Studios, Borehamwood, as a second assistant film editor on a major feature film called *Operation Crossbow*, which starred Sophia Loren, George Peppard, and Trevor Howard, amongst others, and he was assisting veteran film editor Ernest Walter, of *The Inn of the Sixth Happiness* and *The Haunting* fame, among many, many other titles. Well, I never! Unsurprisingly, we got along famously.

There was still the issue of joining the film union, the A.C.T.T. Clearly, Bob Bucknell wouldn't sign anything, so what to do? Well, amongst his other activities, Bob did actually hire out Caledonian's rooms to others. I knew that I had missed some of the great days when I picked up the telephone there and answered it and heard, "This is Carl Foreman, is that Caledonian Films?" Carl Foreman? The producer of *The Guns of Navarone* and the man who actually wrote *High Noon*? Can't be, must be my old Dulwich pal Gerry Powell having me on – he was good with American accents. "Oh, come off it, Gerry," I said, "I know it's you." The voice at the end of the phone was indignant: "I said, is that Caledonian Films? This is Carl Foreman." And it was. I was so embarrassed I didn't know what to say, but fortunately Foreman spoke first. "We were there a while ago with 'The Victors'. Did we leave any cans behind?" Whew – what a pro, no embarrassment whatsoever. "I don't think so. I'll check and call you back." And he left a phone number. When I asked Bob Bucknell he said, bluntly, no, they didn't leave anything here. And then, "But don't you worry about it. I'll call him back." And that's the last I heard of the matter, but at least I got to speak to Carl Foreman just that one time, albeit with decided embarrassment, on the telephone.

But I still wasn't anywhere near to acquiring an A.C.T.T. union ticket, and now I had two possible signatories for my union entry form: Martyn Green and David Lenham, both working on major features at MGM. How could I get the requisite four signatures, plus that of a shop steward? Roy Galloway, the editor at Guild who was also the shop steward there, said that when I left, if I needed his help in any way, to call him, which at the time seemed very kind of him, but I knew that he was gay, and I wasn't keen to contact him. But needs must. So I could, possibly, achieve two signatures, and maybe also a shop steward. (I already well knew that Bob Bucknell wouldn't affix his name to any union form.) But I couldn't lose the chance of both Martyn and David signing, so I went to the A.C.T.T. union offices to get a form. And, maybe, there was a chance of a signature from Derek York, and I asked him the very next time we met up at the NFT, and he kindly replied, "Yes, of course." How to complete the form, that was the question?

Now, I should really recall here what happened just before I secured that job at "Matisse". I had answered a couple of advertisements that I had found in the Evening Standard, the first selling flowers, no less, the second hawking encyclopaedias, both on a door-to-door basis. I started off with the flower selling, but nobody was buying. I only worked Streatham streets locally, of course, and at one of the houses, almost directly opposite my old schoolmate David Trace, the front door was opened by the most lovely girl that I thought I had ever seen. We chatted amiably, but she really didn't want any flowers, and she closed her front door. But I never forgot her. However, I didn't manage to sell any flowers at all, and pretty soon, after about only a week of trying, I gave up. But I never forgot that girl. I mentioned her to David Trace, and he knew immediately who she was. Her name was Andrea Louis, and she did have a sister, but from my description David was able to identify her of the two. I decided to try to see her again, via the same device, but with a different product: encyclopaedias. Not only were the samples much heavier to schlep than flowers, but I was also failing to interest anyone in buying any. And then I pressed Andrea's doorbell. She couldn't have been more friendly, remembered me from my previous call, and invited me in for a cup of tea. All very professional, I had tea with her and then said my goodbyes. I went straight over to David's and told him what had happened. He told me he thought she had a boyfriend, but wished me good luck anyway. Then I got the job with Stanley and Irene at Matisse, and you know the rest, and so I forgot all about Andrea.

That is, until I told David Trace that I was starting evening classes at the Streatham and Tooting Institute in cinematography. "That's where Andrea goes," said David. "You remember Andrea?" Did I? Did I heck!! David said he would speak to her, and see if she'd like me to accompany her to the classes on Monday nights. I said, "Sure," or something similar, so he did. And we met up again, and then, ever afterwards – well, at least for a while, I accompanied the lovely Andrea Louis on our bus ride to Tooting, and picked her up after her classes, and similarly escorted her home, walking her to her front door, and walking away on air. It wasn't exactly a date (I really couldn't afford dates, and maybe she would've said "No", and that would've ended the Monday bus journeys together altogether) but it was a minor source of great pleasure. She did give me some photographs of herself, though. More anon…

I went to the A.C.T.T. and got a form for union entry, and both David Lenham and Martyn Green signed for me, as did Derek York. But where to get an extra signature, not to mention a shop steward? I knew I couldn't ask Bob Bucknell, nor Colin, and possibly neither of them were union members, but I was certain neither would endorse yours truly, for all sorts of varied reasons. But that time at Caledonian I was assisting one Oscar Burn, who had a film career dating back to 1948, when he directed a British "B" called *Castle Sinister*, and, seemingly, had been an editor virtually ever since. So I asked him, but despite his voluminous credits, he had managed to work quite outside of the union, and wasn't even a member, either that or he had let his membership lapse, I can't quite remember, but he certainly couldn't sign a union form for me. What I did learn from him, though, was the editorial slang expression "spike". He asked me to "spike" an audio tape in order to have a sound effect on it transferred for use, and I was too callow and ashamed to ask him what "spike" meant. So I said to him "Do you mean like this?" and promptly tore the tape ahead of the required effect, thus, I thought, placing it at the front of the reel, and therefore easy to locate. "No, you idiot," he said to me, "join it up and I'll show you." Which I did, and he placed two pieces of paper either side of the sound effect that was required, and said, "That's what a 'spike' is." I was constantly learning all the time, but the most important lesson I learned from that exchange was to never, ever use slang, and never abbreviate. Always explain very clearly and precisely what you want from an assistant, and then tell them if they don't understand, don't be afraid to ask. It was an absolutely invaluable cutting room lesson, learned in error.

Meanwhile, back at evening classes, I was gradually learning how to make films, not just merely to watch or criticise them. I was proving popular with Ray, but less so with other class members, or so I thought. For instance, on one particular occasion Ray showed us all a library shot of a lightning flash, and asked us, if we had access to this shot how would we use it in a film, any film? There was a silence, and then yours truly put up his hand. "Yes, Tony?" "You'd put it on the very front, to alert your audience and wake them up," or words to that effect, I said. A silence, then a round of applause from the class. I'd managed to please the teacher and alienate myself from the whole class in one fell swoop!

It became time for us to make a short film, and Ray asked for scripts, and would provide the equipment, and he said that we'd make it extramurally, i.e. out-of-class one day. To my surprise, my script was selected. It was to be a five-minute (or less) filming of a joke: A priest is finishing a burial, looks as though he's forgotten something, turns away, sees a traffic light saying "Cross Now", returns, and crosses himself. The End. I don't know where I got the idea from: all I know is it would be easy to shoot it mute on Streatham Common. And it was. We cast from evening class members. An ex-school friend, Andrew Izod, had access to theatrical props, and came up with a fake tombstone, and we managed to film very quickly on Streatham Common, without permissions, and just managed to finish the shoot before a policeman arrived to scurry us away. It was my very first time as a director, and we edited it on Ray's kitchen table, and since it was shot mute, that didn't take too long to do. I had made a film: it was my very first, but it wouldn't be, as so many amateur films are, my last. What I didn't know, was that it was shot on reverse stock, with no negative, on 16mm. But, nevertheless, I had a film to show. What, of course, I should have done would have been to make an immediate copy, for protection purposes. Maybe Ray should've advised me, maybe he did, I can't remember, but all I had was the one single copy. I couldn't wait to see it projected on a big screen. But how? It only ran about five minutes, if that, and I couldn't afford to hire a theatre, and, although I knew Ray had access to a big screen, I just wanted to look at it first, on my own, privately. I then thought I could kill two birds with one stone. I needed to get Roy Galloway's signature on my union form; he was, after all, the Shop Steward at Guild, and I needed a shop steward's signature. I phoned him, and told him what I had been doing, and he said come over to Guild one lunchtime, and I'll see your short and sign your form. Which I did.

But, in running *Requiescat* (for so the short was pretentiously titled by yours truly) in the Guild theatre, a join broke, and I lost a frame, forever. I was devastated, but Roy explained if you can't shoot on negative, make a copy of everything. I had learned another lesson. And he signed my form as shop steward, so I now had three signatures. I needed one more, and Roy said he'd get it for me. And so, with distinguished Guild editor Max Elliot signing, my A.C.T.T. form was complete. I sent it in.

And it was rejected. On principle. When I queried it, I was told the A.C.T.T. was not admitting new members at the moment. Try again. I could've cried. Still, now I'd made a short film. I was still working at Caledonian, and I was walking Andrea Louis to and from the bus stop. It would've been enough.

But Mummy was now very ill, and home from hospital on, what nobody told me, was merely a respite. Daddy took her on a holiday to Majorca, and it was to be their very last holiday together. Dad himself was going through a difficult financial period, but of course, selfish and self-absorbed as ever, I never really knew anything about it at the time. He'd gone into a tailoring partnership with one Cyril Coulson, a friend, known professionally as Peter Coulson, and had sold his shop at 62, Streatham Hill to a firm set up by both of them, but it didn't work out, and Dad was on his own again, in the same premises. A new tailor, G.S. Evangeli, had opened in Streatham High Road, near to the Odeon, and Evangeli had asked Dad to come in and manage it for him. Dad was now working as a salaried worker, which he hadn't been since his Savile Row days, long before I was born. That didn't work out either, but it paid his expenses. But it really didn't suit him, not at all. He managed to get back the 62, Streatham Hill shop, and began to recommence where he had left off. All this, and Mummy very, very ill. At least my sister Linda was being looked after by Nanna and Auntie Doris, neither of whom knew how ill my Mummy really was. And me… Well, I, in retrospect, behaved like a selfish shit. All I wanted was to get into the A.C.T.T. in case I got a better job offer, and could happily leave Caledonian. How selfish and unthinking can you get? But, of course, no-one had told me Mummy was actually dying, and she did indeed seem much better after the last spell in hospital and the holiday.

And then, suddenly, at evening classes, Martyn Green told me of a feature in the MGM cutting rooms next to his, called *Passport to Oblivion*, on which they were having trouble with their second assistant editor, and there may well be a job vacancy coming up. Had I put my form in? I had, but I couldn't bring myself to tell him that I'd been rejected. What to do?

Meanwhile, at Caledonian, a new British film had taken over a cutting room suite. It was called *He Who Rides a Tiger*, and the editor was one of the greatest of living British editors, the venerable Jack Harris who was then in his late '60s, whose 59 credits included five films for David Lean (most notably, *Brief Encounter*) and three of my own personal favourite swashbucklers, all of which I saw as a youngster on their first release: *Captain Horatio Hornblower, R.N.* (Gregory Peck), *The Crimson Pirate* (Burt Lancaster) and *The Master of Ballantrae* (Errol Flynn). What tales he must have to tell, if I can manage to get them out of him, but, mainly, there was no more distinguished editing name in the country. If I could only get <u>him</u> to sign my next union submission... How to do it? And who else to get to sign alongside him?? And when?

Working at Caledonian with *He Who Rides a Tiger* in the cutting rooms proved to be a delight. Before *Tiger* arrived, everything seemed fraught with panic, largely, I now know, because "panic" was Bob Bucknell's stock-in-trade; he either left everything to the last minute, or bumbled through because he wasn't quite sure how to reach a result. This last, on occasion, proved very fortunate for me. Bob let me do the "cutdowns". I think to Bob it was a relegation, but to me it was a major break. Ambassador Films, a production and distribution company long in Wardour Street, run by brothers Alfred and Gilbert Church, had amassed over about fifty years a prolific library of film, both their own productions, which included Flanagan and Allen features, and various other films that they released, including several series of hour-long "B" westerns. Many of the films they had produced themselves, such as the Tod Slaughter melodramas, or the children's films made at Bushey Studios, had dated badly, but they found that they could still make a decent living by cutting down their varied product for screenings at Saturday morning children's picture shows. And Bob Bucknell convinced them that he had the guy to do it: me!

And so I honed my craft. Bob told me to "get three twenty-minuters" out of such varied product as the Range Busters series of westerns, and the Flanagan and Allen pictures. It wasn't always quite possible, but I certainly managed to create at least two twenty-minute viewable shorts out of all of them. Sacrilege, I knew, but it paid. And I got to know the Churches, who let Ray Selfe and I borrow titles from their vaults, and screen them in Ray's upstairs house cinema. Proper films, like the rare *LeGong*, a colour feature travelogue produced by Gloria Swanson's third husband, Henri, the Marquis de la Coudraye, a rare treat indeed, and another film that I remember we simply couldn't identify, its titles being missing. What to do? I suggested the only person who could identify it would be film historian Kevin Brownlow, who I didn't yet know personally, and Kevin duly came along to West Norwood to view the Ambassador print of what he rightly identified as the 1915 epic *The Juggernaut*, long thought lost at the time. It was Kevin Brownlow who pointed out to me that I may well have been a distant relative of the versatile Hollywood feature director Edward Sloman, who was raised in London's East End, and who Kevin interviewed for his book *The Parade's Gone By*, and who once had a distinguished film career, including such titles as *His Woman* with Gary Cooper and Claudette Colbert, and the Jewish epic *His People*, plus the 1930 Harry Richman musical with a very early Technicolor sequence *Putttin' on the Ritz*, among almost a hundred others, mostly now all lost. In fact, Kevin was convinced of it, although I couldn't be sure, but there did seem to be a slight facial similarity to my own Father, at least. Nevertheless, Kevin and I have been friends and professional associates ever since. Well, almost. He did ask me to appear, when I was bearded, as an extra in *Winstanley*, which he directed. Dressed in canvas rags, I was hit on the head (hard) by another extra. Kevin's only directorial introduction to me, well before shooting, was "Don't shave that beard." The hit hurt, the shot was in the can, I went home. Eventually, an envelope arrived with some frames of the shot. I had been edited out of *Winstanley* completely, but Kevin, ever the gentleman, posted the cut frames to me as a reminder and a "Thank you". I did take off my beard, but grew it again sporadically.

I carried on at Caledonian doing several feature cut-downs while *He Who Rides a Tiger* was being edited by Jack Harris, and whenever I could, I spoke to him, only slightly off-put by his seemingly constant nose-drip, which his delightful first assistant, Lois Gray, said you didn't notice after a while. Oh, really?

The second assistant on *He Who Rides a Tiger* was one Nick Napier-Bell, and he was busy synchronizing the daily rushes, something I'd not yet done, but would be essential to learn if I were to start in features as a second assistant editor, which was my goal. Nick, however, was engaged in many other activities whilst on *Tiger*. He was trying to set up cutting room suites of his own, for rental purposes, and he was also involving himself in supplying 35mm. spacing (for building up feature dubbing tracks) to the studios around town. In other words, to put it mildly, he didn't intend to be a second assistant editor forever. (And neither was he.) So he asked me if I wouldn't mind, as he put it, of doing "a bit of syncing up" for him occasionally. This was a break for me, if Nick did but know it, and he showed me how to "sync" the daily rushes, the sine qua non of the second assistant editor's workload. I watched him show me how you find the frame on which the clapper board closes, and match it to the sound "clack" on the recorded magnetic track. And so I learned what a clapper-board is <u>really</u> for, not merely a symbol of the start of a take, but what activates perfect picture and sound synchronisation, the virtual religion of film editing itself. Of course, I wasn't being paid to do this, but Bob Bucknell wasn't around, so it didn't matter, as long as I pleased Ambassador Films while Colin looked after the C.O.I., it really didn't matter. I can never thank Nick Napier-Bell enough, although I suspect he has forgotten all about those early days, before he created his own empire of film.

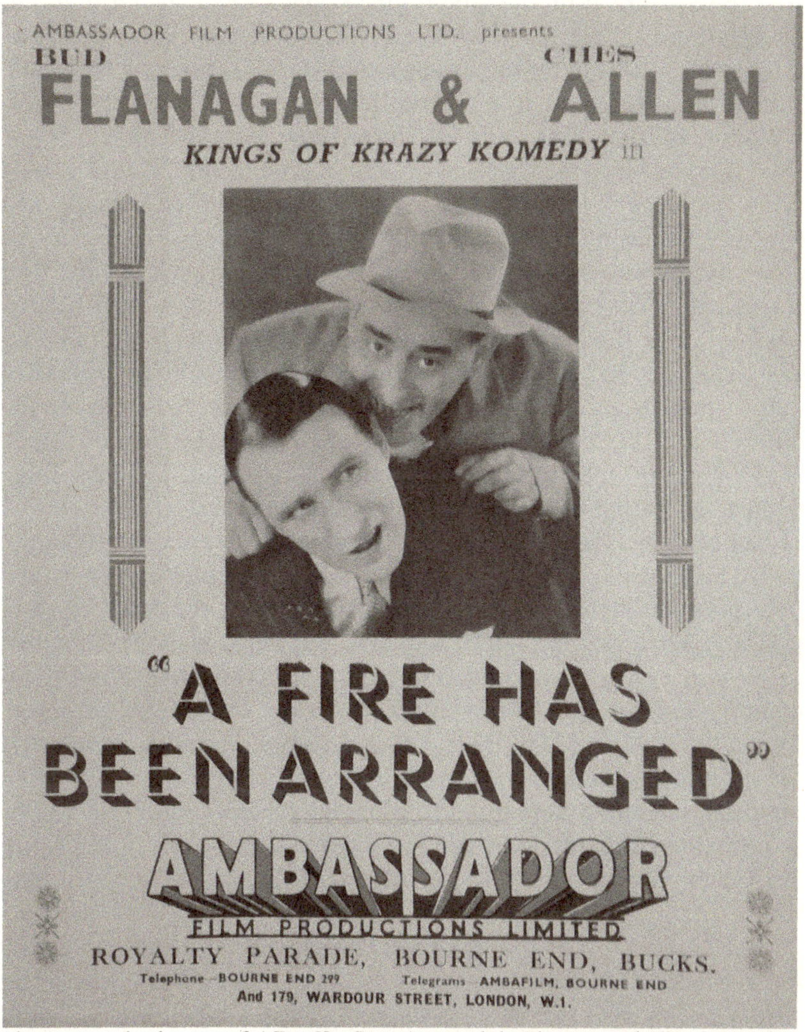

The vintage press-book cover of *A Fire Has Been Arranged*, the Flanagan and Allen feature that I turned into two Saturday Morning Pictures twenty-minute shorts for Ambassador Films, to my aesthetic shame, at Caledonian Films' request.

So now I knew how to synchronise rushes, and also how to edit film. I was now acquiring the technical skill and knowledge that I wasn't actually learning from Ray Selfe's cinematography classes, enjoyable though they were. What to do? What next? I couldn't stay exploited at bloody Caledonian forever, and it seemed that I couldn't get accepted by the union, even if I could get a job on a feature. And then, it all suddenly seemed to coalesce. At evening classes, Martyn Green, still on the epic *Operation Crossbow*, told me that *Passport to Oblivion* were likely to get rid of their useless second assistant editor. He'd only heard it on the studio grapevine, there was nothing definite, but he thought he'd let me know in case I was interested. Was I interested?!? But how to do it? It would mean getting into the A.C.T.T. union first, and then giving notice at Caledonian if I got the job, or would it be the other way around? What to do first, how to do it? The answer: wait and see…

So I said to Martyn, what do you think I should do? Could you get me an interview with the *Passport to Oblivion* cutting room people, or, at least, find out what's going on, because if they fire their second assistant, they'll have to give her two weeks' notice, surely? Martyn said he'd try and find out. I had to think hard and be able to move quickly, if necessary. It just didn't seem possible. Bob Bucknell, who I couldn't wait to put in my past, despite all he had done for me (and despite all the exploitation involved) would be furious, and what if I get turned down by the union again? If I got the job and wasn't in the A.C.T.T., I couldn't accept it, and I could be out of Caledonian for good, jobless and unemployed. Still, first things first, let's get this third union application form into the A.C.T.T. in Soho Square.

I had to move fast, because *He Who Rides a Tiger* were making ready to move out, and I needed those signatures. Surely no-one would turn down a person who had the great film editor Jack Harris as a sponsor, let alone his director, *The Lavender Hill Mob* and *The Titfield Thunderbolt*'s director Charles Crichton, himself a former film editor (for Alexander Korda, no less, titles including *Sanders of the River* and *The Thief of Bagdad*). I set out to woo Charles Crichton. I went to the British Film Institute and bought from them a still of Alec Guinness and Stanley Holloway in *The Lavender Hill Mob*, and asked Charlie Crichton to autograph it to me personally, which he kindly did. After he autographed the photo, I proffered a newly supplied union form, and asked Mr. Crichton if he would kindly sign that for me as well. He laughed, and did so.

Well, Charles Crichton and Jack Harris, no less, endorsing little ol' me. Now, I needed two more worthy signatures. Derek York was in one of Caledonian's cutting rooms making changes to *Séance on a Wet Afternoon*, on which he was the editor, and he kindly signed the form as well. Three ace editors. Could I get another one? Jack Harris suggested his own first assistant, Lois Gray, and she duly signed when he asked her. Now, I needed a Shop Steward. I could go back to Roy Galloway at Guild, I thought, perhaps, but his name didn't seem to help matters the last time. I needed to think.

In the meantime, one night at evening classes Martyn Green told me that *Passport to Oblivion* at MGM were starting to look around for a new second assistant, and were going to give their allegedly useless second her two weeks' notice. Would I be interested? If so, perhaps I had better phone the first assistant on the film, Geoff Brown, and say that I'd heard from Martyn that they might be looking for a replacement. And that I did. Geoff Brown and I made a date for an interview, as early in the morning as possible so as not to interfere with the day's workload. Knowing Bob Bucknell was away on one of his funny shoots, I fully intended to get back to Caledonian as soon as possible. Martyn started work at the normal studio start time of 8.30 a.m., which meant I would meet him at the pick-up point as early as seven o'clock in the morning. This particular time, ludicrously early for me, fazed Martyn Green not a jot. I met Martyn at a pre-arranged spot in South London, and I was really surprised at the distance we travelled before we reached Elstree. Martyn set me at my ease by saying, should I get the job, he would give me a lift there and back if possible, but since it was an 8.30 start I'd better get used to getting up really early. He couldn't guarantee lifts back because they were doing a lot of overtime – "double bubble" as he called it, in film industry slanguage.

We reached Elstree, and drove through Borehamwood High Street, at the end of which I saw many cars and vehicles parked in which looked like a factory, and as we got nearer I could see the clock tower with MGM emblazoned on it, and thought I could just about make out Ivanhoe's castle in the distance, which is what it turned out to be. At first, I had never, ever seen so many cars in one place before, ever, and I asked Martyn what was that, was it a car factory next to the studio? And I'll never forget his answer. "No, that's the studio."

I'd really, truly, never seen anything like it. I'd never seen so many cars. I didn't drive, never wanted to, took a failed driving test once before on which my instructor said to me, "Mr. Sloman, I just want one thing: for you to bring this car back to me in one piece." There's confidence for you! Martyn parked, and checked in, and showed me to the *Passport to Oblivion* cutting rooms, and there he introduced me to Geoff Brown. The meeting, I thought went exceptionally well. I was also greeted, surprisingly, by Lois Gray, who had just recently left *He Who Rides a Tiger*, and had just started working on *Mister Moses*, assisting editor Peter Weatherley: two of the foulest, yet funniest, mouths in filmdom had found each other! It was good that Lois had greeted me – I could see that Geoff Brown was impressed that I knew other cutting room feature people. Shooting on *Passport to Oblivion* had about a month of filming left, and Geoff told me that the title had now been changed. After MGM's success with *Where the Boys Are*, *Passport to Oblivion*, a James Bond-type spy pastiche, would now be re-titled *Where the Spies Are*, and could I start a fortnight from now? I then met the film editor, Bill Lenny, and looked around the cutting rooms a while, and then left, feeling myself in the way, which I guess I was.

Outside the *Spies* cutting room, I found Martyn and thanked him, and he was pleased, and he said it was good that Lois Gray said "Hello" to me: she was very, very popular. I then made my independent very laborious way back to Soho via bus, train and underground. The journey took nearly two hours. Getting the job was one thing, but four hours travelling per day was quite another, but anyway, what to do about the union? It wasn't, of course, ever mentioned, just naturally assumed that I was an A.C.T.T. member. What to do about getting into the union? I couldn't work in a studio without being a fully paid-up member of the film union, the A.C.T.T. itself.

I decided to confront the union head on. I had four very, very decent names on my form: it would've been hard to find better names for an editing submission; all I needed was a willing shop steward. I took my newly-signed form right round to the A.C.T.T. first thing Monday morning. I needed advice. I didn't really want to go back to Roy Galloway, the shop steward at Guild who had endorsed me previously, but I would if I had to. At the Soho Square headquarters, I asked if I could speak to anyone involved with membership about my form, and the desk secretary made a call, and Steve Cox, the editor of those animation films made by Richard Williams and George Duning, came down to see me. He introduced himself, and asked what the problem was. I told him, and he was surprised that I had such distinguished sponsors as both Jack Harris and Charles Crichton. I said, I still need a shop steward, and fast, and explained why. He said, "Give me the form," and I did so. He then took out his own union card, inserted his number on my form, and then signed it. "I'm the animation shop steward," he told me, and "I'll make sure this goes in right away. We're sitting this week, that's why I'm here. You won't have any trouble with those signatures, including mine. I'll make sure of it." I couldn't breathe for joy. I asked him if he'd be in touch with me, and he replied, and I could barely believe it, "You'll have your union card in the post, most likely this week." And that's what happened.

The day that I received my new union card, I asked Bob Bucknell to accept my immediate notice. He wasn't too surprised. "They all leave sooner or later," he said. He wasn't the least bit interested in where I was going. "Just make sure you clean up properly before you go." Well, thank goodness that's over. Fat Colin just grunted, and said nothing, seemingly disinterested. To be fair to Bob Bucknell, he did wish me well when I told him I was going to MGM, and he actually said, "Keep in touch." Suddenly, now I'm leaving, he's behaving like a human being.

At evening classes that Monday evening I told Martyn Green, and thanked him profusely. Hard to tell if he was pleased, or if he sensed another rival in those sacred (to me) MGM cutting rooms. Anyway, he said he would continue to give me lifts to Borehamwood, but that he would soon becoming under notice because *Operation Crossbow* was wrapping up. I'd soon be on my own in one of the world's major film production studios, and, truthfully, I couldn't wait to start.

That two-week wait felt like an eternity. What if my card didn't arrive? There was no going back to Caledonian: I'd be out of work with no job and no union card. I told my parents, and both Dad and Mummy were delighted, pleased and proud for me. They both realised, perhaps more than I did at the time, that working on *Where the Spies Are* would not only be a major first feature credit for me, but would also introduce me to the seemingly glamorous world of freelance film production, and, more importantly, the concomitantly high salary that I was now able to command. Steve Cox was as good as his word. The union card did arrive, properly signed by President of the A.C.T.T. George Elvin, and I had a Union Member's number. I could barely believe it: I could now work anywhere in the world on any feature film at all. Hallelujah!

Back at evening classes, I thanked Martyn Green again, and asked him what he was going to do after finishing up on *Operation Crossbow*. He said he was going to see the world, and that's exactly what he did. After giving me a morning lift to MGM in my first week of work, which was also his second week of notice, he took off for Hong Kong where, I understand, he became a newsreel cameraman. I never saw him again.

MGM. Metro-Goldwyn-Mayer. Arguably the most famous name in cinema and motion pictures in the world. And I – Anthony Barney Sloman, the Yiddisher kid from Forest Gate – had made it, and was going through those famed studio front gates to work on a motion picture that was actually an MGM production, and would begin with that oh-so-famous leonine roar from Leo the Lion himself. I could barely believe it, but I also knew I was there to work. Any of that stupid star-struck movie kid nonsense must go out the window, now and fast.

Well, that bloody journey from Streatham to Borehamwood knocked all the glamour out of it, that's for sure, but the increase in income greatly compensated, as did the pleasure of meeting contemporaries, and future friends, who shared my interests. I became good pals with the other second assistant editors – my contemporaries – in the studio: the serious-minded Peter Watson, who was working on John Ford's *Young Cassidy* (taken over by director Jack Cardiff because of Ford's illness), and also Chris Kelly, son of Tom Kelly, the cameraman who had died as a result of a tragic accident while filming *Duel in the Jungle*, and no less than Ava Gardner's ward as a result, who was finishing up on *The Yellow Rolls-Royce*. Film lovers both, and friends for life, although we don't see each other that often these days, at least nowhere near as often as when we used to meet in the film numbering room at MGM, or in the canteen at lunchtimes.

MGM was thriving then, and I got to visit all of the departments on a professional level, and met many great technicians on a workaday basis. Head of the editing department was Frank Clarke, who was just finishing up on *The Yellow Rolls-Royce*. He was famous for editing the classic war documentaries *The True Glory* and *Burma Victory*, but for me he was more important as MGM's chief editor, for *Beau Brummell* and *Bhowani Junction*, both starring Stewart Granger, and for *Ivanhoe* and *Knights of the Round Table*, both of those starring my other film hero Robert Taylor. You can imagine the conversations I had with him: he had some particularly pertinent things to say about director John Ford on *Mogambo*, that I can't possibly repeat here, but I'm sure he repeated them all when he taught at the London Film School, after he left MGM.

The editor I was assisting was Bill Lenny, and I learned much from him. When he discovered that I had a certain amount of film knowledge, and was attending cinematography evening classes (I never knew when to keep quiet!) he used to send me up rotten, nicknaming me "Eisenstein" and making jokes that I didn't think were funny about my approval, or not, of his own editing. (But he really was a very funny man, deliberately so.) I learned a lot from Bill, and I'll never, ever forget how he taught me how to determine the length of a shot in the edit:--

There was a sequence in *Where the Spies Are* wherein star David Niven is looking out of an aeroplane at a village that has been set alight by the villains. Bill invited me to his side to watch him edit the three shots on the moviola: Niven in his aeroplane, looking out of the window, then the process shot of the burning village which was Niven's point-of-view, and then back to Niven again. "O.K., Eisenstein, how would you cut that together?" said Bill. Well, I thought I knew film, and had read all the books on editing that were available, not to mention books on film theory itself, so I started in: "Well, I think you hold on David, then do a count-down from the point-of-view..." Bill cut me off. "Watch me," he said. He ran the first shot of David looking, then the second shot of the village burning, and kept his foot over the moviola brake. "Cor, Ethel, look at that burning village!" Bill said to no-one in particular, and slammed on the brake. I took a sharp intake of breath at the revelation. "Yup, Eisenstein," said Bill, "that's how you do it. Don't count frames, don't measure lengths. Put yourself in the position of both the characters and the audience. That's all there is to it." Facile, maybe. But true. And no film school in the world could have ever taught me so well. No wonder Bill Lenny was director Val Guest's favourite editor. I learned so much about feature film-making on *Where the Spies Are*. It was the best film school in the world.

Bill Lenny's dubbing editor was James Shields, and Jimmy and I got on famously. He immediately identified me as ex-public school, and asked where I was at. On telling him Dulwich College, he revealed that he was an Old Pauline, that is to say, ex-St Paul's, and he said we always smashed you lot at rugger. And so we bonded. (Jim would later be better known for *Alien* and *Chariots of Fire* and many, many others, but he was not to be confused with the American sound mixer James Shields, of *The Hustler* and *On the Waterfront*. So ignore IMDB's listed credits for him). Jimmy's sound assistant was a nice guy called Peter Connor, and it was to him that I owed my next job.

Meanwhile, *Where the Spies Are* was still shooting, and, as second assistant editor, my key jobs were to synchronise the daily rushes, and attend the evening screening rushes selection by the director and editor at the end of the shooting day, a major first for me. My job was simply to tick the selected takes in the rushes notebook as the material was viewed on the big screen in the rushes theatre itself, and then, after numbering, break them out in script order for the editor to assemble them the next day in the cutting copy. Very straightforward, especially with a director like Val Guest, who knows exactly what he wants to use on sight. No messing around over choices here. Except for one particular evening, when I was horrified by the behaviour of our star, David Niven, whose screen image, as I'm sure you are aware, is nothing but pure charm.

After a run of interior shots with co-star Françoise Dorleac, Niven stood up from his chair in the theatre and said, "Stop the bloody rushes." To me, since I was responsible for talking to the projectionists via the intercom. I looked straight at Bill Lenny, who nodded affirmatively at me. I told the projectionist to hold it. They did, and froze on a frame. David stood up, and addressed Val Guest, the director, who was sitting on the other side of Bill. "Look at me," said Niven, "I look like a fucking turkey. Look at those wattles." Val Guest didn't blink. He turned to art director John Howell, seated below him, and said, "John, is the set still standing?" John replied, "No, Val. They're dismantling it now, as per schedule." Guest replied, "Have them stop, John, put it back the way it was. We'll reshoot tomorrow." Then, turning to face the abashed Niven: "Is that all right with you, David?" The newly-chastened Niven just nodded his head firmly up and down. Guest turned to me: "Restart the rushes, would you please, Tony?" And I did, giving the projectionists the O.K. to carry on.

I did again, however, have another rare opportunity to watch Mr. Niven in action in close-up. There was to be a scheduled screening of the assembled edit of *Where the Spies Are* in a London preview theatre for the U.K. MGM executives, and Bill Lenny asked me to make sure the cutting copy gets to the right theatre well in time. And, as what I thought was a gag, he said, "David Niven is coming with you. Make sure he also gets there in time, too." But it wasn't a gag. The screening was to be at the Anglo Preview Theatre, at the Brewer Street end of Wardour Street. A car had been booked, by the production office. At the appointed time, I packed the film cans into the boot of the booked limousine, and waited, with the driver, for David N. He turned up after a short while, suggested I sit in the front seat with the car's driver, and we set off. We arrived in London, and headed down Oxford Street to turn left into Wardour Street, when David said, "Stop the car right there," pointing to the junction of Oxford and Wardour, "I'll walk from here." I pointed out to him that the preview theatre was just down there on the right, and he said, "I know. I'll walk it. You can walk with me, and he (indicating the driver) can take the cans in before we arrive." A dilemma for me. Do I let our star walk unaccompanied down Wardour Street? – we may never see him again. Or do I deliver the cans myself? The driver then offered to unload the cans himself at Anglo, so I walk down Wardour Street with our star, wondering why Niven wants to do this. And then I found out. He has fans everywhere, and people, mainly women, crowded around him for his autograph. He was in his element. He schmoozed, and smiled, and signed, and, yup, we were twenty minutes late for the start of the screening. Bad manners on Niven's part, but I learned that Val Guest really knew how to treat a star.

So I wasn't exactly at home much, what with evening screenings and overtime, but, on the rare occasions that I was, I noticed how much Mummy's condition had seemed to deteriorate, since her last stay in hospital. She also seemed not to get her words right, and she used to be ever so chatty. Talking about Val Guest, she inadvertently called him Val Gielgud (John's brother, a BBC producer). That wasn't like her at all. Another hospital stay beckoned. On the weekend before she went in, Daddy told me the seriousness of her condition. "They might let her out for Christmas," he said, "but it could well be her last." I don't think the weight of what he said really sunk in at first to my self-obsessed mind, or maybe I just psychologically blocked out those very facts that he was conveying to me. After all, it was only August, and the sun was shining. I had to tell someone, to share my grief, -- I didn't really know what to do. I didn't really feel like crying yet, but I needed a sympathetic shoulder. Aha! Andrea…

The previous weekend Ray Selfe had been setting up a shoot for a film satire of his called *The Colossal Pinavision*, parodying the then-fashionable epic *Cleopatra*, with a Sunday shoot in the middle of Soho Square, with the 20th Century-Fox building behind his cast, who would be aping the famous poster currently boldly displayed in the Fox window, with a reclining Elizabeth Taylor flanked by Richard Burton and Rex Harrison. Ray had found a Harrison lookalike, but asked me at evening classes if I could find him a "Taylor" and a "Burton". Of course, I said, and phoned Andrea Louis and Gerry Powell, thinking my two friends would be ideal casting. They both agreed, and we all convened afterwards. When the shoot was over, I guess unsurprisingly if I'd given it a second thought, Gerry and Andrea went off together. And then it became Gerry who was accompanying Andrea to the evening class, no longer me.

I phoned Andrea afterwards and asked if I could come over. (I thought I might need a female shoulder to cry on.) It was a bright, sunshiny afternoon and Andrea opened the door to me in her bikini. I had never seen anything so wonderful in my life, I thought at the time. She said that they were having a splash-around in the pool in their garden, but that we could talk in the living room. Oh, that bikini! I was utterly mesmerised by a little trail of black hair that began just below her navel and vanished into that very low-cut bikini bottom. I wasn't sure if this was the moment…

We went into her sitting room, and we talked. She asked me what did I want to say, and I told her that I had no-one else to talk to about Mummy's condition. She said that I could always talk to her, and so I did. She clearly didn't know what to say, or how to take it. After all, we weren't exactly <u>that</u> close. But she kissed me sympathetically, and asked would I like to stay and play with her in the garden (Wouldn't I just??), but I declined. And that was the last time I saw her alone. The next time I saw her was on the bus to evening classes with, yup, Gerry Powell.

(But what I never knew until very recently when preparing this actual book that you are now reading, following a Zoom conversation just prior to publication, was that someone else I knew well had also subsequently regularly gone out with the lovely Andrea, and that somebody was none other than my school buddy Nick Nacht, no less, and guess where those two first met? Yup, on that *Colossal Pinavision* shoot that previous Sunday in Soho

Square, where Andrea was Cleopatra, and on which Nick very kindly assisted, unpaid, both Ray Selfe and myself, to get experience of shooting film! Nick only told me about it some fifty years later when I when I informed him that I was writing this very memoir!)

When Mummy went into hospital, Linda went to stay at Forest Gate for a while, and Nanna Morris kindly looked after me, and then Linda came back. I was still working late on *Spies*, but just before Christmas, Mummy was let out of hospital for the festivities. It would be her last Christmas at home, and I think we all knew that, but, selfish as ever I guess, I couldn't seem really able to take it in. Mummy wanted to prepare a proper Christmas, so on Christmas Eve to get us out of her hair she let me take Linda "up West" to see *How the West Was Won*, newly opened at the Casino Cinerama theatre. Of course, with today's hindsight, I probably should have stayed at home to help with the preparations.

The following day, Christmas Day itself, Ray and Jean Selfe had invited me over to their house for a private screening with some friends of theirs for a double-bill of *The Wages of Fear* and what was then called (forgive me) *Ten Little Niggers*, later re-titled, for obvious reasons, *...And Then There Were None*, an Agatha Christie classic. Ray Selfe's copy bore the original title on the screen, and was therefore incredibly rare. I told Dad that I had been invited out Christmas night, and he said that he'd rather I stayed at home. What he didn't -- couldn't -- bring himself to say was that this would almost certainly be Mummy's last ever Christmas, a fact that only he knew for sure. Although I had been duly informed, I had psychologically blocked it out, or, rather, just couldn't truly take in that very harsh real fact indeed. As far as I also knew, my sister Linda had also not yet been so informed either, and was considered too young to guess.

To this very day I regret going to that screening. Why did I go? Well, to see two films hard to see, and in perfect screening circumstances, I guess. Pathetic, now. But to leave Mummy on what might be (and indeed turned out to be) her last Christmas... Dad said again, "Don't go." But I went, and I've lived with that shame and sadness all my life, a shame and a sadness that I never truly experienced at the time, locked as my mind was in a state of disbelief. After Christmas, Mummy went back into the Lambeth hospital, and I returned to *Where the Spies Are*.

Mummy phoned me once, at the studio, and I took the call. Geoff Brown said to transfer it to the next door cutting room, Jimmy Shields' room, so as not to disturb Bill Lenny at work. I took the call there, and Jimmy, professional as ever, stopped his moviola when he realised how serious was that particular telephone call. Mummy told me on the phone, in a voice feeble and weak, that "I'm going down the pan, Tony, I'm going home." I thought she meant that she was getting better, but it wasn't until afterwards that I realised she was trying to tell me that she was actually going to die. We chatted for a bit longer, but I really couldn't make out what she was saying and I truly don't remember anything else of what was to be our last telephone conversation. I hid behind a curtain for a moment briefly to dry my eyes, and then thanked Jimmy for letting me take the call.

Gradually, and slowly, Mummy became weaker. Linda went to live with Auntie Doris at Forest Gate, and eventually stayed there, and went to cousin Della's school with her, but Nanna stayed with us for a while in Streatham. Before Mummy went into hospital that last time I came home one evening to find Daddy playing to her a strange tape of himself talking. I only heard a part of it, but it sounded like a confession. It sounded as though Dad had done something very, very wrong, involving money, and that he was apologising to Mummy. Clearly I wasn't meant to hear any of this, but it certainly seemed very weird to me. I couldn't ask either of them what was going on, but Mummy seemed quite distressed. Dad was just Dad.

With Linda now looked after, Nanna went home, just leaving me alone with Dad who, to my utter horror, was "seeing" a friend, a blowsy lady called Blanche Holland, who, to me, looked like a badly made-up extra from a "B" movie. This can't be happening, I thought, but it was, it was. One night Dad told me he was expecting a ship-to-shore call from Blanche, as she was on a cruise with her husband, and could I not touch the phone if it rang. Well, the phone did ring, when I was in bed, and I got up and deliberately answered it before Dad could get to it. The voice on the phone said would I take a ship-to-shore call, and I was about to say "No" when my Father grabbed the phone out of my hand. His look told me exactly where I stood in this matter. I went back to bed, ashamed for him, hating him for what he was doing, and when he was doing it.

Clearly everything in the world was about to go wrong, and it did, it did. We got a call from the hospital on a Friday night, saying that perhaps Dad should come instantly. He went to the Lambeth Hospital, and then I got a phone call from him saying come as soon as possible. When I arrived at Mummy's bedside, two neighbours, Peggy and Charles, appeared at the same time, but Daddy and a nurse suggested that they leave, and just Dad and I were left.

Mummy wasn't moving. She, I think, was trying to speak, but couldn't. The nurse suggested that Dad and I go to the hospital café, and then come back. Which we did. That, evening, Mummy started losing breath, and Dad and I had nothing to say. Then, near midnight, she breathed her last, her eyes still open. I remembered a Roman tradition of putting coins on a dead person's eyes –why ever would I suddenly remember that? – and then her eyes closed. I gently touched her eyelids. They opened and shut again very quickly. And then she was gone.

We left her there in the hospital bed, and then we could do, or say, nothing. We went to Dad's car, and, as I sat down, I began a crying jag – I cried and cried and cried, and Dad said something like, "There, there, let it all hang out." And then we drove home. When we arrived at the front door of our block, and went up the stairs, to my absolute horror, Dad, who I then realised had been secretly drinking, and was now more than slightly the worse for drink, (I, thoughtless as ever, felt that this was both gross and irresponsible, with not a thought as to how he himself might feel) began to sing, I guess ironically, from *Oklahoma!*, "Oh, what a beautiful morning, oh, what a beautiful day…" Horrified is too mild a word to convey my feelings. We went indoors. We didn't want to wake Nanna – that would wait until the morning. It was half past midnight, on the very eve of St. Valentine's Day.

Funeral arrangements were made quickly. I phoned Geoff Brown at the studio and told him what had happened, and he sent his condolences and said that he would tell Bill Lenny, and not to worry. The funeral was at the Orthodox Jewish cemetery at Waltham Abbey, ironically not too far away from where I was born, and the Streatham synagogue made all the arrangements. I can't exactly remember what happened next, but when we returned to our flat the shiva (mourning) chairs were in place in a semi-circle, and someone from our synagogue was there to traditionally make the cut in our mourning clothes. A whole week of mourning was customary for orthodox Jews, and Dad and I duly sat in the chairs provided, the ones with the sawn-off legs, arranged in a circular shape in our living room. Auntie Doris and Uncle Don soon arrived with Linda, and we cried and cried together. Linda stayed overnight, and, on the 17th, had her birthday. I gave her, sorrowfully, her present that I had bought earlier, Manfred Mann's first album, and it was agreed that she would return with Auntie Doris after the week of shiva was over, and would live henceforth with them in Forest Gate. Don and Doris wanted me to contribute to her upkeep, which I did, sending them, as they requested, a weekly cheque for £3, which was a lot in 1965.

To my surprise, to put it mildly, Dad's "secret woman" Blanche turned up one evening at the shiva with her husband, who happened to be a West Indian. To my own horror, I found buried deep in myself a prejudice that I could not ever have imagined I possessed, but perhaps that was because I felt that Blanche herself should not have been present, let alone her husband, whatever colour he may have been. But we had other visitors, one of them an old flame of Dad's from way back. Her name escapes me now, but I thought she was lovely, cool, sophisticated, and good-looking, and an obvious suitable candidate for Dad's new future. But, as far as I know, they never ever met again. Also, my schoolmate David Trace brought along the current copy of *Films and Filming* monthly magazine for me, which was a genuinely kind and very thoughtful act.

Geoff Brown phoned during that week to ask when was I returning to *Spies* because they were about to get very busy again. MGM's American executive in charge of supervising the editing of every single MGM picture was about to arrive from Hollywood to look at the cut. She was the venerable Margaret Booth, a former editor herself (*Mutiny on the Bounty*, *Camille*, *A Yank at Oxford*), now the high supremo in charge of all MGM product on delivery. Geoff said there would be inevitable changes that she would demand, and he wanted me back. I told Geoff the shiva lasted seven days, and I would be back next Monday. He said, "All right", and would call me Friday to double-check. When he phoned, he told me that Ms. Booth had asked for a major sequence (set in the Royal Opera House, Covent Garden, but not featuring star David Niven) to be removed, and several other alterations, and that we would be re-reeling to accommodate her changes. She was going back over the coming weekend. I was truly sorry to have missed seeing her, and thought about it a lot when she finally died in 2002, aged 104. But I was very glad indeed to be going back onto *Where the Spies Are*. In my personal anguish I feared that I would be fired for taking far too long off work when Mummy passed away.

With Linda safely settled at Forest Gate, and Dad embroiled in heaven-knows-what, I was very glad to be back at Borehamwood. I knew it was what Mummy would've wanted, and I missed her terribly already, but at least she had passed away knowing that her son had made it working where he wanted to be, on a theatrical motion picture feature, a proper job (albeit freelance) with a proper future ahead of him, that's assuming I played my cards right, and managed not to upset anybody.

I learned much from my director Val Guest, who seemed very friendly towards his new second assistant, particularly after I told him how much I liked his *Expresso Bongo*, a key film in my young moviegoing life, although I didn't tell him that, exactly. There was a scene in *Where the Spies Are* that had to be re-shot on instructions from the MGM bosses in Hollywood. It was a fight scene in a garage, and on the floor could clearly be seen an old packet of American cigarettes. I can't remember the name on the packet, but it was a very well-known brand. MGM wanted a re-shoot, with the offending packet removed. Bill Lenny was busy cutting, Geoff Brown busy with running the editing rooms, so Bill and Val asked me to handle it. Basically, to see if the offending cigarette packet could be optically removed each time it appeared, thus obviating the expensive necessity for retakes. MGM at Borehamwood was the only studio in Europe to have its own laboratories and special fx department in the studio itself, and that department was under the great fx man Tom Howard, who had won his Oscars for *Blithe Spirit* and *tom thumb*.

I made an appointment to see the great man, and arrived at the laboratory on the MGM lot a little early. In the foyer, sitting at a table, were two young Americans, who introduced themselves as Doug Trumbull and Con Pederson, and they were over here for work on Stanley Kubrick's new project, a space film called, tentatively, *2001*. Stanley Kubrick! My hero!! (I didn't say). I just asked them all about it, and they told me that, since it was an MGM picture, they would be doing it all here, at MGM Borehamwood. It would be cheaper, and there would be no Hollywood interference. Besides which, Stanley Kubrick now lived over here, after *Dr. Strangelove* and *Lolita*. I hadn't really time to chat with them, but we exchanged pleasantries, and they invited me to look over some time at the sets they were building, which I eventually did. I then went up the stairs to Tom Howard's office, and noticed on the wall a large transparency of the funeral scene from *Doctor Zhivago*, where the young Yuri watches his father being buried. I'd seen the film only a couple of weeks before, at the Empire, Leicester Square, in the 70mm. opening print. The door opened to reveal Tom Howard, who saw me looking at the picture. “Hi,” he said, “I’m Tom Howard. You must be Tony.” Then, looking at the picture on the wall: “Like it?” “Yes,” I replied, “I’ve only just seen it.” “What do you think of the sky?” I looked at the picture. “Oh, David Lean’s skies are always ravishing--” Tom cut me off. “That’s not David Lean’s sky. That’s ours. He just shot the foreground.” And then I knew I was in a den of wonders, a secret world where everything might not be quite as it appeared. I was clearly in the right place to lose our cigarette packet from the fight scene, and nobody would ever notice, and I secretly thanked Val Guest and Bill Lenny for giving me this opportunity. How thankful I would be eventually to know, and be able to work with, the wonderful Tom Howard would greatly show in the next time that I was to work at MGM, on what was to become arguably the greatest, most original, filmed television series of all time, for I would be working virtually hand-in-hand with Tom Howard’s superb FX department on the television series entitled *The Prisoner*.

-----END OF REEL TWO-----

<u>REEL THREE</u>

Where the Spies Are came to an end. I'd missed quite a few evening classes owing to overtime, but I'd made a bit of money in the meantime. What next?

During *Spies* I'd befriended, amongst others, sound editor Jimmy Shields' dubbing assistant Peter Connor, a genuinely nice guy, a little older than me, someone who nobody else at the studio seemed to take seriously. He was professionally sound, but a little lank and gangly, and we had much in common, particularly in music. It so happened that neither of us had a specific girlfriend at the moment, but I knew, thanks to David Trace, a few Dulwich girls, but hadn't asked any of them for a date yet, being, frankly, a little shy (oh, yes!), and also uncertain of how pressure of work would affect my availability at any given time, once I started on *Spies*. Now, a certain new wave of French popular music had beached, and artistes such as Françoise Hardy and Richard Anthony were attracting those of us who were bored by the Beatles and the Rolling Stones' endless cover versions of tracks that we had far better recordings of by their American originators. During *Spies*, on one weekend off, I went to a Dulwich Tennis Club dance with David Trace, and met some of his Dulwich friends, girls, of course, but since I didn't drive and was working very long hours and far away, dating seemed to be out of the question. However, chatting to Peter Connor one day in the *Spies* cutting room, we both mentioned at the same time that Françoise Hardy was coming to play dates in London, and wouldn't it be great to see her at the Savoy Hotel? Peter joked, "Wouldn't it be better to take a couple of girls with us?" I thought it over for a while, and then I came up with an idea: "If I can get the girls, could you get a car?" Peter said he'd let me know, and the awaited eventual answer was "Yes", so I made some phone calls.

I'd been to a few Dulwich Tennis Club gatherings, and had actually entered a competition in which we mimed to gramophone records. I did Elvis' "Stuck on You", and came in second, beaten by one Clive Archer, who mimed grotesquely, I thought, using exaggeratedly "Jewish" gestures, to Adam Faith's "What Do You Want (If You Don't Want Money)?", supported by his regular serious girlfriend Valerie Balchin, who was posed on top of a piano. Valerie was sweet, and we became friends, sort of. Also present was Mandy Mitson, who David Trace had once dated and who, therefore, I knew. I took a chance, and asked both Valerie and Mandy if they'd like to come with me and a friend to see Françoise Hardy live at the Savoy. Would they? Would they just! They were delighted, and so I phoned Peter Connor and made the arrangements.

Well, apart from his car stopping, stuck somewhere around Primrose Hill (and, thank goodness, starting again), we had a great time at the Savoy. However, on arrival at the hotel restaurant, we noticed that everyone there wore evening dress. I said, as a joke, there must be a wedding going on. Was I wrong, and ignorant to boot. I didn't know that evening dress was obligatory then at the Savoy in the evenings. Nevertheless, I had booked a table, and the four of us were shown to our seats. Of course, although both Peter and I wore suits, and the girls looked ravishing besides, we were the only ones there not in evening dress, but Peter and the girls were too decent to mention it in any way. We weren't asked to leave, and we had a great time.

After Peter had driven the girls home to their respective South London abodes, and dropped me off, he said to me something along the lines of "That was wonderful, Tony, just wonderful. I can't thank you enough. One day, perhaps soon, I'll do something for you..." And we said goodnight and goodbye, and I thanked Peter profusely for providing the car.

Where the Spies Are concluded, and we all said our mutual goodbyes. My new *2001* friends Doug Trumbull and Con Pederson took me on a tour of the *2001* sound stages as a farewell. Shooting hadn't yet started on the opening sequence, and I saw men in what looked like monkey suits practising movements on a vast, barren stage dressed as an uninhabited planet. I was privileged to watch the now-classic opening of *2001: A Space Odyssey* actually in preparation before Kubrick began shooting. I said "goodbyes" in particular not just to the *Spies* crew, but also to Peter Watson, Chris Kelly, and all of those that I had grown to know in the cutting rooms and in projection at MGM, and especially to the girls in the offices who had been so kind. One girl gave me a touching, personalised note. If only I had known how she felt earlier...

What to do next? I'd left with what I thought was a lovely bonus: I had never received holiday credits before, having been ignorant of them because of my previous employers' exploitation of me, and now I had a healthy and sufficient amount of money to live on for quite some little while. But what to do? Living alone with Dad was getting to be very, very difficult. He was drinking heavily now. He always liked his drink, but never like this. Of course, I thought, he certainly had reason to put it away as he now did, but perhaps, just perhaps, his current imbibing was just a little too much? Linda was getting on very well at cousin Della's school, and had made new friends, and with my finishing money I could afford to pay for her future at Auntie Doris's for quite a while, or so it seemed to me at the time. Friends and relatives were also being very kind to me. I partook of my first Passover Seder without Mummy at Auntie Fanny and Uncle Hymie's, and spent a fair bit of time with the nearby lovely Traces, David, his sister and his parents. What next?

I was beginning to miss MGM. I had – foolishly for a freelancer – taken the busyness and the convivial company that I had encountered there for granted. I especially missed my once-a-week Friday lunch in the MGM restaurant, where I could afford to sit at the big table where the cutting room staff – editors, dubbing editors, <u>and</u> assistants – all gathered to chat over an extended lunch. There I would encounter, and be befriended by, the experienced and knowledgeable sound editor Peter Musgrave, then working on *The Hill*, who took me into the sound studio where he was shooting "footsteps" tracks, that is to say all the sound fx under dialogue, plus everything else thought needed to enhance a film's soundtrack, and he showed me also The Hill itself, comprised of a very high pile of stones, sand and cornflakes, in order to create the soundtrack for a film whose director, Sidney Lumet, wanted no background music whatsoever.

I also met, over lunch, John Huston's film editor Russell Lloyd, currently editing J. Lee Thompson's *Return from the Ashes*, and, no, I didn't tell Russ Lloyd that I was in the same form at Dulwich College with his son John Lloyd, when the latter was expelled from that venerable establishment for stealing money from blazer pockets left hanging up in changing rooms whilst the owners of the jackets were playing compulsory sports.

I also enjoyed the company of the garrulous Teddy Darvas, whom many of my contemporaries thought boorish, who had worked closely with David Lean on *The Bridge on the River Kwai*, a displaced and volatile central European Jew who was then currently acting as the British assembly editor on Robert Aldrich's *The Dirty Dozen*, a match, some were saying, that could only be made in some demented Hollywood heaven. And there were, for me, also some great events to be witnessed in that studio restaurant at MGM….

The moment when all heads turned towards the door – we had "felt" a definite presence enter, who turned out to be the oh-so-glamorous ex-Queen Soraya of Persia, on the arm of Maximilian Schell, then currently starring in *Return from the Ashes* at the studio. (Both of them shorter than you'd expect.) They positively exuded glamour and class.

The time David Niven, our own star, got up from his table to greet with an embrace Martin Balsam, who had just entered, and with whom David had recently co-starred in *The Captive City*. Martin barely came up to Niven's waist. What was Balsam doing there? Well, he was Stanley Kubrick's first choice for the voice of "Hal" in *2001*, only to be replaced eventually by Canadian actor Douglas Rain.

And most exciting of all? The time *The Dirty Dozen* all turned up for lunch at once, shooting having broken, all in their screen army costumes: one after another – Lee Marvin, Ernest Borgnine, Charles Bronson, John Cassavetes, Jim Brown, Richard Jaeckel, George Kennedy, Robert Ryan, Trini Lopez, Ralph Meeker, Telly Savalas, and Clint Walker, so massive that he had to duck well down to get through the restaurant's entrance! How I missed those days, and still do.

I caught up with all the new movies, and continued with my evening classes, and managed to live with Dad and all his foibles, when I received a telephone call from none other than Peter Connor, wondering what was I up to, and would I like a job? Would I?? It was, apparently, to be the assistant editor to an editor who I'm only going to refer to here as Simon, working on a series of Army commercials at Worldwide Pictures in Holborn, whose previous assistant had just left. I was soon to discover why. Peter didn't know how long it would be for, but if I'd like to do it he'd recommend me, since he said that he himself only wanted to work on features. I told him that I'd like to, what to do next? He said he'd phone Simon, telling him that he (Peter) was otherwise engaged, and would recommend me. Which he did: I was to start the coming Monday, without an interview. All that seemed to matter was that I was a bona fide A.C.T.T. member. At last!

For me, it was better than schlepping to Elstree every day, but that was to be the only advantage. Simon turned out to be a total neurotic. When I arrived on the Monday he greeted me, friendly enough, then sat down in a chair next to the moviola, his head in his hands, shaken, and told me he couldn't do the job. "Why?" I stupidly asked him. "I can't, I just can't," he said, chain-smoking. Suddenly, I wondered what was I doing here? I tried to phone Peter Connor, but there was no reply. I was never to see Peter Connor again.

What to do? Simon told me that the producer, Tony Hearne, was expected to arrive at any minute to view the cut. Only there wasn't one. I said, was there a script? Were the rushes logged? If so, where were they? The answers were "Yes", and "Yes", and (pointing) "Over there". I said that if nothing is assembled then, what is the producer coming in to view? And that's when Simon started shaking and trembling.

Well, they were only commercials, about sixty seconds in length each, so I said that I'd assemble the first one according to script, and we could show that to producer Tony when he came in: just put him off for an hour, or possibly longer if you can. Suggest that he comes in after lunch. And so, when Tony Hearne, a nice, humorous, plumpish, elderly man who smoked cigars, arrived after lunch, there was an assembly cut of the first commercial for him to view. As for me, well, I wasn't sure if I didn't like the way things were going, or if I was actually pleased to be editing this early in my career.

The producer was happy, thank goodness, and suggested that we dub the first one and show it to the backers (who, to my astonishment, happened to be the C.O.I. once again, my old "muckers" from Caledonian) before we attempted to edit the other commercials, and then do them one at a time. Simon agreed, and Tony Hearne left me to deal with the track-laying and to organise the mix. What about Simon, you might be thinking? Well, in addition to his chain-smoking, he seemed to be drinking quite a bit as well. The thought occurred to me that perhaps I wasn't being paid quite enough for this job, but what to do? Simon just told me to track-lay, and to get it dubbed, and then to call Tony Hearne in to look at it, and not to worry about the other commercials. Simon would take care of those. ("Oh, yeah?" I thought to myself.)

Worldwide was next to a building where my cousin Michael, Auntie Becky's son, was serving an apprenticeship, so I phoned Michael and said let's meet for lunch; it would give me a break, at least, from pub-lunching with Simon. Now, in truth, Michael and I had had a strange relationship. He had lost his father in the last ever V2 bombing raid on London, when Hughes Mansions, where they lived, was bombed, and he was brought up by my two great aunts (Nanna's sisters) Aunt Becky (Michael's mother) and spinster Aunt Petsy, and, as a child in Forest Gate, we used to play together. Some weekends I stayed with them and Michael in their home in the East End, in Vallance

Road. We saw each other frequently during our young teenage years, going to the pictures together (*The Vikings* and *The Magnificent Seven*, both films each seen twice), and visiting each other's houses. As Nanna's nephew, Mummy and Daddy were always very kind to Michael, but, unquestionably, Michael's aloofness and peculiarity did not exactly endear him to Auntie Doris, and especially not to Uncle Don, who, on one weekend when we were on an outing to Epping Forest, deliberately left Michael to find his own way back home from a pub there, the "Robin Hood," after we had searched for him when Michael had seemingly taken it in his mind to vanish from our sight. We should have recognised then that Michael needed psychiatric care, but such things were certainly not thought of in our family or, indeed, generally not considered at all in those days. But, although in truth we had little in common, Michael and I still saw each other pretty regularly. We played strange "games" together, invariably initiated by Michael. For instance, we would pretend to be opposing barristers in an invented courtroom drama ("Sir Clifford Richard" and "Sir Martin Wilde" – rock'n'roller me invented the character names), or I'd otherwise be an English flyer being threatened with extreme torture by a Nazi (Michael, of course) in my bedroom, in order to tell the truth (what truth?). Surely, by no stretch of the imagination were these normal "games" for young teenage boys to be playing.

And then, my parents thought it might be a good idea for me to go on holiday with Michael. Now, the four of us family Slomans had had a couple of very pleasant summer holidays in the Channel Islands, and so it was suggested that Michael and I go to Jersey for a fortnight. Which we did. It turned out to be the worst holiday of my life. Michael and I had a room in a very nice, comfortable boarding house: separate beds, cooked breakfasts, and evening meals. On our first few days we explored Jersey island, and swam in the Channel, and then, after about a week together, Michael made what I can only describe as a distinct pass at me. I was utterly horrified. I knew all about "queers" from Dulwich College, but it never, ever occurred to me that my cousin...

Michael had been brought up his whole life by two very strong women, without a father figure at all, and very probably had no friendships with girls. But none of this pat psychology went through my mind as I managed to fight him off successfully, thank God. My first thought was: "We've got another week to go. What on earth to do?" But he was repentant, and said something like "If you don't want to play, I guess it's all over." Whew. But we still had to carry on for a while. I dreaded going to sleep, and tried to stay awake as much as possible. We managed not to see each other so much in the daytime, going our own separate ways. There was, obviously, no-one I could speak to, but I wrote home asking for more money, pleading that I had run out, but actually scared I might need more to just get away from Michael. Anyhow, he made no more such advances, and we returned, never to see each other for a long, long time, and then only on social occasions like weddings or Bar Mitzvahs. But soon enough Michael had a couple of severe breakdowns, and medical help was sought. I did phone a few times in that period to see how he was (there were family rumours of attempted suicide), and eventually we conversed together as though nothing untoward had ever happened in Jersey.

So here I now was, in High Holborn, stuck with a major drunken editor on Army commercials, and my only respite at lunchtime seemed to be my crazy cousin Michael. Oh well, needs must. I phoned Michael after all this time, and suggested we meet for lunch while I was working in Holborn. Any port in a storm. And so we did meet again, for a quick lunch, mercifully brief. He was obviously quite still disturbed, but about what I had no idea, and, frankly, I was momentarily ashamed of myself for not wanting to know. I was just looking for, and needed, a respite from the Army commercials next door. Michael was telling me his very real troubles, and all I could offer was cod psychology. Leave home, I suggested to him, you're a grown-up now. But I could tell that he really wasn't, and probably never would be, and history proved that to be true. My unfortunate cousin spent most of his adult life in and out of "hospitals", as they were called, until mercifully rescued by our mutual cousin Gerald, Aunt Julie's son, she the cousin of Aunts Becky and Petsy, and Michael was to spend the whole of the rest of his life under the beneficent care of Gerald and his lovely wife Margaret, clinging to his Judaism for comfort, and dying, ill, sadly, and without the love and looking-after that he really needed, though cousin Gerry did more than his best, bless him, but Michael was, I think, alas, irredeemable.

Meanwhile, back at the Army commercials, what to do? Simon wanted me to track-lay, but in truth, I had never been a proper dubbing editor, so far. I had laid music tracks, but that was just finding a piece with a decent start and/or a good finish, and matching it to action. As Bob Bucknell taught me: "It fits where it touches." I'd never really laid sound effects, but I'd seen post-sync. fx ("footsteps", or as the Americans call them "foleys", after the man who allegedly invented them) shot, but not track-laid, and I knew about post-synchronised dialogue, but had never fitted it in soundtracks. It was quite clear that Simon, who could hardly stand up owing to drink, was utterly incapable of track-laying, being barely able to edit: he hung up the selections and I joined them up for him. Ergo: a cut! So now it was time to call in Tony Hearne to view that edit. Which I did. More to the point, after viewing it he congratulated Simon and promptly booked the Worldwide dubbing theatre for the mix. Well, at least I thought to myself, we don't have to go too far to dub – we didn't even have to leave the building!

And then one of the most wonderful things in my world happened. I received a telephone call from one Mary Kessel (who I didn't know, and of whom I'd never heard even though her last three films as assistant editor prior to this phone call were *The Grass is Greener*, *The Innocents*, and the Royal Performance Film of its year *Sammy Going South*). Mary said that Peter Watson had recommended me from working in the cutting rooms next to me at MGM, and that she was starting on *Othello* at Shepperton on Monday, and since they were shooting with three cameras filming simultaneously, there would be an awful of of syncing up to do. Would I be interested in starting on Monday? Would I?? I, of course, said "Yes", and asked if she wanted to interview me first, a procedure I was used to. She said "No, just turn up on Monday, it's the first day of shooting." I didn't even think to ask what the money was, but she told me the rate, and I couldn't've been more delighted. I was over the moon, as they say. "See you there, then." "Looking forward to it." "And me." "Thanks again, and thank Peter for recommending me." "You can thank him yourself on Monday." And we hung up. *Othello*! With Sir Laurence Olivier. Blimey!!

Wait a minute. How do I get out of these damn Army commercials? They want me to start at Shepperton Studios on Monday, and the A.C.T.T. notice period on leaving a job is two weeks, either they give it to you, or you give it to them. Either way, it's two weeks' notice, best not to leave them in the lurch and start the following Monday on a better job for better money. Not to mention prestige and the chance to work with the universally recognised Greatest Actor in the World. What would you have done?

It didn't take me too long to think about it. I was working with a neurotically incapable hopeless drunk, but, still, I didn't want to let him down. Nor Tony Hearne, really. I phoned Tony Hearne, and told him about the phone call. "Take it," he said, and asked me just to track-lay that first commercial, so that it could be mixed in my absence, and to concentrate on finding a substitute for myself, to start virtually immediately. He couldn't have been nicer, or more professional. Only thing was, I didn't know enough people then to find a suitable substitute, and I couldn't really lie to whomever I found anyway, that they would have to "carry" Simon. I decided to ask Ray Selfe, my friend and tutor at evening classes, and he said he'd ask around, certain he could find someone. I told Simon, but he didn't seem to care one way or another, and was, as they say, "in his cups" at the time of our conversation. Ray called me back. There was somebody he knew who had worked in features, but he was a bit "funny". Would I like to interview him? I said "Yes" immediately, and so he sent this man – who must remain nameless – along to Worldwide for me to interview him for my job.

I was anxious to get the position filled, so in truth I would have taken anyone, or so I thought. Ray's man telephoned, and we made an appointment, me being very careful to make sure Simon wouldn't be there. I didn't want anyone to meet Simon, and I certainly didn't want Simon to exercise his right of veto. I was actually being a shit, and I hadn't yet spoken to anybody except Ray about finding someone to replace me. Ray's guy turned up for an interview. Yes, he had worked on commercials, and, yes, he knew how to track-lay. He hadn't been an assistant for quite a while. To me, it looked like he hadn't been anything for quite a while. He was ill-shaven, and wore a two-piece suit that looked like it had come from a second-hand shop, or worse. His tie was loose, and, frankly, he looked like he could maybe need a bath. But I had to pass this rotten job over to somebody, and, at the time, I didn't even recall that it was the job that even Peter Connor didn't want, hence me in this particular position. I ascertained that this seemingly down-on-his-luck gentleman could start next Monday, and he replied affirmatively. I really didn't know what to do. I can't remember if I told him he was hired, but that was my intention, and so I asked him to turn up Monday morning and ask for Simon. Which, eventually, he did.

I took Simon's cut and proceeded to track-lay, but of course, I'd never properly track-laid in my life, and this largely consisted of mute shots of cars and heavy vehicles on main roads. Worldwide had an fx library, so I retrieved, and had transferred, various car tracks, and proceeded to lay them. Or so I thought. But I didn't drive, and I didn't know therefore how to synchronise car engine sounds in the correct position for reality. Easy-peasy, once you know how. But I didn't. So I "laid" the tracks on the moviola, not properly marked up, and charted them accordingly. If I could have had a rehearsal, I would have noticed that they were all slightly out of sync., and attempted to correct them, but Simon said a rehearsal would be a misuse of the budget. Which, of course, it would have been, if the tracks had been laid by a professional dubbing sound editor, which I wasn't, at least not yet.

I started on *Othello* at Shepperton Studios the following Monday. It was good to meet up again with Peter Watson, and I couldn't thank him enough, and to meet Richard Marden, the editor, and his first assistant Mary Kessel. Everyone seemed so nice and so professional, it was such a relief, despite the journey from Streatham to Shepperton, via Waterloo, with a bus at the other end. Another four-hour travelling day!

But, in the meantime, what of Dad, in Streatham? There was definitely "something" going on, there were messages on the answerphone for him to call the police. He was seeing various women, and one called Anne, it seemed, quite frequently. The other thing that really horrified me was our shopping. I'd done it when I could, on weekends, and occasionally at evenings, but Dad had started bringing home non-kosher items, pork sausages and bacon and the like. I didn't know what to say or do. I gave some meat he'd bought to Bruno as dog food, without saying anything to Dad. If we were no longer going to have a kosher house, after Mummy's death, I thought at least we could discuss it and see how I felt. I think, with hindsight, I was more revolted at the fact that he was doing it without consulting me, than that he was doing it at all. Who to talk to, who to discuss it with, who would understand? I had no answer, when, surprisingly, I received a phone call from an old card-playing friend of Dad's, Gerry Hart, who was also Jewish, and who wanted to ask what was going on, and how was Dad, what with all his troubles, now that they no longer played weekly cards. Gerry then suggested we meet up, and would I like to come with him and his wife Pam to the opening of a new Covent Garden club that Annie Ross was operating where the American jazz singer Dakota Staton would be appearing? I said "Yes", but it would have to be late one evening, because I didn't get back till about nine-ish from Shepperton. Gerry said that would be fine, bring a date.

So we did. I can't remember the name of the girl I brought along to Annie's Room, and Gerry and Pam brought their two daughters. Gerry and Pam understood my situation. They had lost a daughter of their own, a third daughter, to a dreadful disease, which they wouldn't name, and who I remembered meeting when we both attended Fenstanton. She was then thin and sickly, and clearly not long for this world. Gerry had a solution for me to think over. They now had a spare bedroom, and, if things got worse between Dad and me, I would be welcome to move in with them. Well, this was something, something that I guess would have been inevitable one day, but something that hadn't really actually occurred to me as yet. Leave Dad? A lot to think over, an awful lot to think about.

I asked Dad what was going on with him and the police, but he wouldn't tell me. I remembered the tape that he had played for Mummy, but I couldn't bring myself to mention it. And also Dad was drinking far too much. I should have also asked him about his work I now realise, but, self-absorbed as ever, I never did.

First day at Shepperton was exciting. Remember, I'd joined *Where the Spies Are* when they were well into their shooting: I'd never been in at the start of filming before. Dick Marden proved to be a terrific guy, and well knew how to organise a cutting room, delegate responsibility, and edit the complex three-camera shoot at the same time. His experienced first assistant, effectively my boss, Mary Kessel, was both motherly to Dick, and schoolmistressy to we two second assistants, Peter and I. She told us what the procedures would be: there would be an awful lot of rushes, but most of them would be extremely long takes, so it was mainly just a case of "wind it in" once we had identified the clapperboard. But there would be an awful, awful lot of rewinding the reels, so she hoped we both had strong hands (Mary's little joke). Since there wouldn't be rushes until tomorrow, Dick Marden suggested we all have lunch together, since we may not be able to ever again (he wasn't wrong – the synchronising of rushes took most of the day; the viewing took most of the evening). Mary then took us onto the shooting stage to meet the crew, but the doors were locked because it was a very long take (they were all long takes) so we hardly saw any of that day's shooting, and only managed to meet Maggie Unsworth, the continuity woman who was married to the film's lighting cameraman, the great Geoffrey Unsworth (*2001: A Space Odyssey*, *Cabaret*, *Becket*). Maggie was a delight to work with, and the ensuing daily mountain of continuity sheets almost a joy to receive in the cutting rooms. Mary Kessel sensibly suggested that both Peter Watson and I had good solid breakfasts at the studio, prior to the arrival of rushes, as the sheer amount of rushes received daily would preclude us having a proper lunch in order to be ready for evening screening at the normal rushes time. And, boy, was she ever right!

Dick Marden was fast and very able, and assembled the chosen takes rapidly according to script and continuity order, and kept well abreast of the shoot. Stuart Burge, the director, happened to be a very nice man, and went a very long way back with Laurence Olivier, having appeared in a very minor role in the 1953 film *The Beggar's Opera*, billed fourth in the Wikipedia listing, but frankly, hardly visible in the film itself. A very special bonus on *Othello* for both Peter Watson and me was that we took it in turns to be on the set with the moviola for matching purposes. With very long takes used, floor time was valuable, and sometimes the crew had to pick up exactly where they left off last night on the following morning. So I was fortunate enough to watch Sir Laurence Olivier in close-up action, live. I couldn't believe my luck: I just marvelled at his sheer professionalism, let alone the performance. One day I was at the moviola on the studio floor, placed next to Dickie Bird, the sound recordist, when "Sir", in full costume and make-up, came over to Dick's sound recording station, and stood next to me. "Dickie," Sir Laurence said, "watch me very closely. When I move forwards, my costume clinks. When I touch it, you pull down, and come back up after I move. I'm speaking throughout, but I'll give you a gap. I don't want to post-sync. the whole bloody speech because of a clothes rustle." I was just amazed at this level of professionalism, and actually remember feeling deeply privileged to witness this glimpse into Olivier's craft. I watched the said take very carefully, with one eye on Dickie's hand on the sound pots. Dickie did exactly as per requested. There was no second take. I told Mary Kessel afterwards about this. "Yes," she said, "that's typical Sir Laurence. He hates to post-sync." And he did. When a dialogue line was needed to be retaken, he recorded it "wild" on set, i.e. not in synchronisation in a post-sync. theatre, "dubbing", as it's popularly known outside the industry. I, a neophyte, found this extremely hard to believe. Until Dick Marden tested me out. "Sir" had to do a wild track of a speech that was interrupted during shooting by an overhead light going out with a huge "whoosh". Shooting didn't stop (Stuart Burge knew better) and "Sir" re-recorded the line afterwards on the stage. Dick handed that recording to me to fit. (Remember, we didn't have a dubbing editor yet. I thought one was going to come on later, but it never happened, and I was soon to find out why.) I took the roll of sound from Dick and laced it in the synchroniser, matching the first modulation with that of the sync. take, and wound it through. I wound it right to the end, listening very intently for where it would be necessary to pull it into sync. It sounded like one straight track. I ran it again. Surely that can't be right? Every single wild track needs fitting. I reluctantly interrupted Dick and told him of my dilemma. "That's 'Sir'," Dick replied. "He doesn't like post-syncing. He'll always do a wild track on the floor if he can, and it always matches perfectly: he's so good, no editing is necessary." I was simultaneously amazed and flabbergasted. Dick apologised for tricking me, ever the gentleman. "I knew you wouldn't believe me. Nobody would. You had to find out for yourself."

That wasn't Olivier's only speciality. I caught Mary Kessel hiding a particular take in the cupboard, and asked her what she was doing. "Oh," she replied, "this is a take that I've been instructed to destroy. When 'Sir' threw his gown up as he gesticulated, you could see that he'd blacked-up all over, and that he wasn't wearing any underwear." Blimey! What would "Sir"'s blacked-up genitalia on film fetch at an auction? I thought, somewhat disrespectfully.

We never broke for daily lunch until the completion of the floor shooting, as Mary Kessel had predicted, nor did I actually see that much of Shepperton Studios, apart from our cutting rooms and the soundstage, with occasional trips to the canteen for a quick lunch, where I ran into no less than director Otto Preminger one day, on his way in. I'd just seen his "In Harm's Way" in a super 70mm. premiere copy at the Plaza, Piccadilly Circus on the previous Sunday, my day off, and I couldn't resist telling him how much I'd enjoyed it. "Excuse me, Mr. Preminger, but I saw *In Harm's Way* over the weekend, and I'd just like to say how much I enjoyed it." Preminger stared down at me and patronisingly patted me on the head. "Sank you, mein poy," he said to me, and entered the canteen.

One morning, after I'd finished rushes, Mary asked me to join up a roll of *Othello* out-takes that she had selected, since she had been asked by our producers to choose a series of shots of Olivier in his *Othello* make-up requested by film producer Julian Blaustein, who was producing *Khartoum* to star Burt Lancaster as General Gordon, to see what "Sir" would look like blacked-up once again, this time to portray the Mahdi, a role for which he was under serious consideration. I duly did so, and Mary committed me to a vow of total secrecy as we sent that reel to Pinewood, where *Khartoum* was based, to the attention of *Khartoum*'s assistant editor Nick Napier-Bell, who I knew from *He Who Rides a Tiger*. I was to ensure its delivery, and to receive it back from the car driver on his return from Pinewood, and to absolutely discuss it with nobody, not even Nick. I did exactly what I was told, and, lo and behold, Laurence Olivier did, in fact, star in *Khartoum*, although not with Burt Lancaster, but with Charlton Heston in Lancaster's stead. Apparently, producer Blaustein had wanted to see if Olivier's make-up would show up poorly on the very big screen, since *Khartoum* was to be filmed in Ultra-Panavision-70 and to premiere in Cinerama. As it so happened, our *Othello* also debuted in London in 70mm., a blow-up, though. In those far-off days, there were no issues over a distinguished actor like Olivier "blacking-up" for such roles. I seriously doubt if you'd get away with it today, let alone worrying about how it would look on a very big screen: Olivier as both *Othello* and the Mahdi: perhaps only he could've brought off that particular double act. Sir Laurence Olivier and Shepperton! What a privilege, what an experience for me on only my second feature!

On the studio floor, I became friendly with Frank Finlay, who played Iago, and when he discovered how long my journey was to the studios, he kindly offered me car lifts with him, when he was on call, to Chiswick, where he lived, and that managed to cut my railway train ride in half. What a nice man. As for our Desdemona, I truly had never before heard a woman swear like Maggie Smith. I remember walking past her on the set one day and hearing "Fuck. Cunt. Shit. Damn" come out of her mouth, talking to no-one in particular. I wasn't half surprised!! I also got to know Sheila Reid (Bianca) and Joyce Redman (Emilia) moderately well on set: I thought Joyce Redman was quite positively one of the sexiest women that I had ever seen!

Rex Pyke joined us as a sound editor, and prepared to cut in various necessary sound effects and replacement dialogue re-recordings, and, since we had no actual dubbing editor, Mary Kessel booked a sound studio for us -- the cutting crew – to record all the necessary post-sync. sound fx, plus some off-screen and occasional on-screen crowd voices. Now, that was a very real and valuable learning experience for me. Not only did we record various sound fx and footsteps, but editor Dick Marden also needed some odd vocals, so he asked us editing folk to shoot some dialogue for him to use. If you listen very carefully, you'll hear the voice of yours truly cry out splendidly: "Ho! The Watch!".

Othello came in at 165 minutes, the longest film that I was ever to work on, and therefore the heaviest amount of reels, picture and sound, to carry, when necessary. Peter and I remained on the film well after the shoot, to assist Rex in shooting all footsteps and sound fx under dialogue for the foreign versions, and then to assist running the one big screening for the backers. That sound recording session on *Othello* was the first such I had ever attended, let alone participated in as an artiste. We had to create some additional "footsteps" tracks for some scenes, and I learned a very big sound fx lesson. Dick, Mary, Peter, Rex and I were the "crowd", and one scene had the members of the group shuffling together, then walking away. On "Action" we performed "wild", i.e. not to picture. And I duly walked away into the theatre distance. After "Cut" Dick asked me what was I doing? "I was walking off," I replied, "like the character." "Oh," said Dick, recognising my inexperience in sound, and told me that I didn't have to do that literally, the recordist would "walk" me off if I stayed in the middle, by gradually reducing the sound level. Well, I was embarrassed and flustered, but nobody seemed to mind. (But when I eventually became a sound editor, I learned to always hire the very best most professional footsteps artistes in the business, when I could.)

The other fabulous thing about Shepperton was that, after shooting and rushes were over, we could take a proper lunch break. Peter and I lunched in the main canteen, where frescoes from *The Long Ships* adorned the walls, and we visited the summer sunshine-blessed grassland afterwards, where we saw Pat Boone playing ball with some of his cast members from *The Main Attraction*, and Tony Curtis picnicking with his fellow actors from *Drop Dead, Darling*, which was shooting at Shepperton under the title of *Arrivederci, Baby*.

After the actual editing on *Othello* came to its natural conclusion, we prepared for a major running of the whole assembled cut, and this was to take place at the cinema in the Shell building in Waterloo, opposite London's South Bank. At 165 minutes *Othello* took up many, many cans, with the action and sound still separate. That's 17x2 cans of film that had to be cleaned and beautifully labelled, black for picture, red for sound. That's thirty-four cans in all. That job fell to me.

The producers of *Othello* were British Home Entertainment, BHE, a newly-formed company created to film stage shows and major theatrical events, and it was headed by a very, very distinguished film consortium including the likes of Lord (John) Brabourne and Anthony Havelock-Allan, who were credited as *Othello*'s producers. Both were expected to turn up to this first screening, and there was an interesting whiff of scandal in the air as "the Havelock" (as Anthony H.-A. was termed) was previously married to actress Valerie Hobson, who was now married to War Minister John Profumo, currently engaged in, arguably, the greatest political sex scandal of our time. Since they were all invited to our running, I couldn't wait to see all of them together.

My primary job, however, was to re-label the cans which bore swiftly written cutting room titles, i.e. REEL 1 SOUND; REEL 1 PICTURE; etc. etc., in black and red magic markers. (Traditionally black for picture; red for sound). I remade those beautifully, or so I thought. The screening was in the evening, so I spent all morning remaking the labels in my best hand, and then, satisfied with my work, went off to lunch. When I returned, I was horrified. Mary Kessel had ripped off all my labels! The cans were now unlabelled, meaning, at least, that it would all have to be done again, but also meaning that each can would now have to be opened to identify its contents. I went to find Mary immediately to find out why. "They weren't nearly neat enough," she told me, and produced a stencil. "You should've used this." I spluttered, "But you never said…" "You should've known," she replied. "Now hurry up. The car will be here at three." Thank you, Mary Kessel, I thought. I took the stencil from her, wetted its accompanying pad in the Gents, and proceeded on the long and arduous job of re-labelling every can, making absolutely certain that the correct contents had the correct labels. The car arrived just as I was finishing the very last one, with sore and ink-stained hands: red for sound, black for picture!

The running went well, until a reel was missed out. Mary said "Cut!" into the microphone, and Peter and I rushed into the projection box. No, it wasn't my re-labelling as I'd feared (an instant firing offence, I fantasised), they'd just missed out a reel, their fault, they apologised. Mary was first back to apologise to the distinguished audience, but they were all pros, and the screening, after a very brief pause, continued, but now I knew what it felt like to have your stomach fall out and land on the floor. Loading all those reels back into the car, and then subsequently out again at Shepperton and onto the cutting room shelves in the right order was nothing compared to the absolutely awful day that I'd had, thanks to Mary Kessel.

However, there was one rather pleasant happenstance during *Othello*. Our cutting rooms were in a prime site, should we be inclined to look out over our rushes through the windows to see what else was going on. Early in the morning in a film studio is a great time for socialising, before everybody is trapped on their stages or in their dubbing theatres. Our windows gave onto the paths from the dressing rooms to the stages, although we were winding rushes well before anybody had commenced shooting. But we did see a parade of regular visitors, who would peer in, and occasionally wave and smile at us. *Modesty Blaise* was filming there at the time, and the lovely Monica Vitti would walk past our window whenever she was on call, and would wave at Peter Watson and me. Eventually the waves became blown kisses, and I reciprocated (Peter didn't). Near the end of their shooting schedule, Monica motioned to me to open the window. I shook my head "No". I really didn't know what Dick or Mary would've made of this, so thought that I probably shouldn't. But towards the very end of *Modesty Blaise*'s shooting schedule Signorina Vitti motioned to me one morning to open just the very top of the window. I looked around: no sign of Dick or Mary, so I did. Monica looked in, and said to me, in fractured English, "I just wanted to say 'Hello and goodbye', Tony. This is my last day." She knew my name! Monica Vitti had bothered to find out my name!! I was literally gobsmacked, but managed to stutter out: "Au revoir, Miss Vitti." Wrong language, but the thought was there.

Othello came to a close. Dick Marden invited us all to his bachelor pad for a farewell supper, which he would cook, and said that we could bring a guest, if we had a partner. I didn't at the time, nor did Mary, but Peter and Rex came with their wives. I wanted to bring a girl, because I knew that Dickie was gay, and I, probably foolishly, didn't want him to get the wrong idea.

Nick Nacht had fetched up at a flat in Eccleston Street, Victoria, and was going out with an Australian girl, Jennie Grimm, who also lived there, and I was seeing quite a lot of both of them. In fact, when things got easier on *Othello*, I invited them down for lunch at Shepperton, and they came. It was the first time Nick, a life-long cineaste, had ever visited a film studio. It was the least I could do after he had introduced me to Paris. Sometimes, in the evenings, I used to visit them in Eccleston Street, rather than go home and face Dad, or whatever, and I also sometimes stayed over, and headed to Shepperton early in the morning, well before anyone else got up. So I asked Nick if he wouldn't mind if I asked Jennie to come to Dick Marden's *Othello* farewell party with me. Nick didn't mind at all: they weren't really a couple, he said. ("Oh yeah?" I thought.) Jennie was delighted, especially since it was only over the road. She was, I thought, a sexy little blonde, slightly older than me, and it would send an appropriate message to Dick, if one were needed.

Meanwhile, in the real world, London had become the epicentre of the globe. Not just because of the Beatles, but also for the new fashions, centred on Soho's Carnaby Street, and Chelsea's Kings Road, and there was, quite literally, a whole new wave of music, manners, speech, and conventions. The days of the male of the species being responsible for contraception were over. The newly available feminine contraceptive pill had obviated us fellows carrying around a "packet of three" wherever we, hopefully, went. I kept mine, unused, in my jacket pocket forever. (I did finally throw it away, unopened!)

Sex seemed everywhere, and more than ever, was accompanied by soft drug usage. Although still illegal, pot, or dope, or weed, or whatever you called it, was becoming readily available. "Swinging London" had arrived.

On our very last free lunchtime at Shepperton, the Thursday before the Friday that I was to leave *Othello,* I took a stroll across the vast lawn with Mark Davies, who I knew from MGM previously, and he had a friend with him. Well, blow me down, it turned out to be Peter Cassidy from my old alma mater, Fenstanton Junior Mixed. Peter had always said his dad, Gerry, was in the film business, but I never truly believed him. (His father was Gerry Cassidy, well-known in the industry as the man who ran the Warwick preview theatre in Mayfair). Peter was now in the cutting rooms, working with Mark on *Life at the Top*. And on that stroll on the Shepperton lawn, they offered me something to smoke. Well, I didn't even smoke regular cigarettes, but I was persuaded: it was fashionable, it was hip, but I was stupid – I could've said "No". But they were very persuasive, and it was very "hip". So I took a few "tokes", and felt nothing, except a rather pleasant sense of well-being, and a distinct sensation of being naughty, let alone being stupid smoking an illegal drug in a work situation. But I was leaving the job tomorrow, so what the hey?

But there was one more aspect to *Othello* that was to affect my life forever. On that very last day of my employment, that particular Friday, a large truck parked in the Shepperton grounds in order for voluntary blood donors to supply a pint of blood, an admirable gift indeed to those who would need it, from those who were healthy and currently earning, and so, in theory, could spare it. Well, Mary Kessel being Mary Kessel at her most schoolmistress-like, virtually insisted that both "her boys" – Peter and I – give a pint of blood before we leave the picture. Peter declined, but I wish that I had done so, also, but I recognised that it was my one last chance to show Mary that I wasn't a clod, and duly gave a pint of blood to charity. Big mistake.

The following day, Saturday, I was taking a girl from Dulwich to the Annual Dulwich Tennis Club dance, and during the evening, dancing with her, I felt weak and suddenly I crashed to the floor (not impressive on a date!). David Trace and others rushed over to help me, and in so doing I felt a tremendous pain, and couldn't move my right arm. David (and someone else, I think, but I can't remember. All I know is, it certainly wasn't my date for that evening, who I never saw again) drove me to the nearest hospital, and they put me under and reset my arm, which had dislocated. When I came round, the doctor asked me if I had given blood recently. He said, "Aha!" on being told I had, only yesterday. "You shouldn't be dancing just yet."

And ever since, albeit rarely, about four or five times, that shoulder has dislocated itself, and I've had to have it reset. It almost put me off the missionary position for ever. Thanks for nothing, Mary Kessel (but was it also Heaven's punishment for smoking that single last day illegal "toke", I pondered?).

So *Othello* was over. But what happened domestically, behind the scenes at home, I have yet to recount. Not just because it's hard to remember, which it is, but largely because, psychologically, I'm sure I really just don't want to remember at all, but here goes…

It was difficult, and gradually becoming impossible, for my Father and myself to live together. Less so for me, since working at Shepperton meant that I hardly ever saw him, except on weekends: he worked Saturdays, and we had some occasional overtime at the studio on those days. But when we did overlap, at home in the evenings or on a Sunday, life together seemed just impossible. Dad was drinking heavily, and was clearly involved with – to me – strange women, and then there was that police matter. Gerry and Pam's offer of their late daughter's bedroom was both kind and tempting, but I knew that, whatever else, the hours that I was working would indeed make life there difficult, and deeply unsocial. One evening at a weekend screening at Ray Selfe's, I unburdened myself verbally to Ray and his wife Jean, who then mentioned that they had a spare room in their West Norwood home. It was to have been for their forthcoming child, but Jean had lost the baby in pregnancy. This could be my salvation, but, I thought, not a word to my Dad, just carry on working on *Othello* and see what happens.

What happened was remarkably strange indeed, and I owe a big debt to my fellow co-second assistant editor at the time, Peter Watson. With the hindsight of over fifty years, I can see that what he did was a deliberate kindness, kept secret, but I can see now why he did what he did. Peter lived in Ealing, and every Friday brought into the *Othello* cutting rooms his local weekend paper, to see what films were playing locally, and we discussed them. Ever neat and precise (and therefore perfect for cutting room work), Peter would put the newspaper back in the travel case he carried, and we thought no more of it. But one Friday he left his newspaper on my cutting room bench. Most unlike him. But as I picked it up to give it back to him, I saw that it had been folded open on a specific news page, on a headline – and I can't remember it exactly, which said something like "Streatham Tailor Arrested for Fraud. Ealing Court Verdict." I picked it up, and yup, it was Dad. From what I could gather – and I really can't remember it at all clearly, I must've been in slight shock, and still had cutting room work to do – Dad had been involved in something like fraudulent cheque-passing with a man called Bob Phillips, and they had together conned money out of either a client or customer, or even just a friend, but it was a substantial amount, involving the cashing of a large cheque, and now Dad had been arrested. Apparently he would be bound over, with sentencing to follow. I was stunned, aghast, but it certainly explained a few things, not least of which was that mysterious tape recording that I overheard Dad playing to Mummy about six months before she passed away.

I asked Peter Watson if I could keep the newspaper and he said "Of course". We didn't discuss what he had done. Peter was, and still is, far too gentlemanly and well-bred to have discussed such a thing, but his instinct was absolutely right: I knew nothing about this matter, nothing at all, and yet here I was living with – a criminal! What to do? Well, for a start, just keep on working. But the truth was, I had a choice. With my sister safely ensconced at Forest Gate, I could now either take a room with either Ray and Jean, or with Gerry and Pam, and leave my Dad to his own devices. What about Bruno the dog and Stripey the cat? I didn't know what to do, nor did I know how to move, when to do it, what to take. The only thing I was sure of was that I wouldn't tell Dad I was going, or even where I was going. He had told me nothing, and I sure as hell wasn't about to tell him anything about my intended future whereabouts, whatever they were to be. I did wonder if Auntie Doris and Uncle Don should be told, for Linda's sake, but, coward that I was, I just put off telling them until much later.

And so, in the middle of *Othello*, on a weekend off after the shooting was finished, I enlisted the aid of a friend with a car, and moved in to 127, Thornlaw Road, West Norwood, as Ray and Jean Selfe's new lodger (I found that, in another part of that huge house, there were also other boarders: a very, very old couple who seemed to have come with the house). Ray and Jean were most welcoming, and Jean would cook for me if I let her know if I would be back for supper, and the rent was minimal. But there was a catch, and for me it was a big one: they had no hot running water, so baths were out. In fact, I think the bath itself was used for storage. What to do? Well, that's how you find out who your real friends are. Ray and Jean said I could bring Stripey, the cat, and I managed to put him in a cat-box for transportation, and took him with in the car as well. I had, understandably, but with regret, to leave Bruno behind with Dad. I chose a Saturday because Dad was out on bail, and therefore at work, and not at what was once my home. I was just unscrewing a book stand around about 6.00pm when Dad arrived back. Slightly tipsy, he was aghast, speechless and horrified. I was basically a coward, hoping to be well gone before he returned, but I screwed-up (or did I really want to do it this way, Doctor Freud?). Dad closed the door behind him. "Leave it open," I think I said. He asked me what I was up to, and I told him, but not where I was going or where he could find me. He could call me at Shepperton if he wanted to (he never did). That was it. No "Goodbyes", definitely no hugs, I just went out the door. Now, perhaps I think I should have stayed and offered him some support, perhaps I should have maybe offered help, or some sympathy, or at least discussed the why and wherefore of his problems – I don't know. Those are the questions that have lived with me all of my adult life. I just went, that's all.

Back at Shepperton, *Othello* continued as I have previously described, and, to be brutally honest, I tried not to think about Dad at all. I had a job to do, a difficult journey to make, new relationships to forge, plus now no bathing facilities. I had enough on my plate, more than I could ever imagine. Of course, I eventually had to tell Auntie Doris, who informed my sister. Doris herself didn't seem a bit surprised, but that was a discussion that we never had. I was now effectively paying out regularly, weekly, money to Auntie Doris and

Uncle Don for Linda's upkeep, and now rent to Ray and Jean, not to mention the cost of daily travelling to the studios. I needed another job, and fast.

And then the phone rang. It was someone I'd never met, called Robert Dearberg, who said he'd heard that I was available, and would I like to be his second assistant editor on a film for Hammer that was just returning from a location shoot in the Canary Islands. Tom Simpson was the editor, and he, Bob, was the first assistant. I was excited. I really didn't want to blow it by asking the wrong question. I said "Yes, I'm available. What's the film called?" Bob replied, "*One Million Years B.C.* and can you start Monday week?" Well! Well! Well! Could I? Could I just!!

And so I fetched up at Elstree Studios, the studios of Associated British Picture Corporation, popularly called ABPC, in the very heart of Elstree village, just down the road from MGM up on the hill, where I'd worked on *Where the Spies Are*. MGM, Shepperton, Elstree:-- I was getting around.

The editor I was to work with, under Bob Dearberg as his first, was Tom Simpson, who seemed to me to be a terribly nice man, avuncular and kindly, a far cry from previous editors I had met. He had worked regularly for Hammer, most recently on *The Nanny* with Bette Davis, also with Bob assisting, at Elstree, and, to me, seemed a rather oldy-worldy type of editor. Indeed, Tom's first credits included the 1948 *Anna Karenina* with Vivien Leigh, and the Powell and Pressburger 1949 production *The Small Back Room* (U.S.title: *Hour of Glory*). I was in distinguished company indeed.

One Million Years B.C., directed by Don Chaffey, had just come back from a location shoot in Lanzarote, so there were rushes rolls to sort out. But a selection of takes had already been made by Don and producer Michael Carreras, and, it being a Hammer film, there was no waste, or the luxury of alternate performances. But there was, to me, one totally, unusual aspect to the rushes: – there was no production sound shot. Not just no synchronised sound, but no guide tracks, nor wild tracks either. No sound man on the shoot at all. Ergo, one thing was very clear to me: I wouldn't have to synchronise rushes, unique in features.

So we had a cutting room confab. It seemed that Tom would assemble the film in script order, and then, and I think Tom was dreading it, Hammer's supervising editor Jim Needs would take over and determine the actual cut. (James Needs had been producer Michael Carreras' batman during the war. Some background for editing film!). Bob would effectively look after the mute rushes in order to enable Tom to assemble them, and I would duly file trims, but also look after the incoming newly studio-shot material, and work on the studio floor with a moviola to ensure all studio material matched the location shooting, and also work closely with the special fx team on all the specialised material. But, to my delight, there wasn't exactly a special fx team, just one man: but what a man! None other than the great Ray Harryhausen, the American natural-born heir to *King Kong*'s Willis O'Brien, and creator himself of some of the best animated sequences in cinema ever, using a frame-by-frame hand-animated process that he called "Dynamation". I could hardly wait to meet him, and what a lovely, charming, dignified man Ray turned out to be. We were to work very closely together on *One Million Years B.C.*, and what a pleasure it was. And I was getting paid for this!

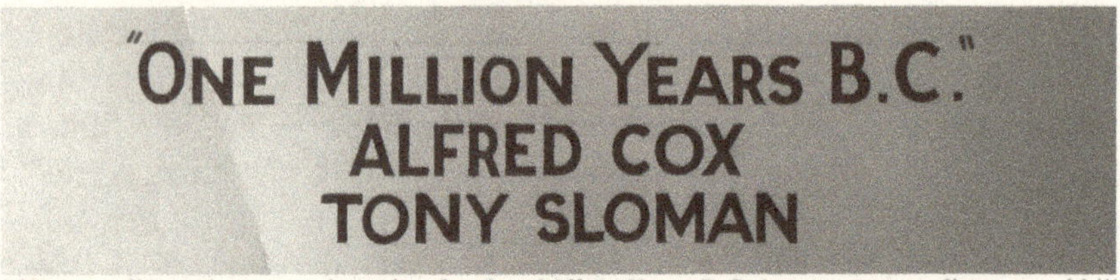

My Elstree studio cutting room door sign for *One Million Years B.C.* As you can see, I'm second billed under sound editor Alfie Cox. It was to be the last time I had second billing.

Still, having a bath was becoming a problem. David Trace explained the issue to his parents, and so I went over to his house one weekend, but I found the whole experience rather embarrassing, though the Traces, really lovely people, didn't seem to mind. I had to think elsewhere. There was Nick, at 8a, Eccleston Street, but there were always so very many people around: it was awkward and embarrassing. And then it dawned on me: the studio itself. And that's what I did – the studio showers once a week (or more if necessary)! Nobody knew, and I suspect if they did, nobody would care.

One Million Years B.C. was exciting to work on in many ways. I spent much of the time on the studio floor with the moviola, showing sequences filmed on location to director Don Chaffey that he had to match with the studio shoot. I thought Don a remarkable man: tall, distinguished with flowing hair and a smart beard and moustache, he seemed to me to have been born out of his time: he would've been secure and happier roistering with Sir Francis Drake and Sir Walter Raleigh at the court of the first Queen Elizabeth, surely. He was a person of extremely good humour, and nothing seemed to faze him: he'd seen it all before. Of course, the atmosphere on set was certainly helped by the fact that none of the actresses actually wore much clothing: you really didn't know where to look!

When Raquel Welch discovered that there was a moviola on set, and therefore she would be able to view herself, she quickly became my new best friend. Not only did she press herself extremely closely to me in my brown suit, but she finally revealed what she was after. She wanted to keep some frames of herself, and could I provide them? "Nobody would mind, would they?", she said, pressing closer to me, in that tiniest of bikinis. (Yes, I did get an erection. Positioned tightly between Raquel and the moviola, this was literally hard work. And she knew it.) I replied that, if she came to me with the producer's permission, of course she could have frames. I was pretty sure Michael Carreras would say "No", as they certainly wouldn't want any unauthorised stills to get out. Raquel, pushing herself so close to me that she was almost on the other side, wouldn't take "No" for an answer, and said she'd see what she could do. I'm sure that she did, and the answer was still

"No". She never asked, nor pressed as close, again. I thought, if that's what she'd do for frames, what exactly did she do to get the part?

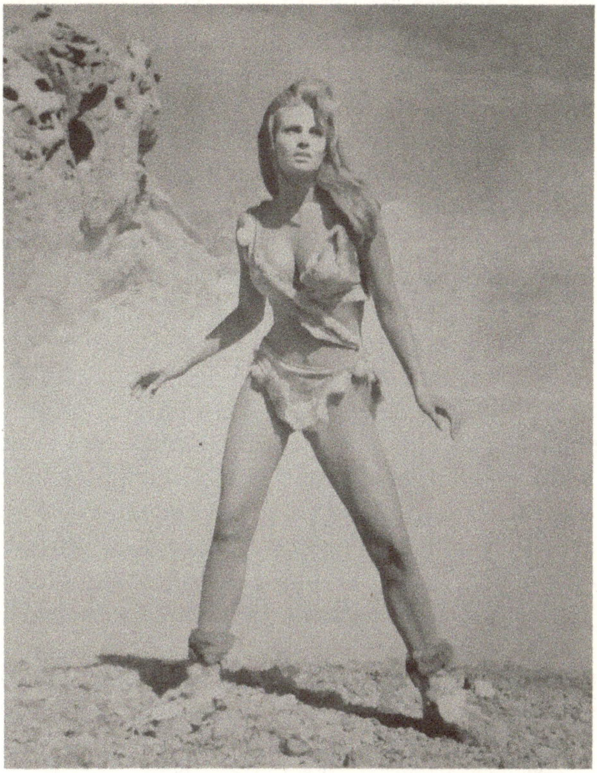

The *One Million Years B.C.* 1965 Christmas card, the first time anybody beheld what was to become that classic still from the shoot that turned the then-unknown Raquel Welch into an internationally world famous pin-up girl.

I learned an awful lot on *One Million Years B.C.* It made me completely forget about not going to film school. What I was learning could never be taught. While Bob Dearberg attended to Tom, the editor, who needed serious attending to daily, I served Tom in quite a different manner. Whatever I was doing around four o'clock, I had to leave the studio and go and get Tom an *Evening Standard* and a bar of chocolate, daily. Protest to Bob was useless: Tom was the Editor, and if that's what he wanted… and so I did, at least until the cut was finished. But this was more than compensated for by my other activities on the movie. I was seconded to the great Ray Harryhausen, and then assigned to take care of all the film's studio screenings, which, of course, were mute, since the film was shot silent, and the dubbing crew couldn't really start until the edit was completed to Hammer's satisfaction. A funny story: I was assigned to show the edit thus far to the designated composer, who turned out to be Mario Nascimbene, the composer from *Where the Spies Are*, who was therefore the only film composer that I knew personally. (He autographed to me the sleeve of my disc of his *The Vikings* main theme.) I was looking forward to meeting him again. Also at the running was Chris Barnes, a Hammer editor who was joining the film to create the sound fx. The running was to be in the main theatre at ABPC. At the appointed time, Mario Nascimbene turned up, and greeted me like a long-lost buddy, and I was very touched. Chris Barnes appeared, and sat next to me in the theatre. I started the show. Now, remember, *One Million Years B.C.* was shot mute. That's awfully, awfully quiet when you run it on a big screen. I'd had a busy weekend, what with taking a bath at Eccleston Street, and dining out subsequently, and promptly fell asleep during the viewing. Chris Barnes woke me up, and handed me a piece of paper which kept me alert throughout the whole rest of the screening. Written on it were just two words: "You snore."

Working with Ray Harryhausen was itself a privilege, and such a nice man. My main function working with him was to be on his own personal soundstage at Elstree with the moviola (as I had previously done on *Othello*) to see where his newly shot material would go into the sequences as cut, and to see how it could improve them wherever possible. Ray needed to see them over and over again and do frame counts before shooting his effects, which he never let me see (the shooting, that is), always sending me outside the stage when he was actually filming: he operated the camera himself, besides doing the physical manipulation of the creatures, and often filmed several times over to achieve the correctness of movement. He didn't let anyone see him do this, ever.

We had some fun, though. One day Ray was working with a live lizard, as opposed to creating the creatures from scratch, and it just fell asleep under the lights. Ray prodded and prodded, but the most it would do would be to roll over and fall asleep. Ray sent me out to the studio canteen to get some green leaves, hopefully to lure the lizard's appetite to make him go into a suitable action. But the lizard again fell, seemingly permanently, asleep. Ray made certain that it wasn't dead, and then sent a message for Michael Carreras, the film's producer, to come down to our set. Michael was busy directing a film on another stage, a film especially written to use again the *One Million Years* production sets. At the time of shooting it was called *Slave Girls*, but it eventually surfaced as, surprise, surprise, *Prehistoric Women*. Ray also called Don Chaffey in for a meeting, and asked me to stay. At the meeting, Ray made it very clear that, if he had to use real animals, he couldn't guarantee not only delivery, but he couldn't even guarantee the material in the required time schedule, and suggested that they drop the whole animated main title sequence intended for *One Million Years B.C.* "And use what, exactly?" said Michael Carreras. Don Chaffey then appeared, summoned from wherever, and said "What about library material?" Michael said that they were unlikely to find anything appropriate, that's why Ray was here, and now even he couldn't seem to be able to meet the Hammer schedule. And then I piped up. I reminded Ray, Michael, and Don of Irwin Allen's *The Sea Around Us* (which I had seen at the Astoria, Streatham, supporting *Dangerous Mission*), which featured the simulated creation of the world, and also the much later follow-up *The Animal World*, on which Ray himself had worked, with a similar sequence. They all just stared at me. Ray spoke first. "Tony's right. That could work. I'll talk to Charlie Schneer (the film's producer) and I'm pretty sure he'll let us use it." And that's what happened. Ray then concentrated on all the rest of our film's special fx, but he did speak to Charles Schneer as well, and the whole of the opening sequence of *One Million Years B.C.* was drawn from material from *The Sea Around Us*. I'm not sure if *The Animal World* was used as well; I think not. I don't want to say here that, uncredited, I saved the day, but I certainly helped Hammer both to save face and keep their budget down. Don Chaffey was pleased, and also I know Ray Harryhausen was happy. Years and years later, when I was elected a Governor of the British Film Institute, I submitted Ray's name for a BFI fellowship, and he was duly awarded one. He said what a great time he had working with me on *One Million Years B.C.* and how grateful he was for my main title sequence suggestion. I, modestly but truthfully, told him how lucky and how privileged I was to work with him. And I really meant it.

There's a slight coda to this story: I was invited, as the elected BFI Governor, to represent the BFI at the celebratory 50th anniversary of *Room at the Top* in Bradford, the town where most of the filming took place. I travelled there by train with the film's cameraman, the great Freddie Francis, and his wife Doreen, who was that film's continuity girl, and co-star Mary Peach, plus director Jack Clayton's widow, *Ben-Hur*'s Haya Harareet. We arrived the night before the screening, and checked in at a chosen hotel. In the morning, I was breakfasting with Freddie and Doreen Francis, when out of the hotel window I spotted Ray Harryhausen, blithely walking towards the Bradford Film Museum, and I pointed him out to Freddie and Doreen. Freddie said that he really admired Ray, and always wanted to meet him, so I rushed out of the hotel breakfast room into the street, and quite, literally, stopped Ray in his tracks. He was surprised to see me, and I told him that I was breakfasting with a great fan of his, Freddie Francis, and would he like to join us? And he did, and it all turned out very pleasantly. So one result of my working with Ray on *One Million Years B.C.* was that I was able to introduce the world's greatest model animator to his fan, one of Britain's finest ever cameramen!

My work on *One Million Years B.C.* was coming to a close, but, after Jim Needs had re-edited the film, and let Tom Simpson go, and it became quite clear that Ray Harryhausen had no further use for my services, such as they were, Jimmy Needs moved me over to help on the dubbing team, mainly to prepare for the 100% vocal soundtrack, writing down and timing all the "dialogue" that would be needed, effectively making me an uncredited dubbing assistant on a second assistant editor's salary. No wonder producer Michael Carreras liked Jim Needs! I was grateful, of course, because working on that particular aspect of film-making – the sound side – had never occurred to me at the time.

I prepared dialogue sheets, and measured the requisite sequences, and prepared cast lists for the sound editors, a very distinguished team of Roy Baker, Alfie Cox and Roy Hyde, whose combined credits would take up far too much space to relate here. All of these veterans were Hammer regulars, and all had one thing in common. To be kind, they were eminently clubbable. In other words, they liked to drink. This conviviality didn't seem to affect their work in the slightest, and I learned another major fact about film technicians: the studio bar was invariably a home from home, at least in those days.

I was pleased to be doing this, because, although there were other assistants, I was given, and was grateful for, quite a heavy workload, and it never, ever occurred to me that I was being exploited. Not only was I preparing the loops to be shot, I was also being entrusted with writing the "dialogue", i.e. a series of grunts and sounds that would match up with the actors' mouth movements, since the film was shot m.o.s. (i.e. "mitout sound", a Hollywood Yiddishism). Also, although producer Michael Carreras had credited himself with writing the screenplay, clearly nobody had written the "dialogue", of which there was none.

Most of the original character names in the script were retained in the post-synchronisation of the dialogue, which is more than can be said of the actors. As far as I know, not one of the actual actors involved in the shoot revoiced themselves. Nikki van der Zyl, a very experienced and talented dubbing artiste, revoiced Raquel Welch, and John Richardson was revoiced by the actor David Graham, perhaps better known today as the voice of *Dr. Who*'s Daleks and most of the *Thunderbirds* characters. Uniquely, since no original sound was recorded during shooting, there was no matching of performance required, and I thought that Nikki and David, who were well-cast by, I think, the dubbing crew, not either the producer or director, did a superb job. All of the voice characters had managed to recreate personalities alluded to in the screenplay, so consistency of performance was easily achievable. Actually, there was one male character who needed revoicing who had no identifiable name, and dialogue editor Alfie Cox asked me to come up with one. I remembered that the 1940 version of *One Million Years B.C.* was produced by Hal Roach, and remembering from my childhood that old "slanguage" called "backslang" ("Pig Latin" in the U.S.A.) that my mother and Auntie Doris used among themselves when they didn't want us children to know what they were discussing, I suggested using backslang, to create the new character name Archoa, which was "Roach" in backslang. And so it came to be. (Bye the bye, an accessible example of backslang can be heard in the "We're in the Money" sequence of *Gold Diggers of 1933*, wherein Ginger Rogers delivers a verse towards the end of the song in authentic Pig Latin.)

Tom Simpson had long gone after Jim Needs' arrival, and Bob Dearberg had taken over the running of the film aspect (as opposed to the sound side) of post-production, and did a superb job of integrating Ray Harryhausen's new material into the cut, supervising the recording of Mario Nascimbene's score and editing it onto the film, and delivering the final print, replete with the new library material, opticals, and both main and end titles. And, as so often happens in the cutting rooms, our intimacy dissipated when the film was over. But Bob Dearberg would, as I would eventually discover, be responsible for securing for me one of the major jobs in my early career, but more of that later. We did see each other socially occasionally: I remember we went to see the then-notorious *Lady in a Cage* together, when it opened in London at the Royalty theatre, converted into a cinema for that very purpose. Banned by the British Board of Film Censors, it received an "X" certificate in London. For what were not yet called film buffs, it was a must-see, and Bob and I really both appreciated Olivia de Havilland being absolutely terrorised in an elevator. We weren't to work together again, but remained good friends. What next?

To be honest, I needed a rest, though holidays weren't in my nature. No freelancer likes to take one, really, unless they have something to go on to. Of course, I had some personal things to sort out, but it wasn't easy to find out what Dad was up to. In the meantime, I saw to it that Linda was secure, and when *Where the Spies Are* played the ABC Forest Gate local, the ABC Upton Park, I invited everyone to come and see it with me: my treat. And so my beloved Nanna, plus a female friend of hers, my sister Linda, and my Auntie Doris and, I think, my cousin Della, all came to see *Spies* with me, on me. They all enjoyed it, but wanted to know why my name wasn't on the credits. I explained that only heads of department were customarily credited (as opposed to nowadays, where everybody seems to be credited), but they all thought that I should have my name on the film; after all, it wouldn't be on the screen without the rushes! I couldn't possibly argue with that.

I decided to look in, after all this while, on Ray's two evening classes, but it soon became quite clear to me that I had outgrown the Monday class. But someone I knew from the Monday class, a waspish dour sophisticate friend of Ray's called Max Burns, was making a film of his own, and was hoping to shoot his own script at Ray's other class, and asked me if I'd like to help with the shoot. I said "Sure", and read the short script he'd written, called *Stones in a Well*, a rather gloomy piece, I thought, largely consisting of inanimate objects remembered, and fantasised over. I was to be the assistant director (to Max), Max would be on camera, and the continuity girl was to be Linda Carpenter who, as far as I knew, used to go out with Ray Selfe's wife Jean's brother, Graham Bottle, and was recovering from the break-up of that affair. We did a couple of days shooting at the Dick Sheppard school in the evenings, and it was clear that Linda and I were hitting it off quite well, both acknowledging that Max needed a lot of looking after. This mutuality of interest bound us closely. Linda was in her young twenties, and extremely bright, and cute, or so I thought, and there was clearly present a welcoming friendliness.

My old schoolmate Nick Nacht, was in Paris again, and, remembering my last visit, invited me over. As we chatted, it occurred to me that if Nick booked a hotel room in a good location, as he did last time, perhaps he could make it a double one, with a double bed, and I might bring a friend. Nick, in his wisdom, said, "Ask her first." So I did. I asked Linda if she'd like to come to Paris with me. No strings, just a week in Paris. She thought about it, and then said "Yes". I, of course, was to pay for everything.

So we did. Nick booked a nice central hotel, and we flew cheaply from Southend Airport, of all places. When we arrived, and signed in, we got to our room and she clocked that it contained a double bed. She explained that she expected two singles, at the very least, or even two connecting rooms, or a suite, or something. But she was here now, and I had no alternative but, guess what, to promise nothing untoward would happen, not even if she wanted it to. Satisfied by this honourable explanation from an ex-public schoolboy, that's what happened. A week in Paris, not even seeing each other nude, sleeping together but apart, pulling away from each other should our bodies touch in the night, not quite what I had expected. Serves me bloody right! But we had a great time, seeing movies, dining with Nick, and prowling the streets. One incident remains in my memory: we visited the Louvre, and looked at everything we could together, but when I turned around at one moment Linda wasn't there. I searched through that particular gallery, and couldn't see her anywhere. I waited and waited, and, truly didn't know what to do. Her French wasn't good (neither was mine!), and time was going by very slowly. Eventually, I decided to speak to an attendant:--

Me: "Pardonnez-moi, Monsieur, mais j'ai perdue ma petite femme quelque place ici."

Attendant: "Quoi?" I tried to repeat myself, and had the distinct impression that he thought I was a mad, or at least a totally irrelevant, Englishman.

Attendant: "Quelle age?"

Me: "Possiblement vingt-et-une."

Attendant: "Sans blague! Vingt-et-une?" And he threw his hands up in the air and walked away, clearly suggesting to me that the twenty-one-year-old girl in question was displaying nothing but good sense in leaving this particular loony English lad on his own in the Louvre. So I left, and went back to the hotel, distrait. However, when I got back, there was Linda, lying on the bed reading a guide book. "What happened?" "Oh, I'd just had enough." So had I. After we returned to London, I never saw her again.

When I got back to Ray and Jean's, something had happened. Apparently my cat, Stripey, had got out and run away. There was nothing I could do. Although Jean had kindly said that she would look after her and change the litter tray in the week I was away, it really was my fault, I knew, for trying to have a "dirty week" in Paris. Fate had once again taught me a sad, tough lesson. I just hoped that Bruno, our dog, was safe with Dad, so I walked down the hill towards Streatham High Road the next Sunday to see if Dad was in, and ran into Bruno, or rather it was the other way around, on the corner where our block of flats was situated. Bruno was clearly glad to see me, but what on earth was he doing outside the flat on his own in the street? I made a fuss of him, and took him inside and upstairs. But my flat key didn't work in the lock any more. I could do nothing but leave Bruno outside the flat. At least he was inside the building. I never saw him again.

When I was working at Shepperton I had bought an old 16mm. projector from one of the theatre projectionists there, and now I had it set up in my bedroom at Ray and Jean's, and Ray let me run 16mm. films that he either had borrowed or owned as long as I didn't disturb anybody. I was running *The Old Man and the Sea*, when Ray knocked on my door one evening and said that there was a telephone call for me. To my great surprise, it was Tom Simpson, the editor from *One Million Years B.C.*, phoning to see if I was available to come and assist him on two pictures that he was editing consecutively, at Merton Park Studios. He was sorry to be offering me the second assistant's position, because he had Ernie Grimsdale as his first, but he would like me to join him. Was I a) free and b) interested? "Not half!", I nearly said – merely, "Yes. Thank you. I'd be very pleased to do it. Starting when?" "Monday week" was the answer, and so I eventually fetched up at the venerable Merton Park Studios, home of those Edgar Lustgarten and Edgar Wallace supporting features, to work on *The Frozen Dead* and *The Curse of the Golem* (later retitled, so imaginatively, *It!*) on the duly appointed Monday, very happy that Merton Park was located in South London, not that far from where I was living in West Norwood. Couldn't be better.

But I certainly wasn't ready for what happened when I arrived. I joined Tom and Ernie in the cutting room block, but not exactly in our designated cutting room. Apparently, Merton Park already had an extant permanent team of staff editors, and they hadn't been instructed to leave, nor given notice, fully expecting to work on our incoming pictures. It seemed that they (Derek Holding, Brian Blamey, Roy Norman and Tony Bray – two very distinguished editors, picture and sound, and their two highly experienced assistants) anticipated that they were going to work on these two new films, although neither of them were actually Merton Park productions, and, quite simply, they wouldn't leave their cutting rooms. Oh.

Tom Simpson, a genuinely patient man at the best of times, said to Ernie and I that perhaps we'd better go and have a cup of coffee in the café over the road while things got sorted out. And so we did. Tom told us, when he eventually joined us, that the crew of four had, in fact, been given their notice, but they'd thought their own jobs were permanent, and that the notice didn't apply to them, apparently. The local shop steward was called in, and the union ruled that, despite their long-term working relationships with Merton Park Productions, this no longer applied to the two new films, which were Seven Arts features, on which the three of us (Tom, Ernie and myself) already had existing contracts by way of our letters of engagement: the four must go therefore, and make room for us. Which they did that day, making a very long day of their leaving, by way of which I got to know all four of them quite well, and eventually was able in the future to hire Derek Holding, who by that time had acquired his rightful reputation as the best post-sync. fitter in the industry, if not the world, as my dialogue editor on *The Company of Wolves*, but that's another story for another time.

The Frozen Dead and *It!*. Well, for a start, I was excited (and hope I didn't show it) because both films starred Hollywood veterans, Dana Andrews in the former, and Roddy McDowall in the latter. If nothing else, I hoped I would get some good Hollywood stories, and I was really pleased to be working at Merton Park Studios. After MGM at Borehamwood, ABPC at Elstree, and Shepperton Studios themselves, Merton Park might seem to be small fry, but to me it was one of the great classic British studios, leaving only Pinewood and Bray at which I hadn't yet worked. But the time would come when I soon would work at both. I never ever quite realised then how fortunate I was.

The Frozen Dead started shooting on the Monday morning that we arrived, and after sorting out the personnel problems that I've described, by Tuesday we were well ensconced and ready for the first batch of rushes. Although filmed in colour, the rushes were printed and delivered in black-and-white for economy, a quite common practice then, but this was the first time that I had ever come across it. What can I say about *The Frozen Dead*, a film about a post-war group of Nazis being resuscitated in England to carry on with Hitler's philosophy? It truly was as awful as it sounds, but I did get to meet, and talk with, Hollywood star Dana Andrews, who was, we understood, still struggling with a drink problem, although you would never guess it behind the semi-Germanic accent he assumed to play Doctor Norberg, the scientist who could preserve the brains of key dead Nazis, and build a future Master Race. The writer-director of this nonsense was one Herbert J. Leder, a gentleman who had made a couple of earlier cheapish horror films, and who would end up teaching film at Jersey City's State College Media Arts Department. Well, you know the old saying: those who can, do; those who can't, teach. If he is remembered at all today, it's probably for directing *Pretty Boy Floyd* starring John Ericson, which was awful, back in 1960.

But I can't say that *The Frozen Dead* wasn't fun to work on, except for one terrible day when I, personally, was responsible for stopping Dana Andrews (*Laura*, *The Best Years of Our Lives*, *Where the Sidewalk Ends*), a major star of my childhood (*Duel in the Jungle*, *Strange Lady in Town*, *Night of the Demon*), from being able to complete recording his post-synchronisation, or, as the Americans say, "looping", in the one day booked for him to do so.

Well, you see, I had been earning decent money with some regularity for a while, and had taken to betting on the two major British horse races, the Derby and the Grand National (a habit I probably inherited from my Father, although, as I have already stated, it was my Grandfather who took me dog-racing, where I actually learned about betting). Merton Park Studios were right next to a betting shop, and so, the lunchtime of Dana Andrews' post-sync., I put a bet on a horse in the Grand National, which was taking place that particular Saturday. I didn't know racing form, so I just chose a horse's name that I liked, and placed my bet. I can't remember the name of the horse I bet on, but it was a hundred-to-one outsider, and, amazingly, a pile-up on the course enabled my horse to win! I knew that the projectionists would know the result, and when they informed me I was flabbergasted. I ran back into the theatre, and told everybody (well, just star Dana Andrews and sound editor Jim Roddan) that I had won the Grand National and that I would like to buy everyone a drink, including the projectionists. Jim said, "O.K.", and off I went to the pub, "The Old Leather Bottle", that was adjacent to the studio. I didn't waste theatre time in asking everyone what they would like. I just said to the bartender "Five of the very best, please. I've just won the National, and have one for yourself." And that's what happened. So I went back into the theatre, and waited for a break in looping, and then took in my tray, and offered everyone a drink. What didn't I know? Well, for a start I didn't know that Dana Andrews had just returned from an alcoholics admission programme in Europe and was absolutely not to partake of any alcohol whatsoever, not just for fear of breaking his cure, but for fear of what may happen to him if he so much as even takes a sip of alcohol. But he took the proffered glass, and he and Jim toasted my win.

And then Dana collapsed. Into a heap, onto the floor, spilling his drink in the process, the very least of my worries. Jim Roddan, no mean drinker himself, recognised the symptoms. He and I helped Dana to a couch, and Jim loosened Dana's tie and opened his shirt. He then, in lieu of a newspaper, waved the dialogue sheets over Dana, and after a few seconds (although to me it felt like fifty years), Dana came round. He had trouble speaking. (At a post-sync. session!!!) He managed to half-whisper; "My cure. It only takes a sip…" And then he collapsed back onto the couch, fast asleep. I didn't know what to do. I felt that my stomach had fallen out of my body, and that, obviously, I would be fired. Thank goodness the director wasn't there. But Jim was professional calmness personified. He merely said, "Check if the theatre's free on Monday."

The theatre was free on the coming Monday, and we re-booked it, making sure with the production office that Dana wasn't needed for shooting. He was only down for filming in the early morning, so we re-booked the theatre for the afternoon. Eventually, Dana came round. He couldn't have been nicer. He explained that they had told him at the clinic what just a whiff of alcohol would do to him, and he hadn't yet had a chance to test if they were right. He then actually thanked me for giving him the chance to see that, in fact, they were right, and could we continue whenever he would be available? We told him that we had already booked the theatre for that coming Monday afternoon, and he was pleased, and asked us to please not to tell anyone what had happened, especially not our director Herbert J. Leder. And we never did. And, boy, did I go home chastened. Wealthy, but chastened. I never bet on a race ever again while working on a picture. Would you?

The filming of *The Frozen Dead* was immediately succeeded by the instant commencement of shooting on *It!*. As soon as the last shot of *Dead* was in the can, the same crew, same editing crew, same studio technicians, moved directly onto *It*!, except for Tom Simpson, who, of course, was still editing *The Frozen Dead*, so former Merton Park editor (remember that first Monday?) Derek Holding was brought in to edit *It!*, and boy, was he fast! I'd never seen editing like that before: no re-edits, the first cut was the director's approved one, and the one that we dubbed to, and eventually the one that was released, (but rushes were, again, in black-and-white although the film was shot in colour). Incidentally, both *The Frozen Dead* and *It!* were actually released cinematically only in black-and-white in America, and didn't appear in colour over there until their eventual domestic availability in VHS and, eventually, DVD. (Thought you'd like to know!)

The leading man of *It!* was Hollywood veteran Roddy McDowall, MGM's young star of *Lassie Come Home* and John Ford's *How Green Was My Valley*, latterly respected as a world-famous stills photographer, and confidence-keeper of most of the major stars, mostly notably, at the time, Elizabeth Taylor. He was also, vouchsafed exclusively to me by none other than Mel Tormé, known in Hollywood as a world-famous secret collector of motion picture films, as indeed was Mel, and had a fine hoard of 16mm. (for which, alas, he was eventually busted). Also, as a piece of trivia, Roddy McDowall was born in England, and I passed, unknowingly, his Herne Hill birthplace on my daily bus journey to Dulwich College.

It! turned out to be truly appalling also, a fit companion to *The Frozen Dead*. But I got to know, and work with, Derek Holding as well as Jim Roddan, and helped out in what was to become a regular cinematic procedure of mine: the locating of library material. The prologue to either *Frozen Dead* or *It!* (I can't remember which) needed a shot of war-torn London in colour, and rather than go through miles of library footage, I mentioned to Jim Roddan the 20th Century-Fox CinemaScope feature, *D-Day the Sixth of June*, which I had never seen, which possibly held appropriate material, and Jim, bless him, said, "Get it in – we'll have a look at it." And so we did, in a comfortable theatre with appropriate alcoholic refreshment, not just the opening, but the whole film! I liked this game.

I'd just also like to record here, quite literally, just for the record, my very first sighting of Roddy McDowall. We – the cutting crew – had gotten used to eating breakfast, before daily shooting commenced, in a transport café directly opposite the studio. It was a regular British fry-up breakfast: egg, sausage, bacon, chips, beans, toast and all the trimmings. I thought it was great, mainly because it meant I didn't have to make breakfast before I left for the studio. I was eating this standard British breakfast when Jim Roddan nudged my arm, and indicated to look up at the front door of the cafe, where there stood an absolutely horrified Roddy McDowall, staring into the cafe and the food on our plates with a total look of incredulity on his face that bespoke "Has it all come down to this?" or, more rather, "After all those years in Hollywood, why the fuck am I here?" Either way, he was a perfect picture, as he turned around and left the entrance, unbreakfasted, clearly facially aware of what he and his career had seemingly sunk to. I'll never forget that look.

Nor will I forget what else Roddy did on arrival. The film's co-star was to be Jane Griffiths, who I saw as long ago as 1954 as Gregory Peck's leading lady in *The Million Pound Note* at the Streatham Astoria, but Roddy McDowall immediately objected to what I understood to be her "bodily aroma", or so it was reported to us. So she was swiftly removed just before the start of shooting, and replaced by Jill Haworth, the English girl who had created the role of Sally Bowles in the hit Broadway show *Cabaret*, and had made three movies for Otto Preminger, including playing Karen in *Exodus*. She and I were the same age, and *It*! was to be the first of three minor horror films that precipitated her decline until her death at age 65. Jane Griffiths, however, died only nine years later at the tragically early age of 45.

Post-synchronising with Roddy McDowall was an absolute pleasure, and it was only after working with him that I learned why he was considered one of the very best in the business. He really was a "see it, do it" artiste: a veritable slew of first takes. The results, shot without the director present, were absolutely flawless, and barely needed fitting. (No, he didn't want to have lunch with Jim and I. Who could blame him?) I've seldom seen anyone so fast, so good, so professional. Roddy may have felt at the time that his career would be virtually finished after *It!* coming, as he was, from a major Broadway stage success in *Compulsion*, but his next film role after *It!* was playing Cornelius in *Planet of the Apes*, and the rest is history (three sequels and one television series). I often wondered if such a stickler as Roddy minded that his name was misspelt in the credits for *It!* as Roddy MacDowall, instead of Roddy McDowall. I just bet he really hoped that nobody he knew would ever see it (or, even, *It!*).

But I can't leave the production of that infamous Herbert J. Leder double bill without mentioning a few other odds and sods. First of all, that dislocated (literally!) head in *The Frozen Dead*, Kathleen Breck, wouldn't go on a date with me, and who can blame her, I hear you think, not to mention the sheer impertinence of a second assistant trying to date a star. Well, if not exactly a star, at least an asterisk. (Old movie joke.) What I didn't know was, that after (or perhaps before) she was cast in *West 11*, she had had a "relationship" with that film's director, Michael Winner, and that might have accounted for her non-fraternization attitude. Or maybe not. After all, she did receive top billing in *West 11*, and now she was playing a disembodied head.

I also learned to keep my mouth shut on set forever during The *Frozen Dead*. As second assistant, one of my chores was to collect the previous day's continuity sheets from the set, and one day during the shoot on set I found myself standing next to assistant director Doug Hermes, a stern-faced veteran from the old school, and we were chatting, and I remarked to him about the shot in question, saying something like "Wouldn't it be better if… (I forget what)?" He said, "You really think so?" Not being at all aware of any irony, or of being "sent up", I replied, "Yes." "Well," said Doug, "You'd better tell the director." Herbie Leder was standing next to Doug, who said, before I could stop him, "Tony thinks it would be better the other way round." Herbie couldn't believe his ears. He just blew his top. I can't recall the exact actual dialogue, but it was on the lines of "Who do you think you are? I'll have you taken off the picture..." etc. etc. I caught Doug smiling: he knew exactly what he'd done: he'd taught me a lesson. Later, Tom Simpson told me that associate producer Tom Sachs had reported the incident to him, and to warn me never to speak to the director on the set ever again, or else. I was well-and-truly warned.

Dana Andrews, however, had become someone with whom I had achieved a new intimacy, after the post-sync. theatre incident. He clearly didn't want any kind of relationship with either his co-stars or fellow technicians, and was friendly and pleased to see me whenever we bumped into each other in that very small studio, and when we did after a couple of occasions, he offered me a lift back into London with him in his supplied limousine. I accepted, and was dropped off close to Eccleston Street, as Dana was staying at a nearby hotel. He also let me sit with him in the back seat (unlike David Niven!) So we chatted about the movies, and eventually I asked him if he had a favourite amongst his films, and he said, "Yes. *Three Hours to Kill"* Well, I thought I knew movies, but I'd never, ever heard of that one. Now remember, this was a real film star, an actor who'd worked with Ford, Hawks, Hitchcock, Wyler, Kazan, Renoir, Milestone, Otto Preminger, and heaven knows who else. He even sang in the most popular version of *State Fair*. So what was *Three Hours to Kill*? And why was that particular film Dana Andrews' favourite?

I paused too long. "Never heard of it, have you?" he said. I replied with honesty, "Frankly, no, Dana. Why is it your favourite?" "Well," he said, "it was because of the producer, Harry Joe Brown. He'd provided me with two lovely leading ladies" (for the record, Donna Reed and Dianne Foster) "and a great location, but he was running out of money, and could barely finish the film. He asked my agent if he could defer my last two payments, and, of course my agent said 'No', and threatened to withdraw my services in mid-shoot, at least that's what he told me. Now I knew Harry Joe Brown had a collection of primeval Mexican artefacts, so I said I'd take a few of those as payment now, and I'd finish the film for him. So that's what happened, and over the years those artefacts greatly increased in value, and now they're worth about..." And he paused for effect. What an actor! "...two hundred and fifty thousand dollars. So that's why *Three Hours to Kill* is my favourite movie — those artefacts just keep on increasing in value".

The Frozen Dead and *It!* double-bill didn't actually get a wide London release, but it did pop up at the independent Old Kent Road Astoria, a cinema I had never previously visited. I like to see everything I work on in a public cinema, but this for me was an especial treat; after all, I had only seen the two films in black-and-white workprints, never in colour, let alone finished and with an audience. I invited my sister – my plan then was to take her to see each film that I had worked on.. We fetched up in the rather unsavoury Old Kent Road for the double bill. There was no getting away from it: although nowadays the two films have a rough period charm, you could argue, back then, when they came out, that they were crap. Linda wondered why I didn't tell her such and I feebly replied you never know when you work on them. I never took her to see anything I worked on again. Oh, and incidentally, a brand-new recently published current allegedly complete history book on Merton Park Studios totally neglects to mention the last two theatrical features to ever film there, which were, of course, *The Frozen Dead* and *It!*.

Out of work, it was time to catch up with my personal life. Dad had been sent to Pentonville jail, a holding prison prior to being moved to Ford Open Prison. I couldn't see him while I was working at Merton Park studios, largely because we were working overtime at weekends, but, truly, that was just my excuse. I really didn't want to see him at all: he had told me nothing of what he was up to, nothing of the trial and sentence, and clearly wasn't the least interested in how I felt, or what was happening to me, but at least Linda was safe and secure with Auntie Doris and Uncle Don, and that's what really mattered. I was making out okay at Ray and Jean's: it wasn't ideal but they were good to me, and I had a back-up of my good ex-Dulwich mates, Nick, David, Tim, Paul, Gerry, and Bruce Elliot, a year younger than us, but a good friend, and Jewish, too. Girlfriends? They came and went – I was arrogant, selfish, movie-obsessed, and, perhaps, just perhaps, not very good company at the best of times.

I remember one time taking a friend of Nick Nacht's, a very nice Hendon-based Jewish girl called Ruth, to an evening screening at the Arts Lab. Well, not exactly an evening, actually an all-nighter, four films shown consecutively in the basement arena, no chairs, just sitting on the floor on hippy rugs. Perhaps not the ideal first date for a guy and a girl? You'd be right. It was kind of O.K. during the first two films, but I decided to get "fresh", as the Americans say, during the third film, *The Caine Mutiny*, which I'd already seen on release. Ruth played along to start with, but then she decided she'd rather watch the film. So we did. I forget what the fourth film was, but we emerged into the Drury Lane dawn, a little bleary-eyed. I took her back to her Hampstead home, depositing her at about eight in the morning. We never dated again. I fetched up at Eccleston Street and told Nick all about my evening: it was too far, and I was too tired, to go back to West Norwood.

The sixties had become a great cultural period for what *Time* magazine called "Swinging London", and, to me, Eccleston Street was a superbly-sited base from which to explore it, being located at the very end of the King's Road itself. With Nick and the gang I frequented the Arts Lab, Drury Lane, of course, plus the National Film Theatre, the Starlight Cinema Club in the Mayfair hotel, the Roundhouse (where I saw Jefferson Airplane plus The Doors with Jim Morrison, in one terrific evening), and as many cinemas and West End theatres as I could manage to visit, not to mention all those private Ray Selfe screenings, where I met many future film critics and film historians. I was in my element, but without a regular girlfriend, although I enjoyed good company with Jennie and her flatmates such as her cousin Helen (we saw *Zorba the Greek* together) and friends like the delightful Marie-Jeanne, plus various relatives and associates, and I also happened to meet up with several other unemployed British film technicians of both sexes for, invariably, very long (and often very drunken) Soho lunches.

My closeness with Nick and Jennie led me to become friendly with the rest of 8a, Eccleston Street, and I was surprised to find that the lease of the Victoria flat was held by a former captain of Dulwich College, John Whitmarsh-Knight no less, who was a Dulwich contemporary of Nick's brother, Andy. John was very amiable, although older than me, and we got on well. He was working in the City, but wanted to be a screenwriter, no less, and had written a screenplay from a Georgette Heyer novel about Charles II called *Royal Escape*. I didn't tell him, but I happened to know that Val Guest, with whom I worked on *Where the Spies Are*, had been trying to set up a film of that same novel for some time, presumably from his own screenplay. I was certainly curious enough to ask to read John's version, and he loaned it to me. I hadn't realised that, at the time, we seemed to have bonded. John asked me about where I was living, and I told him my tale, most of which he'd known already from Nick. I'd been sleeping on the couch at 8a, Eccleston Street occasionally, and John asked me if I'd like to move in. I won't say it hadn't occurred to me, but I wasn't sure. He said to think about it. When did he want to know by? I asked. "When you're ready," he replied. I discussed it with Nick and Jennie, and they thought it a good idea. The other flatmate, Rick, was indifferent: he had a regular girlfriend called Cindy and spent much of his time with her. Well, now, this could be a real turn-up for the books: Ray and Jean had been kindness itself, but there had been certain limitations, some of them unspoken. It was quite clear that the bathroom issue would be resolved, if nothing else, and I would never again share the experience of helping to get the old couple in the other spare room hospitalized, as I once did, when the old man collapsed and wet his trousers. (It was a mild heart attack.) Also, it would free me from the obligations of Jean cooking for me, and/or letting her know when that wouldn't be necessary. I'd lose instant upstairs cinema access, but that was an unexpected bonus anyway. So it all came down to rent, and it seems I could afford it, at least for now. Could the others at 8a put up with my awkward hours? John said they didn't care, to just come and go as I pleased: there were no rules. It didn't take me long to make up my mind. I wasn't working at that moment, and that made it a good time to move.

I asked Ray and Jean if they'd mind, and how much notice would they require. To my surprise, Ray and Jean were happy for me to go, (I guess relieved might have been a better word, but it never occurred to me at the time!) and said whenever I liked, and that Ray would help me move, so a weekend would be best. And so I moved into 8a, Eccleston Street, with four flatmates at the time: John, Jennie, Jennie's cousin Helen, and Rick Homfray, who wasn't always there. It was a tight fit, but it seemed to work. And, by thunder, it was bloody central, and thus I seemed to have grown up at last, and so I said "Goodbye" to Streatham forever.

Just before I vacated Ray and Jean's I received a telephone call from one Bernard Williams, a man that I didn't know, who turned out to be the production manager on a brand-new television series that had just started filming at the MGM Studios, Borehamwood, after a location shoot in Wales, and apparently, I had been recommended to him for work on it. He didn't tell me in what capacity I would be employed, only that it was a newly-created editorial position on a television series, and was I free and was I interested? Well, having just moved into 8a, with a need to contribute to a new tariff of shared rent and rates, it couldn't have come at a better time. "Yes, of course," I said to him, and he then said that he'd like me to come down to MGM and meet up with the director Don Chaffey, who he believed I knew (Did I heck? We got on famously on *One Million Years B.C.*), and also to meet with the show's producer and star, Patrick McGoohan. I said "Yes, of course", once more, and we made a date to meet at the studio the next Monday morning. To tell the truth, I was quite excited and extremely flattered, although I hadn't got the job yet. But who wouldn't be? They had actually asked for me.

But it was television. I hated television, and all that it seemed to stand for. The sheer banality of content, the overall lack of both quality and showmanship, the inevitable catering for the dumbest of audiences. I was a film person through and through. I loved cinema, its history, its talent, everything about it! When I worked last at Elstree there were shows like *The Saint*, *The Baron*, and *Randall and Hopkirk (Deceased)* in production there, and when I was working at MGM Patrick McGoohan as *Danger Man* (*Secret Agent* in the U.S.) was shooting, and I had absolutely no interest in any of them. (Apart from acquiring *Baron* star Steve Forrest's autograph on a studio still of him in *Flaming Star*, acting with Elvis. Most unprofessional of me, I know.) I really did not want anything to do with television, not at least in those days, when the film industry itself in Britain was booming. But I did ask Bernie Williams, what was the name of this show? He replied: "It's called *The Prisoner*".

-----END OF REEL THREE-----

REEL FOUR

It certainly felt good to be going back to the MGM Studios in Borehamwood that October. I had very fond professional memories of *Where the Spies Are*. *Spies* was a very important film for me in my early, formative career, and returning to those studios felt a little bit like going back home, which I was never again able to do in my own real life.

I arrived that autumn day at the formidable building that housed the MGM studio gate, and I enquired at the front desk for Bernard Williams. I was told that I was expected, and that he would come down and show me where to go. "I'll take you on to the stage to meet Pat and Don," said Bernie, who was much younger than I had imagined, and, with that, we went onto the large MGM stage where *The Prisoner* episode entitled "Dance of the Dead" had paused between takes. On our way through the stage we bypassed a strange sight: what seemed to be a row of connecting metallic office drawers, which on closer inspection turned out to be a matte painting, with only the central stack of drawers being actually real, which I would later recognise as a key image used in the opening montage of every *Prisoner* episode, where the word "Resigned" was overlaid onto a portrait photograph of Patrick McGoohan. When we reached the actual huge main set itself (which I eventually found out was the control room of No.2) it was like nothing that I had ever seen before, certainly not for television, a vast open space with sliding doorways within it, almost a template for a science fiction movie set, which, in fact, as I discovered eventually, had been a suggestion for the original design.

I could see the extremely tall and distinguished Patrick McGoohan in the near distance, and Bernie then left me alone and went off to find Don Chaffey. He returned with Don, and also with Patrick, having collected him en route, and Bernie seemed to be dwarfed by having each one either side of him, almost a comic trio. Don grabbed me and hugged me by way of greeting, prompting Bernie to say, "I see you know each other," even though he must have already known that we'd both worked together on *One Million Years B.C.* Don then introduced me to Patrick McGoohan, who, I swear, seemed to be the tallest man that I had ever met. By way of introduction, Don said of me: "He knows everything. He never forgets a frame." And Pat then said, "So you never forget a film?" I said, "I think Don said I never forget a frame," to which Pat replied, "Ah, argumentative at the start, are you? Do you see a lot of films?" (This clearly was not going to be the usual job interview.) I said, "Yes." McGoohan said, "What did you last see?"

I told him the truth, that yesterday (Sunday) I had seen a great double-bill at a London Tottenham Court Road cinema, François Truffaut's *Shoot the Pianist* (*Tirez sur le Pianiste*), and Vittorio de Sica's *Il Tetto* (*The Roof*). Pat threw his head back, laughed, and said to Chaffey, "This is the guy for me, Don!" and they both laughed together. Pat was obviously pleased and happy to hear this, but for the life of me I thought that was rather an over-reaction. Pat asked me, "What did you think?" I replied on the lines that I thought that *Il Tetto* was an absolute masterpiece, and that *Shoot the Pianist* had been overrated, and Pat slapped me on the back – which nearly landed me on the studio floor – and said, "Well, I haven't got the time to discuss this now. Don, talk to Bernie." (As a matter of historical interest, I only discovered in a recent Roger Langley tribute to Patrick McGoohan, that de Sica's *Il Tetto* was one of Pat's favourite films of all time. I had seen it almost by chance the day before my interview, with my afore-mentioned cousin Michael, on a trip up to the West End, because sitting through a good double-bill programme rather than just a single feature meant that I wouldn't have to chat too much, or listen to Michael, so I talked him into seeing that particular double bill of Truffaut's second only feature, and the new picture from the master-director of *Bicycle Thieves*, both of which I really wanted to see anyway, and since Michael wanted to come "up West" and visit with me, he agreed to my choice of programme.)

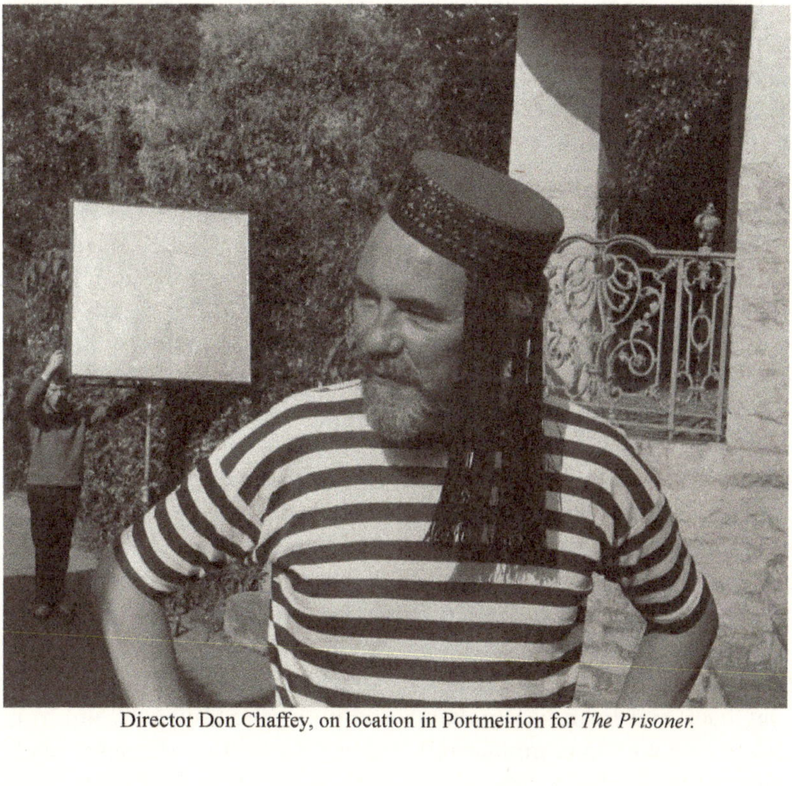

Director Don Chaffey, on location in Portmeirion for *The Prisoner.*

Don Chaffey, after Patrick left us, was approached by the veteran Scottish actor Duncan MacRae, who, to my utter amazement, was camping it up in his canopied costume, and Don joined him, with a wink at me. I had no idea that Duncan was so outrageously gay, having seen him recently on screen as the stern father in *The Kidnappers* (*The Little Kidnappers* in the U.S.), but Don kept his own fake butch camping down to the minimum, impressive though it was, and winked again at me, and said "See you later," and left with Duncan.

I still didn't know what the job was. They had a full cutting room count, and their music editor turned out to be none other than my old friend and colleague Bob Dearberg, who was Tom Simpson's first assistant on *One Million Years B.C.* (directed by Don Chaffey), when I was the second. Could he have been the one who recommended me? I suspected as much, but I never, ever found out, because the very week of my own interview Bob had left his job on *The Prisoner* on account of being offered an actual cutting position: to be the film editor on *The Darwin Adventure*, produced by the distinguished coupling of Irving Lerner and Joseph Strick, a very major career boost for Robert C. Dearberg, so I didn't get to see him again for some time, and I never ever got around to asking Bob if it was, in fact, he who recommended me for *The Prisoner*, although to this day I suspect it was probably a combination of both Bob and Don Chaffey. And I still didn't know what the job entailed…

I arrived in Bernard Williams' office to discuss start dates and, more importantly, money, whatever the job itself was. I went up to Bernie's office to find that the news had already been relayed to him of my being approved, and I met the series co-producer David Tomblin, with Bernie. "What happened?" said Bernie, as if he didn't know. "I think they want me to start as soon as possible," I said. "Can you start on Monday?" asked Bernie. "Yes," I said, not wanting to ask what exactly was the job, but I knew I had to do so.

"What exactly am I being hired as, Bernie?" I asked. I couldn't go on not knowing. "Oh," said Bernie, "didn't they tell you? Film Librarian. In charge of getting all the back projections so far filmed ready for the set, finding library material where it's needed, shooting inserts where required, and matching new stuff to the location shoot where necessary." I tried to take it all in. I think I came up with "Oh…" "And," continued Bernie, "if it doesn't exist, you get it shot. Can you start next Monday?" Of course my answer was affirmative. Now, it only remained to discuss money, for what, as far as I knew, was a non-union, non-guild position. Where on earth did I stand? I wanted the job, of course, but I knew better than to show that to Bernie. They had sent for me, remember. I certainly wasn't going to beg. (At least, that's what I hoped to convey. I also didn't want to talk myself out of the job!). And I was accruing considerable financial expenses: rent at 8a, Eccleston Street, weekly support for Linda to Auntie Doris, and now that bloody journey again every day back and forth to Borehamwood by public transport, not to mention meals, etc. Not that I'm complaining! But just remember, if you're reading this today, that inflation has greatly taken its toll since 1965, and these figures that I'm about to mention might seem ridiculously low now, but in 1965 the average earnings, and therefore the concomitant spending powers, were far less than today's rates.

Now, Bernie Williams was very young for a production manager. He was very well connected in the film industry, being married at the time to Valerie, formerly Norman, sister of broadcaster and film commentator Barry Norman, and therefore also daughter of producer-director Leslie Norman, of the Wardour Street Normans, the suppliers of, amongst many other things, film cutting room equipment. I knew Valerie Williams, of course, when she was the production secretary on *Where the Spies Are*, and now I was having to make a deal with her husband. But remember, on *Where the Spies Are*, as second assistant editor, I was being paid thirteen pounds ten shillings a week, plus overtime, and I'd done a couple of features since then. Bernie Williams offered me sixteen quid a week. I wasn't too happy. They (Pat and Don) clearly wanted me, but I was a snob. I really didn't want to do telly. I made a counter-offer, and thought that if Bernie said "No" then I'm not doing it – there'll be another feature film coming along someday. And also this particular job – librarian – is a non-job. Being a film librarian isn't going to lead to another film librarian job because there ain't one. They just don't exist. Bernie clocked my non-reply. "I'll tell you what I'll do, Tone," ("Tone", he called me!!) "We'll pay you twenty-five, but not yet. If you manage to stay with us, if you're still with us in a month's time after working with Pat McGoohan and Don Chaffey – well, then we'll pay you twenty-five. But right now it's sixteen."

Very canny. We were both roughly the same age, I was only twenty-one, Bernie was twenty-four, the youngest production manager in the business. Patrick McGoohan knew exactly what he was doing: it showed in the art direction, the costumes, the artistes. The sixties were the decade when youth ruled, and Pat wanted to be part of it, forever, and time has proven him right, and wise beyond any normal measure. Bernie and I shook hands. I started the following Monday, arriving to find I had a cutting room allocated to me on the main MGM cutting block, next to the show's editors, Geoff Foot, best known for his work with David Lean, and Lee Doig, a nice man whose background, unsurprisingly, included twenty-one episodes of Patrick McGoohan's popular British television series *Danger Man*, and who began his early career as second assistant editor on the classic *Black Narcissus*. I admired Geoffrey Foot immensely, and when he died at the age of 95 in 2010 I was truly honoured to be asked to write his obituary for *The Independent* newspaper.

Both Lee and Geoff worked together on the first episode of *The Prisoner*, entitled "Arrival". Unsupervised, I reckoned that my first task was to read all available scripts, especially those shooting or about to be filmed, and then to view the edit of "Arrival", not only to get a flavour of the series, but to see what were the immediate needs. They were filming the episode entitled "Dance of the Dead" at the time. I also asked to view any episode that was complete, and Geoff and his assistant Eric Mival told me that, in fact, not one actual episode was yet finished. All of the material that was filmed in The Village, as the Portmeirion location was called, was being assembled, and I could view the first episode, which would make sense, because there was an intended chronological series order. Also, since Bob Dearberg had now left, this would be Eric Mival's last week at being Geoff's assistant, since Eric had been promoted to become the music editor, and, right now, he knew where everything was. O.K., I thought, let's look at that first episode, which was then lined up for me to view in one of the screening theatres on the MGM lot. And so I saw the cutting copy of "Arrival", projected with joins, no sound effects, no main or end titles, and more importantly, no music. All very sensibly shot without either sound effects or jarring "temp" music, just dialogue only, on location. This seemed particularly important, since that location shoot featured the village band continually miming to playing "music", as the McGoohan character, nameless but termed "P" (for "Prisoner") on the continuity sheets, wanders through his new village location, surveying the sights (but clearly not all the sounds) of his new displaced "home".

Now, here's the thing. I'd arrived on the very week *The Prisoner* was without a music editor, and it seemed to me that I could be extremely useful right away. Remember, I was my own boss, unsupervised, providing I followed the shooting schedule and provided the necessary materials. Clearly, with Bob Dearberg gone and, at present, Eric not yet started as music editor, there was a case here to find the music to match the shots. And I knew exactly what would fit those images, and what would be totally suitable, and to this very day I have never been given credit for this major discovery, a key contribution to the look and the very feel of that first scene-setting episode "Arrival", and now a definitive part of *The Prisoner* history, which these days is widespread well beyond any palpable imaginings of its own creators.

The Christmas before her last, my Mother asked what would I like for a present, something that she and Dad would like me to have that I couldn't afford myself. I was so deep into contemporary music, mainly American rock'n'roll, that I truly felt that I ought to get to know more about classical music, not easy for me to have access to back then in the early sixties, and I saw an advertisement for the then brand-new Reader's Digest Treasury of Light Classical Music, a twelve-disc collection that seemed to suit my imagined need. My Mother sent away for it and gave it to me for my present that Christmas. I listened to every track, one of which was Johann Strauss Senior's' "Radetzky March", to which I found myself "diddle-um-dum-dumming" forever afterwards.

And that's how I knew what would match the action of the mute band photographed for "Arrival" perfectly: "The Radetzky March" (J. Strauss, Snr. 1848). I had learned from my experiences with finding music for Bob Bucknell's C.O.I. jobs at Caledonian Films that the secret of finding music for mute material was not merely to find music that would be appropriate, but to find music that would positively enhance the images to which it would be matched. No music sessions on *The Prisoner* had actually taken place thus far, nor as far as I knew was there even a composer as yet on board, so after I viewed the long edit of "Arrival", I suggested to Geoff and Eric, who was at that point still Geoff Foot's assistant, that I knew exactly what selection of music would be absolutely perfect to use over the currently mute "Arrival" sequence, and, if necessary, wherever appropriate throughout the whole episode. Geoff said to bring it in, and he'd try it out. And I did, and he did, not only at the beginning of the episode, but also – inspirationally – throughout Cobb's funeral as well. The result is television history. They initially used a transfer of "The Radetsky March" from my actual Reader's Digest disc for the cutting copy and rough mix, but the March was eventually re-recorded for the *Prisoner* episode "Arrival" itself at a music session arranged by, and conducted by, Wilfred Josephs, since re-recording would have made much more sense: no legal wrangles or royalties paid to the Reader's Digest, or RCA, or even to the Strauss estate if there is one, I' m guessing. And the actual synchronisation was perfect, although I, and quite probably only me, noticed that the bass drum beat never quite exactly matched the visuals of the shots, although the marching rhythm matched perfectly well, so I guess the actual look of the drumbeats didn't really matter, and probably nobody in the world ever noticed, so perfect was the whole overall match of picture and sound. With that "Radetzky March" discovery of mine, I felt that I had already justified my employment on *The Prisoner*. Patrick McGoohan, I was to discover, was absolutely over the moon about the selection of the Strauss piece, but I'm pretty certain that he never knew initially at the time of first hearing that it was my suggestion; my very first contribution to working on *The Prisoner*, and one that, as far as I know, has never ever been divulged until now, for if it had, I'm sure somehow, somewhere, a *Prisoner* buff would have wanted, at least, to discuss it with me, or even try to locate the original recording (not too difficult, try Amazon) to make certain.

So what next? Setting up my cutting room, that's for sure, with a working moviola, synchroniser, and bench, plus all the necessary stationery requirements, plus a copy of all the continuity sheets thus far, and making sure that a daily copy be delivered to me in the immediate future, for it will say on the continuity sheets exactly what I am expected to provide, by way of the screens, for future back projection or via television, (in No.6's house, for example). Also, any signs of additional material that needs to be shot well in advance of its studio need. Plus, of course, any library shots to locate. After all, my professional title on *The Prisoner* is "Film Librarian". Quite a workload, I'm beginning to realise, and an awful lot of new people to deal with, but first of all I'm going to visit the head of MGM special effects, the venerable Tom Howard, with whom I had previously dealt on *Where the Spies Are*, and whose current workload with Stanley Kubrick on *2001: A Space Odyssey* should be coming to a close, freeing him up to help and advise me.

Tom Howard, thank goodness, was pleased to see me again, and we had a long chat. His advice was inestimable, and he outlined to me the procedures I had to take, his main warning being that time was my enemy:

"Make bloody sure that they shoot the material you'll need on the screens well in advance. It's far cheaper to back project them in the shoot than it would be if we had to add them later, superimposed via the labs." Good advice, and all down to scheduling: that would mean a long chat with Bernie Williams as soon as possible.

But even that proved not to be easy. I asked Geoff Foot where might Bernie be, and he said to try the sound guys. It seemed a good way to introduce myself to sound editor Wilf Thompson, and his assistant, who happened to be his wife Mary, so I went along to Wilf's central block cutting room, where I discovered Wilf deep in discussion with Patrick McGoohan, who grabbed me and clasped my hand so tightly I feared for the health of my fingers. "Thank you, thank you, thank you," he said. I wondered for a moment for what, but then it became clear: "That 'Radetzky March', I don't know why I didn't think of it myself!" Well, there was no answer to that: I just breathed a sigh of relief. At that moment, James Mason, of all people, appeared just outside the window, as I looked down he was standing by a soundstage, dressed for his role in the then currently-filming *Stranger in the House*, seemingly much taller than he photographed on the screen. One of my favourites. I must have stared a moment too long, because when I looked back, Pat had vanished. "He can't stand not being the centre of attention," said Wilf. What could you say? I hoped I hadn't offended him. But Wilf anticipated me: "He was just about to leave anyway – don't worry about it. That's Pat." Oh, right…

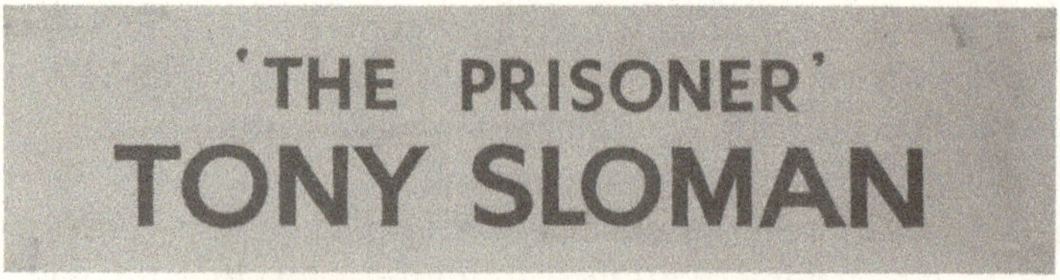

My MGM studio cutting room door sign for *The Prisoner*.

By now, *The Prisoner* series is very well-documented, if not over-documented, and that's all well and good, and both the shooting order and the various screening orders can be verified by various *Prisoner* buffs. There still seems to be some doubt, over fifty years later, as to the "correct" screening order. I find it truly amazing (and, by the by, slightly flattering) that the respect and enjoyment of *The Prisoner* has endured for well over those fifty years: there's no doubt in my own mind that it was the bravest, the classiest, and, without question, the most original television series ever attempted. Anywhere. Absolutely anywhere, at any time. So it's more than just "nice" to know that it is still celebrated, and indeed loved, so very many years after we all sweated blood to try to bring Patrick McGoohan's vision to fruition. It deserved no less.

"Dance of the Dead" was actually the first episode that I worked on, beginning with its MGM shoot on the appropriately numbered stage number 6.

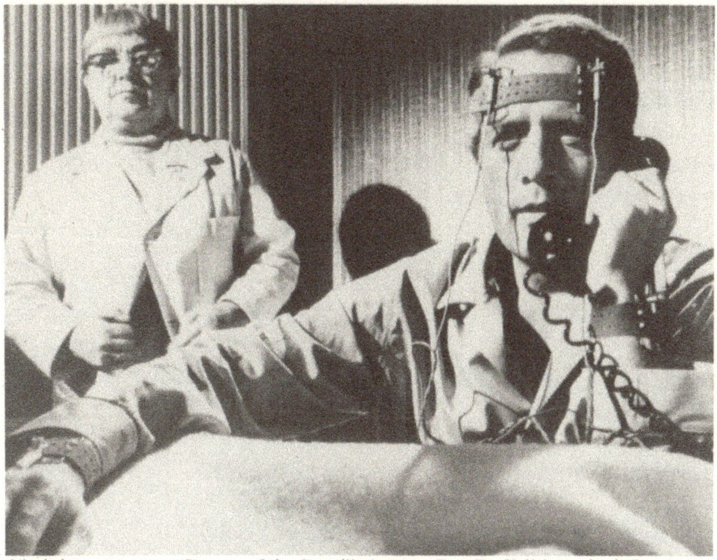

Behind the scenes on "Dance of the Dead". Actress Bee Duffell is to the left.

In the early days, there was little of the extreme pressure that came later on, although, in truth, I had absolutely no idea then that Bernie Williams virtually slept at the studio each night as he prepared the schedule for the series shoot on a day-by-day basis. I truly, in my innocence, had really no idea how very complex an issue preparing each day actually was for this particular production manager. After all, this was by no means a normal, say, five days a week film shoot, nor an ordinary television series with regular and reusable sets and characters. What I will do here now is to lay out very clearly the order of the episodes on which I worked during that major studio shoot. I wasn't on either of the two location shoots in Portmeirion: my work was entirely confined to the MGM studio sound stages, the editing rooms, and the on-site laboratory. To clarify matters, herewith the actual order on which I worked on the episodes, and therefore the correct shooting (and screening) schedule as far as I was concerned, the order to which we were working in full accordance with the original proposed delivery schedule, that is to say the first intended television screening order.

For the record, then, and, at last, finally:--

1. "Arrival" (original title "The Arrival", director Don Chaffey).

2. "Free for All" (director Don Chaffey; credited to Patrick McGoohan).

3. "Dance of the Dead" (director Don Chaffey).

4. “Checkmate” (original title: “The Queen’s Pawn”, director Don Chaffey).

5. “The Chimes of Big Ben” (director Don Chaffey).

6. “Once Upon a Time…” (original title: “Degree Absolute”, director Patrick McGoohan).

7. “The Schizoid Man” (director Pat Jackson).

8. “A Change of Mind” (director Patrick McGoohan).

9. “A. B. and C” (original titles: “Play in Three Acts” and “1, 2, and 3”, director Pat Jackson).

10. “It’s Your Funeral” (director Robert Asher).

11. “The General” (director Peter Graham Scott).

12. “Hammer into Anvil” (director Pat Jackson).

13. “Many Happy Returns” (directors Michael Truman and Patrick McGoohan, credited to Joseph Serf).

Thirteen episodes, thirteen titles. I left after thirteen episodes, as did Bernard Williams. The writing was on the wall. Wilf Thompson left after ten episodes. Bernie Williams was replaced by Ronald Liles, and myself by David Naughton. It’s difficult to really comprehensively account for how the excitement of joining *The Prisoner* turned to such disillusionment towards the end. The real problem for we technicians was that we never really knew, about halfway through the studio shoot, whether or not financier Lew Grade was going to pull the plug on Patrick or not. His money-man Bernard Kingham came down to the studio on several occasions, and we heard back that each episode was well over its projected budget, and few of them were actually completed. Indeed, the very pre-title sequence itself had not yet met with Patrick McGoohan’s approval, and was taking up a lot of editorial time. But for my part, I just carried on. My major problem was liaising with the labs over delivery dates. It was, of course, absolutely crucial that the material to be projected onto the various screens be filmed early, in order that the specific back projection plates be made and prepared well in good time for the shoot, and it was the main part of my job to co-ordinate such, in addition to finding, and if necessary, shooting, the various library shots required. I didn’t have time to leisurely watch the on-set shooting, or socialize, although I did once, on the way back to my cutting room one lunchtime, catch a glimpse of a seemingly quite isolated Eric Portman on the waterside set of “Free for All”, watching the phoney waves, resting his chin on his cane in his solitude, a far cry from the dynamic villain I’d once seen on screen as a youngster in *South of Algiers*. (But in those childhood days I had absolutely no idea of his own personal problems with his drinking or his homosexuality, both now well-documented, and besides, I was far too young then to know about either, anyway).

Bernie Williams had explained the arithmetic involved, since it was his job to plan the production schedule, and there could be no question of waiting for the back projection plates, for which I was totally responsible. Fortunately, MGM had its own laboratory on the lot, unlike any other studio, and liaison there was crucial, but at least convenient. The lab needed at least three days between shooting the material required and its appearance on the screen. Scheduling, therefore, for Bernie and myself was effectively a nightmare (more so for Bernie) because on many occasions the material required on the screen was invariably the same material to be cut to, and therefore, for economy reasons, it should all be filmed at the same time. But, of course, say it all takes place in the same location, say, Number 6's house, then, say, half of it is projected in Number 2's control room, then you can't shoot it all at the same time, since you have to film it three days before it ends up in Number 2's house. Now, you can work backwards, of course: you can shoot the scenes and then decide afterwards which bits would be used in Number 2's room, but since they had to be ordered for back projection, they may well have to be filmed later. The actual scheduling was Bernie's problem, mine was to get the material where it had to be, on time. Mine was not a job, therefore, that anyone had ever done previously: certainly, of course, many, many feature films had utilised back projection, but ours was on a television series, with appropriate television scheduling, at least in theory. We were very much in the hands of the laboratories, quite unlike today where digital technology has largely replaced back projection, and where colour grading and light levels can be controlled via sophisticated computers, and you may not, and almost certainly will not, be shooting on film, and if it doesn't quite work, it's easy enough to fix immediately. But film, 35mm. motion picture film, which is what *The Prisoner* was conceived for, and filmed on, has to have the sequences as required by the script run on a projector behind the screen on view, because it is all done by back projection, and then filmed front projection, although the actual image viewed is from behind the screen, it is actual back projection, not superimposition of any kind. Now, that footage has to be prepared (by me) and to be readily available, in theory, for more than one screening, several takes, in fact.

But several takes with back projection presents a risk that we couldn't afford. Since the image has to be totally still, i.e. without the slight "judder" of a normal film projector, and invariably will have to be an exact match to the cut material either side, the projector itself has a lock-off device. Let me try to explain: every frame of film has four perforations, and normally goes through a projector at twenty-four frames per second, sound speed. But, on a regular projector those frames can't help but judder, ever so slightly, and probably quite unnoticeable to the human eye, but judder they do. Therefore, if you are shooting film-on-film, as *The Prisoner* would have to do, then of course all judder must be avoided, totally. So, here's where we get technical: in order to avoid judder, each frame projected through back projection has to be specially printed, with what are termed "locked-off" perforations, especially printed, specially effective perforations. Therefore, because it is rock solid, because it goes through a back projector without a judder, it's liable to scratch, because of the acute tension. Now, you're filming a film that must never look like a film: it has to look like live broadcast television in Number 2's house. Clear?

So, as a consequence, on the studio floor there's no rehearsal with the back projection, because it goes through the projector gate rock solid in tension which can only increase the chances of the film being scratched, and of course if it is scratched, then that would "blow" the scene totally, back projection and foreground action combined. (Now you know how grateful both film makers and film insurers are for today's digital techniques.) If the back projected scene had sound, then that would invariably be added later, in the cutting rooms.

The resulting method in order to facilitate shooting involving myself and the laboratories meant that two prints of the material required were provided, and only to be used on actual takes, not for camera or actors' rehearsals. Two prints of everything meant that everybody on set was locked into a maximum of two takes only. If something were to happen to the back projected materials, we couldn't go to a third take, because not only is there a chance of visible scratching, but because we are picking up dirt each time we screen it, which would require cleaning, but in cleaning it's possible to get more dust onto it, which, of course, would result in more scratching. If you can imagine all this, just think of my responsibility! I was only twenty-one at the time, and the best thing for me to do was just not to think of what could go wrong at all.

But we made it work. Tom Howard offered the most wonderful support, and supplied me each time I needed a "projjie" with the most careful, most experienced projectionists on the MGM lot, which meant that they were amongst the best in the world. I really don't think to this day that my *Prisoner* directors, even Patrick, bless him, quite knew what I was going through to get that stuff onto the screen, but, of course, making it look easy was all part of the job. No, we never went to a third take, ever, on any of the background projector material. (Although, if you look very, very carefully, on "The Chimes of Big Ben" episode we did have to use a second take which wasn't quite correctly colour-graded: it looks a little "washed out" to me, that's all, but nobody noticed, nobody ever complained.) And then Bernie, good as his word, upped my own salary as he said he would. And, by thunder, I was earning it, and Bernie knew it!!

On the question of some less-than-perfect colour grading in the back projection plates, ultimately, as it always does in movie-making, it all came down to money. The bankers visited the set regularly on Lew Grade's insistence, to speak to Patrick McGoohan about budget over-runs, and, inevitably, Bernie Williams took the meetings. We were about to start shooting "The Schizoid Man", which needed, in the script, a lot of special fx work, and, already the financial over-runs were becoming astronomical. Bernie Williams called me into the meeting with Bernie Kingham, Lord Grade's chief accounts man, and some other *Prisoner* heads of department. Bernie asked us all how could we get out of this position of constant budget over-runs. He looked straight at me, and said, "What are we going to do? How are we going to get out of it? Could we shorten anything?" I had to speak up. "You're talking to the wrong guy," I said. "I can't speed up the labs." Bernie Williams came to my rescue. "No, I can speed up the labs," he said, looking at me. "I can tell them what you can't – I can say we're switching labs if they don't deliver. They won't like that."

I suddenly realised that we were putting on a show for Mr. Kingham. "Are we switching labs?" I asked Bernie W. "No, of course not," he replied, "but you'll see. We'll shave a day off your three-day schedule."

So, a little show for ITC's head honcho. As it happened, Bernie Williams did manage to arrange a two-day delivery for the back projection plates, but, to be honest, I wish he hadn't: the grading started to vary, and the colour wasn't quite perfect. But Bernie did indeed speed up the delivery, and therefore proved to head office what a superb production manager they had hired, but eventually on "The Schizoid Man", which was to be all split screen and laboratory work, I think I proved myself Bernie's equal.

In my pre-shooting meeting with Patrick McGoohan on "The Schizoid Man" I pointed out how extremely complex (not to mention how expensive) this episode would be if it were filmed with superior laboratory optical work, with Pat playing both the roles. There would be absolutely no guarantees that it would be ready in time, at least not from me: the matching lab work could take ages, even if the make-up and costume departments were terrific. Then we discussed how to do it. Now, as you know, I was, and, by the way, still am, a great Stewart Granger fan, and there's a scene in *The Prisoner of Zenda* where Granger as Rudolph Rassendyll walks around himself in his dual role as heir to the throne, which is an amazing technical achievement, but, legendarily, cost MGM a small fortune. Patrick McGoohan then said, "We'll have to do that, without using doubles." So I said to Pat, "Talk to Tom Howard. He's head of MGM special effects. He'll know how." The meeting broke up, and I phoned Tom Howard to expect a call, gently warning him that there was a very real worry about the costing of the sequence. Tom understood immediately.

Patrick returned from his chat with Tom Howard, and told me that we do have to do it cost-effectively with doubles. In the meantime, I'd had a chat with Pat's stand-in, Frank Maher, to ask his advice on how to shoot the sequence, and he said that it would be definitely faster and easier using doubles, just him and Pat. "And cheaper, too." So Patrick, after speaking to Tom, then talked to Frank, who got back to me and confirmed what I'd already anticipated. "But," said Frank, "we'll shoot it in a way that they'll never know."

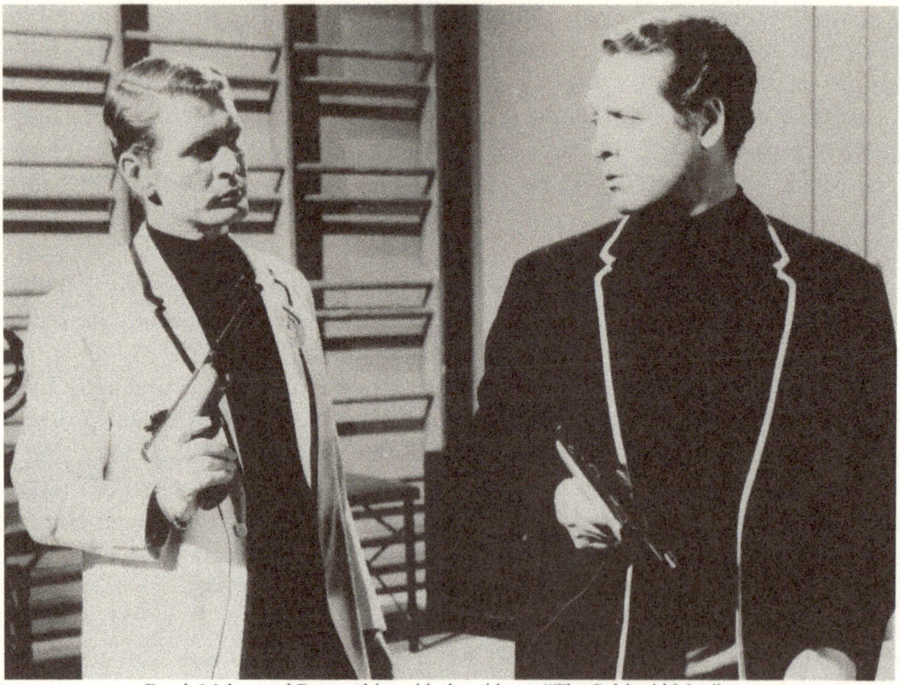

Frank Maher and Pat working side-by-side on "The Schizoid Man".

And that's how I got to direct the Frank Maher side of the screen in "The Schizoid Man". Although Pat Jackson (*Western Approaches*, *Virgin Island*) was the episode's director, he was more than happy to let me "direct" Frank's side of the screen, which we did in a tight and exceptionally finely-tuned double exposure, printed together on a negative with Pat Jackson's own main shoot. Patrick McGoohan loved it, I'm happy to say! (I don't think you can tell where the join is, at least not on television. If you watch that episode on a big screen, that's another story, but, remember, it was first transmitted in black-and-white, on even smaller domestic television screens that those in regular use today).

There were a few other shots that they let me direct on *The Prisoner*. In "The Chimes of Big Ben" there originally was a sequence where Patrick is using a viewing device called a triquetrum, apparently invented by Greek astronomer Ptolemy around about AD 140, that predated the telescope, and he's looking up at the stars. I mentioned this to Bernie Williams, who said that neither a library shot nor a separate shoot was in the budget, so I asked my mates on *2001*, Doug Trumbull and Con Pederson, if they had anything that would be suitable, that Stanley Kubrick a) wasn't using, and b) wouldn't know about if anyone else used it. They asked me what I wanted, and I replied that it was just a simple shot of the sky, seen distantly from a precursor of the space telescope. “A triquetrum?” asked Con. Somewhat surprised, I replied in the affirmative, and Con said, “We’ve got the very thing.” And he opened a very large drawer in his office, and showed me an optical plate master of stars in a black sky. He asked Doug if he could let me have it, and Doug agreed, providing Stanley never, ever found out. So off I go, with this huge matte shot under cover, to my cutting room, and phone assistant director John O’Connor to set up an insert shoot for me as soon as possible for “Chimes of Big Ben”. I’d only need one cameraman and lights. John doesn’t even ask Bernie, he just arranges it and we shoot it that very evening, on our own Stage 6 when the main shoot had finished for the day. I sent the shot neg. to the labs, and the next day, voila! Bearing in mind Doug Trumbull’s warning about Stanley Kubrick, I don’t screen it at rushes, but ask Patrick McGoohan if he has a minute: I’ve something to show him when he next visits the cutting rooms. Curious, he came up that very evening, and I showed him the triquetrum point-of-view shot. Well, he very nearly kissed me! He realised what it was immediately, and was utterly delighted, and told me to send it to Spencer Reeve, who was editing that particular episode, and in it went. At least for a while, because when “The Chimes of Big Ben” was eventually recut, for whatever reason, that triquetrum sequence was no longer included. I never managed to find out exactly why, but it’s now available on a *Prisoner* box set as an alternative “Chimes of Big Ben” edit. I have no idea at all why the sequence had been removed, surely running time couldn’t have been a factor? (Or did Stanley Kubrick ever find out? I never knew.)

The first episode, “Arrival”, was still running at nearly ninety minutes, and Geoff Foot had his work, quite literally, cut out, but eventually he did an absolutely superb job, and no television series ever, to my mind, had a better introductory episode.

Although my job as Film Librarian was to find material, such as the falling tree chopped down in “The Chimes of Big Ben”, courtesy of Ralph Rogers’ World Backgrounds library, I realised that sometimes it would be simpler and far faster to create the needed shot myself. To that end, anticipating other eventual future film project requests, I formed a company with a friend of Ray Selfe’s, a cameraman called Bill Nixon, and it was “The Chimes of Big Ben” that prompted our forming of Earlswood Film Productions, an off-the-shelf company name that I bought in order to get paid for any work we did. In the studio’s shoot for “Chimes”, Pat and Nadia are concealed in wooden crates, and ostensibly get shipped back to the U.K. in a lorry. Well, rather than spend time in film libraries searching for a matching existing extended left-to-right lorry travelling shot, I sent Bill out to shoot one, and he spent a long day up, I think it was the M1, but I can’t really remember, and filmed a beautiful matching long lorry shot that cut in perfectly with the studio material. Don Chaffey was delighted, and I kept quiet about the origin, although Earlswood did bill Bernie Williams. I still have the receipt: I think

Bill Nixon and I split the £6.40 that we charged *The Prisoner*. We never, alas, had such an opportunity again.

I did have another problem, though, on "The Chimes of Big Ben". Patrick and Nadia Gray were to escape from the Village via a boat that Number 6 had put together from an art exhibit he had submitted, and a rocky coastline background plate was needed for the interior studio shoot to match the landscape of the Portmeirion location filming. I had looked at a few from World Backgrounds, and selected a suitable one which was approved by director Don Chaffey, so I ordered it up as a background plate, two copies with appropriate back projection sprocket holes, as per normal. They duly arrived from the labs, and were prepared for shooting. I was busy, the projectionist in charge lined them up ready, and the shot was rehearsed without Pat and Nadia. Next thing I know, I get a phone call in my cutting room from Gino Marotta, the assistant director. "Come down on to the floor, quick – the plates don't work." Knees shaking, continuity sheets in hand, I descend to the studio stage. I look at the set-up. The boat is framed in front of the back projection, but there's a clear gap at the top: the sky doesn't reach the rack-line; you can see the set through the film. Oh my Gawd! The stand-ins for Pat and Nadia are in place, and there's clearly an open gasping space above their heads, and it dawns on me that I hadn't taken proper accounting of the spacial distancing when I viewed the library shot – you clearly couldn't have studio space, not sky, above the heads of the artistes. What to do? Gino was of no help. Brendan, the lighting cameraman, was busy lighting regardless, so I asked the camera operator, Jack Lowin, for any suggestion before Don Chaffey and the principals arrived to shoot the scene.

Well, Jack couldn't have been kinder, more sweetly professional, and more practical. He said to me that if we moved the camera closer, and moved the back projection film one perforation up a sprocket, we wouldn't have a problem. Brilliant! I said, "But what if Don shoots the bottom of the boat – he'll get the rack-line of the next frame in shot, won't he?" "No," said Jack, "because I've moved the camera in. No-one will notice that we've changed the set-up slightly, not even the director." "Let's try it." And that we did, and no-one indeed noticed, unless of course you were on the set, and could see that the actual back projection was out of rack. But, when shot, it looked like a dream, and was used in two separate sequences. What would have happened if we needed a third take? We never did. I could have kissed Jack Lowin, and he knew it, but I didn't! A firm handshake sufficed, plus a hand-clasp on his shoulder and my most profound thanks.

But there was another story that bears re-telling here, especially since it concerns me, and it taught me a very major lesson in film-making:-- no matter what the shoot, however big, however small, never, ever film anything at all without a continuity person present. The episode was the seventh to be shot, "The Schizoid Man", directed by the veteran Pat Jackson, and I was asked to do an insert shoot, in order to facilitate both shooting and editing, for a major sequence involving Pat as Number 6, and a new arrival in The Village, Number 24, played by Jane Merrow.

So, Number 24 is, apparently, a mind-reader, and Number 6 helps her out in testing her alleged powers. I was informed that close-ups of the mind-reading cards held by the couple would be extremely expensive for a main unit shoot, so would I please shoot the inserts of the close-ups of the cards in question, mute, with my hands doubling for Jane's. Working as per script, I received the relevant prop cards from the art department, and production manager and first assistant for the sequence John O'Connor set up a shoot on an empty adjacent stage. I followed the card order as scripted, but what I didn't do, and should have done, was to look at the cutting copy first, and list, and then film, exactly which cards were actually required, and then shoot all of the card shots specifically in the correct order required by the script, and then also shoot any others, as an editing stand-by just in case, with a continuity person present, listing all the cards filmed in detail on the continuity sheets for the cutting rooms. John O'Connor, like every assistant director I've ever met, merely wanted as speedy and therefore as economic a shoot as possible.

Now, I can't exactly remember all the precise details, but I thought that that was exactly what happened. We shot a number of takes in close-up of every single card required, or so I thought. And then I reviewed the edited sequence itself, and my heart just sank: I'd left one out. Without having taken continuity notes, I thought I'd covered them all. I dreaded what would happen to me when the editor found he did not have a close-up of a specific card when the director asked for it. What to do? Well, the only available choice for me was to simply bluff it out. Which I did, the constant dread feeling in my stomach growing daily until I saw the actual edit: There was no need for the missing card! Geoff Foot had cut around it, maybe even didn't notice it was missing, maybe never needed it in the first place. Talk about relief! But a major lesson learned: never film anything, ever, at all, without a proper continuity person present. That's why it's a separate, specialist job, the continuity sheets providing forever a visible record of what has been filmed. I never shot without continuity ever again; the fear of being fired for incompetence never, ever left me. I should've known better. I do now.

There was one other thing that bears mentioning here, and that was my very own worse moment on *The Prisoner*. It was Christmas Eve, or to be precise the very day before Christmas itself, and involved a back projection shot featuring actress Rachel Herbert and a mini-moke. It had mostly been filmed in Portmeirion with Don Chaffey directing, but Patrick McGoohan was himself directing the pick-up sequences at MGM, well and good since he had actually written this particular episode, under the pseudonym "Paddy Fitz". Now, I took my instructions directly from the daily continuity reports, being the sheets supplied by Doris Martin, the series' continuity person, and from the call sheets, prepared by assistant director Gino Marotta. The continuity sheets were read in association with the actual script provided, and from this coupling I would prepare well in advance, in theory, what was needed from my department (i.e. me) for each day's shooting. When a back projection plate was required, it was invariably filmed early, in order to avoid any potential laboratory problems, and in order for the specially perforated print copy to be prepared for projection. In truth, the system worked well, and with the Christmas break now approaching, I made absolutely sure that all the material that was required over the Christmas period, i.e. just before and immediately after the two-day break, was already prepared and ready in my cutting room before we broke for the holiday. Or so I thought.

O.K. It's Christmas Eve. "Free for All" is shooting on Stage 6, with Patrick McGoohan directing it, matching all the studio material to Don Chaffey's location shoot. Eric Mival and I have managed to have a jolly pre-Christmas lunch together in the canteen, where we've been joined by a couple of canteen girls whom we'd been chatting up virtually since we started working on *The Prisoner*. Eric is naturally friendly, but he has a permanent (and very nice) girlfriend that I think he intends to marry (he did), and I am pursuing Pat, a canteen girl who has joined us for a post-Christmas Eve lunch drink, and we've been there so long it's nearly tea-time, and my Pat is, shall we say, getting friendlier and friendlier, when, suddenly, I am interrupted by a phone call from the floor. It's the assistant director Gino Marotta: "Can you come down onto the stage, Tony, to discuss the B.P. with Patrick? Immediately." "What's the problem, Gino?" I ask. "Pat's asking me to ask you to come down," was the reply. Now, in general, I wasn't on the floor when the plates I provided were being shot: my brief, amongst other things, was to prepare future material for shooting, and Tom Howard had always provided a marvellous senior film projectionist to line up and screen all the floor projection materials, back projection, wall screens, and all television screens that were required on the actual set. I could not possibly imagine why I was needed on the floor: I'd already sent down all of the material required by continuity. So, before I actually appeared on the studio floor at Patrick's request, I went via my cutting room and collected all continuity sheets thus far on "Free for All", plus the marked-up shooting script, to take with me to my meeting with "Free for All"'s director, our executive producer and star, Patrick McGoohan.

Now, when you normally walk onto the studio floor of a project currently in production between takes, there's a very busy buzz –people are chatting, props are being lined up, the set is being dressed or re-dressed, the cameras are being prepared for the next set-up – it's noisy. But, when I opened the stage door to the set and walked in, there was silence. Odd, I thought, they surely should be shooting; this was, indeed, a very strange and heavy silence. Not a sound, no-one talking. I walked directly over to the first person I saw: Gino Marotta, the assistant director who had telephoned me in the canteen. Before I could greet him he looked at me and he said, "Now you're for it." And in front of him was the screen, the back projection screen for which I normally provided the images, and there was nothing on it. There were cameras facing the screen all right, but it looked like no filming was about to take place. Patrick McGoohan was the director, and the thought occurred to me that perhaps there should have been a shot of Rachel Herbert and her mini-moke on the screen, but before I could check anything, Patrick's voice boomed out at me, "Where is it?"

"Where's what, sir?" I replied. (I always called the director "sir" on the floor. In this case, he was only "Pat" or "Patrick" away from the floor.) "Where's the bloody shot?" he asked. I said, "Which shot?" "The shot that's supposed to be on the screen," he said. And then it all suddenly dawned on me: he has stopped shooting, and everyone on the studio floor is watching Patrick McGoohan and me. A thought flashes into my mind at this very moment: they've stopped shooting, and whatever it is, it's clearly my fault. How much is this costing Lew Grade? Patrick spoke: "The shot listed on the continuity sheet is not there on the screen." I really didn't know what to do or say, but I had brought with me all the relevant continuity sheets, and there was the most terrible silence while I checked my sheet. I actually said, "Let's check the sheet." I looked at my continuity sheet, and sure enough that particular shot wasn't asked for as a back projection print. All sorts of thoughts went through my mind. I've upset him, it's Christmas Eve, do I say it was never asked for? Will he fire me for not double-checking at the time? Does he want me fired? But, nevertheless, it was clear from my sheet that it was indeed never asked for. I had a moment of inspired genius: "I think we should discuss it with the editor," I said, the reasoning behind my comment was that Geoff would have to edit the shot (or not) eventually. "All right," said Pat. "Get Mr. Foot down here." He spoke to the assembled floor, to no one person in particular.

I had to wait right there in silence, clutching my script and the relevant continuity sheets. I'm thinking that Pat has got something up psychologically: maybe he really doesn't actually want to break for Christmas? After what to me seemed like an eternity, the immaculately-suited Geoff Foot appeared and said, in his well-educated, well-spoken voice: "What seems to be the trouble?" Before I could even open my mouth, Pat snapped, "Where's the shot?" Geoff said, "Which shot?" and he looked at the blank screen, and said, "Do you mean the shot of the girl with the mini-moke?" "Yes," said Patrick, "Where is it?" Geoff turned to me. "Where is it, Tony? Did you order it?" I fumbled with my continuity sheets, and showed the specific one in question to Geoff. In those pre-digital days, the continuity sheets sent to the cutting rooms were carbon copies of the originals, and it was clear that Pat's requested shot was not indicated to be ordered. For whatever reason, if the shot was indeed requested, that request never turned up on my copy of the sheet: the carbon had failed. Geoff Foot took in all this, with only a brief glance at me. I spoke: "It's not asked for on my continuity sheet copy. You can see for yourself." Geoff said, "We can cut directly to it. You don't need it on the screen, we'll just cut to the shot. We don't need a B.P. plate on it."

Pat then said, to my extreme surprise, what seemed to me like a total non-sequitur: "What's all this fuss about the girl?" I just thought to myself, "Patrick McGoohan, what are you talking about??" Geoff Foot looks at me, and kind of half-winks and smiles. Pat then yells, "O.K. everyone. Positions!!" I breathe again. It wasn't until years afterwards that I realised that Pat, as director, was playing for time on the set, probably to determine his next set-up, as some directors were known to do. I wasn't, of course, aware of it then. They filmed the shot without the back projection, and if you view it today, the shot that would have been the plate is, in fact, just cut in, and very effective it is too. It's not on the actual screen at all. It looks like it is, but it actually isn't. Bravo, my grateful respect and thank you, Geoff Foot.

By then it's about half past four on Christmas Eve. I walked back to the cutting rooms with Geoff Foot. He knew how I felt. I thought this is the end of it all. Patrick didn't like what had happened. He certainly didn't like the way I'd brought Geoff down on to the floor, and he didn't say "Thank you, Tony," or "Off you go, Tony," or anything. He didn't dismiss me. He didn't even speak to me. I thought that this was the end of it, I've lost my job. Pat didn't like the way that I'd brought his senior editor, Geoff Foot, down on to the studio floor, away from his cutting bench. I went back to my own cutting room and collected my belongings, in order to spend Christmas at Forest Gate with my Grandmother, my sister and cousins, and Auntie Doris and Uncle Don. I was hardly in the mood for this particular Christmas, my first without my Mother, and also with my own Father currently in prison. Thanks, Patrick.

Christmas Day and Boxing Day passed, and I went back to MGM studios heavy-hearted the next day, ready for whatever the 8.30 a.m., start would bring. In order to get to my cutting room, I had to go past Stage 6, where *The Prisoner* was shooting, but I really didn't want to go past that particular stage. I really didn't want to run into anybody, so I went round the outside of the stage to get to the cutting room block, the only other single way to get to my own particular editing room. There's only that one way to go, and there, standing right in front of me, right in the middle of the only way into the cutting rooms, was Patrick McGoohan. I couldn't avoid him. I couldn't back out, I have to go past him. And we stare at each other. I really don't want to see him, especially since he was responsible for giving me such an utterly miserable Christmas time. He walked up to me – and remember how tall he was – he was in costume, and he walks closer and closer, and hugs me. He puts his arms around me and said, "I gave you a rotten Christmas, didn't I, Tony?" and he flashes that McGoohan smile. I couldn't speak. I didn't say anything. He knew and I knew and I knew that he knew, and I just hoped that he had as rotten a Christmas. I shook myself from Pat's friendly clutches, attempted a feeble smile, and ascended up the stairs to my cutting room. I guessed that I still had my job, and nothing further was ever said.

But I wanted to check out what Geoff Foot did with those Christmas Eve rushes, and when I saw Geoff's edit, it looked just fine. If you know it well enough, you'd notice it's a cut to the action, and not to the screen, but it works perfectly well. Geoff Foot was a bloody good editor, and such a nice man.

Except for the nickname he gave me. I'd grown a then-fashionable beard, replete with sideburns and moustache in veritable sixties fashion, and when we came back after the two-day Christmas break, Geoff repeatedly called me "Rabbi", because of the beard. It wasn't anti-Semitic, at least I didn't really think so, merely good-natured. But it didn't half irk me.

The Prisoner was running out of footage, and so another location to Portmeirion was in order. Apparently it transpired that on the last location there wasn't much to do in the evenings, except, of course, to drink, and Bernard Williams wanted to avoid any possible repetition of that last, so he asked me to choose some 16mm. film prints to send down to the location, for evening viewing. I had already obtained a 35mm. copy of Stanley Kubrick's *Paths of Glory*, which Patrick had asked for, to view before he directed one of his *Prisoner* episodes (no, I can't remember which one — I'm guessing one with long travelling shots, because that's what seemed to interest Pat most about Kubrick's film.) I kept *Paths of Glory* around in the cutting room for some time, hoping to view it again myself, but Geoff Foot saw it there sitting on the side, and made me send it back.

What to choose to send for viewing by a crew far from home? Bernie said keep it down to five titles, in theory roughly one special viewing per week, initially, and nothing too controversial. So I, selfish as ever, thought "What would I myself like to see in the evening after a tough day on location? Easy. An Elvis musical with good-looking chicks, a Jerry Lewis comedy, an "adult" comedy, and, just to annoy our Patrick, something sexually controversial.

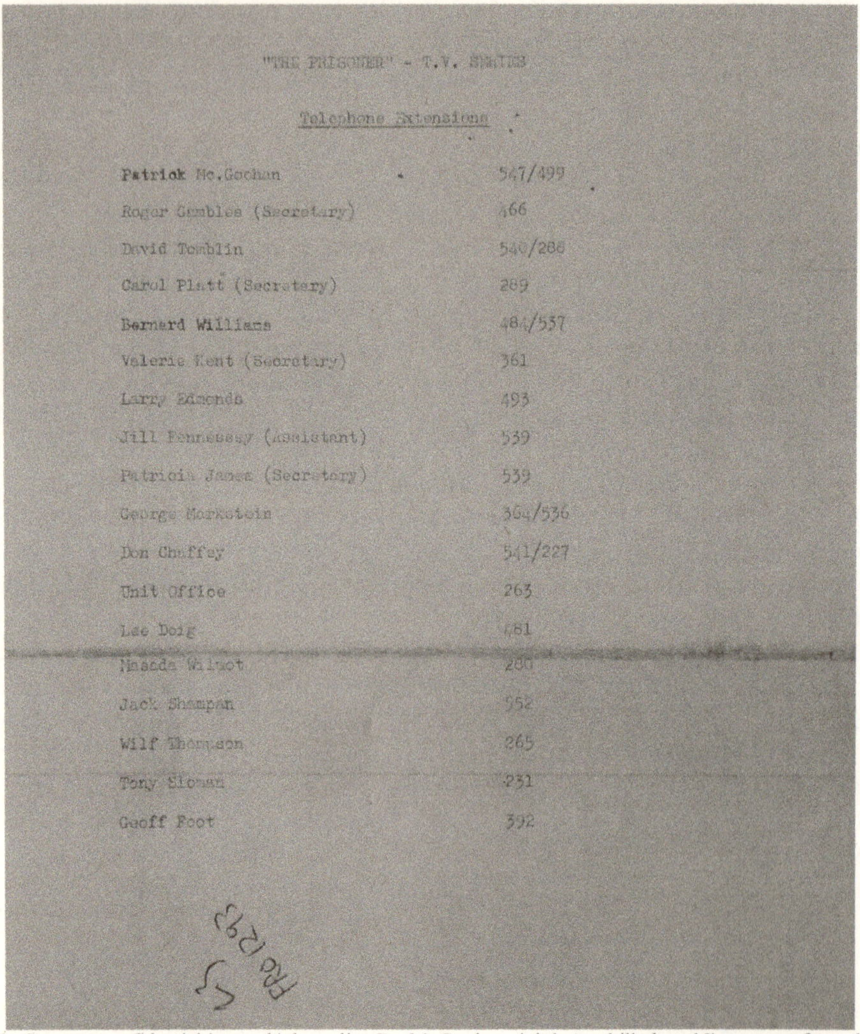

"THE PRISONER" - T.V. SERIES

Telephone Extensions

Patrick Mc.Goohan	547/499
Roger Gambles (Secretary)	466
David Tomblin	540/288
Carol Platt (Secretary)	289
Bernard Williams	484/557
Valerie Kent (Secretary)	361
Larry Edmonds	493
Jill Fennessey (Assistant)	539
Patricia James (Secretary)	539
George Markstein	364/536
Don Chaffey	541/227
Unit Office	263
Lee Doig	481
Mnacda Wilmot	280
Jack Shampan	552
Wilf Thompson	265
Tony Sloman	231
Geoff Foot	392

The Prisoner confidential internal 'phone list. Pat McGoohan rightly top-billed, and I'm one up from the bottom, although I felt that Geoff Foot should have been above me (and above Lee Doig). I don't remember who the "Liz" was whose Frobisher (Knightsbridge) phone number I scrawled upside down on the nearest sheet of paper then available (i.e. my phone list!), but I did occasionally date account assistant Jill Fennessey (539) and renewed my friendship with her later on *The Last Remake of 'Beau Geste'*.

So I did a deal with Ron Harris distributors, and sent down to the second Portmeirion location shoot *Love in Las Vegas* (U.S. title: *Viva Las Vegas*) starring Elvis Presley and Ann-Margret, *Rock-a-Bye Baby* (or could it have been *The Geisha Boy*? Anyway, either way, Jerry Lewis directed by Frank Tashlin), *Period of Adjustment* (by Tennessee Williams; Anthony Franciosa and Jane Fonda directed by George Roy Hill, his first feature), and *Lolita* (Stanley Kubrick directing, brilliantly, James Mason and Peter Sellers: hilariously funny, and jolly likely to annoy Mr. Patrick McGoohan with all his sexual hang-ups!). I have, alas, completely forgotten what my fifth choice was. As far as I knew, they all went down a treat, as I heard from various crew members when they came back, especially *Lolita.* Apparently Patrick McGoohan never went to any of the screenings. Perhaps that's just as well.

But there was a special request from Patrick when they came back to the studio. He had heard of a short film that supported the feature *If...* at the London Pavilion, a half-hour film that got exceptionally favourable reviews, called *29*, or *Twenty-Nine*, and he asked me to get him a 35mm. print to run one lunchtime in a theatre at the studio. I watched it with him, and he was particularly struck by an actor named Alexis Kanner, and it wasn't long before Alexis turned up in a new *Prisoner* episode or two, and a lifelong friendship was born, which resulted in Alexis appearing in three *Prisoner* episodes, one uncredited, plus the feature film *Kings and Desperate Men* which starred Patrick McGoohan, that Alexis Kanner produced and directed himself in 1981.

When *The Prisoner* came back from its second Portmeirion shoot the atmosphere in the studio had definitely changed; it seemed more a question of getting the series finished as quickly as possible, and quality seems no longer to be a priority: the whole series had to be transmitted, no matter what, and there was not quite enough material filmed for the projected run. The overspend and the number of unfinished episodes were causing a major headache for Lew Grade and his bankers. Perhaps it was becoming time for me to move on?

There seemed to be a shortage of scripts. Nobody ever said so in so many words, but we in the cutting rooms were invited to submit story outlines and ideas for future episodes. What looked like a break for us all was actually a desperate race (or ruse) to get the series finished. Were we to be paid for our suggestions and ideas? The matter never arose. Eric Mival thought it was a great idea, and, ever honourable, didn't concern himself with money matters, and tossed off a couple of potential storylines. Ian Rakoff, who was assistant editor to John S. Smith on two episodes and who was already trying to establish himself as a writer, and eventually did so for a while, also submitted a couple of synopses as well. One of his episodes was actually filmed as "Living in Harmony", the Wild West episode of *The Prisoner*, and I presume that Ian got paid for it.

Me? Well, I always hated writing for nothing, although, in truth, I seem to have done quite a lot of it over the years, but I conveyed the idea to my Eccleston Street flatmate, John Whitmarsh-Knight, and he wrote three draft treatments, one of which, set in the tunnels and caves under the Village, I thought very viable, but nothing ever came of it, especially not money. I couldn't let John send them without me contributing in some way, so I did, in fact, submit an idea as well. But in true film industry fashion, neither John nor I ever heard back about our submissions. Perhaps it really was time to move on.

But, of course, not quite yet. At least, not until there's an offer, and then, of course, I'd think about it, or so I thought. But there's an unwritten rule in the freelance business: you never leave a job until it's over, especially not for a better offer. At least, that was the way (so-called) gentlemen behaved. These days, that unwritten rule has gone forever. The change in mores came, I think, towards the end of the Swingin' Sixties: if it's a better offer, grab it with both hands, and to hell with your current employer, who once put his faith in you and paid you a decent salary, and, heaven knows, I saw more than enough examples of that happening, for better and worse. But *The Prisoner* was running out of steam, and it began to show. I had befriended the show's co-creator, George Markstein, a fellow Jew who had based *The Prisoner* on his wartime experiences, and who made a brief, fleeting appearance in the title sequence as No. 6's ex-boss, and I discovered that even he now intended to leave, finding Patrick McGoohan having become impossible to work with, and, indeed, George, a kindly soul, did indeed leave after the first thirteen episodes. George also realised that the show itself was draining Lew Grade's coffers badly, and it hadn't even been screened yet, and it might not be a good programme to be known to be associated with. Rumours were circulating: had Patrick McGoohan gone mad? What was it all about? Was it true that the episodes didn't even make sense? Was any episode actually completed yet? Did it matter?

Nadia Gray. I couldn't believe I was actually working with, standing next to, and actually inhaling the wonderful oh-so-sensual odour of the actress who performed that sultry striptease in one of the seminal motion pictures in my whole life (and also of the whole of the Sixties decade, too), Federico Fellini's *La Dolce Vita* (*The Sweet Life*), the movie sensation of its day. I was introduced to Nadia on the set of *The Prisoner* (episode: "The Chimes of Big Ben") and, truly, had never, ever met anyone quite like her. Magnificently, and perfectly, proportioned, sweet-natured beyond belief (or so I thought), and, quite simply, sexy beyond any measure. Hard to talk sense to when so close, and, frankly, I didn't try. Could this really be the same unremarkable actress that I once saw co-starred with George Cole (of all people) in that British comedy *Top Secret* at the Pullman, Herne Hill?? Harder still to describe her sheer sensual feminine sexuality; the perfume that she used combined with her skin to release a scent unbelievable, the tantalisingly suggestive smell of a very real and tangible sexual woman. Of course, this aspect of Nadia didn't photograph, but every male on the set will never forget it. Especially not Mr. Patrick McGoohan, who had stern, almost Biblical, values when it came to his family life. He had vowed never to film love scenes of any passionate sort, and he avoided sexual temptation like the plague. Almost certainly Nadia was aware of this, and their scenes together just sizzled on the set: Patrick, bless him, couldn't take it.

And so, in "The Chimes of Big Ben", when it came to what should have been quite a tender scene for Number 6, Patrick, to resist temptation, didn't even attempt to film the scene with Nadia. He substituted an unknown extra, wearing Nadia's wig, for the close-up shots, and used Nadia's voice track, recorded separately, only cutting back to he and Nadia when they were a little more apart. None of us had ever heard, or seen, such a performance before: we truly didn't know whether to applaud Pat's ingenious form of sexual resistance, or to berate his professional ability in not being able to handle Nadia. I still think today that the joins don't quite work, but Patrick was the boss, and, if you don't know what's going on, perhaps the sequence works for you. It's lucky it was meant to be a night shoot, and he just about gets away with it. But I never believed it, ever. And I'm sure I'm not alone. Wow: Nadia Gray, and I stood next to her. So she was a mere twenty-two years older than me, but you can look, and want, can't you?

Nadia wreaked a very subtle revenge on Pat's substitution of her in that two-shot close-up. In her very last sequence in "The Chimes of Big Ben" Nadia appears wearing a gorgeous fur coat, unlike any other costume seen throughout the whole series. The coat, of course, was her own, and, if not the very one from the *La Dolce Vita* striptease, then certainly very emotive and evocative of that unforgettably sexy moment in that film when she wore nothing beneath it and then writhed nude on top of it. And she knew it. And so did Patrick McGoohan. What a woman! Patrick McGoohan's pride in his marriage to Joan in an industry well-publicised for its various sexual affairs and entanglements was well-known. Religious reasons were often cited (Patrick was a devout Catholic), but Pat, good-looking and a prize catch, was also all too aware of how on-set sexual antics could jeopardise not only a marriage, but also a production: best not to get involved.

So one evening I actually thought I myself was going to be fired for violating Patrick's unspoken sexual code. A few of us had to work late in the cutting rooms – I can't for the life of me remember exactly why – and I was preparing something for shooting the next day, and Pat was, as was his wont, going through the various episodes with the editors, checking the edits, one after another, with his regular glass of gin in his hand. Now, there was a new girl assistant (who I won't name because she now has a much more senior position in the film industry) with whom I was becoming more than just friendly, and she was also working late, and we had also had a few drinks (though only wine, never Patrick's alcoholic beverage of choice).

I can't remember exactly how it happened, but both she and I ended up on the cutting room floor. At that very minute, we looked up and saw Patrick McGoohan looking in at us through the glass window in the door. We froze for a moment. Pat raised his glass to us and said "Cheers!" Well. Caught by the boss! He didn't have to say, or do, anything else. Shamed and extremely embarrassed, we both stood up, dusted ourselves down, and carried on with our proper work. We both passed Patrick on the way out, and nothing was said, apart from "Goodnight, sir," from me. He just smiled. The incident was never referred to again, but Pat made me feel that I was to be reported to the Head of School the next day, and thoroughly caned, or similar. And, of course, Patrick himself was the Head. (Was playing sex games with an assistant a firing offence? I thought not, even in the perverse world of Patrick McGoohan.) Anyway, it was only flirting.

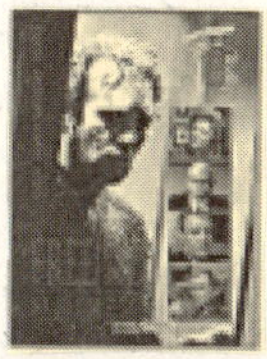

Patrick McGoohan, though, would brook no incompetence, no unprofessionalism, and was swift to remove anyone who didn't fit in with his game plan. I well remember meeting one director who was about to start an episode, in order to discuss, as was my normal procedure, the back projection plates required, and any library shots needed, over and above the obvious demands of the supplied scripts, and we had a very pleasant meeting. His name was Roy Rossotti, and he had directed some second unit for David Lean on *Doctor Zhivago*, having previously worked in the art department on such then-recent major features as *The World of Suzie Wong* and *Lawrence of Arabia.* He seemed to know what he wanted, and we got on perfectly well professionally. However, on my way out of studio that very night I ran into Roy in the car park, and, to my surprise, he was crying. It looked like he'd been crying for a long while: his face was red, and streaked with tears. I immediately thought that he was in pain, and said something like "Hi, Roy, what's the matter?" He told me then that he'd just been fired after his first day of shooting, and was on his way home. I didn't know what to say. I think I mumbled something like "I'm sorry. How awful" or suchlike, but my survival instinct, I'm ashamed to say, kicked in. If the guy was such a loser, I didn't want to be seen with him. I mumbled some platitude, such as "Nice meeting you. I wish you well. Good luck," or something similar, and I vanished into the night. What would you have done? I never saw or heard of him again. I can't even remember which episode exactly he was sacked from, after only one day.

I don't think anybody ever thought Patrick McGoohan was particularly easy to get along with, but it's virtually impossible today to imagine the load that he had taken upon his shoulders. It was becoming clear that there wouldn't be enough money available to complete the series to Lew Grade's delivery requirements, and, at one point, it seemed as though there would barely be any episodes actually finished and available for TV showing. In any order, let alone one that made sense. It became all about money, and Lew was loathe to commit much more to what he clearly thought was Patrick McGoohan's folly, and could break ITC. Patrick, however, had a ruse. He was still in demand for leading film roles, and his plan was to accept, as soon as possible, a decent highly-paid part in an American film, and to use his salary to complete *The Prisoner*, and that he did. We heard that Pat had accepted a key leading role in MGM's *Ice Station Zebra*, directed by John Sturges, and that his salary from that Cinerama epic would go to complete the now-limited series of *The Prisoner*. Patrick would be in Hollywood whilst the completed episodes would be finished to his satisfaction, and on his return the shooting of the final last episodes would be terminated. The series run would be, uniquely, limited to the seventeen currently in production, and this information seemed to be official. Seventeen episodes only, and I was lucky enough to have worked on thirteen of them.

And what memories, most of which I've shared with you, dear reader. But I would be remiss if I didn't share my two favourite moments, although I never realised – how could I have? – that these would be my most singularly fortunate moments on *The Prisoner*, so here goes. Firstly, to relate my very first proper break as a director, offered to me unreservedly by Patrick McGoohan, and secondly, the chance to meet a cast member of, arguably the best, finest and ultimately, greatest and most satisfying motion picture feature ever made, Orson Welles' immortal classic *Citizen Kane*.

Now, I really can't remember the circumstances, but we needed a single shot of Number 6 going up the stairs, built on Stage 6, to ascend to Number 2's house. I was on the stage at the time, and Patrick clapped me on the shoulder and said something like, "You shoot it. The director's busy." I said "When?" and he said "Now, if that's all right with you." Of course it was all right with me, but Pat was in his blazer outfit, and I couldn't help but think the shot required him to be in his "Arrival" suit. I said so. He said, nice as pie, "All right. We'll do it both ways. Both outfits, up and down the steps." And he waved the camera crew over to the fake steps. "Tony's in charge," he said. I ascertained that we could shoot the blazer outfit first, since he was already wearing it, to save time, and then, if he wouldn't mind, he could just pop over to the dressing room, come back, and we'll do it again in the other outfit for insurance. "Anything you say, Tony," Pat said. So we lined up the shot, for Pat to go up those steps, and out of frame, and then back down again. I called "Action," and Pat did the shot perfectly. I knew to get a safety, just in case, and balked slightly about asking for one. Patrick sensed this: "We'll do one more," he said, "for luck." "Action!" And he did another. "Print both," I said. Patrick then said to me and the crew, "Don't move. I'll be right back." And he went off, and returned in his "Arrival" outfit. "O.K. Let's go again," he said. So we did. Up and down the stairs in two takes. "O.K., Tony?" Patrick asked. "All right with me," I replied. "Good," he said, "I'm changing back into my blazer." And he left. I was a director! And, at last, having tasted direction, I knew what my destiny was to be, if I could possibly make it happen, I would.

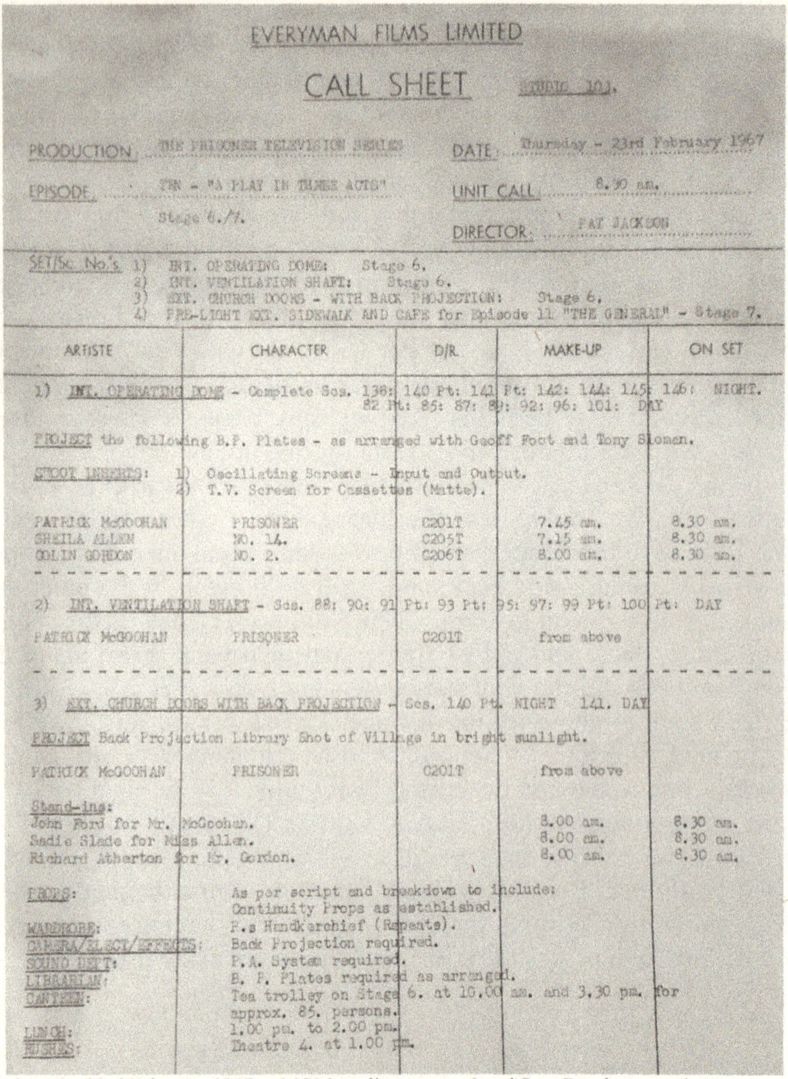

EVERYMAN FILMS LIMITED

CALL SHEET STUDIO 101.

PRODUCTION: THE PRISONER TELEVISION SERIES
DATE: Thursday - 23rd February 1967

EPISODE: TEN - "A PLAY IN THREE ACTS"
UNIT CALL: 8.30 am.

Stage 6./7.
DIRECTOR: PAT JACKSON

SET/Sc. No.'s
1) INT. OPERATING DOME: Stage 6.
2) INT. VENTILATION SHAFT: Stage 6.
3) EXT. CHURCH DOORS - WITH BACK PROJECTION: Stage 6.
4) PRE-LIGHT EXT. SIDEWALK AND CAFE for Episode 11 "THE GENERAL" - Stage 7.

ARTISTE	CHARACTER	D/R.	MAKE-UP	ON SET
1) INT. OPERATING DOME - Complete Scs. 138: 140 Pt: 141 Pt: 142: 144: 145: 146: NIGHT. 82 Pt: 85: 87: 89: 92: 96: 101: DAY				
PROJECT the following B.P. Plates - as arranged with Geoff Foot and Tony Sloman.				
SHOOT INSERTS: 1) Oscillating Screens - Input and Output. 2) T.V. Screen for Cassettes (Matte).				
PATRICK McGOOHAN	PRISONER	C201T	7.45 am.	8.30 am.
SHEILA ALLEN	NO. 14.	C205T	7.15 am.	8.30 am.
COLIN GORDON	NO. 2.	C206T	8.00 am.	8.30 am.
2) INT. VENTILATION SHAFT - Scs. 88: 90: 91 Pt: 93 Pt: 95: 97: 99 Pt: 100 Pt: DAY				
PATRICK McGOOHAN	PRISONER	C201T	from above	
3) EXT. CHURCH DOORS WITH BACK PROJECTION - Scs. 140 Pt. NIGHT 141. DAY				
PROJECT Back Projection Library Shot of Village in bright sunlight.				
PATRICK McGOOHAN	PRISONER	C201T	from above	
Stand-ins:				
John Ford for Mr. McGoohan.			8.00 am.	8.30 am.
Sadie Slade for Miss Allen.			8.00 am.	8.30 am.
Richard Atherton for Mr. Gordon.			8.00 am.	8.30 am.

PROPS: As per script and breakdown to include:
Continuity Props as established.
WARDROBE: P.s Handkerchief (Repeats).
CAMERA/ELECT/EFFECTS: Back Projection required.
SOUND DEPT: P.A. System required.
LIBRARIAN: B. P. Plates required as arranged.
CANTEEN: Tea trolley on Stage 6. at 10.00 am. and 3.30 pm. for approx. 85. persons.
LUNCH: 1.00 pm. to 2.00 pm.
RUSHES: Theatre 4. at 1.00 pm.

Daily call sheet for 23rd February 1967 at MGM studios, stages 6 and 7, at Borehamwood. As you can see, I'm the second item on call No.1. This is for "Play in Three Acts", title later changed to "A. B. and C". Call sheets were delivered to everyone late afternoon the previous day to ensure perfect running of the daily shoot, and were prepared by the first assistant director in conjunction with the production manager. They were our bible. As you can see, I'm on this one twice, so important was my contribution: at the top, in 1) as mentioned, and again at the bottom as Librarian. Interesting to note that rushes were screened at lunchtime. That would indicate that evening overtime was anticipated. (Normal rushes time would be at the end of the normal working day, usually at six o'clock, or to conform with the union 8.30 to 5.30 working day, to avoid heavy overtime payments, at 5.30 prompt. Patrick McG. considered actual lunch a luxury!)

One of the actors in *The Prisoner* episode entitled "Checkmate" (but filmed as "The Queen's Pawn") was the veteran British actor George Coulouris, his casting billed on the episode credits as "Man with the Stick". He had been featured in the last ever episode screened of Patrick McGoohan's previous television series *Danger Man* (*Secret Agent* in the U.S.) entitled "Shinda Shima", and also had been directed by "Queen's Pawn" director Don Chaffey in support to my screen idol Stewart Granger, plus Nadia Gray, no less, in 1965's theatrical melo *The Crooked Road*. Now, this man was also the actor who, to my mind, had played one of the key supporting roles in the whole history of cinema, that of Walter Parks Thatcher, in Orson Welles' *Citizen Kane*, the character who is responsible for removing the very young Charles Foster Kane from his parents, in the opening reel of that film, a scene which terminates with the snow falling on Kane's sledge, prompting the enigma that surrounds Kane's dying word, his pet name for the sledge, "Rosebud". It was George Coulouris, from Orson Welles' Mercury Theatre, who was cast in that 1940 shoot at the RKO studios, under the direction of Welles himself, in whose famous modern-dress production of *Julius Caesar* Coulouris played Mark Antony to Welles' Caesar, a far, far cry from the Manchester where George Coulouris was born in 1903.

I couldn't figure out exactly how I could meet him, but meet him I desperately wanted to, a real-life link to *Citizen Kane*, which not only then was my own favourite film of all time, but it had also just topped the Sight and Sound polls as the best film ever made, and was, at long last, becoming properly recognised. I had first seen it on BBC television, when the BBC acquired the RKO package, and was suitably impressed, but it also taught me never to watch feature films for the first time on a television transmission, and I have tried never to do so ever since. It took a theatrical viewing to fully recognise, comprehend, and simply enjoy *Kane*'s vitality, originality, and sheer on-screen bravado; there simply was no film like it, and I shall be forever grateful to my own Father, who took me to see *Citizen Kane* on the screen for which it was intended, at the first suitable opportunity in my own lifetime, when it played late night screenings only at the highbrow Academy Cinema in Oxford Street, in the early sixties.

And now here I was, working on the very same project as the actor who portrayed Walter Parks Thatcher himself, *Citizen Kane*'s benefactor and surrogate father. Patrick McGoohan must also have known this fact about Coulouris, for Pat was not only a great admirer of Orson Welles as a film-maker, but he himself played Starbuck to Welles' Captain Ahab on stage in London in Welles' famous *Moby Dick Rehearsed* at the Duke of York's Theatre in 1955. Captain Welles and first mate McGoohan – that could indeed explain a lot! I couldn't wait to chat to George Coulouris about *Citizen Kane*, and his working life with Orson Welles.

"The Queen's Pawn" came back for its studio work, and I scoured the call sheets for notification of George Coulouris' work schedule. In the rushes Coulouris was walking with a stick, and I didn't want to inconvenience him in any way, until one day I saw him, make-up towel around his neck, resting in a studio chair. I approached him…

"Excuse me, Mr. Coulouris," I said.

"Uh?" He looked up at me.

"I'm sorry to bother you…"

"Oh," he interrupted me, "I s'pose you're one of those kids who wants to ask me about *Citizen Kane*?" Hmm, that kind of took the wind out of my sails.

"If you don't mind, Mr. Coulouris. You see, I'm working on *The Prisoner*"

"What do you do?"

"It's called the film library. Background plates, and such…"

"Orson would've loved you."

"Oh?"

"Everybody wants to talk to me about *Citizen Kane*. I've made nearly a hundred and fifty films, not to mention theatre and television, but everyone wants to talk about *Citizen Kane*." I didn't quite know what to say. I tried. "But wasn't it the best film you ever worked on?" "Maybe it was. But nobody ever asks me about my own favourite film."

"Oh." (I took the cue.) "What was your own favourite film?" "*California,*" he said. And to my utter shame, at that time of my life, I'd never heard of *California*, major Western that it was in its day, when I was only two years old. "Oh" (a pause from me). "Why was that?" I said, cool, I hoped, as a cucumber.

"I had a great part. I was the villain – fourth-billed – and had a great accent. The Technicolor was fabulous, too." I'd still never heard of it. I didn't know what to say, but, thank goodness, he continued:-- "Made a lot of money on it. Good location, Arizona, good location expenses, nice food." Just then an assistant director came to fetch him, ready for the studio floor. "Nice talking to you, son," said George Coulouris, and I said, "Thank you for taking the time." "Anytime," he said, as the assistant helped him out of his chair, and, aided by the cane that you can see him holding in his episode, he made his way on to the set.

So there you have it. I did actually meet none other than the actor who played Walter Parks Thatcher in Orson Welles' *Citizen Kane*, but did we talk about *Citizen Kane*? Did we heck?! But, as fate would have it, the star of the next feature film I was to work on was in fact Orson Welles himself, although Oliver Reed played the leading role, in actuality, if not in star billing.

It really didn't seem a good time to stay with *The Prisoner*. Before he went to Hollywood, Patrick McGoohan had upset everyone with an episode that he insisted on directing himself, to continue his new bonding with Leo McKern. Filmed as "Degree Absolute", we first knew of it when strange single pages of script started to arrive, often with little more than a couple of lines of dialogue on them. Together, they barely made coherent sense. At least, not to any of us. Patrick's brain was in overdrive, and the two-handed episode drove Leo McKern into a state from which he had to take time to recover for a while, causing a pause in shooting, which eventually resumed with what seemed to be an irredeemable two-handed shouting match. Eventually the episode was re-titled "Once Upon a Time…" and shifted to near the very end of the TV screenings. Leo never really recovered.

As for me, there still were a few things to sort out. The "Many Happy Returns" episode needed some library material for plot purposes, since actual filming of such required shots seemed extremely expensive, and possibly dangerous. I took a meeting early with episode director Michael Truman (although the director credited on screen is Joseph Serf, a pseudonym for Patrick McGoohan) and we got on well together, and discussed sourcing library material involving a person jumping from an aeroplane. As it happened, a new Walt Disney feature film called *Lt. Robin Crusoe, U.S.N.* had opened very recently, and contained such a sequence. I ordered a 35mm. viewing copy, and Michael and I viewed it in a theatre at MGM with Pat McGoohan and Bernie Williams.

The sequence of interest was at the very opening of the film, and Patrick liked it very much. However, Bernie warned him that, even if the Disney people would let us use it, it would be very, very expensive, not just because it would involve dealing with Disney Hollywood to supply the dupe materials required, there probably would be royalties to pay cast and crew on top of that. (But not, I thought, to the original author, who was one Daniel Defoe.) Also geographically, we would have to optically reverse the shots, because the direction was different. If The Village is indeed in the Eastern bloc, as Patrick McGoohan had always intended it to be, then the direction needed for the aircraft from which the jump is made had to be screen right to left, i.e. Eastern bloc to England, which meant that the shot located would have to be reversed, negative and positive both, which would be extremely costly in the laboratories. So, it seemed, *Lt. Robin Crusoe, U.S.N.* was out for several reasons, as usual most of them financial, which at this stage of the production was crucial. The cheapest solution, as it often is, was to shoot the new material needed ourselves, or to find similar footage and to shoot the new required material around it, which is what happened eventually, using the aid of a company that made ejector seats called Martin Baker, and filming was organised actually involving Patrick McGoohan, and shot by our second unit under cameraman Robert Monks, instead of our regular operator Jack Lowin, who did, as usual, the main unit shoot.

But as for me, regardless of the eventual screening order, "Many Happy Returns" was to be the last episode that I worked on. As I've mentioned, nobody on *The Prisoner* at that time ever really knew if the series would be actually completed as planned, or if Lew Grade would pull the plug before the requisite number for a complete series could be filmed. There were no further scripts, script editor George Markstein had resigned over constant arguments with Patrick McGoohan by now, and Pat himself was in Hollywood filming *Ice Station Zebra*, and barely an episode was fully completed and able to be screened as per schedule. Not good. It didn't take a genius to sense that, sooner or later, the plug would be pulled. And also, and I wouldn't have mentioned this to anybody at the time, but Patrick McGoohan's drinking seemed to be getting, shall we say, a little out of hand. I'm no expert, of course, despite the fact that my own Father had a similar problem, but I would imagine that this was also a major source of concern for both *The Prisoner*'s backers and insurers, not to mention the uncredited real executive producer, Lew Grade himself. What to do? Desert the sinking ship? (Yes, there were indeed jokes around the dubbing crew about deserting the 'post-syncing' ship as Wilf Thompson himself also readied to leave *The Prisoner*.)

Then, as it happens sometimes, the telephone rang, and it was dubbing editor Jim Roddan, from *The Frozen Dead* and *It!,* offering me a job as his assistant, on a film called *I'll Never Forget What's'isname* to star Orson Welles, the world's greatest living film director, who was a hero to both Jim and myself. Only he wasn't directing this one, just playing a part; although Welles was top-billed in certain territories, the lead was actually Oliver Reed. I was on the verge of accepting immediately, pending start dates (Jim knew that I had to give at least two weeks' notice), when he told me the director was to be Michael Winner.

Now, Winner had a unique reputation. That his films all made money was beyond doubt, and since he had also helped finance them, that made him a director who would forever continue working, as long as that was the case, and be able to secure major casts. But he had a reputation already, from quite early in his career, for being totally objectionable as a person; difficult, if not impossible, to work with, totally authoritarian and brooking no arguments nor disagreements, and generally displaying no signs of taste (or, cineastes would argue, talent) whatsoever in his work. He had also become known to the outside world as virtually a determinedly one-man anti-Semitism case, I'm ashamed to say. But he did manage to secure great casts, and he was nevertheless a bright, intelligent and witty man, and a movie lover: indeed, he used to regularly contribute to my own favourite film magazine *Picturegoer*. So I said "Yes" to Jim, who then confirmed me with Winner's production manager, and so, albeit somewhat reluctantly, because I wanted to experience, and be part of, the actual termination of *The Prisoner* series when it happened, which we all, rather morbidly, knew would be very, very soon, I handed in my two weeks' notice to Everyman Films. Geoff Foot was not at all surprised, and was the only crew member who wished me luck, but Eric Mival did acknowledge that he was sad to see me go. David Naughton, the second assistant editor on the series, was the ideal and obvious person to take over from me, and he was glad to do so: he actually had time now to list all the possible library shots for future use, something I never actually got around to doing, but for which there was now to be very little future use, if any. (My only real regret on leaving was not being able to supervise the remaining few back projection shots needed. It still hurts me to see, in one particular episode completed after I had left, a character fall to the floor with nary a sound on the back-projected soundtrack. I would have instructed the dubbing editor of that episode to have added a sync. "thud" from a sound library, or to have a suitable noise recorded at a future post-sync. footsteps session, but I was no longer involved by that time).

However, in the future I was to work three more times with Bernard Williams, who, after his sterling work on *The Prisoner*, became known as one of the film world's most respected line producers, a favourite of Stanley Kubrick, working on both *A Clockwork Orange* and *Barry Lyndon*, directly after which he was associate producer on *The Last Remake of 'Beau Geste'*, where I was to meet up with him again in Madrid in 1976, when I went out to Spain as one of supervising editor Jim Clark's assistants. Our next film together was the Michael Winner version of *The Big Sleep*, but although we communicated on the telephone, we never met up in person on that particular movie. We did, though, meet once more at Twickenham studios in 1983, on *The Bounty*, when I was dubbing editor for some early edited scenes before the main edit could be approved. Bernie was line producer for Dino di Laurentiis, and my immediate job was to introduce novice director Roger Donaldson to studio post-sync., and among the Bounty's crew were such then relatively unknown talents as Daniel Day-Lewis, Liam Neeson, and Dexter Fletcher, although the film's actual stars were Mel Gibson as Fletcher Christian and Anthony Hopkins as Captain Bligh, not to mention Sir Laurence Olivier guest starring. I last saw Bernie Williams when we both recorded our commentary tracks for the Network reissue of *The Prisoner* boxed set in London in 2007. He died not long afterwards.

Jim Roddan was pleased when I agreed to be his dubbing assistant on *I'll Never Forget What's'isname* and frankly I was very glad when he informed me that we would be working in the West End, in a Wardour Street cutting room, and our immediate task was to prepare all the necessary post-synchronisation before the cast members departed. The editor was the very experienced and well-respected Bernard Gribble, and the senior dubbing editor who would be joining us was to be Terry Rawlings, who was then just finishing up on Stanley Donen's *Bedazzled*, and who was to have a stunningly successful career later on, his credits including both *Yentl* and *Chariots of Fire* as editor, and *Alien*, *Blade Runner* and *The Great Gatsby* as dubbing editor. Sounded like the kind of people I should be working with, and at last I would be back on a major feature, although still an assistant sound editor, hard to get used to again after my glorious freedom days as virtually my own boss, working to my own timescale, in my very own department, albeit forever uncredited, on *The Prisoner*, rightly regarded today as, arguably, the finest, most original, most creative, and, remarkably, still relevant series that television has ever produced, anywhere in the world. I remain aware today of how fortunate I had been, and how privileged I was to be enabled to create a very viable contribution to a series that I truly believe will endure in perpetuity, thanks to the acuity, wisdom and sheer talent of Patrick Joseph McGoohan, may he forever rest in peace, together with my eternal thanks.

But there was something else that occurred on *The Prisoner* that, many years later, changed my life, and to a degree my current career, and I hadn't really realised that it would not have happened had I not worked on *The Prisoner*, where I met and befriended Eric Mival. Before he started on the series as Geoff Foot's first assistant editor, Eric had taken an educational trip as a student to Russia, not that easy to do in those days. He made a documentary film about it called *Red Reflections*, on which he asked me to do a strange thing. Lacking a close-up of one of his Russians, he noticed that I had a similar forehead and glasses to that Russian he had photographed, and back at the MGM studios Eric asked me if I would mind if he filmed the top of my head to stand in for the missing shot of his Russian. Of course I agreed, flattered, and Eric lined up a shot, with himself on camera. I can't remember exactly, but I think it was in the cutting rooms themselves, and he duly went ahead and filmed me, and if you view it today, it's an absolutely perfect match: utterly impossible to spot. Eric invited along for the shoot his friend, his host and guide in Russia, one Harry Davis, and after the shoot we chatted together. I got on very well with Harry, a fellow Jewish Londoner, and we discovered that we had much in common, not least of all that we both shared a May 6th birthday, and we made plans to visit London's National Film Theatre, where we agreed to meet up sometime in the near future.

I had begun to programme and conduct interviews and film introductions occasionally at the NFT, and Harry, himself an educationalist and teacher, asked me had I ever thought of teaching film (which, in truth, I hadn't), rather than actually working in film. I reminded Harry of the old maxim: "Those who can, do. Those who can't, teach." He laughed, and asked me if I'd like to teach a course in European Film History at Birkbeck University, where he himself lectured. He knew that there had arisen such an opportunity, and he could recommend me if I'd like him to do so. And so he did, and so I did, teaching film in the evenings to students whilst actually working in the editing rooms (cutting an English comedy then entitled *Vol-au-Vent*, directed by John McKenzie, Lewis Gilbert's nephew) during the day. It went well, was quite pleasant, and one of my students actually graduated. Harry himself during the university holidays worked as a lecturer on cruise ships as a guide to the countries visited, and he said to me that, if I would like to, he could put me in touch with his agent, Peter Rushton, with his own recommendation, in order to give cruise ship lectures as he was then doing himself.

And so, lo and behold, I began to work professionally as a lecturer on film on cruise ships, thanks to Eric Mival's friend Harry, beginning in 2007, starting on the Queen Mary sailing across the Atlantic to New York. I couldn't begin to thank Harry Davis enough. And thank you, also, my *Prisoner* confrere Eric Mival, for introducing me to Harry (born Henry) Davis, who changed my life.

The Queen Mary was to be the first of many, many cruises. I became a much-requested speaker. My subjects ranged – or, rather, range – from a three-part history of world cinema, through a series of the lives of famous British film stars, to the most popular, studies of film genres, all lavishly accompanied with suitable relevant film clips projected onto the full-size cinema screens that the ships have in their main theatre on board, invariably followed by a question and answer session and often an appearance or two on the ship's closed-circuit television. At the time of writing I've done approximately sixty such voyages, with an average of giving seven lectures per voyage, to date. Invariably pleasantly accompanied by my wife and partner Simone, we've circumnavigated the world. We've been almost everywhere: from crossing the Atlantic to traversing the Panama Canal; across Europe and into Russia; to the Far East and to the Arctic Circle; across Scandinavia and Arabia, down to Australia and New Zealand, and taking in both French and Italian Rivieras, not to mention visiting my friend Nick Nacht's brother Andy, and his family, in Rio de Janeiro, en route. Of course, we've stopped taking normal holidays. Who on earth would have thought it possible? I regard it as a blessing, for certainly it's a long, long way from being a runner at the Film Producers' Guild, where I began. And I owe it all to the kindly benevolence of the late Harry Davis, who I met through the good graces of Eric Mival, whom I would never have met at all but for working closely together for ITC at MGM's British studios on that most singular television show starring Patrick McGoohan that called itself *The Prisoner*.

-----END OF REEL FOUR-----

REEL FIVE

It was good to be back in Soho. It took less than half an hour to reach the cutting rooms by bus, and we had a traditional 8.30 start, although Jim Roddan invariably didn't turn up until somewhere after nine, to find I had the cutting room all spick'n'span for him, and a cup of (invariably very necessary) coffee ready and waiting. *I'll Never Forget What's'isname* was still shooting on London locations, and Bernard Gribble and first assistant Peter Bond were receiving, and viewing, daily rushes. The only aspect of the production that seemed a little unusual to me was that Bernard allowed Peter to bring his dog into the editing suite daily, and to walk it at lunchtimes.

I did my deal with production manager "Mac" Davidson. As with all Michael Winner films, it was a deal highly frowned upon by the union: a seven-day deal, with no extra overtime paid, and work on weekends, if necessary, included. What to do? I signed, of course, as did everybody who worked for Winner. But at least, thank goodness, the cutting rooms were local, as was the sound studio we were to use, Warwick in Soho Square, with the wonderfully experienced (and extremely cordial) Hugh Strain as the dubbing mixer. Hugh would also record all our post-synchronisation as well, in the same theatre in which he would mix the final dub. Good news all around. Long hours, sure, an illegal deal, that's for certain, but it was great to be back in the centre of town after schlepping to all those oh-so-distant studios by public transport. And, hopefully, I'd be meeting, and working with, Orson Welles; after all, a 100% location shoot invariably meant a lot of post-sync., what with traffic, aeroplanes, trains going by, crowd noises off, and heaven knows what else.

I was well-settled in at 8a, Eccleston Street, and once again able to see films at the National Film Theatre and various other evening venues, although except just when I was getting used to all that, we were faced with a very tight schedule. Understandably, producer-director Winner wanted all the necessary post-sync. recorded and dubbed in, with effects, before showing the cut to anyone, especially to his bosses at Universal, at least not yet. I got the distinct feeling that was because of the adult plot and daring censor-provoking language. (Marianne Faithfull yelled "fuck" a few times on screen – the first time I had ever heard it said, or, rather, shouted, in a film. Winner, like a naughty schoolboy, revelled in its usage.)

So it was all systems go on arrival. Fine by me. Nick Nacht, my best friend from Dulwich and general all-round pal, was now at Cambridge, and invited me up for the May Ball, to go up on the Saturday and stay over after the ball, returning on the Sunday. He would take his girlfriend, and said I could bring one too, and we could take two bedrooms. Sounded good to me, but I was on a seven-day picture deal. It was early in the production, and the workload wasn't heavy yet, so I asked Jim Roddan for his permission to take most of the weekend off. Jim would carry on preparing the recording loops and just hang them up, and I would catch up when I returned. Since no dubbing dates were yet booked, my absence wouldn't create a problem. Or so I thought. Jim agreed, and off I went to hire my evening dress for the Ball, and

I asked a girl friend, an American called Clare, if she'd like to come with me. (So far, our only date thus far had been to see a double-bill of *You're a Big Boy Now* and *The Shuttered Room* on its South London release in Streatham). She couldn't have been more delighted, and we arranged that I would collect my evening dress from Moss Bros, and she could bring her evening gown with her. And so we did, travelling up by train on the Saturday and meeting Nick and his then-girlfriend there, and then checking in to the hotel that Nick had selected, or so we thought. We were just checking-in when the two girls decided that they wanted to share. Serves us right. Nick's and my own naughty plans were thereby thwarted. (That'll teach us!). Nonetheless, we enjoyed ourselves at the May Ball, stayed up all night, and decided to breakfast on the river in the early morning, which we did, in a hired punt.

Gently gliding along the River Cam, we can see a film unit shooting on the river bank. Pulling over, blow me down, it's our very own film unit, with Michael Winner's location associate Robin Douet directing a scene with our film's stars Oliver Reed and Carol White cruising down the river. I can't quite believe it, and, showing off, I wave at our camera crew, and Robin looks over and recognises me, and offers quite a warm "Hello", obviously as surprised to see me there in Cambridge as I am surprised to see him, not to mention our stars. "The May Ball," I explain. "Oh," Robin says, and apologises for being busy, and says "See you around." We watch the shooting for a little while. The girls are suitably impressed, and Nick is, not surprisingly, amazed, and joked that I obviously deliberately set it up. We went back to our hotel, changed out of our evening dress, and headed back to London, a nice time had by all, but, of course, not exactly quite the frolic that Nick and I had intended.

Now, this tale, in true classic cinematic storytelling style, contains parallel action. On his way home that Monday evening, Bernard Gribble's assistant Peter Bond sees our main film unit shooting near Battersea Bridge, near to where Peter lives, so Peter (and his dog) stop a while to watch the filming and say "hello" to our crew. That very next day, Bernard Gribble and Jim Roddan are summoned to appear at Michael Winner's Mayfair office at lunchtime. They duly do so, half-expecting a lunch invitation because of the timing. Bernard and Jim are confronted by a furious Michael Winner, standing behind his office desk, with the two of them stood in front of the desk like naughty schoolboys. "Mister Gribble, Mister Roddan," shrieks Winner, "Why are you sending your assistants to spy on me?" Well, what can you say? Paranoia, you could say that…

Still, I have a very soft spot for *I'll Never Forget What's'isname*, because it was actually filmed in two of my own real-life locations. There's a scene shot in our very own cutting rooms, where you can just about see the back of Bernard Gribble's head behind Oliver Reed on the telephone, as Orson Welles walks past, and the whole of the film's climax was actually filmed at my second home, London's very own National Film Theatre.

The time came to record all the post-sync. dialogue. Winner didn't want to be there for the small-part actors and players, so Jim Roddan took the sessions, with yours truly assisting, over a couple of days at the Warwick sound studios. Oliver Reed was still shooting, so we would record him later on, but Orson Welles was proving to be a problem. Apparently Welles owed money all over town to every single recording studio that existed, for his previous, invariably self-financed, features. At the mere sniff of his name, creditors would come flying out of the woodwork. It was seriously proving very difficult to get Orson Welles into a post-sync. theatre in London. My opportunity to meet and work with him, initially my raison d'être for going back to being a dubbing assistant, looked very close to not ever happening, but what about the picture I'm now on? Surely, he'd have to post-sync. some of his dialogue for clarity?

But we'd already heard how Orson Welles behaved around his director, Michael Winner. Mac Davidson told us that, one day on the shoot at Golders Green crematorium, Welles kept Winner waiting for well nigh on two hours before he actually appeared, and, when he did, he ignored Winner completely and spoke directly to Otto Heller, the lighting cameraman, asking him if that, indicating, was the lighting set-up for the scene, wherein he gets out of his car and crosses to the crematorium. Otto replied that it was. Without a word of greeting to Winner, Welles points to the lights, and tells Heller to move them according to his own instructions, replacing them at different angles, and then saying to Winner, "Michael, is that all right with you?" What could Michael Winner, the director of the film, say to the director of *Citizen Kane*? For probably the first time in his life, Winner showed some humility, and a good deal of common sense as well. Winner replied, "Yes, of course, Orson, let's take the shot." And so they did, Welles' way.

But we still couldn't nail Welles down to post-sync., not anywhere in England, at least. Jim Roddan, wisely, had prepared a list of wild tracks for Welles to record, that is to say, dialogue recorded not to picture, but, hopefully, with exactly the same rhythms and ambiances that would match the unusable, for whatever reason, originals. We never found out what Welles did with that list. We ended up going through all the takes to find his best readings, and sound-edited them accordingly.

Eventually, I was to work with Orson Welles on five occasions: *I'll Never Forget What's'isname*, *Oedipus the King*, *Orson Welles' Great Mysteries* (thirteen episodes, all introduced and bookended by Welles), *Almonds and Raisins* and *Where is Parsifal?,* and I never, ever, met him, not once. However, on *Where is Parsifal*? director Henri Helman and I did get to the Hollywood restaurant where we had arranged to meet Welles in order to discuss the post-sync. session that we had arrived in Los Angeles to record with him, amongst others, only to discover that he had left about five minutes before we actually arrived, and the sight of his departed table was truly stupendous: the remains of several lobsters and chickens, a mess of discarded oyster shells, and an accordingly large number of side dishes, each having suffered severe attacks by Orson. Amazing! No, I never did meet the director of *Citizen Kane*, but I did get to visit his supper table at the legendary "Ma Maison".

I also managed to meet somebody quite remarkable at a post-sync. session for *I'll Never Forget What's'isname*, former silent screen queen and star of *Broadway Melody* itself, Miss Bessie Love, no less. It was a day when we were doing all the small part pick-up lines, and Michael Winner didn't care to be present, so Jim took the sessions. Bessie Love just had one line to record, where she appears in the fake commercial for the fictional Hamayasha cameras that the Orson Welles character has commissioned from the Oliver Reed character. The "commercial" is a ghastly exercise on bad taste (right up Michael Winner's street!) and Miss Love's appearance follows a genuine newsreel shot of Nazi concentration camp activity wherein human remains are scooped up by a bulldozer. Miss Love has one line: "Everywhere you look is history!" Both Jim and I were worried that perhaps she would be both shocked and horrified by the context of her appearance thus – no wonder Winner didn't want to be present.

However, Bessie Love was a pro, and she did it beautifully. I couldn't resist asking her how she felt about her appearance immediately after the extraordinarily tasteless shot of the extermination camps. I should, of course, have kept my mouth shut. "Why?" she said. "Are you Jewish?" I replied in the affirmative, and then she immediately tried to convert me to Christian Science, which she had herself embraced and of which she was a firm advocate. Jim Roddan quietly smiled to himself, and said diplomatically that perhaps we would like to discuss this outside of the theatre. Which we did, but, blow me down, I couldn't rid myself of Bessie Love. To get her to leave me alone, I had to resort to giving her my telephone number (big mistake!), and she would call often, and we would meet up to discuss my "conversion". She clearly had a mission. I couldn't shake her for about five years. (She died, at 87, in 1986, in London.) She was amazingly persistent. We did meet up eventually a few times, and she invited me to some Christian Science meetings. But did we ever get to talk about her Vitagraph years, or her marriage to Howard Hawks' brother William, or even *The Broadway Melody* (her Oscar nomination), or *The Hollywood Revue of 1929*? Did we heck? 156 screen credits, and all she wanted to talk about was converting me to Christian Science!

Michael Winner did, however, want to be present at the re-recording of everybody else's dialogue, which, of course, is only right and proper. He was, after all, the film's director. The only person who would not record her lines with Winner in the recording studio was actress Wendy Craig, who absolutely loathed him, so much so that she wouldn't work if he was present. I have, of course, no idea what was in her contract, but she very firmly held out, and we did eventually post-sync. her without her director present, a first for me, since there was clearly no question of director's choice of takes: like it or leave it. I quietly kind of admired her for that, but I knew it wasn't right. But gradually, working with Michael Winner, I could see how very easy it could be to come to hate him.

Before we started one session at Warwick Studios to re-record, I think, Oliver Reed, Winner arrived early, parked his car outside the recording studio in Soho Square, entered, and promptly gave me a £1 note. "Feed my meter, Tony," he said to me. Well, I didn't drive – still don't – and thought meters only took coins. I asked Michael, "What does the meter take?" and he replied, tersely, "Sixpences, of course. Get change." Somehow I thought this was not part of a senior dubbing assistant's job, so I looked across at Jim Roddan, who said "See you in a little while, Tony" or something like that, a clear understanding to be "Do what the director tells you", so I took the pound note, and went outside to feed Michael Winner's meter. But how? The meter only took sixpences. What to do? It was too early, 8.30 in the morning, to get change at the bank at the side of Soho Square, and I couldn't hang around – Jim needed me in the theatre. There was a sweets and coffee booth open on the other side of Soho Square, so I crossed the Square to it and asked if the man inside would change a pound note for sixpences. "What do you think I am, a bank?" he replied (and who could blame him?). Oh, what to do? I know, I'll buy a sixpenny bar of chocolate, and ask for my change in sixpences with which to feed Winner's meter. And so I did. "What have you got for sixpence?" I said. "Mars do ya?" he replied. I said, only if I can have my 19/6 change in sixpences, please, and thank goodness, he grumpily agreed, handing me the Mars bar and an awful lot of silver sixpences, which I pocketed. I then walked across the square and ate the Mars bar as I went. I fed the meter, and went inside Warwick to help Jim with the session. I was accosted by Michael Winner. "What kept you?" I told him I had to get change (which he must have known) and what I'd just done to get the change to feed his meter. "Where's the Mars bar?" Winner said. I froze: I had to tell him the naked truth. In my mind I went through thoughts: Should I not have eaten the Mars bar? Should I have come back and asked him what to do to get change? Should I have given the chocolate bar to Michael Winner? Should I have asked him what chocolate bar he would have liked if I had to get change? I was, very swiftly, turning into a wreck. And he was waiting for an answer…

"I ate it, sir." I thought adding "sir" would please him: I was so naïve."You ate it?" said Winner. "Yes sir." "Humph!" said Winner and turned tail on me, and we began the post-sync. session. I carried that impression of my director with me throughout the whole time of working on *I'll Never Forget What's'isname*. Of course, almost certainly, Michael Winner never gave the matter another thought. And quite apart from the memory of the image of Oliver Reed asking Winner to leave the dubbing theatre while he (Oliver) spits water all over the theatre floor to simulate vomiting in *What's'isname*, that's really all I can remember of working with Mr. Winner, at least the first time.

The second time I worked with him, on his remake of *The Big Sleep* I didn't actually meet him, but he approved me for the job, and so I spent a week synchronising rushes for a scene between Robert Mitchum as Philip Marlowe, and James Stewart as General Sternwood, in Winner's British remake of Howard Hawks' classic, itself one of my own favourite films of all time. It really was quite something to have the likes of Mitchum and Stewart going through my synchroniser, so thank you, Michael Winner, and, I suspect, thanks also to his line producer, one Bernie Williams.

I had some catching up with real life to do while I was in town on *I'll Never Forget What's 'isname*, despite the everyday work deal. I had to be very frank with Jim, and tell him about my father, because Auntie Doris phoned me to say Dad could now have visitors, having now been transferred from Pentonville to Ford Open Prison, and would I like to come with her, and Uncle Don, who would drive my sister Linda and I down to visit him on a weekend, and of course, I said "Yes". The fact that I felt that I really couldn't face Dad was irrelevant, and a Sunday visit was proposed. Jim said that it would be fine, and that I should go. Thank God I was working with the helpful and understanding Jim Roddan at that time.

I arrived at Forest Gate early that Sunday morning, and Uncle Don drove us – Auntie Doris, Linda and myself – down to Ford Open Prison, near Arundel. It was good to be with my family again, albeit on a trip with a very strange purpose: none of us had seen Dad for about eighteen months, since before his arrest. We arrived at Ford and were asked to wait. Eventually Dad appeared in his prison outfit, I thought perhaps a little chubbier around the waist, but from his manner and attitude you would never believe he thought himself in jail. He was jovial, cheerful, and virtually his old self, making jokes about the prison food, and the ever-present warders, and about his daily routine. You'd think he'd never done anything wrong, let alone let down his entire family. But that wasn't the half of it. To our surprise, we were soon joined by a woman called Anne, who seemed very, very close to Dad. None of us knew what was going on, until a warder said that one of us would have to wait outside to make room for the new guest. Well, I elected to do so, and said my goodbyes to my Father. When the others joined me, it transpired that this Anne was Dad's "fiancée", and she was expecting to marry him on his release. She seemed surprised to see us there. Uncle Don hurried Auntie Doris, Linda and me into his car, and we simply and brusquely said "goodbye" to this Anne. On our return journey, we really didn't know quite what to say to each other, but to our surprise Anne, in her car, appeared in front of us on the way back to London. Although blindingly obvious, none of us mentioned that fact. Auntie Doris made it quite clear what she thought of what had happened, and said to Linda that it made no difference, Linda was as welcome to stay as long as she liked with her and with Uncle Don. I just breathed a sigh of relief at that, and, frankly, could barely believe what I had witnessed that day. Nor did I know what to do about it, if anything.

I'll Never Forget What's 'isname was heading for its final mix, and on the very next day Jim and I received our obligatory two weeks' notices. Some track-laying remained to be done, and Jim in his wisdom had laid up all the originals as well as the post-sync. with corrected "fill", i.e., matching original background sound, so that the director could choose his preferences at the actual pre-mix stage, particularly with regard to Mr. Orson Welles' originals. With Hugh Strain as the sound mixer, there was no longer a need for the dialogue editor, let alone his assistant, to stay on, and Jim and I finished up with a few drinks and very hearty goodbyes.

What next? Well, personally, with what seemed to be going on in my family life, I was disinclined to work immediately. But I still had financial outgoings, regardless of my own new and rather confused family feelings. Once again, Bob Dearberg came to the rescue, albeit indirectly. I received a telephone call from one Norman Cole, who said Bob had recommended me. Bob was working as an editor at Gerry Anderson's *Thunderbirds* puppet studio on the Slough trading estate, and Norman had been asked to take ten minutes out of every completed episode of the series specifically for the American market. Would I like to assist him starting the Monday after I finished on *What's 'isname*? I said "Yes" immediately, without any further discussion: I'd never before worked at the Slough studios; I knew a few of the people there, and I didn't want to decline the job on account of Bob Dearberg's recommendation. I could get to Slough from Waterloo and then connect to the studio bus service. Norman Cole didn't want to meet me before I started, (which I thought a little odd), but it didn't matter. The money was O.K., but, once again, the travelling would be horrendous: Victoria to Slough and back daily. Oh well, I needed to work.

The journey to Slough was bad enough, but I managed to time it so that I could have a breakfast at the station, before departing for Slough. It meant getting up that touch earlier, but it was better than trying to eat something fast first at the flat. The studio itself was on an absolutely huge trading estate, and the air there smelled permanently of sweet chocolate, since the main site on the estate belonged to Mars (memories of feeding Michael Winner's meter!), and that sickly smell pervaded the whole air, even inside the studio itself, albeit less so. I'm certain it never worried the puppet performers. Norman Cole seemed quite amiable enough, although clearly not interested too much in movies, a not uncommon trait in a certain type of British film technician, believe it or not. The job was interesting, and the decision of which ten minutes to remove was entirely up to Norman. Or so I thought. Except on the first day Norman said, "I hear you're good at editing. You view every episode, make notes and take timings, and then give the details to me, and I'll cut them to length." This was somewhat of a surprise to me: I thought I was the assistant, filing trims and taking notes. At least, that's what I was being paid to do. Norman then said to me "Take an episode at a time into the viewing theatre. They run just under an hour each. We should be able to do at least five a day." I had no idea how he had calculated that. Besides, shouldn't he, as editor, be the one to make the cutting decisions, and me the one to file trims and measure and time the results? Anyway, I located Bob Dearberg, thanked him for putting me forward for the job, and asked his advice. He said, just get on with it. It won't last long, and you never know where it could lead. Wise words: if I wasn't careful, I could be working on TV puppet films forever, I thought. But I needn't have worried: I wasn't going to be there that long, but I didn't, of course, know that when I started.

So I did what Norman wanted. I took an episode into the theatre, viewed it, made cutting notes, and came back. The problem was, it seemed to me, that I should be doing this on a moviola in the cutting rooms, where I could go backwards and forwards at my own speed, and time the relevant sections properly, instead of trying to make precise notes in a darkened theatre while the film was still running. I told that to Norman. He said "No", do it the way he told me to. Well, I was his assistant, so I tried my best. It seemed to work well enough with the first episode, but, of course, the timings couldn't be accurate because I wasn't using a synchroniser or a moviola, just projection, and guessing, at that, because I wasn't being supplied with scripts in advance. Also, if I had to be in the theatre all the time, I couldn't help Norman with trims, both finding and filing. I didn't know what to do, but I persevered as well as I could. Additionally, there were no proper canteen facilities in the studio. I wondered why people brought in their own sandwiches, until I realised that the canteen only provided what seemed to be heated-up ready meals, in silver foil. Not exactly what I was used to, nor what I expected. At least I'd had a decent cooked breakfast in the station canteen.

I wasn't ready for the fact that Norman and I got on the same train in the mornings, and, worse, he started joining me for breakfast at the station. That made for a very, very long day in Norman's company, so much so that, after a few days, I couldn't wait to go into the theatre to make my notes, simply to get away from him. But what happened? Of course, what with the long journeys, the perpetual and heavy smell of Mars bars in the air, and the complete lack of any interesting conversation with Norman, I started to fall asleep in the theatre. When I woke up, I'd missed the rest of a whole episode, so I had to ask the projectionist to run it for me again. And again. This was happening too frequently for comfort. Additionally, I'd started doing a very naughty thing. At the station, when I saw Norman, I'd hide, to avoid both having breakfast with him, and having to travel to Slough with him daily. So I became always slightly late on arrival, getting the next train or two, and consequently apologising for my tardiness nearly every day. I couldn't stand it, and my constant dozing off in the theatre meant that Norman was virtually working on his own, and it became very clear to me that he needed me to do what effectively was his job because he couldn't choose the material to delete by himself. At least that's what he told me when he gave me a much-deserved dressing-down for my behaviour near the end of the first week.

But on the Friday of the first week, after the dressing-down, I suddenly felt very ill in the theatre. I don't quite know what it was. I think it was a combination of everything. My domestic situation (finding out about Dad), the constant sickly smell of Mars bars in the air all of the time, the foil-wrapped lunches (which, I'd already heard, had been responsible for several cases of food poisoning), and then pretty regularly falling asleep in the theatre, all began to add up. I didn't want to tell Norman, so I found Bob Dearberg and told him. I didn't have to speak. He said I didn't look at all well, and he'd never seen me look quite like that before, and he offered to drive me to a hospital, and suggested one nearer to London, a clinic he knew in Kensington. He wouldn't take "no" for an answer, and went to tell Norman for me. Norman saw me, and said it was a good idea, and, this being Friday, he'd see me Monday morning.

Bob drove me to the hospital, where I was immediately diagnosed with food poisoning (those foil-wrapped, reheated lunches!) and prescribed medicine and rest. And then I poured my heart out to Bob, who had kindly waited to hear the result. Bob said frankly, that Norman didn't deserve me, that the cutting jobs should be reversed, and he should be assisting me. I thought Bob was right, of course, but what to do? Bob said to take the next offer – it's a busy time, something will come up. "Just leave as soon as possible, or even sooner." I knew he was right. "And don't blame me for getting you the job!" I told him I would never do that, and thanked him immeasurably.

Over that weekend I received a phone call from Jim Atkinson, a marvellous sound technician and drinking mate of Jim Roddan, best known as a wild carouser and girl-chaser, but a brilliantly inventive and witty dubbing editor, who asked if I'd like to assist him for a few weeks only on *Tell Me Lies*, a film version of Peter Brook's stage show, *U.S.*, about the Vietnam War. It would only be syncing and looking after rushes until editor Ralph Sheldon could start working on it, as Ralph was tied up at the moment finishing his previous picture *The Biggest Bundle of Them All*, a Raquel Welch feature. He also added that Jim Roddan had praised me very highly, and, although we had met, he actually couldn't remember me. I said "Yes" immediately, and that he'd recognise me when we met again. Starting when? "Week after next," he said. "Monday week. Sound Associates, Bayswater. They're filming all over London, so it's just syncing rushes, but there'll be a lot of them." I didn't even discuss money. This was a gift from the gods. I knew I really should give Norman and *Thunderbirds* two weeks' notice, but he'd have to make do with just one week, and, I thought serves him bloody well right. (But, really and truly, I should have found out more about that specific job first, more about Norman, and more about the Slough Trading Estate before even thinking about accepting that particular situation in the first place.) Good news, and once again, thank you, Jim Roddan.

I'd actually seen *U.S.* at the Aldwych Theatre in London during its relatively short run, and knew roughly what to expect from the rushes. Multiple-camera contemporary agit-prop cinema with the original cast from the Royal Shakespeare Company, including a virtually unknown Glenda Jackson. This was better than editing puppets! I was really pleased and, to a degree, excited to be back working on something decent with good people, even though I was back again working as an assistant editor, once more just synchronising rushes.

I went in for that one last week on *Thunderbirds*, and told Norman I was leaving, and that I'd had a better offer. He didn't quibble over the one week's notice, indeed I had the distinct feeling that he was rather glad that I was going. I asked him if I should attempt to find a replacement, but he said "No", and it seemed to me that he clearly already had somebody in mind. Well and good. I didn't carp. But I did feel that it was actually professionally up to me to find him a replacement, but he said that it would be taken care of, which led me to think he wanted to get rid of me anyway, and who could blame him? I then worked out the week, and left the Mars-smelling Slough Trading Estate forever.

Tell Me Lies was filming all over London, but our rushes were coming into Sound Associates, a relatively new post-production facility house between Whiteley's store and the Bayswater Road, jolly convenient for me. And probably convenient for Jim Atkinson, my editor, too, but his own personal life was a shade shambolic, and I never knew quite where he would appear from in the mornings, if indeed he did appear, or exactly where (or even how) to contact him in the evenings. However, since the film had no fixed shooting hours, and would often work late into the night on various locations, amazingly the irregular screening of rushes wasn't a problem: we ran when we could, and Jim always seemed to manage to turn up on time, wherever or whenever it was. I co-ordinated the rushes screenings through a very nice assistant director called Peter Sykes, with whom I was to work much later on, and befriended when he became a director on the *Orson Welles Great Mysteries* series back at Caledonian, but I did get a very distinct feeling from Peter that he couldn't wait until the more reliable Ralph Sheldon started as editor on the film, but I wasn't to be around for that.

I'd had a telephone call from Rusty Coppleman, a very distinguished sound editor that I knew of, but hadn't actually met yet, asking me if I was free, and would I like to assist him on a film version of Sophocles' *Oedipus the King*, currently finishing their shoot in Greece, and about to return to Sound Associates? I had been recommended by someone at Sound Associates, where I was already working on *Tell Me Lies*. I told Rusty that I was only on *Tell Me Lies* until Ralph Sheldon started, which Rusty already knew, and he asked would I be free to start in two weeks' time? Would I? I replied formally in the affirmative, thanked him, and we agreed to meet up in the Bayswater complex two weeks Monday to start on the Greek tragedy. As it happened, I didn't have to give my notice: it was anticipated. Jim Atkinson and I were to actually finish the very Friday before I was due to start with Rusty on the Monday.

Rusty Coppleman was a distinguished, well-known and popular sound editor. He had recently had a huge artistic success with his work on *Zulu*, which I admired immensely. No-one who ever saw it would ever forget the remarkable use of sound, particularly the shield noise of the Zulus approaching, which must have been recreated in the studio. Rusty's credits included *The Bridge on the River Kwai* and Gary Cooper's last film *The Naked Edge*, and, unsurprisingly since Stanley Baker was *Zulu*'s producer, a few recent Stanley Baker Africa-based features. I was very flattered to be asked to assist him. (By the way, the International Movie Database persists in listing Rusty as a "her". Oh, no, no.) Rusty said to meet him in the cutting room at Sound Associates, which I did.

The editor of *Oedipus the King* was a very well-meaning man called Paul Davies, who had made his name with the notorious *The War Game* and a couple of Swedish films directed by Mai Zetterling, but clearly wasn't an experienced features editor. Fortunately, his assistant was Garth Craven, a really nice guy who would go on to a very distinguished Hollywood career, primarily as director Sam Peckinpah's editor, and with whom I got on terribly well. *Oedipu*s went smoothly, and Rusty and I bonded, our Jewish backgrounds melding. (Although Rusty's was very strictly closet Jew.)

Oedipus moved along very professionally, and Paul Davies and I became friends, of sorts. Post-production, with Rusty and director Philip Saville (another closet Jew!) also went smoothly, and most of the recorded original sound could be kept, since the Greek location was far from any traffic noise. There was a very limited amount of post-synchronisation, but the most interesting part of the post was the post-sync. of a virtually then-unknown actor called Donald Sutherland, who played the Leader of the Chorus, and had a pronounced Canadian accent. Philip Saville tried to get Donald to modify this at the post-sync. session, which took place at the Anvil dubbing theatre, in the great Denham studio complex that once housed Alexander Korda. Donald tried very hard, but couldn't quite achieve what Philip wanted. For my part, I didn't think Donald stood out particularly in the company of fellow North Americans Christopher Plummer and Orson Welles, but Philip was clearly worried. In the middle of the recording session, Philip started giving Donald elocution lessons. Now remember, at this point in his career, Donald was virtually unknown, though I had seen him on stage in a reading of Edgar Lee Masters' "Spoon River" at the Royal Court, alongside Betsy Blair, and fellow Canadians Bernard Braden and Barbara Kelly, where he more than held his own.

"Tee, Ta, To, Too," said Philip. "Enunciate." Donald enunciated as well as he could, but it still came out Canadian. Several attempts proved little different. Rusty, quite rightly in my opinion, suggested recording it anyway, just so that we had one to use, without bird noise and heavy open atmosphere, and so we did. But we never used it, at least not then. Philip sent Donald home, and asked if we could get a matching replacement, right away if possible, while we have the studio time. The producer then called in Patrick Allen, that slant-jawed British actor well-known as a voice artiste, and Patrick came in and redid all of Donald's lines. And so, in the final approved mix, Patrick Allen's voice replaced that of Donald Sutherland's as the Leader of the Chorus. But then, as can only happen in show business, the completely unexpected occurred. An offbeat comedy that Donald Sutherland had made one film after *Oedipus the King* was released, and became a worldwide success, turning Donald Sutherland into an internationally famous film star, and that film was called *M.A.S.H.*, which Donald followed with the almost equally successful *Kelly's Heroes*. Donald Sutherland had become a major star of his era. And so the inevitable happened: Rusty got a call to replace the Patrick Allen re-voice in *Oedipus the King* with Donald Sutherland's own post-sync. Fortunately, the very wise Rusty Coppleman had laid up the Sutherland post-sync. as an alternative, just in case, but it was never mixed, and certainly wasn't there in the premiere run at the Odeon, Haymarket. But eventually a remix was organised, and Donald's vocals were put back, now that he was a star. I doubt if *Oedipus the King*, excellent though it was, ever returned its money, let alone made a profit, but at least you can now see it with an early performance by the young Donald Sutherland, using his own voice at last.

While we were on *Oedipus* it was announced that Frank Zappa and the Mothers of Invention were to make their U.K. debut at the Royal Albert Hall, and I was anxious to see them, and asked Rusty if he'd like to come with, and he said he would, and our director Philip Saville said that he'd like to join us and bring his girl friend, who turned out to be Diana Rigg. The show was terrific, and famously culminated in the Mothers burning the U.S. flag on the Albert Hall stage, and being subsequently banned from ever appearing there again, but what I remember most about that particular evening was Philip offering to buy us all a drink in the interval, and, as I helped him at the bar, I caught sight of him sneakily borrowing the money to pay for the drinks from Diana; in fact, she proffered the money to him: after all, he was probably waiting for his last payment on *Oedipus*, and she at that time was very famous as Emma Peel in *The Avengers*.

As I mentioned, Rusty Coppleman and I got on very well professionally. I learned to anticipate his needs, and we thought alike in choice of materials. I upset him once at the dub, and I did something that I shouldn't have, and accordingly learnt a lesson. We were doing the final sound mix at WorldWide, in Holborn, where I had previously worked on those dreadful Army commercials, and Rusty had left me to supervise some pre-mixes, which involved creating matching backgrounds from sound loops that Rusty had prepared and charted. Straightforward enough. But the dubbing mixer, Peter Gilpin, didn't particularly like one background loop on a scene – "Too many sheep" – and wanted to change it, was it all right to do so? What I should have done was to immediately telephone Rusty in the cutting room, and ask him if it was O.K. But I didn't. (I don't know why.) I said "Yes" to Peter, and we mixed with a different loop. When Rusty came into the theatre for the playback, he said, "Who changed the loop?" Peter Gilpin said, "Tony." Rusty just looked at me. I couldn't bring myself to say, in front of Peter, that it was Peter who didn't like it. I don't know why I couldn't, but that clearly wasn't the issue. Rusty said, "Why didn't you call me first? Now we'll have to use that background every time we go to that location, won't we?" "Yes," I replied, shamefacedly. "Don't ever do that again," said Rusty to me, in front of Peter, teaching me a lesson, because amateur psychologist Rusty well knew that, if he berated me in front of the senior mixer, I'd certainly never do it again, ever. But what only clever Rusty himself knew was that specific background never recurred in the film, and that particular sheep loop would never ever be needed again. But in future, as a dubbing assistant, I always referred every single theatre query to the dubbing editor in question. I learned a tough, though some would think obvious, dubbing lesson from one of the best sound editors in the business. I'd never make a dubbing theatre decision again without consulting my head of department. Who on earth do I think I am?

Towards the end of *Oedipus*, Rusty Coppleman received a telephone call that would change our lives, his and mine, forever. It was from producer Alan Clore, saying that his line producer, Andrew Braunsberg, had suggested Rusty as film editor, not sound editor, although that too if he'd like, on a brand-new "Swinging London" feature, with exceptional design and music, to be called *Wonderwall*, to be directed by Joe Massot, an American living in London whose short film *Reflections on Love* was up for Best Short at Cannes. Rusty assumed, because of its high music factor, that there was some mistake, that he was wanted as sound editor, but no, Andy Braunsberg assured him that they wanted Rusty to actually be the film editor of *Wonderwall*. After a moment's pause, he accepted.

He told me about the phone call while we were finishing *Oedipus*, and then asked me if I would like to be his first assistant editor. "We'll get a cheap second to do rushes," Rusty added. Would I like to be his first? Pull me down from the ceiling! Would I heck! Promotion indeed!! First assistant on a brand new "Swinging London" feature! Trying to contain my enthusiasm, I thanked him immensely, and spluttered out "Yes," and "Thank you," again. "We start as soon as possible, right here at Sound Associates, as soon as we finish *Oedipus*. We'll need a very inexpensive second assistant." Talk about life-changing…

So we boxed up *Oedipus* and, with Paul and Garth, committed it to the Universal vaults. Paul, although I think slightly jealous if not peeved, wished us luck, and we started searching for a second assistant, a very inexpensive second assistant, and both Rusty and I preferred a girl. Sexist, I know, but making tea was never part of the job that I ever felt comfortable with, and Rusty, in his wisdom, knew it. We received copies of the script, from its translator Alain Passes, credited to one G. Cain, which turned out to be the nom-de-film of the great Cuban Marxist writer Guillermo Cabrera Infante, who director Joe Massot knew from his previous work teaching film at the Instituto del Cine in Havana, where Guillermo had been the Director. It was all very interesting. The film was to be shot entirely on London locations, but with the main shoot at Twickenham studios, so once we had completed *Oedipus* and found our second assistant, we were to base ourselves at

Twickenham, already the hippest studio in England, being Richard (*The Knack*) Lester's home studio and therefore also the home of the Beatles' first two features *A Hard Day's Night* and *Help!*. This was to be the beginning of the Beatles' connection to *Wonderwall.*

In the meantime, *The Prisoner* was receiving its television premiere, Sunday nights on ITV, and, to me, was totally absolutely revelatory, although I think to the television audience at the time it was both baffling and confusing. Of course, although it hadn't occurred to me then, but most viewers, including myself, watched those first transmissions in black-and-white; colour TV sets then were by no means common, and *The Prisoner* lost much of its visual wealth, accordingly. But for me, the real revelation of that first transmission on that particular Sunday in September 1967 was the voice of Fenella Fielding, no less, broadcasting throughout The Village. I had never heard it before: the scenes in which it was used were all shot mute, and stayed such whenever I saw the completed cutting copies. Remember, I wasn't working on the sound side. The scenes involving the loudspeaker voice were all edited to a precise length, and then the dialogue was written, and recorded, to fit the final edits. What a revelation it was to me! Not just because it was Fenella, who I adored, and eventually got to know quite well via BAFTA members screenings, but because they were exactly what the episodes needed: a unifying aspect that could symbolically knot The Village together, an all-embracing new tone that could both identify The Village to its inhabitants, and, perhaps more importantly, unite the minds of the television viewers. To me, it was utterly revelatory, and brilliant! Truly, simply brilliant! The icing, if you like on *The Prisoner*'s cake, written, timed and voiced to perfection. I never found out who cast Fenella: I suspected casting director Rose Tobias Shaw, but long ago I learnt never to put anything past Patrick McGoohan.

But, when *The Prisoner* series first played, I was unable to watch each episode straight through. Being a rock fan, and living in Victoria, I could only watch the first half-an-hour of *The Prisoner*'s Sunday debuts, because I invariably had tickets for Sundays at the Saville, the one-off rock shows at the Shaftesbury Avenue theatre then under Brian Epstein's management, and saw Jimi Hendrix, Procol Harem, Traffic (their debut), Eric Clapton, and several visiting Americans on those Sundays which always clashed with *The Prisoner*'s first television broadcasts. Well, London was swinging, and everything on television would be repeated sooner or later, wouldn't it, though? But it was a tough call, a really tough call.

And then, one night after a Hendrix gig, the house lights at the Saville came on, and a voice from what was Brian Epstein's box made the following announcement: "Ladies and gentlemen, we regret to inform you that Brian Epstein was found dead at his home earlier this evening. Please leave the theatre quietly." "Shock" simply doesn't do justice to what we felt then and there at that historic moment in Brian Epstein's own theatre: I had wondered why his usual box was empty that night. But on Monday morning I was back at Twickenham with Rusty, and our brand newly-hired assistant Bridget Reiss, who was to become my dearest, closest, wisest friend, and who would, one day, eventually give me an instruction that would change my life for the inevitable better, for always and forever: an instruction to drop the immediate seemingly urgent film workload for once, and go and race after the girl that I would eventually marry, before she gets away. Bridget was, as ever, absolutely spot-on.

We started on *Wonderwall* at Twickenham studios on the first day of shooting, which took place on a glamorous indoor set designed by Assheton Gorton, just coming off *The Knack* and *Blow-Up*. *Wonderwall* also had very special contemporary décor and set design by The Fool, alias Simon and Marijke, a Dutch pair of artists who were funded by the Beatles and who designed the costumes worn by them for their TV broadcast of "All You Need is Love," and also both the decorations to John Lennon's piano and George Harrison's guitars and his bungalow. The Beatles themselves funded The Fool's fabulous Apple Shop in Baker Street, which swiftly became known as the Beatles' own shop, to the private opening of which, on December 5th, 1967, Rusty, Bridget and I were invited, whilst working on *Wonderwall*, as guests of Apple Corps.

Wonderwall was very, very much of its time: psychedelia was the watchword, and the slim plot involved "Professor" Jack MacGowran becoming obsessed with his model girl neighbour, played by Jane Birkin, who was then married to James Bond composer John Barry, long before she recorded the notorious "Je t'aime…Moi non plus" with her later lover Serge Gainsbourg, and she had been prominently featured in Antonioni's *Blow-Up*, one of the quintessential Swinging London movies. Appropriately, Jane Birkin's character name in *Wonderwall* was Penny Lane, so the Beatles were "dans le vent" on this film, already.

We screened the cut one time early on at the producer's request for film star Richard Harris, who turned up at the screening slightly worse for drink, and he then proceeded to crudely pursue Bridget, to her distress. He called her "Little Bo-Peep", and, quite literally, chased her round the theatre foyer. Rusty intervened, and Bridget hid in the Ladies loo. Harris then seated himself in the theatre, and I started the screening. Harris fell sound asleep during the running, snoring, and Rusty wisely sent "Little Bo-Peep" home.

Rusty Coppleman worked hard and effectively, and we soon had a viable, if only slightly overlong, decent edit. To celebrate the cut, director Joe Massot treated the three of us in the cutting room up to London's ultra-fashionable King's Road to celebrate, at the most fashionable of all restaurants then, Alvaro's. We were visited at our table by Joe's friend, the lovely Jacqueline Bisset, not yet a star just after *Cul-de-Sac*, and a good few years away from *Bullitt*, and when I was to work with her many years later in Puerto Rico on *Fascination*, when I was post-production co-ordinator for Goldcrest, we both recalled with pleasure that particular day at Alvaro's.

Joe Massot had another reason for taking us to lunch at Alvaro's, not just to be trendy. He told us there that the Beatles themselves would like to see the film as currently edited, with a view to possibly composing the music. After all, Apple, the Beatles' company, had a financial interest in it, via Simon and Marijke, and they would like to see it in its present state, without any temporary music that we might be tempted to dress it up with. The Beatles want to see *Wonderwall*!!! We could hardly believe our ears. But nobody could have taken this amazing news with a more professional calm than Rusty Coppleman, easily one of the coolest film technicians ever, and Rusty just said to Joe, "Where would they like to see it?" Joe just said "Somewhere in town. I'll find out when." And he did.

Rusty had already decided that not only would he be the film editor of *Wonderwall*, but he would also be the sound editor, even though it was extremely unusual, if ever done before on a feature, for the same person to both cut and dub at the same time, but Joe and Andy were agreeable. It made sense. Rusty said we would need to take on a footsteps editor, to record and edit all the post-synchronised sound fx, and to prepare the music and effects track without dialogue for the foreign version, and asked me if I knew anyone, since he didn't want to employ any of his own sound editing contemporaries on his first film editing job. I thought for a while, and then suggested my good friend and associate from *The Prisoner* Eric Mival, a fine technician, and, more to the point, a person of excellent contemporary taste. Rusty agreed, met with him, and so Eric joined we three for a lifelong friendship, I'm happy to say, which actually suffered an appalling hiccup with me on the *Strange Report* television series, but more of that later. Eric joined us at Twickenham, a very amiable cutting room set-up. Although Eric thought of himself primarily as an editor, he was perfectly able and comfortable with recording and creating the international sound effects track, and clearly got on very well with Rusty. Without doubt, Eric's own contribution to *The Prisoner* was considerable, both as Geoff Foot's assistant, and latterly as music editor, and therefore I thought he would be a great asset to us on *Wonderwall*, but, it could be argued, he was perhaps personally just a little too "square" for those swingin' times.

The booking was made. We would screen *Wonderwall* for the Beatles at the Bowater House viewing theatre, in Knightsbridge, at an afternoon viewing, and Joe Massot would be there, introduce us to the Beatles, watch the film, and discuss it with the eight of us afterwards (Rusty, me, Bridget, Eric, and the Beatles, no less). We arrived at Bowater House earlier in the day to meet the projectionists, and to put up the first reel of *Wonderwall* to check the theatre sound levels. At this stage, both picture and sound were still separate, although in synchronisation, as it was convenient that, should suggestions for change arise, the suitable edits could be carried out well before the final mix. At present, of course, there was no music, not even temporary music tracks laid, as sometimes occurs.

The Beatles arrived, all four at once, together with Joe Massot, who introduced us to them, and we duly shook hands with John, Paul, George, and Ringo. We managed to pretend to be cool, calm and collected, as if this happened to us every day. Joe showed everybody into the theatre, whilst I went to check that the projectionists were ready. We then ran the film. I must say that I thought it felt slow, but perhaps that was just viewing it without any music. Anyhow…

Afterwards, all four Beatles thanked us personally, and Joe ushered them out, accompanying them to wherever the post-film discussion (to which we weren't invited) was to take place. On their way out, the Beatles themselves could not have been nicer. It was still daylight outside, about four o'clock, and, as I held the Bowater House street door open for Ringo Starr, he said to me, in that unmatchable Liverpudlian accent, "Y'know, Tony, I always think it's going to be dark when you come out of the pictures." We laughed. I shook his hand and we said our goodbyes. Little could I then guess that Ringo and I would work together in the future on two separate occasions, on one of which I was to be Ringo's choice as editor.

Our screening took place on a Friday. On the following Monday, in our Twickenham cutting room, Rusty Coppleman took a telephone call from our producer, Andy Braunsberg. Rusty turned to Bridget and me after he put the phone down, and said, "You'll never guess what. George Harrison wants to score the picture. On his own, without the others, and he wants to come in for music spotting as soon as possible."

Well, we were flabbergasted, and, of course, pleased and surprised. But before that could happen, there were the new editing notes to be taken care of. After the screening, John Lennon had said that the front was too long, and that you needed to get to the Jack MacGowran character sooner, and, at the theatre, everyone there generally agreed with him, all excepting Eric Mival, who really annoyed Rusty. Eric, of course, should have kept his own mouth shut: his opinion was neither required nor requested at that particular time. Rusty, effortlessly political, said to Eric something like "We'll discuss it later, Eric, not right now" (i.e. "Shaddup. You're only doing sound. Listen to what John has to say. After all he's not only a Beatle, he's also Apple, the part-financiers of the movie"). Eric, no fool he, withdrew from all conversation as the Beatles made ready to depart.

So, George wants to score the picture. Who, in the whole world, in their right mind, would turn down a Beatle? Joe came in to discuss the changes, and agreed on a general slight shortening of the viewed edit, mainly at the front, as per John Lennon's suggestion, and Rusty estimated how long the changes would take, and ultimately proved to be absolutely spot-on in those estimates, and we duly made ready for music spotting with no less than George Harrison himself, at that very moment arguably one of the four most famous (and most talented) musicians in the world, let alone also one of the most famous people in the whole universe. A day was put aside for George's arrival, and the film was to be screened in the cutting room, where timings could be accurately taken, alongside music cues, and that was to be my job, starting Monday week, in order to allow Rusty a full week to do the changes. He did them in three days, and we viewed the film on the screen. It not only moved faster, it clearly looked better, and it was obvious that the music would benefit it, even enhance it. I made rough music notes on Rusty's instructions during the screening, and we looked forward to George Harrison's arrival.

Came next Monday, and came the rains. George Harrison arrived soaked through, sockless, and his Indian-style slippers virtually destroyed by the Twickenham mud that he had to walk through in order to reach our cutting room. Bridget immediately made him a cup of tea (he didn't drink coffee), and the conversation was, first of all, about his shoes, and not at all about the film, or scoring, or recording, or anything remotely to do with the film. After explaining why he couldn't get another pair of shoes right away ("I'm too famous. I can't even go to a shoe shop without being mobbed") Bridget came up with the brilliant bright idea of making him a new pair out of the cardboard Technicolor rushes delivery boxes: they wouldn't get him very far, but they'd get him to his waiting car with dry feet. In the meantime, he could view the film with Rusty while I made notes. George was absolutely delighted with this idea, and promptly took off his own ruined footwear and threw it into our waste paper basket. Bridget then produced two Technicolor rushes boxes, and asked George to stand on them, which he did. She then took a black magic marker pen and drew around the shape of his feet, then placed the box tops over George's feet, and cut off the sides. "All done," she said, and with that, while George and Rusty ran the film on the moviola, reel-by-reel, and I took music notes, Bridget made "shoes" out of the cardboard boxes. When we had finished, George was absolutely delighted with his new "shoes", made out of Technicolor cardboard rushes boxes, which were held together with film joining tape, not ordinary mere Sellotape, and he wore them with pride all the way to his parked car, from the cutting rooms right across the length of Twickenham studios. Of course, everybody stared at him from their respective windows, but George was clearly used to that. He thanked us all, and I told him that we'd send him the requisite footages and a copy of the film, and we would all be in touch very soon, whereupon he invited us to the opening of the new Apple store in Baker Street. The film music session was to be arranged at Abbey Road Studios, and our liaison would be musician and composer John Barham, who turned out to be an incredibly nice man and a lifelong friend: I last saw him, sadly, at Bridget's funeral, not six months after he, Bridget and myself had met up for an Indian meal in Soho, only a few recent years ago.

George Harrison recorded much of the *Wonderwall* music in India, at HMV Bombay, with John Barham, who had himself studied music composition under George's sitar teacher, the great Ravi Shankar. The recording of the film score is particularly well-documented, and the very strong Indian influence continued throughout the London recording sessions. The only problem – and it was a considerable one – was that most of the recorded music didn't adhere to my supplied music timings, and would need to be subsequently edited in order to fit the film, which Rusty did admirably in order to accommodate George's suggested music cuts. The proof, as they say, of the pudding is in the eating, so I would suggest to anybody cavilling about cutting Beatles music, just watch the movie, don't necessarily just listen to the soundtrack on its own, brilliant though it is. After all, George Harrison was pleased when he saw it with the film. I don't think that he was necessarily cut out to score motion pictures; thank goodness for John Barham, and, of course, Rusty Coppleman, whose contribution to *Wonderwall*, I felt from my privileged position, was always shamefully underrated. Today, *Wonderwall* is mainly remembered for its soundtrack album being the very first release on the Beatles' brand new Apple label, numbered SAPCOR 1, which came out on November 1st, 1968.

There was another additional bonus that occurred whilst working with George Harrison. All four Beatles had just completed a film for television called *Magical Mystery Tour*, the contents of which had been kept very secret. No-one had seen any of it at all, and rumours were abounding. Just before Christmas, delivery took place, and each Beatle received a completed 16mm. show print for themselves. One day on his arrival, George brought his brand-new unscreened copy into the cutting room, and asked us if we'd like to be the first to view it; it hadn't even been previewed yet. George himself hadn't time to see it as he was off to India, so he thought we might like to borrow his own copy and be the first people in the world to see *Magical Mystery Tour*. Would we?? Wouldn't we just??!! I said "Yes, please" first, but Rusty didn't want to be held responsible for keeping the print over the Christmas holidays, so he asked me to take it home with me, guard it well, and bring it back after the Christmas gap, if that would be all right with George, who then said that he was happy to leave it with me, and he'd want to know what I thought of it when he returned.

Well!! First kid in the world to see *Magical Mystery Tour*: Me! (And Bridget too, of course). So I took the print home and secretly arranged to view it, not on my own projector (that could cause damage) but on the big screen late at one of the all-night screenings at the Arts Lab in Drury Lane, providing that they gave an assurance to tell no-one. And that's what happened: they just slotted it in, unannounced, between a couple of late night features. What a rare and classic privilege for me: I couldn't thank George Harrison enough. To see (and hear) new Beatles product before absolutely anybody else – well, there just ain't the words! As for myself, truly the most significant aspect of working on *Wonderwall*, apart from the sheer pleasure of the workload, and, of course, meeting for the first time, not only Bridget, but actually all four of The Beatles themselves, and then working intimately with none other than George Harrison, was that it was the very first motion picture on which I received my own on-screen credit: Anthony Sloman. It looked bloody good on the big screen, and, boy, was I proud.

By the way, whilst working on *Wonderwall* my right arm re-dislocated itself – thanks again, Mary Kessel – and I turned up one Monday morning at Twickenham studios with the arm in a sling. I was still able, just, to manage coffee in the studio canteen when I suddenly felt a great thump, and subsequent pain, on the shoulder that was in the sling. I'd been clapped on my bandaged arm by none other than Laurence Harvey, with whom I'd exchanged friendly regular greetings previously. He obviously thought it was a wizard prang to bash someone whose arm was in a sling. What a sadist! He was at the studio completing *A Dandy in Aspic*, having taken over after the original director Anthony Mann had died during production; I suddenly had second thoughts about my friendship with this very distinguished Jewish actor that I had so admired for *Room at the Top*, *Expresso Bongo*, and *The Alamo*, and I immediately lost all interest in seeing *A Dandy in Aspic*, and still never have.

As an interesting aside, *Wonderwall* not only had its premiere internationally at the Cannes Film Festival on May 17th 1968, but it opened in London at a brand-new cinema run by the Compton group, the four-screen Cinecenta, in Panton Street, in London's West End, just off Leicester Square, that following January, a purpose-built house preceding the then-new trend of halving or quartering the larger type of cinema that used to be used for full cinema circuit releases, and foreshadowing the current multiplexes. Before I finally left employment on *Wonderwall*, it was my job to check the levels of presentation (picture and sound) at the Cinecenta, and to see *Wonderwall* through all four of its simultaneous premieres. I'm happy to report, it passed with flying colours.

There was a postscript to working on *Wonderwall*. In the context of the film itself, the central character Oscar, played by Jack MacGowran, sneaks into the film next door (via the *Wonderwall* itself) and hides in a large and very colourful psychedelic wardrobe, designed by Simon and Marijke themselves. A key plot point. Now, during the filming I, very briefly, had dated Sally Waxman, the daughter of *Wonderwall*'s fabulous, indeed legendary, cinematographer Harry Waxman (*Brighton Rock*, *Sapphire*) and when the filming was over, and the set was being deconstructed, Sally suggested that I try to acquire the actual *Wonderwall* wardrobe itself, for keeps, and install it in my Eccleston Street home, a brilliant idea that seriously never would have ever occurred to me: to keep the set itself as a souvenir! Assheton Gorton gave his permission, Sally organised a pick-up truck, and we drove the wardrobe to 8a, Eccleston Street, where it rested in all its psychedelic splendour. However, just before I had to move from Eccleston Street, I arranged to place it – I thought temporarily – with the British Film Institute, who seemed pleased to store it for me in their vaults. The person I was dealing with organised the pick-up, and an exchange of letters granted me access whenever I wanted, and an ultimate collection at a later date to be determined. I placed inside it a package of original black-and-white *Wonderwall* production stills showing the wardrobe's usage in the film, and off it went to the BFI storage facility.

Several years later I was approached about my work on *Wonderwall* by a Belgian group involved in a Beatles chronological encyclopaedia, and I mentioned that I happened to own the *Wonderwall* wardrobe, and they made plans to come over to England to see it. However, when I called the BFI, they said they had no record at all of such an item. I described it in detail, and mentioned the included stills. They referred me to the stills department, which

I promptly visited, and where I found my precious *Wonderwall* stills with "Property of the British Film Institute" now stamped on their backs. I remonstrated, but they clearly didn't believe me. Not at all. They were rude and unpleasant. I then spoke to the BFI vault keeper, who said that they'd searched for the wardrobe as described, but that he had no record of it whatsoever. I offered to come down and look, but it seemed that that was the last thing they wanted. I next spoke to the then-current head of the BFI, who not only didn't seem at all interested, but brushed me off as clearly being a nuisance. And that's how the matter still stands today. The *Wonderwall* wardrobe, designed by The Fool for Apple, is, as far as I know, still held in the British Film Institute classic props collection, but nobody can identify it, they won't let me come over and investigate without permission (whose permission?), and they wouldn't even attempt to look for it after I pleaded with them to search. What to do?

Two other little tales before we leave *Wonderwall* completely. Before the titles appear on any film, the proposed title lists are invariably shown to everybody credited, to make sure of correct spelling and nomenclature. When the *Wonderwall* main titles were circulated, and returned to the cutting rooms, there was a major query from none other than George Harrison, who wanted to talk to me about them. He was concerned that both cameraman Harry Waxman and editor Rusty Coppleman had initials after their names, B.S.C. (British Society of Cinematographers) and G.B.F.E. (the then newly-formed Guild of British Film Editors) respectively. George pointed out that the Beatles had received each an M.B.E. from the Queen in the most recent New Year's Honours List, and he would therefore like M.B.E. (Member of the British Empire) after his name in the *Wonderwall* front credits. Who would disagree with a Beatle? I duly amended the list, after, of course, getting Rusty's permission, accordingly.

One sad memory of *Wonderwall*: Twickenham editors often lunched at "The Turk's Head", an amiable pub just a little way off the beaten track in St. Margaret's, and, one day, working with George Harrison, George suggested that he take us all, Rusty, Bridget, me and himself, to lunch, and we suggested "The Turk's Head", which was used to celebrity visitors, and the landlord would find us a quiet table where George wouldn't be disturbed. We normally walked there, but George insisted that we all go in his limousine, which was parked outside the studio. We piled in, and George duly instructed his driver. On the way, we passed the St. Margaret's railway station, which displayed a newspaper bulletin outside: OTIS REDDING DEAD. George had the car pull up, and sent me out to get a paper. I bought two, and gave one to George and read the other one myself, unable to take in the news. I had seen Redding just recently, performing as a guest with the Tamla-Motown tour at the Hammersmith Odeon. He was only twenty-six, and, as so often tragically happens in America, it was in a plane crash. None of us felt like going on to lunch at "The Turk's Head" at all. George was visibly shaken, and Rusty suggested we go back to the studio, which we did. The other, and perhaps, strangest, of all my stories about working on *Wonderwall* is a uniquely personal one, and deeply life-affecting, and certainly shows that the Good Lord certainly does move in the most strange and mysterious ways…

Jim Atkinson, with whom I briefly worked on *Tell Me Lies*, had come up to Twickenham for a visit to see friends, and, discovering that I was there working on *Wonderwall*, suggested that we meet up for a drink at the end of the day, about six o'clock after I'd finished work. I agreed, but didn't really want to meet in the studio bar, knowing Jim's capacity for alcohol, and so we agreed to meet in the nearest pub to the studio, in St. Margaret's. I get to the pub at six, and no Jim: I'm not surprised, he never had any regard for punctuality. I buy myself a coke and look around the pub, and I see a familiar-looking man drinking at a table in the corner. Blow me down! It's my Father, drinking a beer alone. I can hardly believe it. I thought he was still in prison, serving his sentence, let alone drinking at a pub in Twickenham! He seemed to be on his own, so I approached him, gingerly, "Dad?" Julian greeted me warmly, with a handshake and a hug, as though nothing had ever happened between us. "What are you doing here?" I spluttered. "I live just up the road," he said, "and I thought I'd pop in for a pint, get some chish and fips over the road, and take them home." (He wasn't drunk: he always called them "chish and fips"). "Where's home?" I said feebly, when what I really meant to say was, "When did you get out and what the hell are you doing here?" Unperturbed as ever, and seemingly thinking seeing me here in a Twickenham pub was the most natural thing in the world, he explained that he was now living with the woman that I'd met at Ford prison, Anne, and they lived just down the road, in Richmond. He didn't mention when he was released from Ford, or ask me about Linda, or how she was, or anything realistically sensible. I asked him for a contact telephone number, aware of Jim Atkinson about to arrive any second, and asked him had he telephoned Auntie Doris, or even Linda? He hadn't yet, he replied, but he was going to. I was too flabbergasted to make anything like sensible conversation, and then I glimpsed Jim in the doorway. I told Dad that I had to go, and left him in the bar with only a handshake (I couldn't think straight), and I accosted Jim in the pub doorway, and said we have to go somewhere else, there's someone here I don't want to see. Jim said something like "Happens to me all the time, matey," and we repaired to the Twickenham Studios bar.

Jane Birkin, our star of *Wonderwall*, had yet to reach international stardom, and was at the time married to composer John Barry, who wanted to produce films himself, and, unusually, could actually afford to part-finance them owing to the accumulation of vast recording royalties, largely from the James Bond film soundtracks. Joe Massot, *Wonderwall*'s director, was very aware of this potential new source of film finance, and wanted to follow up *Wonderwall* as soon as possible. As I understood it, either Guillermo Cain or his translator Allen Passes had found a story called "The Southern Thruway" by a contemporary of Guillermo's, the Argentinian writer Julio Cortazar, about a symbolic permanent traffic pile-up, and it was shown to Joe Massot, who persuaded John Barry to option it as a follow-up to *Wonderwall*. But then several things seemed to happen at once. First of all, Joe told Rusty and me that he'd like us to work with him on his next film, called *The Jam*, about a huge symbolic traffic jam. The screenplay was already written, and that John Barry was thinking of co-financing it with Andy Braunsberg, if *Wonderwall*'s line producer, who was Andy himself, could find the rest. It seemed that Alan Clore, who was, in fact, financier Charles Clore's son, who had backed *Wonderwall*, would not back anything again so soon after his producing debut. But what no-one knew, especially not Joe Massot, was that Jane Birkin and John Barry were on the verge of a marriage collapse, largely because of Jane's new interest in singer Serge Gainsbourg. Now, somebody, and I don't know who, showed the screenplay of *The Jam* to Jean-Luc Godard, then a filmmaker so successful that he could raise instant finance for whatever next project he wished to make.

And so, without, as far as I know, either Joe Massot or John Barry ever being aware at the time, Jean-Luc Godard very, very quickly arranged finance for, and subsequently began shooting on, a film entitled *Week-end*, about a symbolic massive motor car pile-up, which was apparently based on a novel by Julio Cortazar. Yes indeed, Joe Massot's proposed next feature film, the very one that Rusty and I were looking forward to working on. I eventually saw *Week-end* when it opened, and noticed that Cortazar was uncredited. Jean-Luc Godard took the screenplay credit for himself, and the film premiered at the Berlin Film Festival in 1968, making it a very fast shoot indeed. I knew how I felt about it, and I couldn't help but wonder how Joe Massot must have felt: the era of peace and love and psychedelia seemed well and truly over.

Wonderwall turned out to be one of the last nails in its coffin. Rusty Coppleman returned to sound editing, and amassed well over forty screen credits. A lovely man, he and his wife Sylvia also ran a sideline in health products, both of them fully practising the lifestyle that they themselves promoted. A really nice pair of people, with a combined warmth and humanity genuinely rare in the film industry. If Rusty had only been film editor on *The Jam* as well, who knows what paths his career would have taken?

Wonderwall was briefly revived, both on film and DVD, in 2014, with a (to my mind) totally unnecessary replacement of the stunning original George Harrison opening music, a new track by an utterly forgettable pop group called The Remo Four, and the DVD itself was accompanied by a booklet written by none other than director Joe Massot. It seems to have sunk without trace. But, and somewhat amazingly, the same could not have been said of Joe Massot. In 1980, Joe Dunton, the great film camera pioneer, self-produced a dynamic musical record on film of the then-current ska and bluebeat bands, entitled *Dance Craze*, and invited me to be one of the editors, since they'd shot too much material for just one to handle. I was extremely flattered, and said that I'd love to, and asked him who was the director. "He's not that well-known," said Joe Dunton, "His name's Joe Massot." To Joe Dunton's surprise, I told him that I knew Joe Massot, and had actually worked with him before. But wise Joe Dunton also knew Joe well, and very sensibly kept Mr. Massot at arm's length, and he wasn't on many of the *Dance Craze* shoots, a couple of which I directed. He did, however, appear for some studio shooting, and eventually turned up for the West End screening of the final 70mm. print that we delivered, and, ever the Joe Massot that I knew, claimed complete credit for directing *Dance Craze*.

How to follow *Wonderwall*? Well, the answer, once again, was provided by a sudden, and well-timed, telephone call. This time from a very distinguished veteran sound editor indeed, Arthur Ridout (*The Crimson Pirate*, *Reach for the Sky*), asking if I'd be at all interested in assisting him on a film on which he was to be one of the dialogue editors at Pinewood Studios. I'd been recommended to him by Jim Roddan, who was a friend of the film's director, Ken Hughes. The film? A new musical entitled *Chitty Chitty Bang Bang*. Would I? You betcha.

It felt good to be working at Pinewood Studios. At last I managed to tick off the last major British studio on the list. Pinewood was so busy that summer that Arthur and I were assigned to a caravan, behind the main editing block: that was O.K. by us. Fewer disturbances from kibitzers, and easy access to the canteen. Arthur was happy to be left alone, because he had another agenda, which suited me just fine: he intended to listen to the live radio broadcasts of the current cricket Test Matches while preparing the dialogue loops, and sending me over to whichever sound studio we ended up at to actually shoot the material, under director Ken Hughes's supervision, although, as it turned out, Ken Hughes wasn't too interested in recording the post-synchronisation either, and only turned up for a couple of sessions: Lionel Jeffries (until Ken got bored), and the film's two child stars (ditto). Quite a responsibility, then, for yours truly, and now I knew why Jim Roddan had recommended me to Ken Hughes. Arthur Ridout listened to the radio on his headphones, and I never knew quite how he could hear the dialogue necessary to be re-recorded on the magnetic soundtrack at the same time, but he did, and never missed a catch.

Artistes' dates were booked where we could get in. Pinewood itself was very busy, and so recording dates were booked at Anvil, in the old Denham studios, and at the Gate studios in Elstree, opposite the Danziger Studios, once the main Elstree Studios. The artistes were booked by our production office, and I went off with the cans of loops, and Arthur remained happily in the caravan. Quite a responsibility for me, taking my first post-sync. sessions alone on such a major feature.

The first such session turned out to be joy itself. *Chitty Chitty Bang Bang* contained a well-chosen supporting cast of well-known, and well-loved, comedy character actors, and most of their scenes were played together, en masse. There would be no rewriting of dialogue, just re-recording for clarity, which meant recording them all separately in order to control the sound balance at the final mix. My intention, therefore, was to do just that, to record them all separately. But they all arrived together, and the hardest part of my job was not just to record them, but to separate them in order to record them. I hit on a wheeze, or so I thought: to keep them in the studio canteen until called separately, record them individually, and then play back the recordings all together to hear how it sounded. But when I list their names, you'll realise just how difficult it was to control such very funny men: Benny Hill, Davy Kaye, Max Wall, Bernard Spear, Alexander Doré, and that utterly incomparable Stanley Unwin, that master of gobbledegook and doublespeak, who actually spoke like his theatrical personality in real life (and who could, fortunately for us, re-create it exactly at will). Nevertheless, they all behaved exceptionally well, and I had a distinct feeling that they were all much happier with me there, instead of the presence of the film's director.

However, director Ken Hughes did indeed turn up for the next two sessions. He phoned to say that he would be arriving late for his session with Lionel Jeffries, and would we mind waiting and not shooting until he arrived, and so I had the opportunity to chat to Lionel about his then-recent work in *Camelot*, a film that I loved, and admired tremendously, and Lionel was very forthcoming about his working in Hollywood on the Warner Bros. lot, and so I managed to enjoy a coffee with one of my all-time favourite character actors, until the director arrived and we proceeded to go to work. Lionel Jeffries made the whole session an absolute joy. Such a professional. Nothing was too much trouble, and his synchronisation was perfect. Not only that, but he totally managed to vastly improve his own performance in the post-sync., and director Ken Hughes was delighted.

We eventually just had one more session to do on *Chitty*, and this was to take place at the Gate Studios in Elstree, with the two featured principal children in the film, Adrian Hall as Jeremy, and Heather Ripley as Jemima. On the day, they arrived together early, accompanied by a chaperone. What should I do? I couldn't really start without the director present for all sorts of obvious reasons: not only were they under-age children, but they had already taken direction from Ken. It wasn't my place to, if necessary, re-direct their performances, in any way, shape or form. Any choices, or changes in readings, had to be approved by the director: that's his job. Well, fortunately the sound mixer was used to minor dilemmas like this, and, knowing that the day would be spent recording children, had set up a small cricket area, replete with stumps, for them to play in until we got started. Heather and Adrian loved this, and when Ken Hughes finally arrived they invited him to join in. What do you do? I joined in too, of course, and a jolly time was had by all. We then stopped for tea, and then Ken said, "We'd better do some work." But what a clever Ken: knowing they had never done post-synchronisation before, he now had them ready and relaxed to do anything. "Who wants to go first?" he said, and they were now both keen and eager to start.

Ken had had enough by lunchtime, and told the chaperone to take them to the studio café, and he'd be back after lunch. Then, quietly, he turned to me and said something like "Let's pop over the road to the studio café there, give us a break. Jim Roddan tells me that you and I could talk movies until the cows come home." Suddenly, I had a new friend, a director whose work, especially *The Trials of Oscar Wilde*, I had admired very much indeed. I was flattered. So we got in Ken's high-powered sports car, and drove over to the old Elstree studios, parked outside the canteen, and went in. We walked up to the counter, chatting away, got our food, and sat down to eat. After a while, I looked up and saw at a nearby table a girl that I used to date, who once was a very good friend, the rather voluptuous Lucy O'Sullivan, a former assistant editor.

I'd taken Lucy to *The Talk of the Town* one very special evening to see the one-and-only Judy Garland. Judy's reputation had preceded her, there was even a chance that she might not show up at all, and sitting at the table next to us was Lonnie Donegan, who was ready to go on if Judy didn't show. Lucy and I finished our meal, and waited. And waited. And the one thing we didn't particularly want to do was to see Lonnie Donegan, whom I quite liked, but who held no interest whatsoever for Lucy. We stayed, with one eye on the clock. Judy Garland was due to go on at eleven o'clock, it was now half-past eleven. We waited, and waited. Then, around midnight, Lonnie Donegan at the next table got up with his guitar, clearly intending to perform. As he did so, there arose cheering and clapping from the wings, and suddenly there was Judy, at twelve o'clock midnight, exactly one hour late. What to say? She was magic, as wonderful as only she could be: the very, very best. She apologised for being late, and put on a show unequalled by anybody else, ever. So Lucy and I saw Judy Garland. (By the way, it was my second time. I'd previously seen Judy at the London Palladium, from the very back of the upper circle, the only seat left in the house after queuing that particular Sunday. Judy also started late then as well, but she had graciously waited for two people to fill the two empty seats in the very front row of the stalls, although I didn't know that at the time. With my theatre binoculars, I saw those two particular seats filled, as Noël Coward escorted none other than Marlene Dietrich to their prime front row positions.)

Anyway, back to reality, as Ken Hughes noticed my greeting, and said "Ask her over." Ken's reputation as a womanizer had preceded my meeting him: I knew about Ken's predilections from Jim Roddan, who was best man at one of Ken's weddings. Anyway, I invited Lucy over and she joined us. We were chatting away, when she excused herself to go to the Ladies. Ken then said to me, not so under-his-breath, "I bet she wears red knickers." I said, "What?" "Bet you she's wearing red undies. She's the type." I said something like, "Are you serious?" He said, "Yes. A fiver." Well, without asking him how he intended to find out, I said, "You're on." So he gets up and goes off in the direction of the ladies toilet. He comes back and says "You owe me a fiver." Clever... What I didn't do at the time, not so naïve as I obviously seemed, would have been to say something like "How do you know? Where's the proof? Have you got a photo or a shred of the panties?" No. Schmucko here believed, of course, that the Director was right. I handed over a fiver, and Ken took it. Lucy returned, and said she was late and had to go. Nice seeing me, nice meeting Ken Hughes. We said our goodbyes, and she kissed both of us, and then we drove back in Ken's sportster and completed the post-sync. recordings on *Chitty Chitty Bang Bang*. And as for me, I'd lost a fiver and never knew if Lucy was wearing red panties or not. And as for Ken Hughes…

Ken Hughes has professed that he never really liked *Chitty Chitty Bang Bang*, but its longevity of popularity proved that he must have done something right. I was invited to the 70mm. premiere at the Astoria Cinema, Charing Cross Road, and I must say that *Chitty* looked, and sounded, superb, if perhaps a trifle overlong, and I was very proud to have worked on it.

Amongst my hippy wanderings that magic summer at such venues as the Arts Lab in Drury Lane, Better Books basement in Charing Cross Road, where "underground" films were screened and poetry readings took place, and UFO (pronounced "Yewfo") in Charlotte Street, I ran across a film maker called Anthony Stern, who had run off some reels of 16mm. film in San Francisco, and was looking for an editor to, as he said, cut them together. We met up again, and he asked me if I would like to work with him. I said, "On what?" and he pointed directly with glee to the UFO stage whereon the Pink Floyd were performing, bedecked with bubble-lamp glowing lights (shades of *The Prisoner*) and flashing colours. He had secured the rights to use a piece of music by the Floyd entitled "Interstellar Overdrive" that hadn't yet then been released, and he asked me if I'd like to cut his film to the music, and he offered to pay me to do so. Since I'd only recently finished on *Chitty*, I said, "Yes, let's discuss it," or some words to that effect.

It transpired that Anthony had managed to secure a grant from the British Film Institute Production Board, provided that we work under their supervision in their cutting rooms in the well-named The Cut, in Waterloo Road, opposite the Old Vic Theatre. I said that would be fine with me, and that I'd probably need an editing assistant. Anthony said, although he hadn't budgeted for one, it would make sense, so I asked my very good friend Nick Nacht, who wanted to work in film, if he was interested in assisting me on *San Francisco*, and he agreed to do so, and so we moved into the BFI cutting rooms in Waterloo.

In the next cutting room to us was another young film maker, a year older than me, called Tony Scott, who was working on his own BFI-financed short called *One of the Missing*, an American Civil War drama. His brother, Ridley, was already involved in making commercials. Of course, in time the two of them would become amongst the world's most successful and prolific film directors, with Tony directing such films as *Top Gun*, *Days of Thunder* and *True Romance* before committing suicide in 2012. The films officer at the BFI Production Board at the time was Bruce Beresford, long before he became known as the leading Australian director of such films as *Tender Mercies*, *Driving Miss Daisy* and two Barry McKenzie features, and it was to Bruce that we were answerable.

Anthony Stern, through, I think, a friendship with the Pink Floyd's Syd Barrett, was allowed to do whatever he wanted with "Interstellar

Overdrive", and, as I understood it, the intention was not to cut the music to the film, but to edit the film to the music, which Stern left me alone to do. His exposed "film" contained lots of flash frames, blurred shots while he was trying to focus, and also what seemed like endless stretches of blank spacing, obviously unexposed or fogged film. I cut all of that stuff out, and the film then moved like psychedelic clappers to the music. Synchronisation, as the term was generally understood, was out of the question, since nothing had been filmed to the music: it fitted where it touched. When we had an edit that palpably "worked", Nick and I called Anthony in to watch it.

Anthony was absolutely horrified. "What have you done?" he shrieked. "Nothing really," I replied. "I've just taken out all the blank bits, all the pieces of leader left in, all the blurry shots—" I got no further. He accused me of removing the soul of his film. I suggested that we show it to Bruce Beresford, to get his opinion. Which we did. Bruce, a lovely chap, of course didn't really have an opinion: What could he say? We'd all seen material like this at the Arts Lab, or at Better Books. In that particular world, Andy Warhol was Eisenstein. Bruce wisely suggested that perhaps I had better put it back the way it was. "Back into rushes?" I asked. Anthony Stern said "Of course, that's the way I shot it." Well, there was no arguing with that. We hadn't had it rubber-numbered, so Nick just handed me the trims in the order of the laboratory key numbers, and I reassembled it back exactly as it was when it first came to me. Back to rushes. Anthony Stern was pleased, Bruce Beresford was gratified, and we were asked to leave the picture on Friday. And so we did. And if you see *San Francisco* at its screenings today, including a recent one I attended at the Regent Cinema, Oxford Street, it looks exactly now as it did when I first saw it: a roll of uncut rushes, with a Pink Floyd soundtrack that doesn't synchronise to anything in particular on the screen, perhaps best viewed through a specific psychedelic haze of smoke or perhaps an injected substance.

One strange point. I hadn't seen Anthony Stern for approximately fifty years prior to that recent screening, and he says he still can never forgive me for the loss of his camera. I hadn't got a clue as to what he was talking about, until he said, "That Tiffany. I never got my camera back. That arsehole." And then it all came back to me, but I never knew what he was talking about until he told me. Living at 8a, Eccleston Street, off the Kings Road in the psychedelic Sixties, I had many, shall we say, strange visitors, often friends of friends with nowhere to sleep in London, overnight strays and stragglers. One such strange being was Kit Marryat, a distant descendant of the writer of *The Children of the New Forest*, who stayed over one night. I can't remember whose friend he actually was, but he brought with him a fellow called Tiffany, who had a flat off the Kings Road, and he stayed over with Kit. They left the next morning, and during the day I had discovered some flat items were missing, amongst them my record player and a set of John Whitmarsh-Knight's kitchen saucepans. It was Jennie who alerted me to the absence of the record player, so I phoned Kit and told him what had transpired. Blithely, he said, “Oh, yeah. Tiffany.” “What??” “Better go round to his place before he sells them. That’s how he makes his living.” So we met up, and Kit was right, and I managed to retrieve the stolen goods before Tiffany could sell them. I vaguely recall that Anthony Stern was there the previous evening, but, since he’d taken me off his film that very next day, I had no reason to see him again. What I didn’t know, until approximately over fifty years later at that Regent screening, was that Tiffany had half-inched Tony Stern’s 16mm. film camera as well. Because at the time Stern and I weren’t at all on speaking terms after he had effectively thrown both Nick and me off his picture, I had no reason to see him further at all. Much later on, I happened to read a report of Tiffany’s death in the London Evening Standard, and felt moderately sorry, but I hadn’t seen him for years, and certainly didn’t want to. I never, ever, knew that he had stolen Anthony Stern’s valuable movie camera, along with his other “trophies”. The Sixties certainly had much to answer for.

Respite from all this hippy-dippy nonsense came with a telephone call from my old friend from *The Prisoner*, Eric Mival, wondering if I would like to join him on a new television series at Pinewood, as his dubbing editor. I certainly would, and was absolutely delighted to be asked. Apparently, the American producers involved wanted new, young British talent, and to have two young editors alternating their sound editors, of which I was to be one. This seemed to be a major break for me, and, although I really wasn’t too keen on doing television, I certainly didn’t imply that to Eric. I couldn’t thank Eric enough. Sound editor on a television series, at last. O.K., so it wasn’t a feature film, but it was a career promotion.

We were to be based at Pinewood Studios where the series entitled *Strange Report* was to be largely filmed, although there would be a fair amount of location shooting, and the show's star was the very distinguished British actor Anthony Quayle, as the forensic expert Adam Strange (hence the title), supported by newcomers American Kaz Garas and the very British Anneke Wills as regulars. An ITC production under Lew Grade, the producer Robert “Buzz” Berger and supervising writer Edward de Blasio are perhaps better known today for helping to create a little television series called *Dallas*, which followed ours. The idea, then, was to aim for the international market, and, in so doing, hire a younger and more trendy crew than usual to help enable decent foreign sales. After all, English productions in this era of “Swingin’ London” ruled the entertainment roost, or so it seemed to many Americans. But *Strange Report*, in actuality, turned out to be as “square” as they come. A fairly typically English policier series, it lacked the necessary dynamic novelty values for longevity in the long run. However, neither content nor creativity were my concerns at the time.

In charge of us Brits was the extremely experienced and talented former editor Brian Smedley-Aston, who was employed as second unit director on *Strange Report*, and who would, in fact, make his own directorial debut with two episodes of the series. In conversation, Brian told me that I could choose my own assistant. Having just finished up on *San Francisco* with my old schoolmate Nick Nacht, I offered Nick the job of assisting me at Pinewood. I did know that he wasn't in the union, but we hadn't had any trouble on the BFI job, so I thought (foolishly) that we'd get away with it.

So Nick started with me at Pinewood on our first *Strange Report* episode, ultimately titled "Cult: Murder Shrieks Out", and it went very well indeed. Nick did some post-sync. as well, and it is his voice that can be heard at the very beginning of that episode calling out "Lars is back! Lars is back!". That was to be Nick's major contribution to the series. Associate Producer Barry Delmaine had found out that Nick was not a union member, and in those days no-one who was not in the A.C.T.T. could ever be employed in a studio. (Remember my own problems in securing a union card?) Barry asked me to ask Nick to leave on the following Friday. I had no option but to do so, and Nick, though not well-pleased, had little alternative. He had made good friends in the short time that he worked on *Strange Report*, including my old mate from *The Prisoner*, Eric Mival, who was responsible for my, and indirectly therefore, Nick's employment, and he'd befriended music editor John Taylor, of whom much, much more later. But what to do? I needed an assistant in a hurry, and we had a tight schedule to meet.

I phoned Bridget, and, ever-helpful, said she'd help me out, but only for a very limited period. She, too, didn't want to do television, didn't want, particularly, to be a dubbing assistant (as opposed to a picture assistant), and wasn't too keen on working at Pinewood. Oh. But, thank goodness, she did come to join me on *Strange Report*, but she made it very clear that it would only be for a little while, whilst I found another assistant to take over. She knew Eric Mival and had assisted Brian Smedley-Aston on a film after working me with on *Wonderwall*, so she wasn't too unhappy, but she, like me, didn't particularly want to do television. At least, not then. Bridget joined me on the episode "Racist – A Most Dangerous Proposal", which reunited me with my old *Prisoner* acquaintance, Jane Merrow. It was at about this time that there were to be some new changes at 8a, Eccleston Street, and ironically, they involved another actor from *The Prisoner*, Michael Billington from the episode called "A Change of Mind", where, in the beginning of which, he played a woodland man who, with another, has a very proactive fight with Patrick McGoohan as Number 6.

I first met Michael Billington at a screening at Ray Selfe's private cinema, when he was accompanied by Josephine Blake, both of them currently then appearing in the musical *How to Succeed in Business Without Really Trying* at London's Shaftesbury Theatre. Mike turned out to be quite a movie buff, although that term wasn't invented then, and, needless to add, we got along famously, and not just because I had both seen and liked *How to Succeed…* when it first opened in the West End. We met at subsequent screenings at Ray's, and it eventually transpired that Mike was looking to base himself in London. He had been cast in the new MGM epic *Alfred the Great*, which was to be filmed in Ireland, and he wanted somewhere semi-permanent to return to, and I needed a flatmate, so Mike moved in. He had been dating

Liza Minnelli, and wanted to be close to London's Chelsea/Knightsbridge area, near to where Liza's mother, Judy Garland, no less, was currently living. Liza was one of Mike's many sidelines, since he had also been dating Barbara Broccoli, daughter of James Bond producer Albert R. "Cubby" Broccoli, for some time. Indeed, since Sean Connery had declined to play James Bond any more after *You Only Live Twice* in 1967, Michael Billington was considered the number one contender for the screen's most popular hero, and there was a two year gap between *You Only Live Twice* and *On Her Majesty's Secret Service*, but when the role was filled, despite all of Mike's screen tests (more than any other actor) for Bond, the part went to the former male model George Lazenby, best known for the "Big Fry" commercials on television, who had to be revoiced as Bond, until Roger Moore took over. When Moore wanted to leave Bond, Michael Billington was once again tested, for *Live and Let Die*, and then for both *Moonraker* and *Octopussy*, but he never played James Bond, merely a small part in *The Spy Who Loved Me*. But he was a good friend to me, in more ways than one, as we shall see.

Meanwhile, while Michael Billington was in Ireland, although he paid his rent regularly, thank goodness, even though he wasn't in London, I was progressing, if that's the word, on *Strange Report*: at least I was always professionally on time, and always met the dubbing dates, and, thus far, caused no trouble. I think the most distinctive contribution I made to *Strange Report* was taking Adam Strange's taxi out into the Pinewood countryside to shoot every possible taxi sound effect ever needed. Invariably, the taxi run-bys were filmed mute, including the opening title sequence in Whitehall, and no wild tracks, i.e. non-synchronous sound tracks, had been recorded for them. It seemed silly to me to spend time and money on taxi sound effects when we had the actual taxi in the studio, so I asked the producers if I could take out the taxi one afternoon with a sound man and record everything that we could possibly need. They were delighted with the idea (no payable sound royalties if we owned the tracks, which we indeed would), and so I took a driver and a recordist into the Bucks countryside and returned with the taxi reels of runbys, brakes, and stops and starts that you can hear throughout the series.

But here's where it all went sour. Eric Mival and I had been good friends since *The Prisoner*, and Eric, a very decent soul, had also befriended John Taylor, the *Strange Report* music editor, as had I. John had quite an industry pedigree: he was the son of actor Michael Rennie, who had become a major 20th Century-Fox star in Hollywood, hence John's adopting an incognito surname, although, once you knew, John was the spitting image of his father. John's mother was Renee (hence Michael's adopted surname) Gilbert, the sister of *Alfie* director Lewis Gilbert, and the cousin of not only character actor Sidney Tafler, but also the pop singer Anne Shelton and her sister Joy. It was John who told me that Lewis cast Sidney Tafler in every single one of his own films for luck – watch very closely and you'll spot him every time. Quite a pedigree, Mr. Taylor, *Strange Report*'s music editor. Of course, the whole family were Jewish, and both John and I recognised a common bond.

Now, the *Strange Report* crew were deliberately hired young, on producer Norman Felton's instructions, in that time of "Swinging London", hoping that none of the perceived and traditional bland English filming methods would creep through to damage U.S. sales. Anyway, Eric Mival, the other dubbing editor Martin Clarke, plus the alternating editor Keith Palmer (who was, in fact, Jim Roddan's former regular assistant before I happened along), music editor John Taylor, plus second assistant Roddy Hay, and myself were all much, much younger than the regular television filmed series editing crews (cf. *The Prisoner*). And, therefore, we were perhaps a little bit more irresponsible, although we always met our delivery dates on time. But one day, Eric Mival announced that he was going to take a long weekend off, in order to celebrate the anniversary of his wedding to his wife, Penny. We, especially my assistant Bridget Reiss, who knew them both very well, were all delighted, and we wondered amongst ourselves just what exactly we could do to celebrate this fact, without disrupting our own production schedules in any way. Well, I have to take full blame for what followed, and I still shamefully regret it to this very day. At Eccleston Street, I was using flat cleaners from an agency that prided itself in being able to supply anybody for absolutely anything, and it occurred to me to give Eric a big anniversary surprise, and I discussed my idea with music editor John Taylor. Are you ready for this? I thought that it would be an absolute hoot to hire a stripper dressed as a bride to perform a striptease to music in our cutting room that very evening before Eric left for the weekend. Wouldn't that, to use then-contemporary slang (borrowed from "Pal Joey"), be a gas?

Well, of course John Taylor was quite the wrong person to ask. A known lecher, and quite the exploiter of every girl he'd ever met, he readily thought that it was a splendid idea, and agreed to split the cost. The only thing we had to do was not to tell Eric, and we did manage to keep it from him. We did, however, check with both Barry Delmaine and Brian Smedley-Aston, our respective department bosses, that it would be all right with them, and they both gleefully agreed. Only my assistant, Bridget, queried the gag on grounds of taste and, frankly, stupidity. I should have listened to her. Of course, she was absolutely right.

We booked the stripper for five o'clock on the Friday before Eric was off for the weekend. John and I bought some noshes, sweets, crisps and things, ready to put out, and Barry and Brian contributed some wine for a toast. The other dubbing crew, Martin Clarke and Roddy Hay, plus the other editor Keith Palmer and his assistant Eddy Joseph, were duly informed, and all thought it would be a jolly good wheeze.

Came the day. And perhaps here I should state, before describing what actually happened, what I didn't know about Eric Mival, although why I didn't know it I truly don't know, just living in my own particularly selfish bubble as ever, I guess. But Bridget, who had worked with Eric closely before, did know. I, on the other hand, having worked relatively closely with Eric on both *The Prisoner* and *Wonderwall*, did not know that he was none other than a deeply committed religious Christian, with very firm and clear-sighted views on morality, and especially deplored what was happening in the world, what with "Swinging London", freer censorship in cinema, and the increasing use of sex in advertising, to say the very least. Would that the obviously totally self-obsessed me had only stopped to think…

The time came. The girl arrived, and brought with her a portable tape player to play a rocked-up version of "The Wedding March". She changed into a cod wedding dress, that clearly came apart bit-by-bit, if she had only been allowed to complete her act. Eddy Joseph, the series' second assistant editor, was appointed to round up Barry Delmaine, Brian Smedley-Aston and all the rest of the editing crew, who arrived in my cutting room to find glasses of wine available. I was then to fetch Eric, and John would start the "show" by pressing the "play" button behind the "bride", and the music would start. Bridget, the only girl present, kept herself well to the back of the proceedings. I should've guessed.

I collected Eric from the next door cutting room, saying that we had a little surprise for him for the weekend, and brought him in. The moment he appeared, John Taylor pressed the button, and the rocked-up Wedding March began to play, and the girl began her strip dance. Eric was appalled. No, he was beyond appalled. He yelled at John and me: "You monsters, have you no respect?" or suchlike, and attacked the tape machine, switched it off, and tore the bride's veil from her face. "So that's what you think of me?". Well, to say we were surprised would be an understatement. Eric was in tears, visibly and palpably hurt. I wouldn't have had that happen for the world – I was speechless. Eric banged his hand down on the cutting bench so hard I was sure he had hurt himself – "Fuck you all!" he shouted, and left. Bridget, wise beyond her years, grabbed me and said, "Go after him," which I did, and saw him headed for the car park. I went back, grabbed Bridget, and said, "He's getting in his car. Can we follow him, and intercept him? I'll apologise." Bridget said, "We can try", and we reached the car park, and got into her car just as Eric was driving out of the studio gates.

Bridget gunned her motor, and we followed Eric, overtaking him somewhere on the main Pinewood road, and forcing him into a side road: great driving from Bridget. He got out, and we confronted each other like gunfighters in a "B" western. I began, something like: "Eric, I'm so sorry, I could never have—" and he cut me off. "Heathens. You and that John Taylor. No respect, none at all" (at least he didn't say "you Jews", I thought). "I am so, so sorry," I said. "I really didn't think—" "No, you bloody didn't. Is that the way to celebrate a marriage? Is it? Is it? Is it?…" What could I say? I had destroyed a friendship, rightly earning approbation for not thinking, or even guessing, what Eric would have thought, nor even taking into account whatsoever the very fact that Eric would have considered that what John and I thought was just a bit of fun would be virtual religious heresy because of the sanctity of the marriage vows, and consequently therefore total gross blasphemy of the highest order. What was I thinking? Well, of course, I just wasn't thinking. Not at all. And now I've ruined his anniversary, not to mention our friendship. And as for our working relationship… After all, he got me this very job. Oh my Gawd! Bridget witnessed all of this, and approached Eric, almost defending me, there on the grassy verge as traffic roared past in the late Friday rush hour. She said – quite rightly – that I was thoughtless, silly and childish (the word "sexist" hadn't yet been invented) and would never do anything like this again (she was almost right), but that I'd learned a lesson, and it would stay with me forever. Eric mellowed: she had expressed his thoughts exactly. Anger was not part of his make-up: forgiving was a key tenet of his Christianity. And so, he forgave me, there and then, thanks, I think, to Bridget. I waited for what seemed to me an eternity, but was actually just a very long moment, and then Eric got back into his car, said, tersely, "Goodbye", and drove off. Bridget said to me, "I'll take you back to the studio. We've got some cleaning up to do." I couldn't thank her enough, and didn't try. And now, for me, all of those previous happy memories of working with Eric Mival on the greatest television show of all time (as we both thought of it, in our mutual shared experience) *The Prisoner* itself, were unfortunately tarnished, because of my later sheer, thoughtless stupidity. It would take nearly fifty years for that particular wound to heal…

Back at the studio nearly everybody had gone home: it was a Friday night, after all. John Taylor, who could behave like a gentleman when it suited him, had waited for us. He echoed my view that Eric's behaviour was totally unexpected, but pointed out that we had learned a major life lesson: never take anything for granted, especially concerning sex (and he would know!), and never, ever, try to second-guess anyone else's tastes. Bridget had had enough, and left us with "I'll see you Monday morning", and I vaguely remember John and I finishing what remained of the bottles of wine. I never found out what happened to the stripper. Did she finish her act for what was left of her audience? How did she get home? Where did she change? Did she get supper, even? All I knew was that I had paid for her services in advance. Just as well.

In case you're wondering, Eric Mival reappeared Monday morning, and business went on as usual. Nothing more was ever said about the previous Friday, but I thought I could detect a slight false bonhomie in his attitude towards me in the future. He and Bridget seemed closer than ever in their friendship, but maybe I was just imagining things. Bridget kept true to her original plan to leave as soon as possible, and did so when I was able to hire Beverly Baker, the daughter of sound editor Roy Baker, who I knew from *One Million Years B.C.*, to assist me, and so we got through *Strange Report*, but it was not, alas, the success that I.T.C. had hoped for, and never went to a further series, the sixteen that we delivered was the whole works, and eventually became a very minor collectors cult series, and you can currently find all our hard work available in an excellently produced Network boxed set.

The relationship that really gelled on *Strange Report* was between me and John Taylor: we had a lot in common, mainly that celluloid was in our blood. Although mine was straight off the screen, John had family connections that I could only wish for, and, as *Strange Report* lurched towards the end, he and I made our plans for the immediate future. Mainly, now with our recently acquired decent salaries, plus overtime and holiday credits, we had both earned some real money, and felt we needed a holiday. Neither of us had ever been to the Cannes Film Festival, and we decided to give it a go. The previous year's Festival had been abandoned, disrupted by political riots, and the current one would be a spiritual rebirth, incorporating a new section, the Directors Fortnight.

I mentioned this to Michael Billington, who thought it would be a great idea, and he agreed to drive me there and back. Also, he thought he knew of a boat that we could stay on. John Taylor's uncle, the film director Lewis Gilbert, also had a flat in Cannes, and John would sound him out about staying at his place. Mike Billington's contact came up trumps, and Mike and I set out, Mike driving of course, for the South of France, with a view to us kipping on his friend Peter Halliday's yacht, nearby in Antibes harbour. We'd spend the two weeks there, and drive back through Paris. John Taylor, and *Strange Report*'s assistant editor Roddy Hay, would make their own way to the Riviera to stay with Lewis, and meet up with us in Cannes. The Film Festival officially opened on May 8th, and we aimed to get there a day before. All well and good, and Peter Halliday's fee for use of the yacht was negligible.

Mike and I arrived in Cannes, and easily located Peter's yacht thanks to his excellent directions, and proceeded to unpack. To our surprise, later that very evening John and Roddy showed up, without a place to stay: Lewis Gilbert wouldn't arrive until the next day. Peter was generosity itself, and, before I could stop him, found myself sharing the yacht's dining room table turned into a twin-sleeper, me and Roddy Hay, whilst John Taylor had the bed intended for me! They could've slept in their car! But at least it was only for that one night, and Mike and I barely saw John and Roddy again.

To me, Cannes couldn't have been more exciting. It was the year of *Easy Rider*, and Mike and I managed to gatecrash both the first screening and the subsequent press conference, and got to meet Dennis Hopper, Peter Fonda and Jack Nicholson, and hung out with them on and off during the whole Festival. I also managed to get to see the Monaco Grand Prix without any real bother, and watched Graham Hill win in his Lotus, with John Surtees and Jack Brabham bringing up the rear. I had never really been interested in motor racing before, despite the fact that race ace Stirling Moss was actually a distant cousin of mine, on Dad's mother's side. I'd never met Stirling until very recently, a year before his death, when we found ourselves seated opposite each other in our shared Mayfair doctor's waiting room. I couldn't resist introducing myself to him, and he was genuinely pleased to meet part of his long-lost family. We discussed various Mosses that were our relations, and we parted.

Back to Cannes. Mike Billington, unsurprisingly, spent most of his time chatting up random "actresses", and I didn't initially spend too much time with him. I saw a lot of movies, including the premiere of *Sweet Charity* in 70mm. (albeit irritatingly with some songs removed for the French release), plus the incredible *Antonio des Mortes*, and our own entries of *If...* (which won) and *The Prime of Miss Jean Brodie* (featuring Pamela Franklin, in the nude, no less!), and *Easy Rider*, the revelation of the Festival, twice. It was also the year of *Z* and *My Night with Maude*, a truly great selection, indeed. And I had some adventures, too. At Caledonian Films I had done some censor cuts for Bob Bucknell, in particular a couple of films, *Aimez-vous les Femmes*? (*Do You Like Women?*) and *Caesar the Conqueror*, for independent film distributor and film maker Antony Balch, who had achieved a sort of notoriety in England for distributing the previously censor-banned classic *Freaks*. Tony Balch was very pleased with the way that I had edited the cuts, as no joins were visible. I ran across him again on the Croisette in Cannes, and he asked me what was I doing here, and he said he was on his own, and would I like supper? Would I? Sure, and he took me to "La Mère Besson", just off the Croisette. We were shown to a table, and Antony ordered that day's house speciality, then he nudged me and pointed at the table directly across from us. I could hardly believe my eyes: There, in front of me, were none other than Luchino Visconti and Federico Fellini, two of the world's greatest-ever, and most certainly most famous, Italian directors, sharing what looked like a huge bowl of bouillabaisse, dipping portions of it into their respective soup bowls, wearing napkins tucked around their necks, and obviously having a jolly good time! Ah, Cannes, I was clearly in the right place at the right time! (However, during that supper, Tony Balch, to my surprise, tried to seduce me. I told him, very frankly, that I wasn't gay, to which he replied, "But how do you get on with girls who don't have anything between their thighs?" I replied something like, "Just fine, thank you. That's what I like." He never pestered me again, and we said our separate goodnights.) I saw Tony later in England, at the National Film Theatre after seeing Marlene Dietrich in *Morocco*. He was pleased to see me, and reminded me of that special evening at La Mère Besson. I thanked him again, and he told me that he was dying. I didn't know what to say. He died of stomach cancer, aged forty-two, in London, soon afterwards.

Meanwhile, back in Cannes, I noticed that, almost wherever I went, whether with Mike or anybody else, I invariably ran into a very small production unit filming. We got chatting to them, and so I met Tony Klinger, the son of Roman Polanski's English producer Michael Klinger, Tony's cousin Mike Lytton, and their cameraman Austin Parkinson, and they were, in effect, filming the festival. At least when they could, because they didn't have permits, but they sure had chutzpah! I came across them pretty regularly, outside the Pavilion, in the Rue d'Antibes, gatecrashing beach parties; they were everywhere. Mike and I got on well with them, and we often shared sandwiches and gatecrashed receptions together. (They carried a movie camera, so invariably were allowed in). In fact when there were days when we didn't see them, we went looking for them, and often found them at the British stand, reloading or checking their equipment.

Eventually, it was time to go home. We'd had a few adventures and a few thrills, and we'd come across John Taylor and Roddy Hay a couple of times. What we'd noticed in particular, all four of us more or less independently, was that, although Cannes was a festival dedicated to the art of the film, there seemed to be the most amazing number of sex films screening, from all countries, but interestingly, nothing significant from Britain, where a sex film could be made very cheaply and also pick up the Government's grant for low-budget British films. Mike and I thought this an avenue well worth exploring when we got back. We saw a few of the sex flicks, and the standards were very low. We knew we could do better than that ourselves: all we needed was the finance. But we didn't really give it a serious, second thought. At least, not then.

It was soon time to depart, but before we actually did, Mike wanted to go up into the mountains, and so we were directed to a café in the hills where film people used to go. We went to where we were shown, and accidentally bumped into a man who was leaving as we entered. "Sorry," we three all said at once, being British, and we all laughed. Approaching the bar, the barman asked us if we knew who that man was. "No, of course not," we said, but the barman replied, "That's Gram Gram," or that's what it sounded like to us: "Gram Gram?" "Oui," said the barman, "Le Troisième Homme". "Graham Greene!" I exclaimed, trying to get another peek at the departing guest. And indeed it was. Well, how about that? We thanked the barman for pointing him out, and the barman asked if we were here for the Festival, and we replied that we were. "Ah," he said, "I used to be in the pictures." "Oh really," we said, "What did you do?" He then went on to tell us, in very broken English, that he was a camera operator on films about thirty years ago. "Per'aps you have heard of Jean Renoir?" Blimey, we thought, not half! "I used to work for him. I operated on some films before the war. Per'aps you have heard of them? *Toni*, *Le Crime de Monsieur Lange*, *La Vie est à Nous*?" Heard of them?! "Those are great classics," I said. "What happened?" "Ah," said the barman, "My camera arm went. I couldn't hold it steady any more, and also they said I was a communist, so here I am." What a story. We, of course, bought him a drink, and he said "Thank you." And we left. Afterwards, Michael Billington said, "I bet he tells that to all the girls!"

On the last day of the Festival, Mike and I decided to fulfil a mutual private fantasy; we would drive along the Riviera to Menton, to pay tribute to our shared screen hero Errol Flynn, and visit his infamous yacht the Zaca, and see if it was still moored in the harbour at Menton, where she had been left since Flynn's death in 1959, allegedly held ransom for Flynn's many debts. We drove along the coastline on a beautiful day, and espied the Zaca in the harbour: we both recognised it immediately, for it was the very yacht that Flynn had leased to none other than Orson Welles, on which he filmed much of *The Lady from Shanghai*. We got as close as we could, and we saw that the vessel was in quite a deteriorated condition: paint peeling, timber flaking from the masts and sides, but, nevertheless, the ship still resonated for us with its last scandalous images, of the legendary Flynn partying with his latest and last lover, the seriously under-aged beauty Beverly Aadland. And then eventually, with a last wave in salute to the greatest screen swashbuckler of them all, Douglas Fairbanks and Stewart Granger notwithstanding, we said our goodbyes to the Zaca, and returned to Cannes. Years later we heard that the Zaca had had to be exorcised, the sounds of the long-deceased Flynn and his nightly ghostly carousings being repeatedly heard regularly along the Riviera shore.

Mike and I left Cannes after the final day of the Festival, and we drove back via Paris, having to drop off a newly-collected girlfriend of Mike's at her home in the centre of town. Mike's "goodbye" took an eternity, and when he finally emerged from the girl's house, I pointed out to him that, since this was the very last day of no less than Jacques Brel in the Paris production of *Man of La Mancha*, surely Mike could have let me go to the theatre matinee whilst he was saying "goodbye" to his newly-found friend? His response was both cynical and mysterious: "You just never know."

And so we set off for London. We had no idea what on earth had happened to John Taylor and Roddy Hay during the Festival in those far-off days before the invention of the mobile phone, and I never did find out.

-----END OF REEL FIVE-----

REEL SIX

Back in London, Michael Billington picked up where he left off with Liza Minnelli. One day he returned her to her mother's flat in Chelsea, then he himself returned to Eccleston Street, and said, "You'll never believe what I've just seen..." Of course, I could indeed hardly believe him when he told me that, when Mike dropped off Liza, he was invited in for tea, to watch her mother, Judy Garland, playing chess with none other than Vivien Leigh, who was in fact the actual owner of the flat. (Two-time Best Actress Academy Award winner Luise Rainer also lived in the same block, as I was to discover later when I visited her there to discuss a potential interview). What can you say? Garland and Leigh must have known each other since 1939, that annus mirabilis in Hollywood, when both were at MGM, Judy Garland as Dorothy Gale, Vivien Leigh as Scarlett O'Hara, *The Wizard of Oz* and *Gone with the Wind,* at the same studio at the same time.

Mike was settling down to be a most interesting flatmate, to say the very least. Once he turned up with actress Vivien Merchant, with whom he had just finished filming *Alfred The Great*, who was in the throes of despair over her husband Harold Pinter's various affairs, when Mike mentioned that I owned a 16mm. copy of Olivier's film *Richard III.* That perked her up. "That's one of David's favourite films," she said, ("David Baron" being Pinter's acting nom-de-plume). "Can I buy it from you?" (to me), "I'd love to give it to him as a present." Well, I thought, a couple of key points: 1) I'm in illegal possession of it. I bought it from one of Ray Selfe's contacts, and in those pre-video days ownership of copyrighted 16mm. film prints could get one into serious trouble with the police; and 2) Nick Nacht had split the cost with me, and it was expensive: £100. I'd have to ask Nick if he wants to sell, and we hadn't even viewed it yet! Nick eventually agreed, and we sold our Technicolor and VistaVision 16mm. copy of *Richard III* to Vivien Merchant for what it cost us. We never got around to watching it, and I never saw Vivien again (except on the stage).

Michael Billington and I had learned much from our trip to Cannes. Not just the world's leading film festival, Cannes is also a major film market, where independent film makers can display their wares, and where studios can show off new product. But what Mike and I really registered was the astounding amount of low-budget semi-pornographic films for sale, most of which would never play in the U.K. even with substantial cuts, owing to our strident censorship rules. We were wondering if we should try and make one, just for money, of course, not for any particular career satisfaction.

At least, that's what we were thinking about when I received a telephone call from producer Michael Klinger, who said that I had met his son Tony in Cannes (indeed I had) and that he (Michael) would like to meet me to discuss something. Well, I was very impressed: Roman Polanski's producer wants to meet me? And, mercifully, it wasn't too far to go. Klinger lived in Grosvenor Square, near the American Embassy, in a block of flats which Frank Sinatra once kept as his London base and housed there his many mistresses (though not all at once!). Michael Klinger said that he wanted to meet me that very evening.

I turn up at the Klinger Grosvenor Square residence and am greeted by Michael's wife, who says, "I've heard a lot about you. Come in." And there, next to his Dad, stands Tony Klinger, who I haven't seen since Cannes. Michael grabs my hand warmly, and says, "You know my son, I believe," and that's the opening of the conversation. We sit down, and Mrs. Klinger offers me tea or coffee. "Coffee, please," and off she goes to the kitchen. I have no words for the style of the flat: Jewish baroque, I think, would sum it up: a burglar would have a fine old time here, I thought. Everything seemed to be gold, or at least gilt. The paintings on the walls were classy, the furniture immaculate beyond measure. If I had ever dared to imagine what a wealthy English film producer's home would look like, then this would match the dream perfectly. What was I doing here, summoned as I was?

Michael, his son Tony, and I are seated facing one another. Michael says his son tells him I'm in the business, as an editor. I reply in the affirmative, adding (you never know) "When there's work, yes." "You saw what my son was doing in Cannes?" asks Michael. I replied that we met only occasionally, but I had a pretty good idea: He was documenting the Festival. "Hah!" says Michael, "Documenting! How would you like to edit it? All the material." Well, there it was. A job offer, from a real film producer. Albeit the offer was to cut his son's movie, and not one of his own, but nevertheless... Before I could answer, Michael said, "You're not busy at the moment, are you?" I couldn't deny that, even if I wanted to. He continued, without waiting for my response. "No-one is, the week after Cannes. When can you start?" I replied, as soon as we can agree on terms, and when I can get an available cutting room. Michael asked me to find one, and start next Monday. I said that I'd like an assistant, and then I turned to Tony K. and asked him if his rushes were numbered and synchronised, and where were they? "In the bedroom," was his reply, and he didn't know what numbering and synchronising meant, "The sound is together with them, it's all on quarter-inch." "Then it has to be transferred. We'd better try to get cutting rooms in a place with sound transfer facilities." Michael Klinger was getting bored. "Good, it's all settled then. We'll talk about your deal tomorrow." And so I left the plush apartment in Grosvenor Square, and started work at Sound Associates in Bayswater on what was eventually to be called *The Festival Game*.

Since this was virtually an amateur job, I called Nick Nacht and asked if he'd like to assist me, and he happily agreed, so we began the following Monday, transferring all the quarter-inch tape sound onto 16mm. magnetic and began synchronising. Not easy, when most of it (except for some interviews) lacked clapperboards, and required lip-synching or finding a suitable noise on the recording with which to synchronise. Thank goodness Michael Klinger didn't ask for a proposed time schedule.

It was good being back at Sound Associates in Bayswater, and bloody convenient, too! Nick and I were on a deal, but overtime doesn't matter so much when you're working close to home, as we both were. In the meantime, Michael Billington and I hadn't given up on the idea of making a cheap British sex film, and then selling it at next year's Cannes. We needed a writer: I didn't want to even attempt it while I was busy with the Klingers, and Mike was going into *Incident at Vichy* at the Phoenix, with Alec Guinness and my old acquaintance Doctor Adam Strange, better known to the general public as Anthony Quayle. From Arthur Miller, this was indeed a touch of class for Mike, as he waited to hear if he was going to be the next James Bond. Mike didn't actually say that he now was no longer interested in making a sex film, and so I still considered him as the potential director of whatever came about as a result of my investigating the possibilities.

I'm not quite sure how I met the writer who wanted to be known as "Andrew Best", but I'll honour here the original promise I made to him about disclosure, and only refer to him as "David". David was an American who had made a quarter-of-an-hour short film about the Bonzo Dog (Doo-Dah) Band, an eccentric British pop group who had featured in the Beatles' *Magical Mystery Tour*. Their members included Neal Innes, Vivian Stanshall, Roger Ruskin Spear and Legs "Larry" Smith, and the short was entitled *The Adventures of the Son of the Exploding Sausage*, and somehow, somewhere, I was invited to a private screening, probably at the Arts Lab or Better Books, and so I met David, who both wrote and directed it. I never asked him how, or even why, a New Yorker like him got involved. When I told him that I was an editor, he told me he also edited his film, and we bonded. We had lunch together, and chattered about what he wanted to do over here, and, since he was a writer, I broached the subject of the project that I was planning with Michael Billington, a sort of *Tom Jones* but played as a contemporary sex farce, not period. He seemed interested, and remained interested even when I told him we had no money to pay a writer. This didn't deter him, and I said, can you come up with a story? And that's how we left it.

Until I heard from him again. He said, "I've got an idea, but I can't afford to write a treatment, much less a screenplay, for nothing." I said to write down the idea, and let's meet and discuss it. And so we did. David came up with the title: *City Suite*, and the simple tale of a country bumpkin (shades of *Tom Jones*) who comes up to London to bring his sister the tragic news that their mother has just died, and that they must make the most of what's left of their lives together. So far, so good, but it didn't sound quite like a sex flick to me. I then showed it to Michael Billington, who, after all, was going to direct it, and he thought it was very promising. But David didn't want to take it to a first draft script stage. In fact, he asked me to do that, and, if it actually got going, to credit him and give him a percentage. I agreed, and assured him that, if and when, then the writing contract would be drawn up professionally by a film lawyer. So we had made a start. But *City Suite* would have to wait until after *The Festival Game*, at least.

When Mike and I were in Cannes, Michael received a phone call from Sylvia Anderson, the wife of Gerry Anderson, producer of the television space puppet show *Thunderbirds*, asking Mike, who she knew to be a James Bond probable, if he would be at all interested in appearing in a live action version of *Thunderbirds*, to be called *UFO* ("Unidentified Flying Objects"), and could they meet when Mike came back from Cannes. Mike told me all this, and I said something like "I bet she was impressed that you were at the Cannes Film Festival", and Mike was, as ever, not sure if she would have been, but I guessed that someone who had only produced puppet films would certainly have been impressed by having to call a Cannes Festival number to reach an actor. When we returned, Mike had a series of meetings with Sylvia, and, as was Mike's way, they became the very closest of friends. *UFO* was to be a family series, if not actually child-orientated, and Mike was, not unsurprisingly, now having serious second thoughts about *City Suite*, let alone making his directorial debut with such a motion picture.

In the meantime, *The Festival Game* was progressing nicely. Also based at Sound Associates, a little down the corridor from us, John Cassavetes was supervising the editing of his new film *Husbands*, and the film's editor was the very distinguished British film editor Peter Tanner (*Kind Hearts and Coronets*, *The Cruel Sea*) who I knew from my days at Elstree. One day, Nick and I were chatting to Peter in his cutting room, and when we left to walk along the long Sound Associates corridor back to our own cutting room, we saw at the end of the corridor, advancing towards us, the *Husbands* team of no less than John Cassavetes, Ben Gazzara and Peter Falk. As we walked towards them we all resembled a Western movie showdown. Nick and I pointed our right fingers, gunmen-style, towards the trio. They responded, and a "shoot-out" took place, replete with improvised vocals from those three very distinguished Method actors. "Phew!" "Blam!" "Bang-Bang" etc., and we reciprocated. Eventually, Peter Falk, Ben Gazzara and Nick fell "dead", and John Cassavetes and I "blew" into our fingers, victorious. We all stood up straight, bowed to each other, and passed on our respective ways down the corridor. What a grand moment!

I learned something on *The Festival Game*. There was a shot of Spanish dancing, and it wasn't filmed sync., i.e. with clapperboards, so there was no way of synchronising it, without a reference shot, i.e. a 'clap'. Since the dancing was so fast, it was impossible to isolate a specific sync. point; it all sounded alike. When we achieved a first edit, and showed it to Tony's dad Michael Klinger, I left out the dancing music and effects because it would have taken me too long to attempt to find a suitable sync. point in time for the screening. Michael asked after the sound, and I explained the problem to him. His reply was a salutary lesson to me: "Sync. doesn't matter. Just wind it in anywhere, nobody will notice." I did, and he was right: it looked just fine. We decided to go without any commentary, using the interviews as narration, and what classy interviews they were: Charlton Heston, Omar Sharif, Jack Nicholson and Peter Ustinov, to say the least. All needed name captions, in case anyone in the world didn't know who they were. And I learned another important lesson in editing...

I contacted title designer Brian Stevens, who I knew from *He Who Rides a Tiger*, and he was happy to do the job for the very little money offered, and we duly marked out the relevant lengths for the title captions. Now, the film was shot on sixteen millimetre, and the framing, which, to be honest, was rather catch-as-catch-can, filled the classical square frame. It never occurred to me, although I should have asked, whether or not it would ever be projected theatrically, conventionally at a wide screen ratio, since all cinemas were now totally converted to widescreen, except for those repertory and archive houses that I tended to frequent, which could show all ratios. I think that I'd actually assumed that *The Festival Game* would be a television special, but I never thought to check the future release pattern, nor did Brian Stevens ask me. All of the titles came in, and they looked fine. Jack Nicholson's was a little low in frame, so as not to completely obscure his face, but it looked all right on the moviola, so I cut it in, along with the others. What, of course, I should have done (which would have cost) would have been to project them all on a big screen in a wide screen ratio to be absolutely certain of their clarity when projected theatrically, or at least measure them accordingly, but I just didn't think, and Michael and Tony seemed very happy.

However, Michael had managed to secure an Odeon cinema circuit release for *The Festival Game*, which, of course, was British quota and a goodly length (55 minutes) to accompany a very long feature. It went out on release supporting *Krakatoa - East of Java*, which I had previously seen on its West End run in Cinerama. I popped into the Astoria, Brixton to catch *The Festival Game* there, and guess what? Yup, I died a thousand deaths when Jack Nicholson's name came up on the lower part of the screen, the wording split completely in half. It just hadn't occurred to me to allow for wide screen presentation! But nobody, neither punters nor projectionists, seemed to notice, and there was never any referral back to me. I'm sure the film looked just fine on television (square screens in those days!) or on 3 by 4 domestic video, and there was certainly never, ever, any comeback from the Klingers, thank goodness.

While I was at Sound Associates, finishing *The Festival Game*, Peter Lodge, who both owned Sound Associates and was also our dubbing mixer on *The Festival Game*, said that he had another short film coming in, and would I like to edit it? Without even asking what it was, I said that I'd love to. He then told me that he had already recommended Peter Dansie, who ran a film numbering service based at Sound Associates, and I pointed out to Peter that Pete, a nice enough bloke, had never edited before. (And I hated myself – temporarily – for doing that. But it's a business). Peter Lodge then said he would set up a meeting between myself and this film's producer, Jon Penington, who had also recently produced a most successful short called *The Plank*, also by this new film's director, Eric Sykes, and this short would be a follow-up. Frankly, with *The Festival Game* newly completed, I was delighted.

But before we finally leave *The Festival Game*, it was thanks to Michael Klinger that I was able to meet, and to shake hands with, one of my own favourite writing heroes, the action novelist Wilbur Smith, whose book *When The Lion Feeds* I had taken out of the Streatham library while I was still at Dulwich, and loved it so much I read it twice. Now world-famous, *When the Lion Feeds* was his first (and to me, still his best) novel, and the film rights were acquired by Stanley Baker, but the film proved uncastable (although singer Tom Jones was once mentioned for the male lead), and has still not yet been made. But Michael Klinger picked up the rights to two subsequent novels, *Shout at the Devil* and *Gold Mine* (eventually filmed as *Gold*) and, while we were working on *The Festival Game*, entertained Wilbur Smith at his Grosvenor Square flat, and I happened to be there at that time, and met him, shook his hand, and thanked him. I'm not sure if he totally believed me when I said I loved *When the Lion Feeds* and read it twice, but at least I got to meet the great Wilbur Smith, so thank you, once again, Michael and Tony Klinger.

I got on well with producer Jon Penington, who was pleased that a professional who had just finished a short film with Michael Klinger wanted to edit *Rhubarb*, for such was the title of the upcoming project, and suggested that I meet the director, Eric Sykes, for his approval. I had been a fan of Eric Sykes from way back, watching his television shows regularly, and admiring his radio work, and also the attempts by MGM to turn him into a film star in such comedy vehicles as *Invasion Quartet* and *Village of Daughters*. Jon eventually did arrange an introduction, and I met Eric, who was profoundly deaf, one evening at a rushes running of *Rhubarb*'s daily shoot. It was, unsurprisingly, shot mute. When Jon Penington discovered that I had previously been a sound editor, he immediately gave me the job. I was unaware of the irony at the time, but I gradually realised that I was to be Eric Sykes' ears, as well as his editor.

But *Rhubarb* was still shooting, and Eric Sykes himself wouldn't be free for a few months. In the meantime, there were a couple of other jobs that came along. The new Roger Corman film *De Sade* had come into Sound Associates, and needed a fast dub. It had been filmed in Germany for the American company American-International, where Roger Corman himself had taken over the direction from, allegedly, a much-troubled Cy Endfield, who had just, apparently, sat on the side of the set having a nervous breakdown during the film's shoot, and now AIP wanted it finished, and fast. It was already edited, and they had sent it to Sound Associates to complete the sound work quickly. The editor was Max Benedict, who I knew well from the National Film Theatre, and when Peter Lodge suggested me, Max, apparently, was very pleased. So I got the 'phone call. Besides, Eric Sykes was still shooting, wherever and whenever he could round up his cast and locations.

A very experienced American sound editor from Edit International in Hollywood called Ross Taylor (*The Exorcist*) was sent over by AIP to make sure everything went smoothly on *De Sade*, and I duly split the dialogues, most of which were useable since it was a studio shoot, and I got on board John Taylor to handle the music, which was scored by Billy Strange. It was a handsome-looking picture, starring Keir Dullea as the Marquis de Sade, with

Senta Berger, Lilli Palmer, and Anna Massey, but eventually was barely released and did little business. However, I did get on very well with Ross Taylor, and I took him to the Starlight cinema club, where we saw *How to Succeed in Business without Really Trying*, on which he'd worked but hadn't yet seen, and I also got a really great previously untold Elvis story out of Ross, who had just completed the sound on what would turn out to be one of Mr. Presley's worst-ever movies, *Charro*. I, naturally, asked Ross what it was like to work with Elvis Presley, and Ross said that Elvis couldn't have been more professional, except for one awkward moment of misunderstanding during the shoot. It was near the end of the shooting day, and Elvis overheard director Charles Marquis Warren say that he'd just like to get one more shot to get in the can before breaking: "Let's do the big head shot". Elvis overheard this, and thought that the director was calling Elvis a "Big Head", not knowing that it was merely U.S. film slang for a close-up. Elvis went into a sulk, and wouldn't come out of his trailer without an apology from the director. Eventually, all was explained, and Elvis returned, and he himself apologised for his own lack of movie slang knowledge. (That's an Elvis tale that you won't find anywhere else!)

In the meantime, back at Sound Associates during our work on *De Sade*, I expounded to John Taylor just what I had in fact learned from our Cannes experience, and told him that I had commissioned a treatment for a proposed sex movie. He said to let him know what happens, and that he might be interested in working on it, perhaps, someday.

Rhubarb was still shooting, and I received an offer to be the sound editor on *Ride the White Horses*, a Ford Motor Company production, directed by Peter Gold. I accepted, and we did a very fast sound mix with John Wood at the De Lane Lea dubbing theatre in Dean Street. Although sports, let alone sea sports, were far from my favourite subject, Ford seemed pleased with the result. However, I wasn't invited back to work on Peter Gold's next project, on which he was the editor, a much-troubled Peter Sellers film, *The Blockhouse*, which was barely released at all.

And, at last, *Rhubarb* had finished shooting, and was ready to edit. There was a script, but it was more a collection of gags, and Eric Sykes just, initially, wanted it assembled in 'script' order. Which I did. But without sound, it wasn't all that funny, despite a fine cast of comedians, because the actual gag was that the word *Rhubarb* was to replace all dialogue, and since the film was shot mute, the gag wasn't there. At least, not yet. But it seemed very funny, mute nevertheless, very funny indeed.

Eric Sykes and I were getting along famously. He was the best kind of director for an editor to work with: he let me edit it the way I wanted, what I thought was best for the scenes (there was still no script), and then he came in, viewed it, maybe viewed it again, and then asked for whatever changes he wanted, and he was invariably absolutely right in his choices. I got the distinct impression that he was actually more interested in the process than in the result. I had hired a new assistant to help me, Caroline Pick, who would eventually go on to become a distinguished commissioning editor for both BBC and Channel 4, and she couldn't have been more welcome. She was patience itself, which was very necessary with Eric Sykes, both for his almost total deafness, and his penchant for very large cigars.

Caroline and I went through the whole thirty-seven minute running time edit approved by Eric, to identify and, hopefully, eventually record the whole cast saying 'Rhubarb' whenever they spoke. Eric loved this idea, even though it was, of course, originally his, merely refined. We then set about locating all the various cast members, and recording them in the nearest available dubbing theatres. This lead to some very memorable moments. It was easy enough to set up a recording session at Sound Associates, with such luminaries as Harry Secombe, Jimmy Edwards, Hattie Jacques, Graham Stark, and even Johnny Speight, but Kenneth Connor presented a problem. He was at Pinewood Studios filming *Carry On...Up the Jungle* at the time, and producer Peter Rogers wouldn't let him off for our post-sync., unless we booked the Pinewood post-sync. theatre and grabbed Kenny when the floor assistant director said it was O.K. to spare him for a few moments. So that's what I did. I had never been on a *Carry On* set before, ever. Why would I ever have been? I was certainly no fan of the crude but massively popular film series. So I went onto the set, having prepared the dubbing crew in the theatre for a quick, and sudden, shoot. On the studio floor I introduced myself to Kenneth Connor, and, fortunately, we were on the stage nearest to the dubbing theatre, so it wouldn't take long to get Ken there and back. But what, of course, I hadn't reckoned with, was the fact that the shooting of the *Carry On* crew was astoundingly fast. Shoot the rehearsal, then one extra take only, and then only if absolutely necessary, was the directorial style of former film editor Gerald Thomas, brother of the *Doctor* series director Ralph Thomas. Kenneth was in almost every shot, and, whilst it was not too disturbing for me to be hanging around the scantily-clad Jacki Piper and Valerie Leon on the set (the latter of whom I got to know quite well when we both lectured on cruise ships a decade or so later), I was beginning to wonder if Kenneth Connor would ever be let out. Suddenly, I felt a hand clap on my shoulder. It was Jack Causey, the assistant director: "Take him now. Get him back bloody quick". I went over to Ken Connor, who was still in costume, who said "Should I change?". I said "Wouldn't bother – it's voice only" and he laughed. We scooted over to the post-sync. theatre, and the moment we arrived the sound mixer put up the first loop. Ken was really fast, and I started to play back the first one, but Ken said "No time for playback, they'll kill me if I'm not back immediately. You listen after I'm gone. If I have to redo anything I'll come right back". And that's what we did. All of Ken Connor's own "Rhubarbs" weren't heard by him until he actually saw the film. But a delay in my leaving led to a quite unexpected bonus for me…

As I left the dubbing theatre on my way to the outside, I ran into none other than Katharine Hepburn, in costume for *The Madwoman of Chaillot*, currently shooting at Pinewood. She accosted me: "Is this right for the looping theatre?" she asked in that magnificent but ageing oh-so-recognisable voice. I pointed to the door I had just come out of, opposite to the direction in which she was facing. "It's just over there, Miss Hepburn," I said, and made to open the heavy door for her. "Oh, don't bother" she said, "I can open it for myself. Thank you so much". I stood back. She smiled at me. I smiled back. "Bloody hell" I thought, "I've just met Katharine Hepburn". And she seemed much shorter than she photographed, as they invariably are.

Working with Eric Sykes was such a joy, full of quite delicious surprises. For instance, once, in editing a close-up of him, I had cut the shot too short, and had to rejoin a trim. In my hurry I had misjoined it, using the wrong trim which made Eric do a sudden jerky face movement, as a result of a few missing frames. I was embarrassed and hurried to correct it, but Eric stopped me. "No, don't fix it, it'll get a good laugh", he said. I was about to protest, but realised that he himself laughed when he saw the jerky move, and this man knew about comedy audiences like nobody else. So I left it, and it still embarrasses me, but Eric was bloody right; it does get a very good laugh every time!

Eric shared an office with *Till Death Us Do Part* scriptwriter and wit Johnny Speight in Orme Court, Bayswater, at the offices of their mutual agent Norma Farnes, and Eric often went back there after an editing session towards the end of the day. One evening we were working a little late, and I had intended to take my assistant Caroline to the Notting Hill Gate Classic cinema after we finished to show her my own favourite-ever Western *Rio Bravo*, which was playing at the late night 11.00pm house. Eric overheard us talking about this, and said why don't Caroline and I pop over to the nearby Orme Court and have a quick drink with him and Johnny before going on to, as he called it, "the flicks"? Hard to say no to a director's request such as that, so we said we'd see him there later, and then go on to the pictures, and so we turned up at Orme Court that evening at about eight o'clock.

Eric and Johnny were drinkers, and that's an understatement. They loved their booze, and, by the time we arrived, they had both gone through several cigars and, I'm guessing, at least a couple of bottles of wine. They welcomed us like long-lost family; they couldn't have been nicer or indeed more welcoming, and Eric himself was full of praise for our work. But, with Eric deaf and seemingly the worse for drink (although he had a capacity I had never previously before witnessed in anybody), and Johnny Speight utterly self-obsessed, but nevertheless very, very funny, this hardly seemed a convivial place for Caroline and me to be, but the film didn't start until eleven o'clock, so we had about 90 minutes to kill. Should we stay? Or were we but intruders in a private evening of two of the most talented, and funniest, men in show business? I made my apologies, as though ready to go, but Eric and Johnny wouldn't hear of it. They put their respective arms around Caroline, and topped up --yet again-- our glasses. It'll come as no surprise to you, dear reader, that I can't remember what we were drinking, but I think it was a very excellent Chianti. I'm not sure, though, and it didn't seem to matter at the time. All sorts of 'nibbles' were on hand, and so this seemed to be our supper also. Eventually, we left them, virtually sozzled in their respective chairs, and made, or rather tried to make, our way out. Only I couldn't seem to stand up. Eric and Johnny didn't notice, but Caroline, bless her, helped me up and out. We said our goodbyes, Eric and Johnny took turns in kissing Caroline, and we left. It was late, and a taxi was the only recourse to get us to the Notting Hill Classic, where we arrived in time, and I bought two tickets for *Rio Bravo*, not just my own favourite Western, but a film I firmly believe is one of the greatest ever made.

We went into the cinema, sat in the centre of the third row of the stalls, and, apparently, I fell asleep during the main titles. Caroline, wisely perhaps, didn't wake me. I woke up as the curtains closed over the end titles, and had difficulty, to say the least, in moving. Caroline helped me up, got me outside, and hailed a taxi. I couldn't speak either, but it didn't seem to matter. She put me in the taxi and told the driver "8a, Eccleston Street" which actually wasn't too far away. I still couldn't manage to speak. Caroline said "See you Monday morning". I'd forgotten it was a Friday night. I spent the weekend sleeping it off, and mentally vowed never, never, never, ever to drink that much again, ever. It cost me *Rio Bravo*, at least, and it could have destroyed my career. Thank you Eric Sykes and Johnny Speight. (And God bless your memories, both).

Working with Eric Sykes couldn't have been more pleasurable. As we approached a final edit, he started taking myself and Caroline out to his regular lunchery, Bertorelli's in Charlotte Street, where he had a table permanently reserved for him, and where he could smoke his beloved huge cigars well away from the other guests. He was the most wonderful raconteur, and one of the funniest men who ever lived. Sometimes we were joined by Johnny Speight, and once by their agent Norma Farnes, who told me "Eric really likes working with you", which made it all worthwhile.

Eric's deafness meant he couldn't attend the post-sync. sessions, which actually only consisted of the actors saying various versions of *Rhubarb*, but it meant that I got to meet, and to direct, some of my comedy heroes: Harry Secombe, Jimmy Edwards, Hattie Jacques, and, of course, Eric Sykes himself, when he actually managed to turn up. He could never hear playback of course, although we did offer to turn the level to maximum in order for him to hear, but it meant that we would all have had to leave the theatre at such a level, which would cost time and money, so we didn't, and Eric just trusted me to okay the looping.

Ditto the actual dub. How do you mix your tracks to the director's liking if the director is stone-deaf? Although Peter Lodge of Sound Associates had gotten me the job, I felt that he was not the kind of man who would be gentle or sympathetic to a deaf director with no sense of time. I did, however, speak to him about mixing at his theatre at Sound Associates, of course, but he wasn't keen. Frankly, this pleased me, and I booked a dub with David Maiden at De Lane Lea, a young mixer I had worked with before, who was very talented and, more to the point, patient. Jon Penington was working to a very small budget, and I could see how, if we weren't very, very careful, there could be dangerous, and therefore expensive, overruns in the dubbing theatre. It's not often, if ever, that one works with a totally deaf director. Mixer Dave Maiden and I met for a chat before we started, and we agreed on a format: to mix the picture normally, until we (i.e. Dave and I) were happy with it, and then exit the theatre, and then play it back to Eric at an extremely high sound level that only he could hear, intolerable to others, and then carry out his subsequent notes afterwards, mixed at a normal level, and then play back again ultra-loud to see if he was happy with the results. And so we did. But with one very happy substantial difference. Eric Sykes was so pleased with the mix that he wanted no changes at all. He asked to see and hear it again, and we duly played it for him at the level as before, with Dave and myself leaving the dubbing theatre and waiting outside. When it was over, Eric came out and gave us both a hug. It made our day.

Eric wanted to show the completed *Rhubarb* to his very good friend and golfing partner, none other than Mr. James Bond himself, Sean Connery, and I arranged a screening which only Sean and I attended. Sean enjoyed *Rhubarb* very much, and afterwards, we had a drink and a chat with Eric. Sean and I turned out to have a lot in common in our taste in movies, and attitudes to film-making, and there and then Sean offered me the editing job on his forthcoming film production of *Macbeth* for Rank, with his then wife Diane Cilento as Lady M. and Eric Sykes as Banquo. I couldn't have been more delighted, and accepted instantly, thanking Sean. I asked when he would start, and he told me that Rank were waiting for the bank's approval of himself as director in addition to playing the leading role. But we all knew that, with James Bond's box office clout, there wouldn't be a problem. We all shook hands and went our separate ways, and *Rhubarb* came to a close, only to turn up on ABC circuit release as British quota support to *Spring and Port Wine*, where it reached quite a substantial audience.

Two codas to *Rhubarb*. A few months later, I ran into Sean Connery in, of all places, Woolworth's in the Kings Road. I was flattered that he recognised me and remembered my name. I asked him what was happening with *Macbeth*, and he replied that Rank had pulled out, and said they had made no money with the first of their new production programme, a remake of Hitchcock's *The Lady Vanishes*, and they were stopping all future productions, except for the *Carry On*s. What he added about British film producers, I couldn't print here. We shook hands and he said "Sorry" and "Goodbye". A nice, smart, funny man, Sean Connery, with a great passion for film. I never met him again.

There were just a few days left before we closed down the *Rhubarb* cutting room that Friday after the final mix, and Eric was about to start recording a brand new television show that Johnny Speight and he had written for London Weekend Television called *Curry and Chips*, to be recorded at the Lee International Studios, Wembley, and he invited Caroline and myself along as guests to watch the recording, and have a final farewell supper afterwards to say "Goodbye", with him, Spike Milligan, and their agent, who was also the show's producer, Norma Farnes. We were to meet him there, where he was already in make-up and costume, which we did, and he began to lead us through the corridors to our seats.

But on the way, lying horizontally across the corridor, we could see the figure of a man directly in our path, wearing a dark suit and a red Egyptian fez, his feet towards the right, his body effectively blocking our path. He turned out to be none other than Eric's old friend and comedy rival, the great Tommy Cooper. "Ignore him," said Eric to us, me and Caroline, Norma and Spike, and Eric paved our way by being the first to step over the prone body, and we duly followed. It seemed a good gag at the time. We watched the recording of the show, which was very funny, and Spike was brilliant, but its racist language raised some hackles, which was, of course, just what Johnny Speight had intended. After Eric had taken off his make-up and changed, we joined him outside his dressing room and we all headed for the exit.

In front of us, in the same corridor, lying down once again horizontally on the floor across the corridor, but this time reversed, his head where his feet were on the way in, and vice versa, was Tommy Cooper again, prone as before. And once again Eric said to us, clearly loud enough for Tommy to hear "Just ignore him". And so we carried on, and went for a nice Indian post-show supper. Nothing else was ever said about Tommy, or his whereabouts, and the gag remains one of the funniest, and most inspired, pieces of comedy that I have ever witnessed. A great gag from a truly great comedian, and I'm absolutely sure Eric Sykes thought so too. "Just ignore him." I'll never forget it.

Rhubarb over, I had to concentrate on what was happening at Eccleston Street. Mike Billington was now involved in very serious discussions with the Andersons, Sylvia and Gerry, and was absolutely sure, although not yet confirmed, that he had a leading role in their upcoming television series *UFO*, and start dates were being discussed. As far as I was concerned, that meant the rent and rates would be paid, guaranteed. What, then, of *City Suite*? Mike and I spent some time with Ray Selfe discussing Ray's own role on the proposed project. It seemed only fair to have him as cameraman, but if Mike was directing and I was editing, it also seemed a good idea for Ray to produce it as well, and that's what we both proposed, and we put together a presentation package. Andrew Best's treatment was a cracker, and could be filmed easily in just a few locations, basically three different houses and a couple of clubs, with some local exteriors. It could be shot in under three weeks, if properly scheduled and suitably cast. Of course, it would help if we had a script to present, and I approached Andrew Best to see if he would write up his treatment on spec.

David (Andrew's real name, remember?) said that he had just received an amazing offer from the States asking him to join a brand-new show for children that would encompass many of David's keen social ideas, entitled

Sesame Street, and he was going to accept, but if I wanted to take the treatment of *City Suite* to script form, he wouldn't mind, as long as he received some payment, and credit (as Andrew Best), if, and when, it got going. We agreed in principle, but there was no exchange of letters at this stage.

I was temporarily quite flush, having worked virtually non-stop since the beginning of *Strange Report*, and decided on two things: if Mike agreed, I'd take the *City Suite* treatment to a screenplay, and we'd schlep it around Wardour Street, and see if we could find any takers. Mike would still be the director. In hindsight: naive, or what? I also proposed a rough budget and shooting schedule, which I could prepare myself once the screenplay was completed. I wrote the central character Bob for Michael Billington to perform, although I knew he wasn't going to both play the lead and direct. I also wrote the locations for those that I knew we could use: my flat, Ray's house, and one other local apartment, plus a couple of Soho clubs and streets. Casting would come later – we didn't need stars, that's for sure, but I liked to write with images in mind, so I mentally cast people that I knew. It all took time, which at that moment I had in scads. When she knew what I was up to, Bridget Reiss was a tremendous help, supportive and friendly, I couldn't have wished for better company. She even offered her own flat as the third location needed, as she had a boyfriend elsewhere and could stay with him while we were shooting, if we ever got to that eventuality.

With the locations blocked out, I could plan a shooting schedule, and write accordingly, and so I did. It took about five weeks, with revisions, a total of two months in all to write the first draft screenplay of *City Suite*. At the same time I researched those film companies that might be interested in producing and releasing an extremely low budget British sex film, available as a British quota feature, and thus able to receive the Government's Eady payout for British films made in Great Britain. My hopes were high, but that's all they were, just hopes.

And then, a lot of things all happened at once, the most important of which was that Gerry and Sylvia Anderson had achieved ITC backing for their series *UFO*. Blimey! The company that once backed *The Prisoner* were now going to make a science fiction series romp with real live actors playing roles intended once upon a time for painted wooden puppets with strings!

Since we now had a script on *City Suite*, our original treatment would also serve as a guide in presentation. I cobbled together a front page production budget, and proposed a cast list of roles and a list of required technicians. With Mike directing, most of the cast and crew could be sourced from Ray Selfe's film classes, or so I figured, and that would keep the costs down. No-one would know that it was a non-union shoot until it was over and finished. I set about identifying possible punters. Their names were well-known to any reader of *What's On In London*. I enlisted Antony Balch's advice, and we both came to the same conclusions: Gala, Border, Miracle ("If it's a good picture, it's a Miracle"), Compton, and Butcher's. A motley bunch. Oh, and maybe New Realm.

I then put together a presentable package: the screenplay, the synopsis, a front page budget and a plausible schedule. In truth, much of this was guesswork, but I was relying on back-up from Mike as director and Ray as producer and cameraman. I thought I was doing an awful lot as just an editor! Ray and I bought an off-the-shelf company name, Liongrange, from the firm that my old Dulwich schoolmate, Howard Rogg, was now employed by, a firm of solicitors in Regent Street (which was convenient) called Malcolm Slowe, whose son, I was to find out eventually, Martin Slowe, handled the ownership, ironically, of the lease to 8a, Eccleston Street, and who would eventually cause a major change to my own life, for the better, although nobody could have possibly foreseen that at the time. The package was ready to present.

Mike Billington and I went for a walk down Wardour Street ("The only street in London that's shady on both sides," as film industry legend has it) and surveyed the windows of the companies that I've mentioned above. Did they look as though they had heft, did they look as though they needed product, did they look as though they had money to spend? We left our packages with Border and Miracle, and made an appointment to see the twin heads at Eagle, who, when we met them, weren't impressed at all to say the least, and were unaccountably rather rude besides, so we didn't bother to leave them our presentation package.

Then, something that I thought truly amazing happened. Mike was called for a costume test for *UFO* at Pinewood, and got the job! He was to play a leading character called Colonel Paul J. Foster, and had to sign a run of the series contract, which he did. He told me that he wouldn't be able to direct *City Suite* if it happened. I reminded him that his name, biography, and credits were part of our presentation package, but he didn't seem too concerned. Understandably, to a degree, he was over the moon having just secured a starring role in a brand new television series. He'd have money for life! But what about me and Ray and *City Suite* if it happened? "You can figure it out", he said. "Well", I thought to myself, "at least I won't have to worry about the rent any more". Little could I guess…

Somewhat surprisingly, I received a phone call from one Barry Edson at Miracle Films, asking Mike and I to pop in and see him, which we did. It seemed that Miracle could use a very cheaply made British sex film to be a quota supporting flick to their imported French product, most of which starred the likes of imitation Brigitte Bardots, in order to claim the quota money. If we could make *City Suite* very, very cheaply, and also on the quiet, Miracle might be interested. Think about it. Which we did, very quickly, in a Wardour Street coffee bar. It all depended on the start date. If it clashed with Mike's starting *UFO*, then he suggested I direct it. "They won't know and they won't care," he said. Well, now...

In the meantime, Barry Edson, who turned out to be a major mine of film information, and a cineaste in his own right who would eventually work for the British Film Institute, had consulted the heads of Miracle, Phil Kutner and Michael Myers, and had made an earnest recommendation, that, if it was cheap enough, it was well worth making for the Eady money alone. Anything else would be sheer profit. Miracle, i.e. Kutner and Myers, liked the sound of that. Oh, and they also wanted a slight change of title. After considering *City Sweet* instead of *City Suite*, they came up with *City Sweet and Sexy*, and eventually decided on *Sweet and Sexy*. Could we make it for under £20,000? My answer, of course, was "Yes". It, perhaps, should have been "You betcha!!" Barry said he would get back to me.

I conveyed all of the above to Michael Billington, who suggested we meet up with Ray Selfe as soon as possible, because he, Mike, now feared that he wouldn't be able to direct the film because of the start of *UFO*. What he didn't say was that, of course, at present directing a sex film would not exactly be good for his new image, and could perhaps possibly cost him his new job. We met up and decided that, if we got a go-ahead, to say nothing about Mike's plight at all, and carry on with me directing, Ray lighting and operating, and cast it cheaply and shoot it quickly. And, with an awful lot of acrimony, that's what we did.

Mike went off to do *UFO*, which, by the way, had three episodes directed by *The Prisoner*'s David Tomblin, no less, and helped us, if 'helped' is the right word to use in retrospect, with two very key casting elements. Mike's own *UFO* stand-in Robert Case to play the hero in *Sweet and Sexy*, and a co-star of his in the series, the American redhead Quinn O'Hara, to play our leading lady, and what I couldn't possibly foresee, not just in the film, but for quite a while in my own life, totally unpredictable at the time, for sure.

Barry Edson arranged a meeting between Phil Kutner and Michael Myers, the heads of Miracle, and Ray Selfe and me, and we apologised for Michael Billington's absence, saying he was working at the time, which, in fact, he actually was. We talked start dates, and crew standards. Miracle weren't particularly interested in the cast, as long as all the women took their clothes off. They wanted us to use Humphries Laboratories, where they had a deal, and they didn't care where in London we filmed. They weren't even particularly interested in seeing rushes either. They had a permanent staff editor, John Pipkin, who would edit the film and be credited as Associate Producer for Miracle, and they would require daily progress reports. What about copyright clearances? I told them that the original author of the story was now in New York, and they instructed us to get our lawyer to secure the author's signature on a letter of approval, and legal certification that it was indeed his original story, as soon as possible, before any monies could be released. Howard Rogg was both surprised and delighted to be sent to New York for a day by Malcolm Slowe to ascertain that Andrew Best was actually a real person, and that he had written the original story of *City Suite*, and also further that he had no objection to my screenplay that was adapted and based on his original treatment being filmed as *Sweet and Sexy*.

Well now, "Andrew" signed all the prepared documents with a will. I took advantage of Howard's trip to ask him to please bring back a copy of the U.S. release of the soundtrack album from *Easy Rider* for me, which featured on its sleeve the original film poster that was used at Cannes; the English sleeve being clearly just a cheap design. Howard did so, and I figured if everything else on *Sweet and Sexy* collapsed, at least I now had a groovy American pressing and an original sleeve of unquestionably the hippest film soundtrack of the moment.

Events moved very fast. Mike Billington swiftly secured his *UFO* stunt stand-in for the lead in *Sweet and Sexy*, promising him that we could schedule around him where necessary. His name was Bob Case, and he was more than happy to do both nude scenes and violent stunt work for next-to-nothing, provided he could have his mates do the stunts with him. Sure. Double sure – in spades: in fact, just what we needed!

UFO had already started shooting, and, I guess unsurprisingly, Mike Billington was already involved with a few of his leading ladies, and since he was still living with me at Eccleston Street, I got to know a couple of them very well: Gabrielle Drake, who was an absolute honey, and Quinn O'Hara, who I knew by screen reputation from *A Swingin' Summer* and *The Ghost in the Invisible Bikini*, cult classics both. I didn't mind so much Mike bringing his girlfriends back to 8a, but I was beginning to resent the fact fact that he was using my records and record player to, I'll use a nice word, seduce them. I was particularly annoyed when my Ben E. King *Spanish Harlem* L.P. was set to replay over and over again my favourite tracks while Mike was making out with Quinn O'Hara on the downstairs couch. No, I wasn't watching, but I could hear perfectly well from my upstairs bedroom. Everything!

However, when Quinn discovered what I was up to, she, unbelievably, said she'd like to be in my film. I said to check with her agent, the venerable Eric L'Pine Smith, and she did so, and she told me that when Eric knew that I was the director, he said something like "Fine, it's about time. You're in good hands". Oh, really?

I then met Robert Case. He looked fine. Could he act? Did it really matter? The main thing about him was that he didn't mind doing the sex scenes. In fact, he said he looked forward to them, and could recommend one of his old girl friends to play a leading role if I wanted. Did I just? It sounded like excellent chemistry to me: sex scenes with people who knew each other just makes my job easier, if not redundant. (But I wasn't wise enough then to realise that sex scenes between people who don't know each other very well, or even at all, are much, much more exciting both to film and to watch). Ray and I cast Bob Case and his Susanne on the spot. Perhaps we should have heard them test-read first, but, frankly we were just glad to get a cast who would do sex scenes. Anthony Balch recommended Cathy Howard, from his *Secrets of Sex* flick, and lo! we had our principal cast.

With Bridget's and Ray's homes providing two of our three principal indoor locations, it only remained for me to suggest 8a, Eccleston Street as the third. And then a very, very strange thing happened: Michael Billington, now starring in *UFO* at Pinewood, decided to move out. For good. He clearly didn't now want anything at all to do with *Sweet and Sexy*, or even me apparently, even though at one time he couldn't wait to start directing it (and Miracle still didn't know he wasn't going to do so). He packed up his things, gave me a cheque for an advance up until the end of the month, moved out, and I never saw him again.

By the way, *Prisoner* fans, the lighting cameraman on Mike's *UFO* series was none other than *The Prisoner*'s great Brendan J. Stafford, and the camera operator was my old mate, and perpetual saviour, Jack Lowin. It was Jack in particular who lingers in my memory, not just for saving my bacon on "Chimes of Big Ben", but for a long-running gag on *The Prisoner* shoot: when a set-up is ready to be filmed, it's customary for the first assistant director to call out "Mark it!", an instruction for the clapper-board to go in to commence the shot. On *The Prisoner*, I forget on which episode, but one definitely directed by Patrick McGoohan himself, assistant director Gino Marotta called "Mark it!" and a tiny voice, which turned out to belong to Jack Lowin, said "Harborough". Pat McGoohan burst out laughing, and Gino called "Cut!". The crew looked at each other, and Jack's expression was that of a very naughty boy. Patrick, still laughing, embraced Jack, and said "That's very funny, Jack". The rest of us present were embarrassed, and didn't know where to look. Jack's unwanted addition of "Harborough" to Gino's cry of "Mark it!" obviously really struck Patrick's funny bone, and he became more relaxed than we had seen him for a long time: perhaps the astute Jack had sensed that that would've been very necessary, sooner or later. Anyhow, for a while afterwards, Pat instructed Gino to call out "Market Harborough" before the clapperboard went in, prior to "Action!". (By the by, Market Harborough is a town in Leicestershire, famous for the training and operations of the R.A.F.'s Wellington bombers during World War II). I could have done with Brendan and Jack on *Sweet and Sexy*, although I did work once again with Jack Lowin on another British sex film, *Can You Keep It Up For A Week?*, directed by my old cutting room mate Jim Atkinson, but Jack and I, alas, never managed to meet up on that little epic.

Back to *Sweet and Sexy* – my first day of shooting did not go well. It was a scene in Ray and Jean's house, featuring Bob Case and veteran British actress Rose Alba, but on the very first day of shooting, our star Robert Case didn't show up. I tried to cover, filming all of Rose Alba's singles, but I noticed something was very, very wrong, and it wasn't only Bob's absence. Ray Selfe, our producer and cameraman, seemed to have been drinking, something I could have never, ever, have expected, and certainly couldn't have imagined, having been a boarder in his house and a student in his film classes. I never saw him take a drink. But this very morning it was quite clear, quite clear. I'm not a psychologist, but I guess he realised he had taken on a lot more than he could handle, and was compensating. But it was first thing in the morning, and we had a full day's shooting ahead, and, at present, our leading actor hadn't even turned up. What a first day for my feature directing debut! What to do?

We lined up to shoot every possible angle on Rose Alba, but Ray was clearly not happy. Nevertheless, we got some fairly usable footage, and, at about eleven o'clock in the morning, Bob Case turned up: "I'm sorry. I overslept, and then I couldn't find the location". None of that mattered, at least he was here. I set about shooting his reversals with Rose first of all, but, in doing so, I noticed that Ray's camera line-up in order to match Bob and Rose's eye-lines when filmed didn't seem quite right to me. He had, in film industry parlance, "crossed the line", making the material filmed decidedly uncuttable. I didn't know what to do – I had to point it out. I took Ray aside to suggest this, and then I noticed, although he hid it well, that he was, in fact, slightly drunk. And this was only our first morning. We carried on shooting, and, although Bob and Rose were excellent, I knew that this would be a nightmare to edit if not reshot, and called over Ray to have a private word. He was brutally honest with himself. "I think we need a cameraman", he admitted. I asked the assistant director to contact the union, and find out who was available and could start immediately, if not today, then first thing tomorrow morning, and Ray agreed to this. (So not only would Miracle discover they hadn't got the designated nominated director, Michel Billington, but they also hadn't got the designated cameraman. If they ever found out, I wouldn't have been surprised if they pulled the plug immediately).

I had as my assistant directors two extremely efficient film buffs. My first was introduced to me by Caroline Pick, whose boyfriend I think he was, Neil Kirk, and my second went under the nom-de-film of Robert Aarons, but in fact was one of Australia's leading writers on film, and would eventually himself direct, under his own name. My production manager was the experienced Simon Willson, who I knew from *Oedipus the King*, and together, or separately – I still don't know to this date – they all helped me immensely by finding for us an excellent camera operator in John Barnard, who had just finished covering the Olympics in Mexico for the Samuelsons, and who saved my bacon, thank God. I would, and did, use him again.

The other main technical problem with *Sweet and Sexy* was the sound. The sound man was Ray's wife Jean's brother, one Graham Bottle, and it didn't come up to feature standards, shall we say to be kind. Worse, Graham actually told me off on set for shouting an instruction to an actress over one particular scene, when she wasn't speaking. Didn't he know about 'fill', or more to the point, didn't he know about post-sync.? Eventually, the whole soundtrack needed to be re-created, which was just fine with me, because we recast all the voices, except Quinn O'Hara's, with professional voice artistes. Bob and absolutely all the other men were brilliantly revoiced by Paul Angelis, perhaps better known as the voice of Ringo in *Yellow Submarine*, and all of the women, except for Quinn, were revoiced by the 'voice of them all', the wonderful, extraordinary Olive Gregg, whose professionalism can be heard in almost every British feature film of note, although seldom, if ever, credited. Her performances vastly improved any film she worked on, certainly including mine, and, equally important in film production, the synchronisation was flawless. What talent, and what professionalism: a real, unsung heroine.

There was a problem with Miracle's editor, our associate producer, John Pipkin. A jolly nice fellow-well-met sociable sort of a guy, he had absolutely no idea of how to run a feature editing room, and clearly couldn't handle, let alone assemble, daily rushes. Ray, as producer, had complicated matters by having the 35mm. rushes reduced to 16mm., in order to facilitate, he thought, the edit at a lower price. He didn't ask me about this. Of course, eventually we would have to conform the 35mm. film as shot, and provide a fully mixed soundtrack on 35mm., so why not just leave it alone? It wouldn't save any money, and eventually, when I, very reluctantly, took over the editing from John Pipkin, that's what we had to do, involving double negative cutting, first of all the 16mm. and then the 35mm. conform, complicated by track-laying on 16mm., eventualising in a 35mm. mix to secure a married print. Whew! And why? Because my producer Ray thought it would save money.

So I took over the edit, enlisted Caroline to help me, plus another excellent person in Ciarin Scott, and also Martin Amstell, who, much later, became the Head of the London School of Film Technique, as my dubbing editor. His assistant was the very excellent John Hackney, who rightly told me off when I, quite out of order, asked him to kindly pick up something for me from the chemist. "I'm not your servant", he said, or words to that effect, and he was right. (But he did it, just that one time).

Ray Selfe and John Pipkin had, unbeknownst to me, become allies. Allied together in one major cause: they both hated me. Ray felt that I had abused his good nature and all the benefits of his previous help and advice, not to mention his letting me have a room in his house, and John Pipkin merely felt I'd abused Miracle, who were, after all, his permanent employers, and that he'd been virtually elbowed out of the production, which I'm afraid, was true. Things came to a head at a post-production meeting, where Ray, John, Barry Edson, Martin Amstell, and myself were present, to discuss full post-production completion of the project. It turned into a heated shouting match, largely because, as it became clear, both Ray and John didn't really know what they were talking about. At one point, John Pipkin actually got so annoyed that he said to me, "Take off your glasses and I'll hit you". So I did, as a gesture, and, bloody hell, he hit me, full in the face, in front of everyone else, with a vicious fist. No-one helped me as I crashed to the floor. They were all, I think the correct term would be, gobsmacked. Ray Selfe, my mentor, landlord, friend, and current ersatz father-figure, did nothing. Trying to preserve what little dignity remained to me, and in considerable pain, I sputtered, "Right, now that that's over, let's get on with the post-production schedule". But I learned my lesson: a freelancer should never, ever joke about scheduling with a regularly paid member of staff of the company which pays the bills, especially when that company had hired the said person as the film's editor, and who had not only first replaced the original nominated director, but also then taken over the actual editing. Nuff said.

Sweet and Sexy was completed. There was some press, and the National Film Theatre wanted to screen it, and programmed it accordingly, with a planned interview with me afterwards. But Ray saw to it that that didn't happen and withheld the film copy, to my acute embarrassment, and tickets were refunded. I never spoke to him about it, ever. The next problem was the censor: *Sweet and Sexy* was banned from public exhibition, to our surprise and horror, and actually refused a certificate in October 1970, completely. It was resubmitted four months later, and the British Board of Film Censors requested over forty minutes to be removed. Forty minutes! Miracle appealed, and the Censors' original request was reduced to the actual editing out of twenty-one whole minutes of material, in order to secure a U.K. Censor's "X" certificate. And that's what happened. *Sweet and Sexy* eventually premiered at London's Cameo-Royal in a double bill as late as March 1972, its running time greatly reduced. However, in this current age of the DVD, and its predecessor, the so-called Home Video, *Sweet and Sexy* became readily available to buy or rent, but, and a very big "But", producer Ray Selfe had seen fit to take it upon himself to remove the whole first reel of the film, eliminating not only his own name (which I feel certain was his main intention), but of course, everyone else's, including, most annoyingly, mine. I always greatly enjoyed that credits sequence, which had absolutely nothing to do with the story or plot of what followed in *Sweet and Sexy*, but was merely, quite simply, the credits projected over the sensuously dancing body of a then-fashionable King's Road model known only as "Fred", completely irrelevant, of course, to what actually followed in the film, but who cared? Where's that lost first reel now?

Oh, and a minor detail on *Sweet and Sexy*, especially for *Prisoner* fans, with which to conclude. In the "Prohibition" Club sequence, where Cathy Howard makes her voluptuous night entrance, if you look very carefully, you'll spot a bartender in the distant background, moving a glass across the bar in half-shadow. This "actor" is none other than Bill Merrow, the father of *The Prisoner* and *Strange Report* actress Jane Merrow. He at the time, I believe, ran a West End employment bureau and just happened to be in that particular club when we were shooting. Don't ask me why, but when I learned whose Dad he was, I put him in the picture!

-----END OF REEL SIX-----

REEL SEVEN

What to do after *Sweet and Sexy*? The film was still having trouble with the censors, and it was also made very clear to me that Miracle certainly didn't want me involved with any of that. Fine by me. Towards the end of the final mixing, Phil Kutner bearded me in his den at Miracle, and said to me, very, very, seriously, like an avuncular Jewish elder, "Tony, what went wrong?". I told him the truth, without naming anyone in particular, and replied that we delivered on time as per contract, and only very slightly over budget, which in actuality means that an original film budget of – would you believe it? - about £15,000 went skyrocketing to around about £20,000. It was also British Quota, and therefore guaranteed to benefit from available Government funding when released, all of which monies would go directly to Miracle. But Phil got all paternal and said that he didn't like what had happened, especially not between myself and Ray (interestingly, he didn't mention Michael Billington). And what did I do then, the schmucko? Would you believe that I actually pitched him another picture, to star Carroll Baker, who had descended to Italian smut by then, and who I could deliver very cheaply. He was appalled, and we parted company for ever. But Ray Selfe kept in touch with Phil Kutner and Michael Myers, and I think to his wife Jean's dismay (for which she surely blamed me, alas), Ray continued with quite a substantial, if not necessarily lucrative, career in and around British sex films, sourcing material for documentaries and eventually running his own professional sex cinema. I don't know if he kept up with his teaching at his various evening classes.

It seemed to me that the best thing that I could do, career-wise, would be to make another movie, any type of movie, as soon as possible. Word had gradually gotten about in the industry that I had directed, so it was now unlikely that the telephone would ring again offering me cutting room work, or, frankly, anything else. I'd developed a professional friendship with one of the *Sweet and Sexy* actors, the former stunt man Jason Twelvetrees (his surname borrowed from the onetime Hollywood screen star Helen of that ilk), whose real name was actually Christopher Gregory, and we'd taken to playing snooker on occasional afternoons, in Eccleston Street opposite the flat. Jason wanted to be a screenwriter, and we tossed around some movie ideas. I told him of the parameters of a commercial plot that I was looking for:-- sex, sex, and more sex, but nowhere near quite as obvious as in *Sweet and Sexy*. I couldn't face more trouble with the censor: it was bad enough as it was, and Wardour Street would almost certainly already know about it. He suggested something else: not lots of girls, maybe just one, an identifiable young woman that an audience could feel for, and her sexual adventures. I pointed out the possible problems with the censors. "But it's a tale of redemption", said Jason, as he potted his ball. I asked him to write me a one page outline, and he did so, and called it "Karen", and it wasn't bad, but Jason didn't feel he could write a full screenplay, at least, not without being paid, and, frankly, who could blame him?

While I was editing *Rhubarb* I became friendly with an assistant editor called Ean Wood, who worked in a cutting room just down the corridor from us. He was a tremendous film enthusiast (they still weren't called "buffs" yet), having studied at the then-new London School of Film Technique in Brixton, and was a great radio and jazz fan, and we just clicked. He was married to photographer Frazer Wood, and I got to know them well socially. After Ean finished *Far From The Madding Crowd* with Peter Tanner, we used to meet up regularly, usually at the National Film Theatre. As he also wrote professionally, I told him my tale, and asked him if he'd like to take "Karen" to a screenplay. He asked to read it first, naturally (but at least that showed he wasn't greedy), liked it, and said "Yes". So he took away with him Jason's outline, and gave me back six very detailed pages of notes. I then asked him if he'd like to turn it into a script with me gently guiding him, as per the expectations of the audience. Even though he protested collaboration, we got on just fine, and he delivered a very plausible screenplay, but he didn't want his name on a sex film, so he chose "James Pillock", and we changed the title of *Karen* to *The Loving Game*.

I needed a producer, or thought I did. Now, who could be a front man, who could schlep our project around Wardour Street? There was already some interest from E.J. Fancey at Border Films, who had offices virtually next door to Miracle, for whom we made *Sweet and Sexy*, and they also needed British quota product. I was still in touch with *Strange Report*'s music editor John Taylor, who always wanted to produce, and he knew all about my problems with *Sweet and Sexy*, and he offered to help to produce *The Loving Game*. Well, I thought he certainly <u>looks</u> like a producer, and as Michael Rennie's son and Lewis Gilbert's nephew, his contacts might well be useful in setting up the project. And so, armed with nothing more than a script, a synopsis, and a rough budget front page, John and I made an appointment to see Mrs. Negus-Fancey at Border Films, and, to my absolute surprise, she said "Yes" almost immediately, provided that we brought it in exceptionally cheaply and showed the script to the censors first, to get their approval and avoid all the awful problems (she'd done her homework) that had occurred on the last film. John and I couldn't have been more delighted, then she added, "But of course we'll need a stand-by director if we're not satisfied with Mr. Sloman's rushes". Without blinking an eyelid, John justified his position in my mind by saying "Would you accept Lewis Gilbert as stand-by director?". Mrs. Negus-Fancey was surprised. "Of course, but we'd need to have it in writing". "You shall," promised John, and we made our exit. John telephoned his Uncle Lewis, and we then all had a very pleasant lunch together, wherein Lewis gave his word that, if Border were dissatisfied with me or my work in any way whatsoever, he would assume direction of the film. Lewis then assured me that, having met me, he knew that wouldn't be necessary, but, as he said, "It'll get you the money". I couldn't thank him enough.

(But eventually, I could, and did. I organised an on-stage lecture by Lewis combined with a season of his films at London's National Film Theatre.

I interviewed him on stage, and I myself was introduced by none other than Lewis' star of *Alfie* and *Educating Rita*, Michael Caine, who actually asked me at the pre-show reception if I minded that he – Michael – could introduce Lewis first, and then me? As if I minded!! And in the audience at the lecture I managed to secure, and introduce, a star from each of his movies, from Earl Cameron to Virginia McKenna, Shirley Anne Field to Max Bygraves, and I'm happy to report that Lewis himself was delighted. For me, it was the very least I could do).

Mrs. Negus-Fancey put her daughter Judith Smith on *Karen* as executive producer, but she didn't take a screen credit. She did, however, change our title to *Sex in the Suburbs*, but that seemed to last for about a week, although we did achieve a feature picture spread in *Films and Filming* as such, and a search for a new title commenced.

I'd learned a very bitter lesson from *Sweet and Sexy*; quite simply, just hire the best people that you can afford. Everybody wants to work, and it's never worth hiring your friends unless they're bloody good at what they're hired to do. So I went to the very best cameraman that I knew, the great Harry Waxman who had worked on *Wonderwall*, and whose past credits included such films as *Sapphire*, *The Roman Spring of Mrs. Stone* and more recently *There's a Girl In My Soup*, a talented man who I knew could glamourise the cheapest of interiors, and who could make all women look gorgeous. And to my amazement, he was free at the time and agreed to do it (and not just because I once dated his daughter some years before). In actual fact, Harry had a real revelation during our shooting. He confessed to me after a few days of filming Luan Peters, our leading lady, that he was actually falling in love with her. "I can't help it, Tony" he told me. I said to him that his secret was safe with me (and of course I knew that it would be jolly good for the picture!). I was glad for him, truly.

John Taylor and I had put together a very viable tight two-week shooting schedule, and we started casting, and that's when I realised what the attraction of producing was really about for John M. Taylor. I won't go into too much detail here, but we did eventually have to cast one of his 'discoveries' in a supporting role. (We had to revoice her eventually, though, using our make-up lady Olwen Griffiths, an excellent actress herself, who had appeared with none other than Hollywood star Van Johnson at the London's Adelphi theatre in *The Music Man*, to whom she later introduced me when he appeared in a charity show in London). I'd seen Luan Peters in the Miracle film *Man of Violence* and was very impressed. She had a real star quality, and considerable low-budget production experience. I thought she was a film star in the making, with the right role. The Fanceys allowed me to do all the casting, and so I met Luan, and we clicked, professionally, that is. No need to do a screen test, but she did offer to do something for me personally, that I just couldn't resist. She offered to show herself to me completely in the nude, just so that I could be sure. She came over to my flat in Eccleston Street, stripped off completely, and did a couple of brief twirls. Not only did she have the job, she had my heart. We got on terribly well professionally, and she was an absolute joy to work with. It wasn't until she died, only recently, that I discovered that her real name was Carol Hirsch, and that she hailed from the East End. Hence that special bonding? (And Harry Waxman too?). I should have guessed...

With John Taylor himself casting from all of the model agencies in London, I was left to cast the other roles, and here seemed a chance for me to pay back in kind some of the folks who had afforded me such pleasure during my coming-of-age days in the cinemas of Forest Gate and Streatham. For the leading male role I cast the well-known Australian actor Vincent Ball, who I remembered from *A Town Like Alice* and he proved an absolute pleasure to work with, and didn't seem to mind at all when he had to take off all of his clothes and run around in the nude in a muddy field on location in a key sequence – what a pro! I also cast James Hayter, who alas, was probably just a shade too elderly by this time, and he had to have his lines propped up in front of him, unseen by the camera. Nevertheless, he was my first Friar Tuck (in Walt Disney's *Robin Hood*), and had worked with all my favourites: Stewart Granger in *Beau Brummell* and Burt Lancaster in *The Crimson Pirate*, plus directors John Ford (*Gideon's Day*) and Howard Hawks, no less, (*Land of the Pharaohs*). But sadly, by the time I came to work with him, he could barely remember his lines, let alone tell tales of his glorious past. I had to delete one scene of his, and I'm sorry today that I did so.

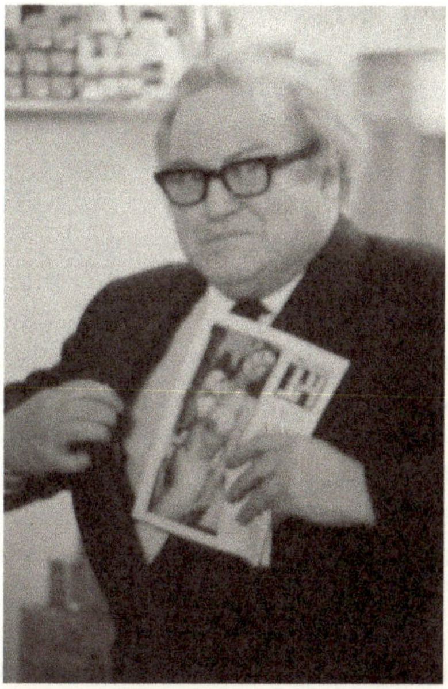

James Hayter (Friar Tuck to Richard Todd's Robin Hood in my childhood) in the scene that was deleted from *Not Tonight, Darling!* I cast him, of course, and I regret that I cut the scene, and feel today that I should have left it in, regardless of quality. But you can never go back... (This is the only surviving photograph of that scene, and it has never previously been published or printed anywhere).

I also cast British veteran, Bill Shine, and thereby hangs a tale. I had to have a very early casting session one day, because, since we weren't actually shooting yet, I was still signing on at the local unemployment office on Wednesdays, which is what I was about to do after this one particular casting session. I interviewed Kevin Colson, who I'd just seen on stage in *Robert and Elizabeth*, but he was far too beefy and really too young for the role, and then I saw Guy Middleton, an English veteran who might once have been perfect, but he was much, much older than his photograph, and, alas, far too rheumy around the eyes, and then I saw Bill Shine, who was perfect. So, that done, the company car then drove me to the Westminster Labour Exchange, where I promptly joined my S to Z queue. And who was in front of me at SH (directly in front of SL), yes, you've guessed it, Bill Shine himself, signing on unemployed! We had a good laugh together, and subsequently bonded for life: the actor just cast, and the director who just cast him, both signing on as unemployed, same time, same day!

Another venerable British actor figured in another related tale. Although, as director, I didn't have to take a medical fitness insurance examination for *Sweet and Sexy* (I briefly wondered if Michael Billington had ever taken one), I certainly had to make that trip to Harley Street to prove that I was healthy enough to guarantee to Border Films that I could complete the forthcoming production. I passed with flying colours, but couldn't resist asking the examining doctor if there was ever an occasion when a candidate, either actor or technician, ever actually failed the insurance test, and to my surprise, he told me the following, I'm sure once highly confidential, story:-

"I don't know if you've heard of an actor called Bobby Newton" he said, "I think he was called Robert Newton professionally". "Yes, I certainly have", I replied, remembering well the first time I saw Robert Newton, as Long John Silver in Disney's *Treasure Island* at the Forest Gate Odeon, and then catching up with his wonderful performances in such as *This Happy Breed*, and, of course, *The High and the Mighty* on release. Not to mention his unforgettable Bill Sikes in *Oliver Twist*. "Well", confided my doctor, "He arrived here for an early morning appointment for *Around the World in 80 Days*. He was clearly well drunk by ten o'clock, and arrived with each hand on each of the portals of my surgery door, in order to steady himself in the doorway. He then fell in. My secretary heard the thump, and came in to help me lift Mr. Newton onto the couch. He was dead drunk. I examined him, and could tell that he probably hadn't very long to live at all, let alone complete the arduous schedule of *Around the World in 80 Days*.

"So what did you do?" I asked. "I had no choice", the doctor continued, "I called the producer who sent him to me, Michael Todd, and warned him that this man was uninsurable, and would not live longer than a few months more, in my opinion". "Goodness," I was mesmerised, "What happened?". "Mike Todd sent a car round to pick him up, and put up a personal bond with his own money that Newton would complete the film's shoot, and Newton died the day after he had completed his performance schedule. The film won the Oscar for Best Picture". Well, I thought to myself, that's the kind of story you don't hear every day.

We put together a very professional crew on our film. I hired John O'Connor, formerly of *The Prisoner*, as my production manager, and it was good to work with him again. Martin Amstell came on board as sound editor, and my old Shepperton friend and mentor in hippiedom, Mark Davies, credited under his real name of Martin Davies, was our Art Director, although in this particular instance art direction largely consisted of just set decoration and dressing, as I had now learned to use real practical locations, and not merely to shoot in available people's flats. In fact, our first interior location yielded a marvellous background for our main title sequence, an original (but uncredited) painting by actor Keith Michell, which we were allowed to use, and we further discovered that the house next door belonged to actor Gary Raymond, who made himself known to us when we were filming. A very nice man, it was a real pleasure to see him recently back on stage in *Follies* at London's National Theatre.

We also managed to secure the currently popular band Thunderclap Newman (of "Something in the Air" fame) to play a couple of tracks from their latest L.P. in a day shoot guest spot at London's then-fashionable night club La Valbonne, and also hired some absolutely terrific professional models, including top calendar darling June Palmer, plus Nicola Austine and Samantha Bond to provide a sensually alluring work-out in a Kensington gym. These girls were marvellously professional to work with, but, perhaps not surprisingly, producer John Taylor's specific casting of Nicki Howorth required the very necessary revoicing job that I mentioned earlier, and I'm particularly pleased to say that one female casting of mine, who was credited on the film as Amber Harrison, went on from us to much further fame, courtesy of sex impresario Paul Raymond, who renamed her Fiona Richmond.

We were required to film an additional much more sexually sophisticated version for foreign market sales, and so 'James Pillock' wrote in a torrid party scene. Somebody – I can't remember who it was - it could have been my wonderful assistant director Gerry Harrison - secured a marvellous threesome, two men and one girl (you could term the sequence 'double entry' – it's only available abroad, alas merely glimpsed in the U.K. version). One of the men turned out to be experimental music composer David Vorhaus, for me a person of great interest, for he was the son of the veteran, and eventually tragically blacklisted, distinguished Hollywood director Bernard Vorhaus, whose film credits stretched from 1927's *Steppin' Out* to his last two films, both made in Italy, 1953's *Roman Holiday* and 1954's *The Barefoot Contessa*, on both of which he was reduced to working under a pseudonym, credited as Piero Musetta, as first assistant director to distinguished directors William Wyler and Joseph L. Mankiewicz, respectively. But for me, Bernard Vorhaus will always be remembered as the director who gave a very young English cutting room technician his first break as a film editor, and that man's name was David Lean.

The filming on what was now called *Not Tonight, Darling!* went extremely well, and so did the post-production, since, or perhaps because, the film editor was Ean Wood, who had written the whole thing as 'James Pillock'. Helping our sound editor Martin Amstell with the post-sync. dialogue I hired Peter Elliott, who I'd met on *The Prisoner* episode "A. B. and C.", which Pat Jackson directed, and on which I was on the set for much of the shooting. I recall one sound-related happenstance on that very set to this day: the clapper-board went in to announce the take, and suddenly my attention was drawn away from my constant, and alas unreciprocated (save for a smile or two) gaze at cute and sexy actress Bettine Le Beau in her French maid's costume, as director Pat Jackson then, rather loudly, broke wind, and then called "Action!". And then I learned something. If you've a fart on the way, do it between the clap and "Action". If you hold on till after "Action" you could ruin your own take. Food for thought, and another lesson learnt on *The Prisoner*. (Yes, I know the dubbing editor could cut out the sound of the fart if it was in the clear, but it could easily fall over dialogue and then you're into post-sync. and atmosphere "fill", and all of that, of course, costs time and money. Nip it in the bud like Pat Jackson did, if you can).

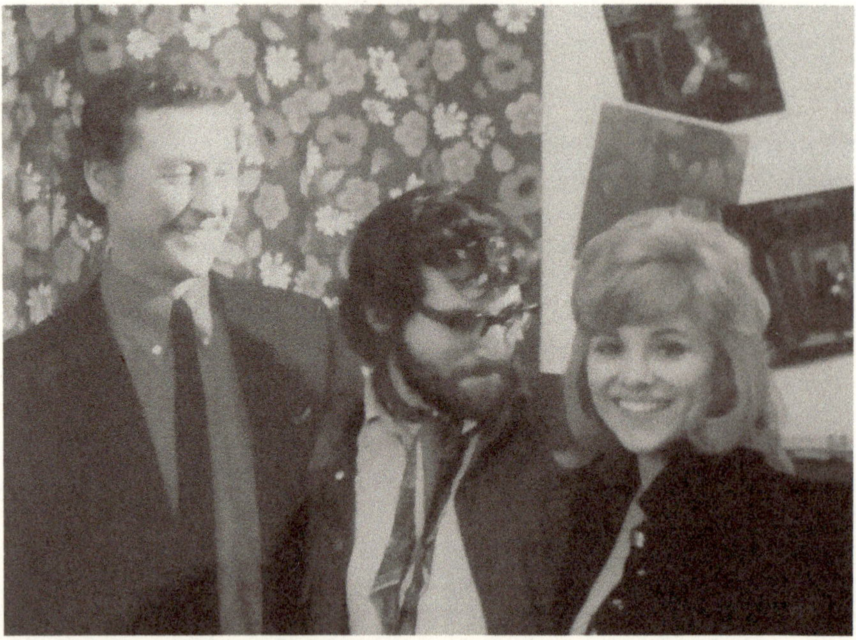

End of a day's shooting on 1971's *Not Tonight, Darling!*, with the director (yours truly!) happily sandwiched between his two stars, both Vincent Ball and myself saying a warm and affectionate "Goodnight" to lovely Luan Peters, her coat already on, anxious to go home after a hard day's shooting on a rented flat location.

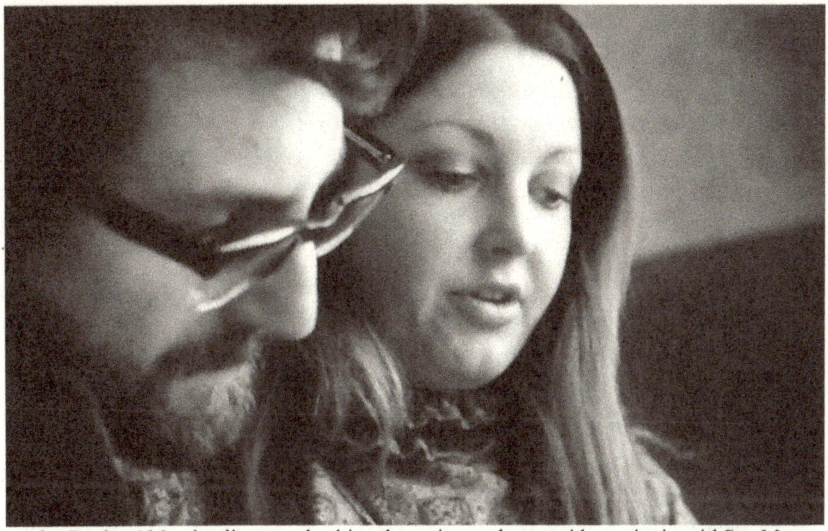

Not Tonight, Darling! Me, the director, checking the script on the set with continuity girl Sue Merry, who I had previously met and worked with on *Wonderwall.*

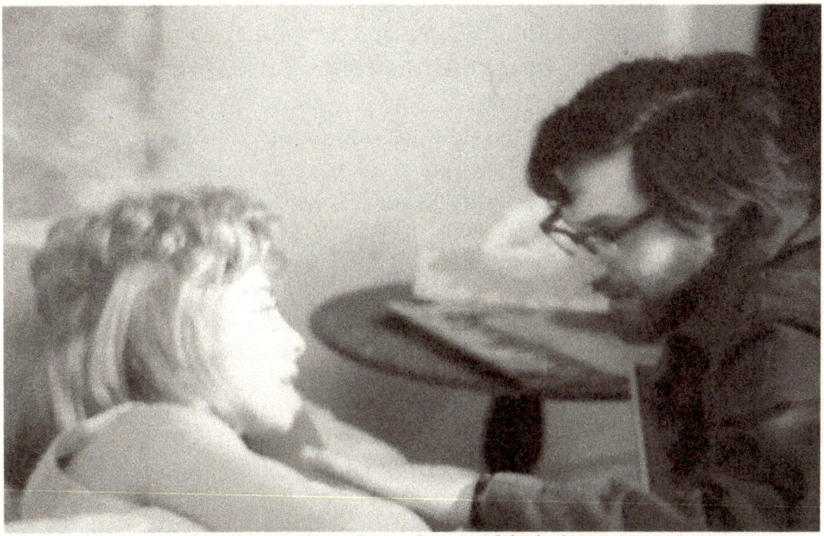

Me directing Luan Peters for one of the bed scenes.

After saving my musical bacon, to coin a phrase, on *Sweet and Sexy*, I hired Denis King again to score *Not Tonight, Darling!*, and he did an absolutely superb job. Hard to reconcile this talented film composer with that youngest King Brother on the piano who featured on two big record hits of my youth: "A White Sports Coat (and a Pink Carnation)" and "Standing on the Corner". Thanks again, Denis.

Unlike *Sweet and Sexy*, *Not Tonight, Darling!* moved swiftly to closure, and managed to open in London's West End well before the earlier title, which was still enmeshed in censor problems. I can never quite remember what opened with what: I think *Not Tonight, Darling!* was twinned with *I am a Nymphomaniac*, and *Sweet and Sexy* was with *The Lustful Vicar*, but it could have been the other way around!

Meantime, I was having, shall we say, domestic troubles. My new flat-sharing mates were a pair of Elaines, one blonde, sexy, and ultra man-bait, the other, her friend, bespectacled and sweet. I can't remember how I met them, but I needed flatmates fast, since Michael Billington had flown the coop, for reasons of paying the rent alone, if nothing else. Whilst I was in production, I had more than all the social contacts that I could handle. I was also seeing more than a little of Quinn O'Hara, my luscious American star of *Sweet and Sexy*. We had become good friends – no, really, – and she had developed a not unwelcome habit of discussing her very varied London love life with me, and thus we became very close pals. There wasn't a part for her in *Not Tonight, Darling!*, and she was seemingly sensible enough and also experienced enough not to cramp my style in any way while I was shooting the film, but she did stay over a couple of nights. After all, Quinn O'Hara did have, what was to me, a very interesting past: she was once engaged to Fabian, a now largely-forgotten American pop idol who once had a 20th Century-Fox film contact, who co-starred in such major films of my teenage youth as *North to Alaska* (with no less than John Wayne and Stewart Granger), and *High Time* (with Bing Crosby), plus his very own starring vehicle *Hound Dog Man* (once intended for Elvis, hence the title).

Quinn also took me to Hyde Park one damp Sunday morning to watch a group of American showbiz ex-pats play baseball, and she introduced me there to Ty (*Bronco*) Hardin, plus some Hollywood heavyweights: Sandy Lieberson (partnered at the time with David Puttnam), Louis M. "Deke" Heyward of American-International Pictures, and Arthur Kananack, whose obituary I would one day sadly write for *The Independent* British newspaper, and send to his sons. All became useful contacts.

Then suddenly, amazingly but unfortunately, the two Elaines were gone from my flat, rent unpaid, rates forgotten. A flit – no forwarding details, no available telephone numbers, not even a couple of I.O.U.'s. Shit! I was right in the middle of finishing *Not Tonight, Darling!*, supervising the editing, recording all the post-sync., music scoring, plus colour grading, and shooting the main and end titles. So I was kinda busy right at that very moment, and that was when Quinn O'Hara suggested that she move in with with me. Aha, so that was it! Did she not remember, or prefer not to remember, that, when we first met each other, she was dating (and I use the word very loosely) Michael Billington, my previous flatmate, when they were both in the same *UFO* episode, and when they, shall we say, consummated that friendship on my living room couch? That's a tough memory for me to forget. But, on the other hand, even if she did take a room, could our own friendship survive the paying, or eventual non-paying, of rent? What if she couldn't get work? What if? What if??

I had another domestic problem as well, a family one. My sister Linda had by now left school, and was about to be employed in entertainment poster design in the West End. It was a very good job at a well known agency specialising in film poster art, well-paid, and she suggested that it might be a good time, and also the right time, to leave Forest Gate, and move in with me, since she would be earning a very decent wage. I could hardly say "No". And all that occurred absolutely simultaneously with Quinn O'Hara wishing to leave her own temporary base and to move in with me as well.

Quinn was very well-behaved during the shooting and post-production of *Not Tonight, Darling!*. She was busy with her own life and contacts, although I did on occasion receive a telephone call in the middle of the night, when she'd got herself into what we could term a situation, largely of her own making, from which she simply couldn't extricate herself. So perhaps it would be better if she moved in with me. (But, frankly, although I didn't know it at the time, she was largely herself to blame for most of her strange situations. It's called a drinking problem). I spoke to my sister about it all, and, it being the Swinging Sixties remember, she thought that it might be a fun idea. And, well yes, that's how it started off, but I was not, by any means, emotionally or financially, ready for the many and varied problems of living with Quinn O'Hara, let alone with my sister, in the same apartment. Eventually, I guess of course, Quinn and I ended up sharing the same bedroom, and, yes, the same bed. My Swinging Sixties sister thought nothing of it – it was I who was uncomfortable, and that discomfort manifested itself in many differing ways.

But, first and foremost, I needed to work. Directing two sex films wasn't doing my editing career any good at all. Quinn's contacts proved interesting, but they didn't amount to anything, only to contacts introducing me to more contacts. It was beginning to seem that the people I was meeting, and was being introduced to, hoped that I might be able to help them, rather than the other way around, and I was running out of money. However, living with Quinn, with hindsight, was both educational and fun at the same time. My sister was quite self-contained, or so I thought, and largely kept to her own friends and boyfriends, about whom I knew it best to ask no questions. Quinn, herself, however, was a sexual education in one. In those "Swinging" days, I'd gotten used to girls being on the pill, which was new then, but normal now. Quinn, however, still used a douche, a convoluted rubber device that looked as though it belonged in the Ark. No amount of persuading would endear her to go onto the pill ("I'd throw it up with the booze."), and so, what can I say? Our sex life was never less than extremely interesting, and I'll leave it at that…

One day, Quinn had an interview with film director Michael Winner for the only female part in *Lawman*, a violent Western to star Burt Lancaster. Quinn was understandably anxious about the audition, and started alternately swigging wine and smoking dope before leaving the flat for the interview. I couldn't manage to dissuade her from either. I urged her again not to go to the audition, but nevertheless she went off in a taxi to meet Michael Winner as arranged. Sheree North eventually played the role.

I was now beginning to feel that my new flat-mate wasn't exactly working out, despite the occasional bonuses. She wasn't earning regularly, and didn't seem able to get work, although I was impressed by the one evening when she telephoned Bob Hope personally, and asked him to send her some running money. Quinn told me that she had toured the Vietnam bases with Hope, and that he had promised her solemnly that, if she ever needed cash to get herself out of any trouble, to call him. And she did, and he came through. But I was already beginning to seriously worry: that's a call you can't make twice, I thought to myself. (And what exactly did she get up to with Hope for him to even make that offer? But that was definitely not my concern, and I certainly didn't think about that at the time).

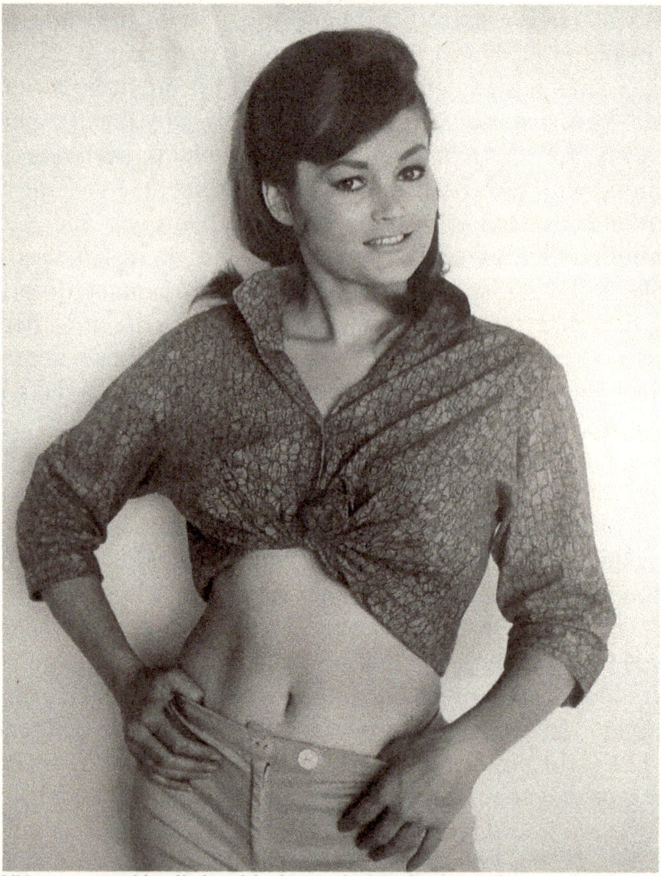

Quinn O'Hara, captured by distinguished portrait show business photographer Frazer Wood, who was married at the time to film editor Ean Wood, both writer (as "James Pillock") and film editor of *Not Tonight, Darling!*.

And then it happened. I guess it was inevitable, but I wasn't ready, although, had I the presence of mind, I guess that I could have predicted that something similar to what was about to happen was on the cards. But, for all my sophistication, faux or not, I really couldn't possibly have predicted what was about to occur between myself and Quinn O'Hara. But I should have guessed. After all, I certainly wasn't keeping her in the manner to which, I'm sure, she thought she was entitled.

My old school friend David Trace was holding a party to celebrate his new flat in Croydon. I can't remember whether at that time if he was about to be married, had just gotten married, or was merely living with, his sweetheart Lindy Armstrong, who was then also a good friend of mine, thanks to my relationship with David. The subsequent happenings somewhat have fogged my memory. David will hate me for writing this, but he really is one of the nicest, sweetest, warm-hearted persons on God's earth (except though when he's in a temper, but he usually has a bloody good reason to be in that temper!). And I was invited to their party. He did say to bring a friend, and so I brought Quinn. Big, big mistake. From the very moment that we arrived, she started drinking heavily, and she began to treat me (in front of all my ex-Dulwich College schoolmates) like her "gofer", or rather more like her servant, demanding drink refills about every five minutes, or so it seemed, and dragging every male, whether available or not, onto the dance floor, one after the other. In short, she was a minor sensation, but not in a good way. "Watch her," warned David Trace to me, "Or take her home pretty damn quick". What I couldn't bring myself to say to David was, "Easier said than done". I'd seen Quinn drunk before, but never like this. I hadn't ever witnessed previously this particular aspect of her apparent nymphomania, obviously fuelled by alcohol. And, heaven only knows, this was most definitely not the place to discover it, emphatically not among my old school friends and former classmates: not just David, but Tim, Gerry, Paul and some various other brothers and sisters. Exactly what was I thinking, bringing a nubile red-headed Hollywood drunk to a Dulwich College reunion party? Well, I continued to freshen up Quinn's glass for a while, but gradually diluting the contents. She could tell, of course, and began to berate me for so doing, in public. That's when I knew it was time to get her out of there and take her home. But then she spotted a latecomer to the party, a fellow called Colin Turner, once in my school class, always an outsider at Dulwich, aloof, and I thought, slightly odd. Certainly never a close friend of mine. But Quinn was a highly experienced gold-digger, and could smell money wherever, and she headed straight for Colin. She threw her arms around him and they danced, I thought, quite a bit too close together, certainly for a first meeting. I didn't know what to do. I felt that I'd been cuckolded there and then, and indeed <u>had</u> just been cuckolded, but I didn't quite know it quite yet. David Trace said to me sharply to get her out of here, <u>now</u>. I approached Quinn with a fresh glass of scotch, and she took it from me while still in Colin's arms, downed it in one, and gave me back the empty glass. That's it, I thought. Humiliated in front of some of my oldest and dearest friends. How do I get her out of here? But it was very apparent to the room what, in fact, was actually happening: that I was being very, very publicly cuckolded (the only term that applied), and that I was helpless, totally helpless, and, alas, also socially emasculated in front of my contemporaries.

It wasn't long before the gold-digging Quinn left the party with Colin, whose super-expensive car was waiting to whisk her away. I was hurt, broken, shamed, and embarrassed. Gerry Powell and David Trace spotted this, and both offered to drive me home. Since David was the host, I accepted Gerry's kindly lift. He drove me all the way back from Croydon to Eccleston Street, clapped me on the shoulder, and said something like "Don't worry, they deserve each other". I went to bed, alone of course, and I never saw Quinn O'Hara again. David Trace (what a gentleman!) phoned me the next day, the Sunday, and said how sorry he was, but not to worry; nobody blamed me. Well, that's something, I suppose.

I'd managed to obtain a job at Gerry Poulson's television commercials company as an editor, and was busy with such name brands as Twix, Fragonade, Mon Cheri and Curly-Wurly, but my thoughts, perhaps unsurprisingly, were with Quinn. While I was at work one day, Quinn came back to the flat and cleared out all her stuff, and left her keys on the kitchen table. She did, however, say "Goodbye" to Linda, but left neither forwarding contact address nor phone number.

That following week I was in Shepherd's Bush on some business for the commercials, and I popped into the Record and Tape Exchange in the Shepherd's Bush Road at lunchtime, as was my wont, to see what fanciable second-hand disc bargains were available. Flicking through the 'new arrivals' box I found a very familiar grouping of long-playing records: the American soundtrack LP album of *A Swinging Summer* (Quinn O'Hara's debut feature) plus some other albums that Quinn once had, and once, or so I thought, cherished. So she had to sell her LP collection. To raise money to live? But Colin was surely rich, wasn't he? What happened, then? I wondered. I bought Quinn's copy of "A Swinging Summer" for myself and left the Shepherd's Bush Record and Tape Exchange with my one concrete souvenir of having lived for a while with Quinn O'Hara, my oh-so-glamorous Hollywood star of *Sweet and Sexy* (although I know for a fact that somewhere in a drawer of mine she did leave a red casual jacket that once upon a time belonged to Fabian Forte!).

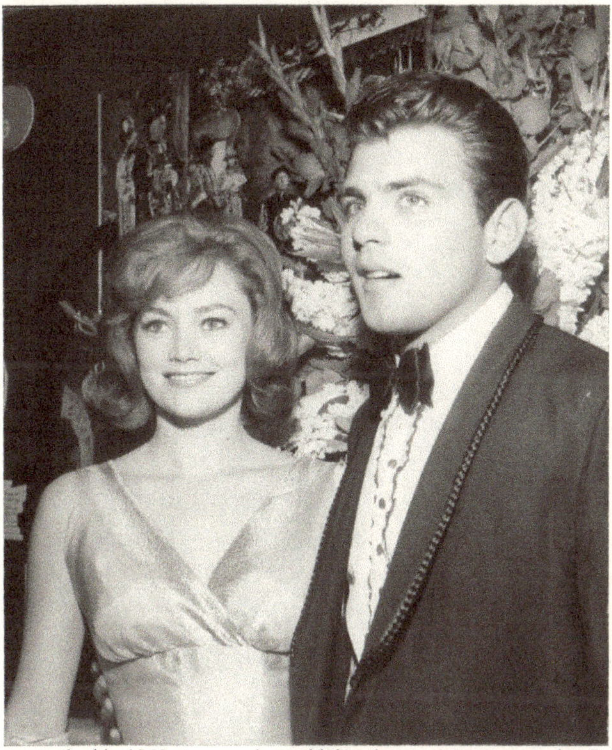

Quinn O'Hara, photographed in 1963 at a premiere with her then-constant companion Fabian. Their dating period lasted from March 1963 until July 1963, that's four whole months and two whole days, a long time for Quinn in those heady days, whose later dating partners would include none other than Frank Sinatra himself. *Sweet and Sexy* was a long way off her horizon then, and eventually she had it deleted, alas, from most of her available filmographies.

-----END OF REEL SEVEN-----

REEL EIGHT

So, suddenly I had neither work nor income. It wasn't going to be easy to find the money to pay both my rent and rates. My father's brother, Basil Sloman, had invited my sister Linda to visit him and live with his family in South Africa for a while, and hopefully find work in Johannesburg. It was an attractive and adventurous proposition, and Linda decided to accept it. We threw a 'goodbye' party for her at 8a, Eccleston Street, and off she went, quite happily. But financially I was now, as they say, in 'shtook'.

It was clearly time to attempt another film, although I knew that the two I had already made were not exactly, to put it mildly, the kind of cinematic product that, particularly in prissy England, would really serve as calling cards, however cheaply and well-made they were. No matter how successful their eventual box office, they were, nevertheless, of a not-to-be-discussed and quite disrespectful genre. (Although in those days it wasn't yet termed 'genre'). Accordingly, I'd just made a couple of dirty sex flicks.

What films did I want to make? To be frank, I didn't really know. I didn't feel that I had what you might term 'a calling'. I wasn't an "auteur". I just wanted to make movies, and I knew how to. I met up with some of Quinn's contacts, and no less than Louis "Deke" Heyward of American-International said that, although they were moving their production base back to the States, they were still looking around for product, and he liked what I was doing (and he knew I worked cheap). He asked me what would I like to make, and, thinking, I guess, of both *Scaramouche* and American-International's own excursions into costume drama, which included the *De Sade* that I had worked on, and more specifically, and more notably, *The Witchfinder General*, I said something like, "Period horror, with drama and glamour". He smiled and seemed pleased, as they used to say in slang, at where I was coming from. Since Deke's real name was Lou Horowitz and he had been a scriptwriter for *77 Sunset Strip* and had produced the U.S. DJ Dick Clark TV show, we were sort of cross-generational soul mates, and bonded. He gave me good advice: find a subject with a broad universal appeal, or something highly-specialised, such as horror, and send it to him. No guarantees. Well, I sort of knew that, but I thanked him anyway. "And send my warmest regards to Quinn". I thought, "Oh, yeah?...".

But Deke was right, I needed a workable screenplay that I could show around, using my two inexpensive features as a calling card. Deke's own big hits were costume horrors – perhaps that's where I should be heading. I needed to identify somebody who would ideally write for nothing, at first at least. Someone with a wild imagination, someone who could write effortlessly, creatively and ideally with a sense of humour and a moderate interest in period drama. Who else but my old pal from *The Prisoner* Ian L. Rakoff? And he also actually had something to show that he had written, that episode of *The Prisoner* called "Living in Harmony", the Western that Ian had originally entitled, after the first lyric line of the *High Noon* theme song, "Do Not Forsake Me, Oh My Darling", a title nicked by Patrick McGoohan for another of the later *Prisoner* episodes. I had the distinct feeling that Ian was not only unhappy about the title theft, but about the whole manner in which he was treated as a *Prisoner* writer. Well, that's TV for you: everyone's disposable. Ian seemed to me to have become of late slightly bitter and broody, but nevertheless he was still good company, and, much more importantly, still talented, but would he work for nothing? I was broke, after all. Soon find out...

I had known Ian Rakoff from when he first joined *The Prisoner*, when he was assistant film editor on two episodes, "It's Your Funeral" and "The General", and I had been in touch with him, on and off, over the years since then. I knew that he was a sort of protege of director Lindsay Anderson, and that he had worked on Lindsay's *If...* as an assistant editor, and *If...*, of course, was one of the major successes of the Cannes Film Festival that Mike Billington and I had gatecrashed. Ian had also edited a well-regarded short film called *The Burning* directed by a young Stephen Frears, and had actually assisted on *Magical Mystery Tour*, so he had achieved some sort of pedigree. Would he work with a young and broke sex film director? I couldn't help but keep that question in my mind as I approached him for a meeting.

I called my last producer, John Taylor of *Not Tonight, Darling!* (not to mention our editorial collaborations to both *Strange Report* and *De Sade*) and told him of my current problem, and suggested we meet up together and discuss it. Unsurprisingly, he wasn't busy himself at that moment, and was more than happy to discuss working together again. Especially on a rather slightly differing project from our last combined effort. Further to that, before I could suggest a meeting to talk about a current project, John suggested that I might like to come over to have supper with him and his mother and to meet his father, Michael Rennie, who had just ended his contract with 20th Century-Fox, and who was visiting Britain and seeing his family for the first time in ages. Wow! I was delighted, but, of course, pretended to be very cool about meeting his famous Dad. To me and, of course not only to me, Michael Rennie was a big star. Not just for *The Day the Earth Caught Fire*, one of the greatest ever mid-fifties science fiction features, but also for playing St. Peter in the first-ever film made in CinemaScope, *The Robe*, and its sequel, *Demetrius and the Gladiators*, and for also co-starring in a run of early Fox 'Scope pictures: *Seven Cities of Gold*, *Island In The Sun*, *Soldier of Fortune*, *Teenage Rebel*, plus, of course, *The Third Man* television series. A real life movie star! Also I was looking forward to meeting John's mum as well, Lewis Gilbert's sister.

We had a delightful home-cooked meal at Mrs. Taylor's, and I met Michael Rennie, I swear the tallest man I've ever seen. We chatted away, and I asked him what his favourite of all his films was. He replied "*Dangerous Crossing* with Jeanne Crain". He pronounced his co-star's first name as "Jeannie". Unfortunately, I had never heard of the film. That must've shown on my face. "You've never heard of it, have you, Tony?" said Michael Rennie. I confessed that I hadn't. "It was the one directly before *The Robe*", he said. "Jeannie and I had one picture each left on our Fox contracts, and Fox had this huge set that they had especially built for their *Titanic* left over, so they put us together on a picture using that leftover set. Fortunately, we had a very good director, Joseph Lewis, and a nice, tight schedule, and we had a very good time". Well, well, well, I thought, and after all those big pictures, too. (I eventually picked up a vintage copy of *Picture Show* magazine with a glamour still from *Dangerous Crossing* as its cover picture, with Michael Rennie and Jeanne Crain gazing at each other. Look very, very closely at their eyes. Is that merely acting?).

Michael had to leave early, and John and I walked him to the car park. He was going one way, and John was going to drop me off at my flat. Michael and John embraced, and Michael kissed John – it was very moving, and I was touched to be able to witness it. What we weren't to know was that that was the last time John was ever to see his father. Michael Rennie died of emphysema on that very trip to England in Harrogate, Yorkshire, later that year. I was reminded of a time on *Strange Report* when John used to give me a lift to Pinewood, collecting me from Hammersmith. One Monday morning, while I was waiting, I noticed that the Ritz cinema over the road was playing a film called *Kill or be Killed* (the U.K. title for the Italian gallo *Death on the Run*) all of that week, and the name of top-billed Michael Rennie shone above that of co-star Ty Hardin from the poster on the side of the cinema. John pulled up, I got in the car, and pointed out to him the name of his father on the poster. John Taylor looked up, nodded, said nothing, smiled, and drove us off to Pinewood.

John was very interested in whatever project I was planning with Ian Rakoff, and was keen to come on board as producer. I told him that I had no money whatsoever, and couldn't pay Ian, or even front up money to pay for a script or synopsis. John said that he's take care of that, provided it wasn't too expensive, and we never discussed it again. My deal was to work with Ian and find a suitable, commercial subject. I couldn't have been more pleased. Still broke, but glad to be back in harness, especially with people I knew who could deliver and had worked with before, although there couldn't be much more disparate work than *The Prisoner* and *Not Tonight, Darling!*, and I should know!

Ian was pleased with the meeting, at which I explained, approximately, what I was after. Deke Heyward had made it very clear to me what he could sell, and, because Quinn O'Hara had made *Cry of the Banshee* for him, and I had seen it, I thought I knew what he wanted. I explained to Ian that we were after a period sword-and-sorcery flick that wouldn't cost too much. A few special effects, but generally an atmosphere of mistrust and doom in, say, 12th century Britain. Ian pointed out that I hadn't mentioned sex."That too" I said, "But it's not a sex film". "Just horror, then," joked Ian. "Well…" I started to say, but Ian knew almost exactly what I was after: something that could star Vincent Price or perhaps Christopher Lee, with lots of dark atmosphere and a fairish sprinkling of sex and violence: "When do you want me to start writing?" "Now would be good", I replied.

And so Ian delivered the script of *Maudric* (the central character's name) virtually a month after our conversation, and I thought it was bloody good, and told him so, and so did John, although I was never certain if John ever read it right through, but that didn't matter. What next? Well, first off, we copyrighted it, and then I sent a copy to Deke Heyward in Hollywood. That was the first disappointment, no acknowledgement of receipt, and the script never came back. I sent out copies to several U.K. agents that I had had personal dealings with, and all, without prompting, took considerable time in getting back to me, if at all, and all said the same thing, that it wasn't for them. I thought of getting a star attached, and sent it to Christopher Lee to play the lead. To my surprise he 'phoned me back, and said that he'd like to do it, but that he was also very heavily booked up in advance, and please to call him when the money is in place, and to use his name if I thought that would help, but no, he wouldn't give me a letter, or a commitment in any way in writing. I thanked him, but recognised a "Thanks, but no thanks" when I got one. In the meantime, I was very, very broke, and signing on again at the local unemployment exchange (No, I never ran into Bill Shine there again, ever, but I did meet film editor Max Benedict almost every Wednesday and we'd have a coffee together regularly). I also currently had no flatmates, and the rent and rates bills were now increasing somewhat alarmingly. I was, unsurprisingly, starting to get letters from the landlord. Still, I thought, *Maudric* would happen soon. It's got to, it's just got to.

But *Maudric* didn't happen soon. *Maudric* didn't happen at all, but it did give me one wonderful, stupid moment. At the time, Elizabeth Taylor and Richard Burton were the talk of the town, and were staying in London at the Dorchester Hotel. Richard Burton would be splendid as *Maudric* himself, and of course it would take our picture up a notch. How to get a script to him? Simple. Just wait at the Dorchester and put it in his hand. Or so I thought. I arrived at the Dorchester, script and covering letter in hand, and went straight to the front desk. "Is Richard Burton in?" I asked the desk clerk, who replied, "No, Mr. Burton and Miss Taylor have gone out for a long lunch. They will be back around two-thirty". "Thank you". It was nearly noon. I went for a walk with the script. I really didn't just want to leave it for collection; if they were coming back, I could put it straight into his hand, or so I thought, and Ms. Taylor (I can't remember if she was Mrs. Burton or not at that time) would be a splendid choice as co-star if we could afford them, of course. But if he showed interest, who knows?

I came back to the Dorchester around one-thirty and sat in a chair in the lobby, directly opposite the front entrance, and sure enough, after about an hour, appeared Richard Burton and Elizabeth Taylor, who both looked far, far shorter than I'd ever imagined, and, shall we say, perhaps a little the worse for drink? I was impressed, but also, frankly, a little bit cowed at the same time. They went to the reception desk to collect their keys. I couldn't do it. I simply couldn't find the nous to put my script into the hands of these two seemingly quite drunken people, no matter that they may be possibly the biggest stars in the world at that moment in time, and could help me out of my financial predicament with a mere whisper. I watched them get into the lift, stagger, and vanish. I then went to the reception desk and left the script in a marked-up envelope for delivery to their room. Of course, I never, ever, heard from them at all. Nor their agent neither. John Taylor said that he would call them, or at least the hotel, later, to see if they received the script. I don't know if he ever did, or what happened. He never called me, and that was virtually the last I ever saw of John, except years later, when quite out of the blue he invited Simone and I down to his new home near Chichester to meet his wife and recent offspring, and that was the very last time I met up with John M. Taylor. *Strange Report*, *De Sade*, and much more importantly, *Not Tonight, Darling!*, all seemed so very, very long ago.

Just when I desperately needed cash, I received a 'phone call from someone I hadn't seen for a while, that extremely tall and jolly nice cutting room fellow called Roger Guertin, who asked me if I was free, and if so, would I like a job? Would I?? He obviously, thank goodness, hadn't heard about my new career as a sex film peddler, and he told me that he was at De Lane Lea on a film entitled *The Manipulator* starring Stephen Boyd and Silva Koscina, with Michael Johns as the dialogue editor, and they needed another dubbing editor. Would I be interested? I said an immediate "Yes", and I started the following Monday in a cutting room next to Michael Johns, with Liz Osbiston (one of the twin daughters of the distinguished editor Alan Osbiston of *The Guns of Navarone* and *The Victors*, amongst others) as my assistant. I felt that I was back home again. (Or, at least, back in the film business). *The Manipulator* was a German-backed international adventure flick, and was no masterpiece, to put it mildly, and was eventually known worldwide, if at all, by its subsequent retitling as *African Story*, but, for me, it was that one very special thing: a source of income, But what could I say to Ian Rakoff? Only the truth, and I suspected the author of *Maudric* wouldn't warm to it.

But Ian Rakoff seemed to be a body quite used to coping with disappointment. He couldn't have been more philosophical, or more generous in his world outlook. His attitude seemed to be, if it happens, it happens. At least we had a good script, and we knew it. Indeed, Ian began to joke about the script, referring to *Maudric* as "More Dreck" ("dreck" being Yiddish for "manure"; in other words "more shit", ergo: "More Dreck"/"*Maudric*". Well, it seemed amusing at the time). I had to tell Ian that I would be starting work on a feature at De Lane Lea, and he actually seemed pleased for me. He didn't even mention John Taylor, nor even seem to care as to what would become of *Maudric*. He obviously had something else up his sleeve, and he certainly wasn't about to divulge what it was, at least not to me. I would find out in due course.

Just prior to commencing work on *The Manipulator* I was on my way home to Eccleston Street one day when I ran into a man in the doorway of 8a who turned out to be my then landlord, Martin Slowe. He was terribly polite, and asked me what was I going to do about the rent that was owed to date. I told him that I was just about to start a new job, and that I would be able to pay him something at the end of the month. That didn't seem to please him too much, and he duly informed me of how much was actually owed. I shouldn't have been so surprised, but I had lost count. It seemed an absolute fortune to me, now without flatmates. He answered my unasked question: if I couldn't come up with the balance by the end of the month, I would be served with a writ. I would then have to appear in court, and he would abide by the court's decision. "Hello, debtor's prison" went through my mind, but at least *The Manipulator* was about to pay something.

Work on *The Manipulator* proceeded apace, and pretty soon we were in the dubbing theatre. This mix was being overseen by the film's German producer, one Stanley Norman, and in a sequence in one of my reels a steam train transects a railway crossing, and Stanley asked for a railway crossing sound effect, a bell or an extended whistle. We were about to break for lunch, so rather than send his request to Cinesound at Elstree, I remembered where there was indeed such a sound effect, in the sound library of my old apprenticeship stomping ground, no less than Caledonian Films at 22, Greek Street, just a street away from where we were now dubbing in Dean Street, and that very visit there to find a sound effect would, amazingly, turn out to govern my future existence, both professional and financial, and to create new bonds of friendship for life.

Well now, Caledonian Films had changed considerably. I entered, walked up those oh-so-familiar stairs, and introduced myself to the two new people who seemed to be in charge: an amiable long-haired semi-hippy in cowboy boots called Richard Bedford, who introduced himself as the editor, and a likeable friendly soul called Geoff Hogg, who I assumed at the time to be Richard's assistant editor. I told them what I was after, and they invited me in to have a search. When I last saw it, that particular sound effect was filed under the *Telegoons* fx, and, lo and behold! - there it was, still in the cardboard box where I had filed it. I ran it on the nearby moviola to be certain, and, sure enough, it was perfect for *The Manipulator*'s railroad crossing. I was pleased, and got to chatting to Geoff and Richard, both ex-Kay's laboratory hands, who had taken over Caledonian at Thomson's request from my old boss Bob Bucknell, about whom they shared exactly the same feelings as I did, and to Thomson's delight, they had turned Caledonian around into a profit-making entity. As I chatted to both Richard and Geoff, it turned out that we all shared similar tastes in, and attitudes to, movies, together with a deep and profound abiding love of cinema. We made a tentative date to meet up again at a later time, because I had to get back with the sound effect, have it transferred, lay it into the track, and mix it into the picture. Richard said to give him a call, and when I told him that I owned a 16mm. colour print of *Rio Bravo*, he said to bring it over one weekend and we'll screen it at Caledonian. And we did, and thus began a lifelong friendship, but, sadly, Richard's own life was cut tragically short. However, Geoff became a bosom buddy, and nowadays we still meet up and go to "The Pictures" together.

The month on *The Manipulator* went by quickly. We finished the film and I made new friendships with Liz and Michael, but in the way of freelances, hardly saw them again, although I seem to vaguely remember coming across Michael Johns, just one more time, and I that I upset him over something, but I truly can't remember what it was. It was good fun, however, working with Roger Guertin, and we became friends. I invited him to screenings at Ray Selfe's, and I remember, to my shame, prevailing on Ray to lend Roger a print of "Sands of Iwo Jima", John Wayne's wartime Oscar-nominated performance, but Roger unfortunately sadly mislaid it, and Ray was, rightly, furious, and I seldom saw Roger again. I don't know if Roger ever compensated Ray for the loss, and it left me feeling very bad about introducing anybody to anyone, for a very long time.

And then, somewhat surprisingly, I received a telephone call from Ian Rakoff, a phone call that didn't mention *Maudric* at all. Ian was currently working on a feature film with his old mentor Lindsay Anderson which was called *O Lucky Man*!, a sort of sequel to Lindsay's international success *If...*, which featured so strongly at the Cannes Festival that I visited with Michael Billlington, and Lindsay now had a rather strange request: there was to be a sequence in *O Lucky Man!* wherein our hero, once again portrayed by Malcolm McDowell, visits a porno club with his mates, and Ian Rakoff had immediately thought of me because of my two recent feature films, and had recommended me to Lindsay to shoot the required material, since Lindsay had asked him if he knew anyone who could film sex stuff. Lindsay himself, who was not-so-openly gay, said that he felt that he couldn't do it justice, or, as I suspected, he just didn't want to waste his own time filming it, undoubtedly feeling that it would be more than a little bit beneath him, and also that it would also be far cheaper just to get somebody in to shoot the necessary material, rather than have to source it from somewhere else, and then having to negotiate for the rights to be able to use it, let alone the duplication costs of laboratory matching in order to integrate it into the film proper... Definitely cheaper just to quickly shoot something.

I knew Lindsay Anderson slightly, and Lindsay remembered me from our meetings over coffee at London's National Film Theatre, and also from Derek York's private screenings at Derek's flat, and he thought it would be a very good idea to have me shoot his little sex film sequence, and that was the gist of the message conveyed to me on his behalf by Ian Rakoff. Unsurprisingly, it didn't take me more than a couple of seconds to say "Yes" to him, if indeed that long, and to tell Ian to convey to Lindsay that I'd love to do it, and I thanked Ian for suggesting me. Ian said that he'd get back to me with dates, but it wouldn't be immediate, probably in a few weeks time, since Lindsay had to clear it with his producing partner, the actor Michael Medwin, who, with Albert Finney, had founded Memorial (named after London's Albert

Memorial) Films, and were the actual producers of *O Lucky Man!*. Ian said he would arrange a date to discuss exactly what Lindsay wanted.

Couldn't be better timing. I had just received a court summons to appear at Bow Street Magistrates Court in Covent Garden to answer to non-payment of rent monies, which, of course, I duly did. I told the Judge, when asked, that I was a freelancer in the film industry, and had a short job coming up. The Judge seemed very experienced in these matters, and instructed me that I must now take, and indeed apply for, any job available, whether film or television or whatever, no matter how menial it may be, and pay back the bulk of my earnings to my landlord, Martin Slowe, until the escalating debt was paid off. (Phew! At least he didn't throw me out of house and home). The Judge also asked me if I had an agent, and since I replied that I did not, he suggested to try the Union notice board, because the A.C.T.T. displayed a regular weekly listing of industry vacancies at their Soho Square offices, and, even if a listed job may not actually seem suitable, to apply for every single vacancy listed, regardless. This was my sentence, and I had the distinct feeling that this particular judge knew the freelance show business territory very well; at least I wasn't going to jail for non-payment of debt, which was what I feared. I left the courtroom trembling slightly, and headed over to the A.C.T.T. offices to look at the list of current vacancies, and I asked for a copy to take away. There were some assistant editor vacancies listed at the BBC, all of which I wrote away for, listing my now not inconsiderable editing credentials.

In the meantime, *The Father Christmas Film*, for such was it termed in the *O Lucky Man!* shooting schedule, was to consist of a party scene in which the drunken revellers watch a raunchy stag film, a sex flick to be shot by yours truly. The discussion I took with director Lindsay Anderson could not have been briefer: "You know what I need," was about the gist of it, and indeed it turned out that I did: Father Christmas comes down a chimney with his sackful of sex toys and meets – surprise, surprise – a beautiful Babe at the bottom of the chimney. After swapping mutual greetings, Santa shows her a giant phallic sex toy, and they fool around with it for a while. He then removes his famous red coat and wraps the Babe in it. He then satisfies her (we assume) in a classic manner. Both Santa and the Babe achieve simultaneous satisfaction. End of…

I told Lindsay that I could shoot that in a day, and all he said was "Go ahead", and if necessary he would liaise with me via Ian. Oh, and by the way, Michael Medwin, *O Lucky Man*!'s co-producer, would like to be present at the shoot. Fine with me. He who pays the piper, as far as I was concerned, can call any tune he so desires. I was given a production office in Memorial's Hammersmith headquarters, and I duly began to crew up. There was no prescribed shooting date, just to deliver as soon as possible. (It was also in my financial interest to do so). First off, get the shooting script written. Which I did, overnight. To my surprise, Lindsay Anderson wasn't the slightest bit interested in vetting it.

Now, casting. "Santa" needed to be a fearless actor, with absolutely nothing to lose. Although he'd be bearded, and therefore difficult to identify, he must be willing and able, if not to actually engage in faux sexual activity of the bump-and-grind variety, with (hopefully) an elegant, good looking, semi-nude female partner, he would also have to flash a giant phallus, although not necessarily, in actuality, his own. There was, in fact, a film modeller called Christopher Fowler, who I would later encounter again on *The Company of Wolves*, who was known for specialising in creating such items. I called him on the phone, and he said that he would more than delighted to come and show me his wares.

Which he did. I selected one extremely hefty looking giant vibrating phallus, and we discussed fees and shooting dates, because Christopher wouldn't let his creation out of his sight. I then realised that I needed both a production manager, and also a production secretary, both of whom could be absolutely trusted to maintain a vow of silence where this rather particular specialised production was concerned. I had an excellent production runner on *Not Tonight, Darling!* called Sean Redmayne, who also appeared briefly in the film, and he had been working (heaven knows doing what) with John Taylor in the interim, so I called him to manage my forthcoming day's shoot, and he was delighted. As production secretary, although actually my personal assistant, I needed somebody who I could trust absolutely, and would keep 'mum' about the whole high-falutin' endeavour, so I called on my very good friend Nick Nacht once again, and he, too, was pleased to come on board: after all, working on a Lindsay Anderson film meant 'prestige'. All our other arrangements on *The Father Christmas Film* would be looked after by *O Lucky Man*'s associate producer Basil Keys, whose other film industry connections included both his own two brothers: Hammer producer Anthony Nelson-Keys, and popular novelist and sometime film director John Paddy Carstairs. Basil Keys clearly had every intention of being present at the shoot, and why not?

Casting? Well, I think it was actually Sean Redmayne who came up with the perfect candidate to portray Father Christmas: that alleged notorious friend of H.R.H. Princess Margaret, the one-and-only John Bindon. Bindon was a tough London ex-gangster who had made a few films; he was discovered by Ken Loach and featured strongly in *Poor Cow*, and then appeared in *Performance* and *Get Carter* among others. But it wasn't merely his acting talent that got him well-known in the industry; there's just no other way of putting it – it was the reputed size of his penis. And, also, his infamous trick of balancing a number of beer-glasses on it when erect. He sounded like the ideal actor for what we required. Sean arranged a meeting in a Knightsbridge pub. Johnny Bindon was most convivial, and, flattered, readily agreed. He asked who the girl would be, and I told him that she wasn't yet cast. He suggested his then girlfriend, the fashion model Vicki Hodge, blue-blooded daughter of the Second Baron of Chipstead, Sir Rowland Hodge. I said that if she'd like to do it, we'd love to have her aboard. Johnny Bindon said "She'd do it for me", and we shook hands on the deal. John, Vicki, and I next met in the costumiers Bermans and Nathans, and we chose the necessary costumes: a Santa Claus outfit, and a lovely, but completely see-through, nightie. They tried them on, and to me they couldn't look more perfect. I thought Lindsay would be pleased as well.

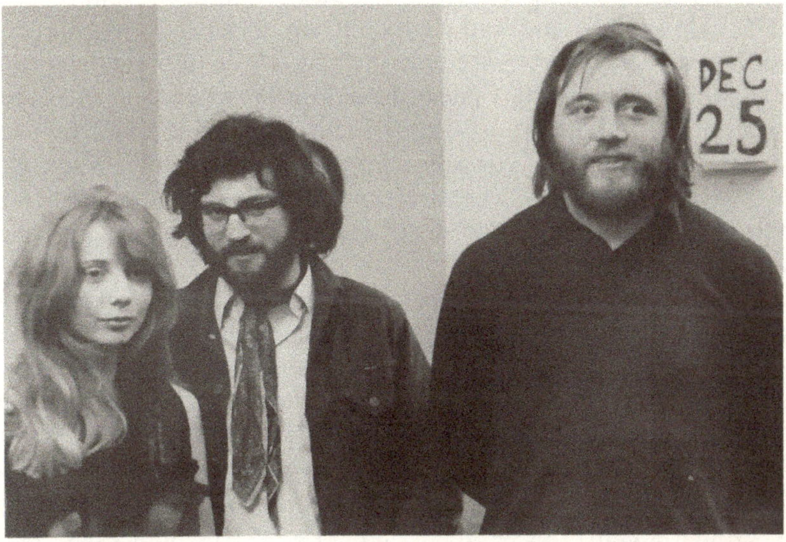

Actress Vicki Hodge, director Tony Sloman, and Vicki's then boyfriend actor John Bindon on set. Check out Johnny Bindon on the internet: his life story is more incredible than any movie!

The times and dates were fixed to shoot *The Father Christmas Film*. It was a very simple shoot: Santa Claus comes down the chimney, takes the giant phallus out of his bag, the girl indicates that she'd rather have the real thing, Santa puts the phallus back into his sack, and opens his red coat to reveal (off-screen) to the girl his real genitalia. She gasps with delight, and they end up copulating in Santa's sack. Not a problem to shoot. I hired my cameraman from *Not Tonight, Darling!* John Barnard, who had been Harry Waxman's camera operator on that film, and we did several takes of everything, without sound. I covered it pretty thoroughly: big close-ups, regular close-ups, mid-shots from all angles, and, of course, a jolly good master: full coverage throughout. The excellent Olwen Griffiths, also from *Not Tonight, Darling!*, did the make-up (such as it was) for me once again. Basil Keys came down to watch the shooting and brought our co-producer Michael Medwin with him. Ian Rakoff was nowhere to be seen, neither in pre-production, nor at the shoot.

I edited it myself the following day. I had checked that Lindsay Anderson didn't want to view my rushes, as long as Basil Keys had okayed them, which he did. After a longish lunch with the *O Lucky Man!* cutting room staff, most of whom I already knew, I had a cut ready to show by the end of the day, and that's when Ian Rakoff reappeared. He said Lindsay had asked Ian to run the cut that evening for Michael Medwin, but they didn't want me to be present. Odd, but okay I guess, at least they can say whatever they think if I'm not there.

The next day I received a phone call from Ian as I was packing up the cutting room. In short, it went something like this: "Lindsay hates it. Michael is going to do a reshoot. He's casting now. See you around". And he hung up the 'phone. Whaaat?? I called Ian back. He was both brusque and rude. "I got you the job, didn't I?" he said, and went on to say that at least we all got paid, didn't we? Not a "Sorry" or a grace note in sight, not an apology in earshot for this treatment of me. I should, I guess, have known better than to expect any sympathy from Ian Rakoff. It just wasn't in his make-up, he was far too self-obsessed to waste time on sympathy for others, especially when he was presumably working under direct instruction. Therefore I had no choice but to accept this decision and bite the dust, and so I duly packed up, thanked everybody, and left the building.

I told Basil Keys my tale, and he informed me that, when Michael Medwin saw what we were actually up to, he wanted to do it too, and was now, at that very moment, casting girls for a new shoot, with himself playing Santa Claus, as a gag. Some gag, I thought, just a dirty old actor-turned-producer playing games. Did Lindsay know? Did Lindsay care? Did it even matter? I got paid, everyone else involved got paid, and if you see *O Lucky Man*! today there's so very little of the *The Father Christmas Film* visible in the final edit that it really doesn't matter a hoot as to who shot what, but I still well remember how they treated me after that shoot and subsequent delivery, and my old *Prisoner* buddy Ian Rakoff should have been heartily ashamed of himself for the way he dealt with the matter. It surely wouldn't have hurt him to offer an understanding "Sorry", or at least to have shown some sympathy to a fellow film-maker. Some fifty-odd years later, I brought up the matter at a celebratory re-screening of *O Lucky Man!* at London's Regent repertory cinema in Regent Street. Ian just brushed me off with a desultory quip: "That's show business," he said. No, Ian, it's not, and it dented your image with me forever, is what I didn't say, nor that it had shamefully tarnished our post-*Prisoner* relationship as well, alas. Some things still hurt, even fifty-odd years later; there are ways of doing things, even in the show business.

However, quite three years after *O Lucky Man!*, I was surprised to receive a telephone call from Ian Rakoff asking me if I was available to work. It was a television film directed by Tony Scott entitled *The Author of Beltraffio*, based on a Henry James story for French television. Ian had been hired by editor Pam Power as the sound editor, but had limited experience in that area, particularly when up against the clock. I was surprised to receive the phone call, but, all past problems set aside, I was available, and I helped out Ian by laying up his dialogue tracks for him. He thanked me, and I got duly paid.

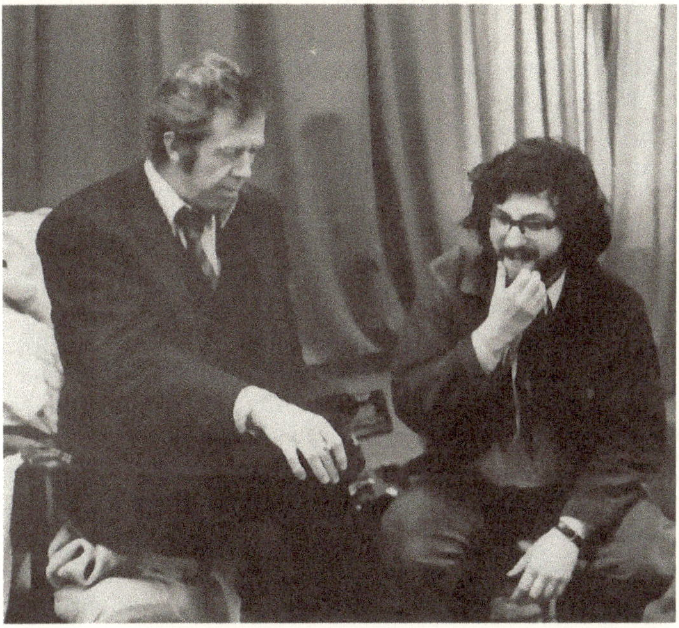

Michael Medwin, former actor but now producer of *O Lucky Man!*, confers with me between takes. Little could I imagine what was going on then in his mind!

The story isn't quite over. Yup, I had managed to alienate, or fall out with, at various times, both Eric Mival, one of the nicest, most genuine people on God's earth, and Ian Rakoff, no less, who has his own particular problems to handle, with both of whom I will forever share the privilege and immortal legacy, along with editor John S. Smith, of being the only four current surviving members, as far as I know, of *The Prisoner* cutting rooms, a rare privilege that I think we four might well have acknowledged would perhaps have happened in time, but in truth we were all far too busy occupied working on *The Prisoner* itself to ever consider any possible likely heritage, let alone its truly remarkable fan loyalty, and its well-deserved, seemingly eternal, longevity.

Oh, one slight coda. Eventually I worked as an editor for RAI Italian Television, based off Bond Street, on a short television programme entitled *The New Swinging London*, in 1983. I was waiting to meet the film's director Ascania Baldesseroni, when in walked the cameraman on the shoot, none other than David Naughton, the very person who took over *The Prisoner* Film Librarian position from me all those many years ago at MGM Borehamwood, when I left. (It must have been the fastest cutting room promotion in editing history, for David to go from second assistant editor to Film Librarian on my departure!). He was, as ever, smoking heavily, and I wasn't exactly sure that he recognised me, as I clapped him on the shoulder and called out "David!", but he recovered quickly, and said "Hello" all right, but I think that he was more than just a little bit embarrassed to be recognised by me. Anyway, at that moment our director appeared, and David duly went off with Ascania. "See you around," were his last words to me. I never saw him again.

After *The Father Christmas Film* I did indeed revert to becoming, once again, an assistant editor, at the BBC this time though, for I did as the judge indicated I should, and eventually managed to pay off the debt to Martin Slowe, who I would later meet in my life in a quite different context, on occasions when I attended the Liberal Jewish Synagogue in London's St. John's Wood, where he had become the President. The Lord certainly does work in the most mysterious ways, as I was indeed to find out when I started work at the BBC on the *Man Alive* series, produced by Desmond Wilcox, on the episodes called "Could Do Better" and "The Right Time to Die", which we were editing in cutting rooms at Shepherd's Bush, but had to screen to Desmond Wilcox at the BBC's Kensington House for final approval...

Kensington House turned out to be very interesting indeed. Desmond Wilcox's offices were adjacent to those of Esther Rantzen, television pundit and star of her own popular programme *That's Life!,* and it was no mere coincidence that their offices were adjacent. Everybody knew that they were a couple. Everybody at the BBC that is; I neither knew nor cared. At least, not until the tea-trolley came around. As assistant editor, it seemed that one of my functions was to fetch tea for the editor that I was assisting, a nice man called John Billingham, plus our series producer Desmond Wilcox, and take the teas into them while they were viewing the edit. At around about the same time, I noticed an especially attractive young girl fetching Esther Rantzen's tea, and also getting herself something to eat at that same particular tea trolley. This went on for a couple of times during the screening, both of us arriving at the tea trolley at the same time. She was so lovely, I just had to chat her up, and I eventually asked her out.

Her name was Simone Cécile Posner, and we were married at the Liberal Jewish Synagogue, St John's Wood on the 7th of August 1977, and afterwards we had a catered reception at BAFTA, followed by a honeymoon in Paris, and are still married, amazingly, with two now adult sons, at the time of writing.

So there you are. If you happen to have a bottle of champagne in your refrigerator, take it out, add orange juice to make a Buck's Fizz if you wish, and join me in toasting the memories of all of those good people that you have just read about. Let's drink to our bygone friends on *The Prisoner* first of all: Here's to Patrick McGoohan, Don Chaffey, Bernie Williams, Geoff Foot, Lee Doig, Pat Jackson, Bob Asher, George Markstein, Frank Maher, Jack Shampan, Gino Marotta, Jack Lowin, Bob Dearberg, Doris Martin, Fenella Fielding, and, of course, Mike Billington, bless 'em all, who have all ascended to that ultimate screening room in the sky, and to all those talented others, also, alas, now no longer with us, with whom I had the privilege and the pleasure of once working alongside: George Harrison, Philip Saville, Joe Massot, Val Guest, Jim Roddan, Jim Atkinson, Max Benedict, Rusty

Coppleman, Eric Sykes, and yes, even Michael Winner. And a very special remembrance greeting to Bridget Reiss, forever sorely missed, who managed to make every single day that oh-so-much brighter for her very presence. Cheers, all!

As for me, well, I've been very, very fortunate, not to mention very lucky, and, yes, I guess there probably is enough memory material available for another volume, if requested, but nothing else could really compare with those rare privileged and highly precious days on *The Prisoner*. Nothing ever will. Be seeing you…

-----END OF REEL EIGHT-----

REEL NINE

APPENDICES AND CODA

Tony Sloman : Filmography

1964	Assistant Editor Caledonian Films, London
1964	2nd Assistant Editor *He Who Rides a Tiger*
1964-65	2nd Assistant Editor *Where the Spies Are*
1965	Assistant Editor Army Commercials (Worldwide, C.O.I.)
1965	2nd Assistant Editor *Othello*
1965-66	2nd Assistant Editor and Assistant Sound Editor *One Million Years B.C.*
1966	2nd Assistant Editor and Assistant Sound Editor *The Frozen Dead*
1966	2nd Assistant Editor and Assistant Sound Editor *It!*
1966-67	Film Librarian and Director of Insert Material *The Prisoner* television series: Episodes: "Arrival" "Dance of the Dead" "Checkmate" "The Chimes of Big Ben" "Once Upon a Time…" "The Schizoid Man" "A Change of Mind" "A,B, and C" "It's Your Funeral" "The General" "Hammer into Anvil" "Many Happy Returns"
1967	Assistant Dialogue Editor *I'll Never Forget What's 'isname*
1967	Assistant Editor (U.S. versions) *Thunderbirds* television series
1967	Assistant Editor *Tell Me Lies*
1967	Assistant Sound Editor *Oedipus the King*
1967-68	Assistant Editor *Wonderwall*

1968 Assistant Dialogue Editor
Chitty Chitty Bang Bang

1968 Editor
San Francisco

1968-69 Sound Editor
Strange Report television series
Episodes:
Report 5055: Cult "Murder Shrieks Out"
Report 1553: Racist "A Most Dangerous Proposal"
Report 2493: Kidnap "Whose Pretty Girl Are You?"
Report 7931: Sniper "When is Your Cousin Not?"
Report 4977: Swindle "Square Root of Evil"
Report 8944: Hand "A Matter of Witchcraft"
Report 4821: X-Ray "Who Weeps for the Doctor?"
Report 2641: Hostage "If You Won't Learn, Die"

1969 Editor
The Festival Game

1969 Sound Editor
De Sade

1969 Sound Editor
Ride the White Horses

1969 Editor and Sound Editor
Rhubarb

1970 Director, Editor, Co-scriptwriter
Sweet and Sexy (a.k.a. *Foursome*)

1970-71 Director
Not Tonight, Darling!

1971 Editor Television Commercials:-
Twix, Fragonade, Curly-Wurly, Mon Cheri.

1971 Sound Editor
The Manipulator (a.k.a. *African Story*)

1972 Director, Script
The Father Christmas Film
(insert for *O Lucky Man!*)

1972 Assistant Editor
Man Alive television series
Episodes: "Could do Better" (i)
"Could do Better" (ii)
"The Right Time to Die"

1972 Co-scriptwriter
Maudric (unrealised)

1971 Assistant Editor
Panorama

1972 Editor
World Cinema : Pandora's Box

1972 Editor
Hold It! (uncompleted)

1972 Co-scriptwriter
Kiss Yesterday Goodbye (unrealised)

1972	2nd Assistant Editor *Vault of Horror*	
1972-73	Assistant Sound Editor and Assistant Editor *Son of Dracula*	
1973	Assistant Editor *Man Alive* television series Episode: "Pop into Your Local Before it Disappears"	
1973	Assistant Editor *Tuesday Documentary*: "The Big Eat"	
1973	Sound Editor *Man in the Woods*	
1973	Sound Editor *Tuesday Documentary*: "Graham Hill's Shadow"	
1973	Sound Editor *Orson Welles' Great Mysteries* series Episodes:	 "Battle of Wits" "Come into my Parlour" "A Terribly Strange Bed" "The Monkey's Paw" "The Dinner Party" "The Inspiration of Mr. Budd" "Captain Rogers" "La Grande Breteche" "For Sale – Silence" "Unseen Alibi" "Death of an Old-Fashioned Girl"
1973	Editor *Orson Welles' Great Mysteries* series Orson Welles' first thirteen narrations	
1973	Sound Editor *Money with Menaces*	
1973	Editor *An Invitation to the Wedding of HRH Princess Anne and Captain Mark Phillips*	
1973	Sound Editor and Post-Production Supervisor *The Big Cats of Africa*	
1974	Sound Editor *Weekend Guest*	
1974	Editor ILEA productions for ETV: *Social Studies: Teaching* *Social Science for Teachers* *Parents Need to Know: Schools* *Parents Need to Know: The Parent's Role* *Persuasion II* *Tooting Police Station* *North London Polytechnic* *My Street, Your Street* *Loaded Language*	

1974	Assistant Editor *Can You Keep It Up For A Week?*
1974	Editor *Can You Keep It Up For A Week?* X trailer *Can You Keep It Up For A Week?* U trailer
1974	Sound Effects Editor *'Nasty' Nastase*
1974	Assistant Sound Effects Editor *Children of Rage*
1974	Sound Editor *The Way South*
1974	Editor *Canterbury Walk*
1975	Editor *One Road Leads to London*
1975	Editor *Vanessa Redgrave's Nursery School*
1975	Assembly Editor and Sound Editor *The Economist*
1975	Editor *Keep Britain in Europe* Programme 1 *Keep Britain in Europe* Programme 2
1975	Sound Editor *Watch Out!*
1975	Screenplay and Co-original story *Walk Into My Past* (unrealised)
1975	Sound Editor *The Memory of Justice*
1975	Editor *Alice Cooper: Welcome to my Nightmare*
1975	Screenplay *The Marvellous Land of Oz* (unrealised)
1975-76	Assistant Editor *John and the Magic Music Man*
1976	Assistant Editor *Circasia*
1976	Screenplay *Poison in the Mind* (unrealised)
1976	Assistant Dialogue Editor *The Pink Panther Strikes Again*
1976	Assistant Sound Editor *The Author of Beltraffio*
1976	Trailer Scriptwriter *The Eagle Has Landed*
1976	Sound Editor *Summer of '76: The Fun of the Fair*
1976	Assistant Editor *The Last Remake of 'Beau Geste'*

1977	Editor *British Airways Leisure Flight*
1977	Assistant Sound Effects Editor *Valentino*
1977	Assistant Editor *Where We Live* Programme 4 *Where We Live* Programme 10 *Where We Live* Programme 12 *Where We Live* Programme 14
1977	Sound Editor *The Cat and the Canary*
1977	Editor *Where We Live* Programme 15: "Around and About"
1977	Screenplay *Strangers* (unrealised)
1977	Sound Editor *Perkembangan Alamiah* (*Natural Development*)
1977	Additional Assistant Editor *The Big Sleep*
1977	Associate Record Album Co-ordinator *Equus*
1977	Additional Assistant Editor *Caravans*
1977	Screen Treatment *Magpie* (unrealised)
1977	Sound Editor *Count Dracula*
1977-78	Sound Editor *The Class of Miss McMichael*
1978	Sound Editor *Son of Hitler* (a.k.a. *Hitler's Son*)
1978	Sound Editor *Summer of My German Soldier*
1978	Screenplay *Partners* (unrealised)
1979	Editor *Radio On*
1979	Screenplay *The Great Oregon Kidnap Caper* (uncompleted)
1979	Trailer Editor *Zulu Dawn*
1979	English Dialogue Editor *Deathwatch*
1979	Editor *Trucking*
1980	Post-Production Supervisor *European Folk Tales*

1980	Editor German television commercials: "Sport Billy", "Shuard", Spielzeitung"
1980	Screen Treatment and Adaptation *Moonlighting* (unrealised)
1980	Dialogue Editor TV Version *The Rose*
1980	Trailer Script and Trailer Editor *Prostitute*
1980	Trailer Editor *The Long Good Friday*
1980	Post-Production Supervisor and Director Arabic Versions *Go for Goal!* (Films 1 to 8)
1980	Editor, Trailer Script and Trailer Editor *Dance Craze*
1981	Additional Sound Editor *Shock Treatment*
1980	Screen Treatment and Adaptation *Empress Josephine* (unrealised)
1981	Editor *Making Merry*
1981	Editor Artiste's Tests (Ingrid Bergman) *A Woman Called Golda*
1981	Director Teaser Trailer *The Mouse and the Woman*
1981	Editor *The Visit*
1981	Producer/Co-screenplay/Co-original story *O to be in England* (unrealised)
1981	Additional Assistant Editor *The Secret Policeman's Other Ball*
1981	U.K. Casting Director *You Asked for It!*
1981	Release Script Editor *Blood Tide*
1982	Associate Producer *The Merry Widow* (unrealised)
1982	Promo Scriptwriter and Promo Editor *The Nutcracker*
1982	Editor *Workseekers*
1982	Finalist *Film Buff of the Year 1982*
1982	Sound Editor and Trailer Editor *Ascendency*

1982	Editor
	Television Commercials:
	Hartley's Strawberry Jam
	McCain Morjuice
	Steiner Furniture
	Cadbury's Dairy Milk Chocolate
1982	Editor
	Almonds and Raisins
1982	English Dialogue Editor
	Tenebrae
1982	Sound Editor and Post-Production Supervisor
	Palms and Dates
1982	Editor for RAI
	Pterydactyl
	Thermography
1982	English Dialogue Editor
	The Scarlet and the Black
1983	Editor
	Starship
1983	Co-screenplay
	White Edge (unrealised)
1983	Additional Sound Editor
	The Bounty
1983	Editor for RAI TV
	The New Swinging London
	Paula Fille Della Torre
	Wrong Mothers and Daughters
	Profumo
	Magic Eye
	Pubs
1983	Sound Editor
	Man on the Screen
1983	Editor Teaser Trailer
	Supergirl
1983	Editor Teaser Trailer
	Lionman II – The Witchqueen
1983	Dialogue Editor
	The Master of Ballantrae
1984	Sound Editor
	Where is Parsifal?
1984	Supervising Dubbing Editor
	The Company of Wolves
1984	Sound Effects Editor and Sound Editor TV version
	Mata Hari
1984-85	Dubbing Editor
	Shadey
1985	Dubbing Editor
	Billy the Kid and the Green Baize Vampire
1985-86	Dubbing Editor
	Act of Vengeance

1986	Co-Screenwriter *Art Attack* (unrealised)
1986	Dubbing Editor *Born of Fire*
1986	Screenplays *Catwalk* (unrealised) *Fifth Avenue* (unrealised)
1986	Editor *The Pink Floyd : On The Run*
1986	Elected Members' Governor The British Film Institute
1986-87	Dubbing Editor *Empire State*
1987	National Film Theatre Programmer *Sondheim on Film* (season)
1987	Guardian Lecture Interviewer Stephen Sondheim
1987-88	Sound Editor *The Fruit Machine* (U.S. title *Wonderland*)
1988	National Film Theatre Programmer *Marilyn Monroe and her Generation* (Three-part season)
1988	National Film Theatre Programmer *Meet Whiplash Walter* (season)
1988	Guardian Lecture Interviewer Walter Matthau
1988	Guardian Lecture Interviewer Mickey Rooney
1988	National Film Theatre Programmer *Robert Morley : The Englishman's Englishman*
1988	Guardian Lecture Interviewer Robert Morley
1988	Dubbing Editor *The Last Warrior*
1988	Museum of the Moving Image Programmer *Directors One to One* : David Lean and Hugh Hudson
1988	Editor Main Title Sequence *The Last Emperor* (German version)
1988	National Film Theatre Programmer *David Lean : Director's Director*
1988	Guardian Lecture Interviewer Sir David Lean

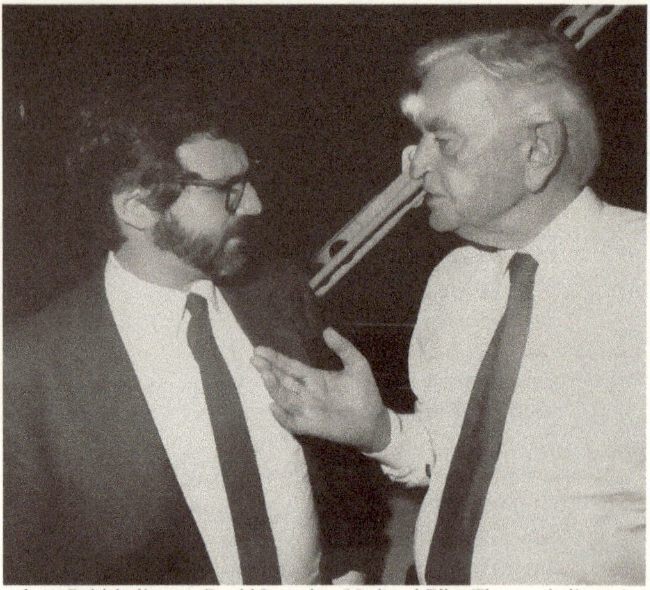

I got to programme my hero British director David Lean in a National Film Theatre dedicated season which I curated. Here we are conferring after I interviewed Sir David on the NFT stage.

1988	Dialogue Editor *Tank Malling*
1989	Dubbing Editor *London's Burning* Series II
1989	National Film Theatre Programmer *Feet First : The Choreographer as Director – Busby Berkeley to Bob Fosse and Beyond* (Parts 1, 2, and 3)

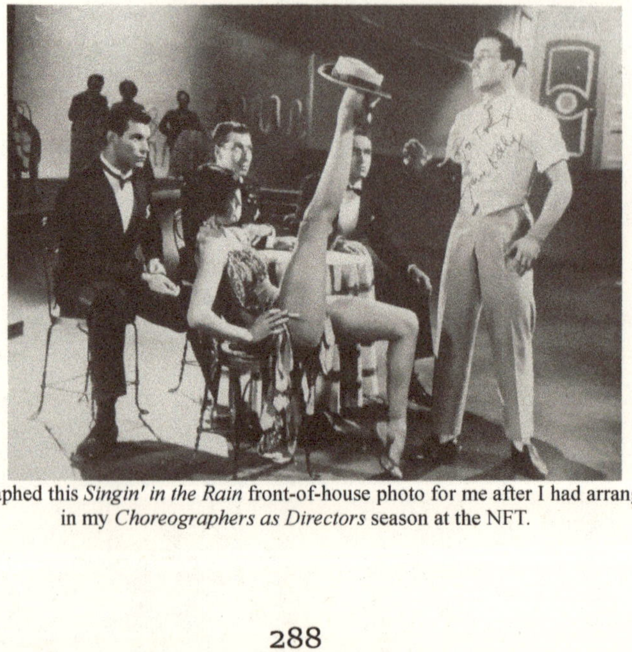

Gene Kelly autographed this *Singin' in the Rain* front-of-house photo for me after I had arranged his section in my *Choreographers as Directors* season at the NFT.

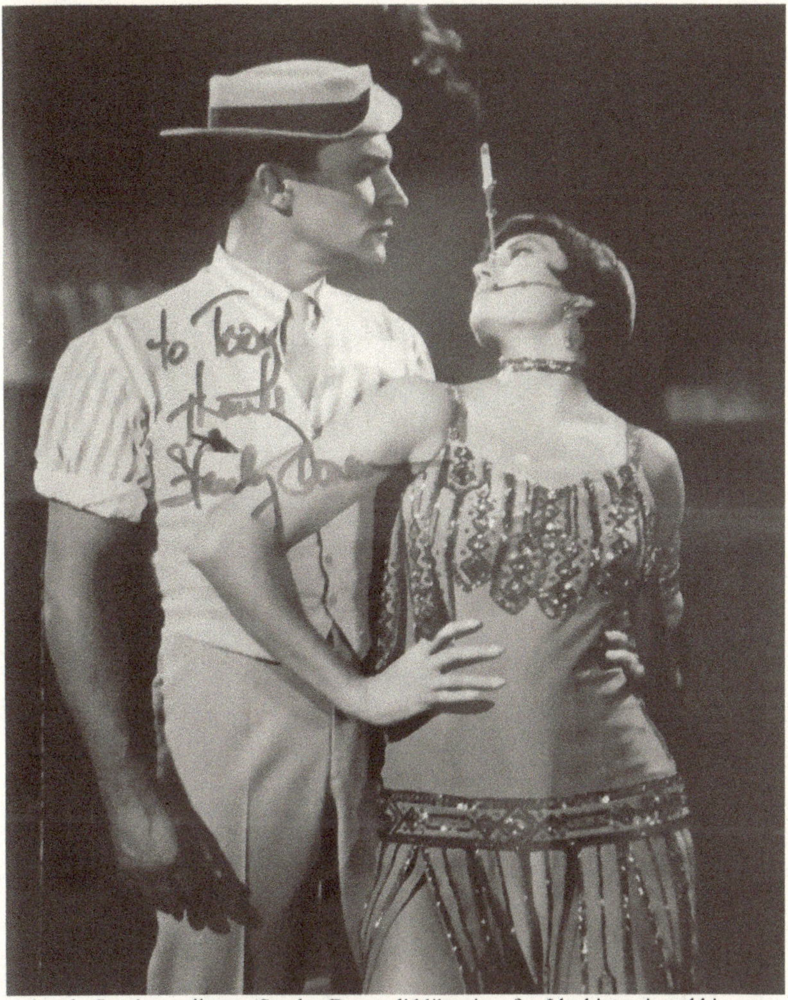

And *Singin' in the Rain*'s co-director Stanley Donen did likewise after I had interviewed him on stage, also at the NFT. I had the opportunity of telling both Kelly and Donen that I thought *Singin' in the Rain* not just my own favourite film but easily the best motion picture ever made.

1989	Sound Editor *Istanbul*
1989	Museum of the Moving Image Programmer *Directors One on One : John Schlesinger and Jack Gold*
1989	Screenplay Co-writer *Atlantis* (unrealised)
1989	National Film Theatre Interviewer Richard Todd

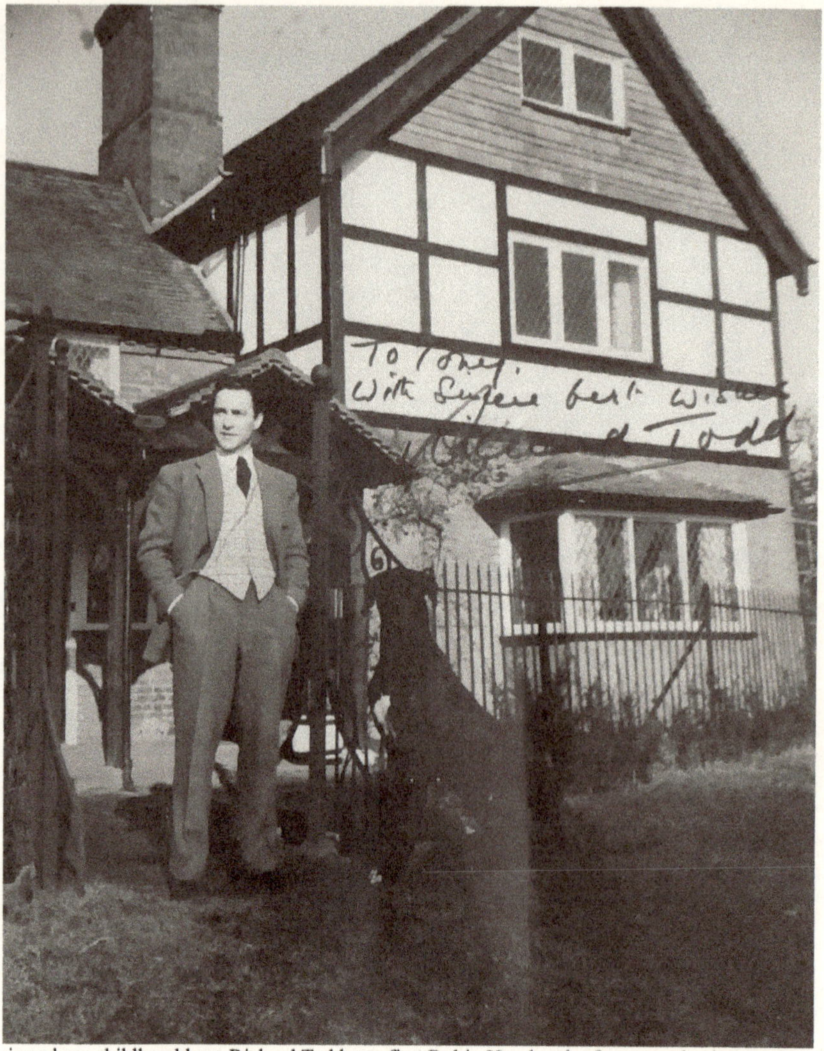

I interviewed my childhood hero Richard Todd, my first Robin Hood and, of course, also known for portraying "Dam Buster" Guy Gibson, on the NFT stage, too, and did a couple of radio broadcasts with him.

1989	Museum of the Moving Image Programmer
	Directors One on One : Robert Parrish and Clive Donner
1989	National Film Theatre Programmer
	Midsummer Music 1 : A Busby Berkeley Bonus
	Midsummer Music 2 : An MGM Cavalcade
1989	Editor
	Absolut Vodka : Absolut Silence
1989	National Film Theatre Programmer
	People We Like : Terence Stamp
1989	Guardian Lecture Interviewer
	Terence Stamp

1989	Screen treatment co-author *Go Away, Little Girl* (unrealised)
1989	Editor BBC programmes *Anarchist Rap, Safe Sex, Battered Women*
1989	Editor *Maggie's Secret* (a.k.a. *The Rape*) (uncompleted)
1989	Guardian Lecture Interviewer Stanley Donen
1989	National Film Theatre Programmer *The Steven Spielberg Factory* (Parts 1 and 2)
1989	Museum of the Moving Image Programmer *Directors Talking to Directors: Bertrand Tavernier and Peter Duffell*
1989	Editor BBC Training Films *Clingfilm* and *Reebok*
1990	Broadcaster for BBC Radio Scotland *Head On – Reputations : The Marx Brothers*
1990	Editor *Funeral Games*
1990	Co-author *A Chronicle of the Movies*
1990	Broadcaster/Writer for The Derek Jameson Show *Movietime*: Frank Sinatra Esther Williams Gary Cooper Ann Miller Glenn Ford Charles Walters Hal B. Wallis Debbie Reynolds
1990	Promo Script and Editor *A Rage in Harlem*
1990	Promo Script and Editor *A Woman at War*
1990	Guardian Lecture Interviewer Ann Miller
1990	Broadcaster/Writer *Christmas at the Movies*
1991	Broadcaster/Writer for The Derek Jameson Show *Movietime:* Judy Holliday Richard Widmark Sal Mineo Jane Powell Danny Kaye
1991	Editor *Lost in Siberia*
1991	Editor/Co-Producer *Assassin of the Tsar*

1991	Additional Editor *The Cursed Days in Russia are Back Again*
1992	Trailer Script and Trailer Editor *Lost in Siberia*
1992	Trailer Script and Trailer Editor *Assassin of the Tsar*
1991-92	Executive in Charge of Production Spectator Films U.K. Producer: *The Cherry Orchard* (unrealised) *Trotsky* (unrealised)
1992	Producer/Screenwriter/Original Story *Toymaker : The Legend of Father Christmas* (unrealised as yet)
1992	Producer/Writer/Editor *Celluloid Phoenix – the 25th Anniversary of the Cannes' Directors' Fortnight* (uncompleted)
1992	Elected Members' Governor (Second term) The British Film Institute
1993	Associate Producer *Wake Up World*
1993	Broadcaster/Writer *The Musical World of George Sidney* *The Musical World of Michael Curtiz* *The Musical World of Arthur Freed*
1993	Contributor/Co-Author *Enter the Dream House*
1994	Editor *The Bad Seed*
1994	Post-Production Supervisor *All Men Are Mortal*
1994	Supervising Editor and Post-Production Supervisor *Jamila*
1994	EPK Producer *Haunted*
1994	Guardian Lecture Interviewer and National Film Theatre Season Programmer Lewis Gilbert
1995	Director and Interviewer *The Prince of Wales' Business Leaders' Forum Partnership Symposium at the Commonwealth Institute*
1995	Sound Effects Editor *Talk of Angels*
1995	Feature Films on Television Reviewer *Radio Times* (1995 to current)
1995	Course Lecturer Birkbeck College, University of London "Post-War European Cinema (1945-present)".
1995	Post-Production Supervisor *Space Truckers*
1996	Associate Producer and Editor *Vol-au-Vent*

1996	Production Supervisor *Devil's Harvest*
1996	Post-Production Supervisor *Bolt*
1996	Assistant Dialogue Editor *'B' Monkey*
1996	Post-Production Supervisor *Driftwood*
1996	Trailer Script and Trailer Editor *Driftwood*
1996	Production co-financier *Rhythm and Blues*
1997	Editor and Associate Producer *Hard Edge*
1997	Post-Production Dialogue Editor *Killing Time*
1997	Additional Dialogue Editor *Clockwatchers*
1997	Lecturer, Anamorphic Symposium at Pinewood Studios *CinemaScope and Beyond*
1997	Post-Production Editor *No Way Home*
1997	Production Budget *Not Their England* (unrealised)
1997	U.K. Promoter Compugraf, Istanbul
1997	Editor *Alone*
1997	Lecturer at University of Bristol *Visions of Light : Cinematography*
1997	U.K. Production Executive *Debris* (uncompleted)
1997	U.K. shipping agent *Seven Years in Tibet* *Donnie Brasco*
1997	Editor *BFI Fellowships :* Sydney Samuelson Bernardo Bertolucci Thelma Schoonmaker
1997	Sleeve Writer MGM Home Entertainment, Warner Home Video *MGM Greats, MGM Westerns, MGM War, MGM Epics*
1998	Post-Production Supervisor and Risk Manager *Married to Malcolm*
1998	Risk Manager *Something to Believe In*
1998	Risk Manager *Looking For An Echo*
1998	Post-Production Adviser *Gunblast Vodka*

1998	Risk Manager/Production Executive *Dark Summer* (a.k.a. *Innocents*)
1998	Risk Manager *Monster by Mistake* (Television series)
1998	Risk Manager *Kimberley*
1998	Risk Manager *A Map of the World*
1998	Risk Manager *Special Delivery*
1998	Risk Manager *Daring and Grace – Teen Detectives* (Television Series)
1998	Post-Production Titles Editor *Dancing at Lughnasa*
1999	Risk Manager *Back to Sherwood* (Television series)
1999	Risk Manager *A Rumor of Angels*
1999	Risk Manager *Monster by Mistake* (Television series)
1999	Broadcaster *What a Carry On!*
2000	Script Editor *Strokes* (unrealised)
2000	Risk Manager *Green Sails*
2000	Risk Manager *Graham Kerr's Gathering Place* (Television series)
2000	Co-Risk Manager *The Visual Bible* Episodes : "Mark", "Luke", and "John" (uncompleted)
2001	Risk Manager/Production Executive *The Dinosaur Hunter*
2001	Co-Producer *Johnny Hit-and-Run Pauline* (unrealised)
2001	Co-Producer *A Walk in the Sun* (unrealised)
2001	Post-Production Executive *To End All Wars*
2001	Co-Producer *Toscano* (unrealised)
2001	Script Editor *Money to Burn* (unrealised)
2001	Post-Production Executive *Fascination*
2001	Broadcaster/Interviewer (BBC2) *Living Famously : Vivien Leigh* *Living Famously : Clark Gable*
2001	U.K. Co-Producer *Precious* (unrealised)

2002	Visual Effects Producer *Sherlock* (a.k.a. *Case of Evil*)
2002	U.K. Producer *The Baker Street Irregulars* (unrealised)
2002	Promo Producer *The Living Dead* (uncompleted)
2002	Producer/Interviewer *More Bang for the Buck*
2002	Producer *Love/Sick* (unrealised)
2002	U.K. Producer *Tarrant on TV* (for Nordisk)
2002	U.K. Producer *Family Flaw*
2002	U.K. Producer *Tale of a Dog*
2003	Editor and Post-Production Supervisor *Souli* (a.k.a. *Le Dernier Souffle*)
2003	Post-Production Executive *The St. Petersburg-Cannes Express* (uncompleted)
2003	Post-Production Executive *Belle*
2004	Post-Production Executive *Blessed*
2004	Elected Member The International Academy of Widescreen (National Film and Photography Museum Bradford)
2004	Visual Effects Producer *Summer in the Golden Valley*
2004	Producer *Gatecrash* (unrealised)
2004	Producer *Doctor Blood* (unrealised)
2004	Lecturer (for WEA) *Palaces of Dreams : Picture and Sound*
2004	*World Movie Magazine* writer Sunset & Wardour weekly column
2004	Programmer for the 1st Dubai International Film Festival *Tribute to Omar Sharif*
2005	Editorial Consultant *Backwaters*
2005	London International Film School Lecturer in Post-Production
2005	U.K. Producer *C'est pas moi, C'est L'autre*
2005	Co-Producer *A Tribute to Otto Plaschkes* (BAFTA)
2006	Promo Director *Mary Read*

2006	Promo Director *Moll Flanders*
2006	Co-scriptwriter *Nightingale* (unrealised)
2006	Supervising Editor *Lost in Siberia – The New Edition*
2006	U.K. Producer *The Devil's Chair*
2007	Supervising Editor *Tied to a Chair* (a.k.a. *Spring in her Step*, also a.k.a. *Springtime in Autumn*)
2007	Production Budget *Tovarich, I am not Dead*

… and so, from 2007, as related, I began to give lectures on cruise ships, almost continuously, as a result of Eric Mival, music editor on *The Prisoner* no less, introducing me to Harry Davis, who was responsible for my being introduced to an agent who booked lecturers for luxury cruise ocean liners, and I have been doing so ever since, having now completed well over sixty such voyages, and all because of my friendship with Eric Mival, on that much-loved and well-respected television series entitled *The Prisoner* oh-so-many years ago : I have much to be thankful for. What to add? Well… Be Seeing You... everywhere!

Three lists, in conclusion:-

ALL-TIME TOP TEN FILMS

Singin' in the Rain
Citizen Kane
Scaramouche (1952)
Rio Bravo
Red River
Meet Me in St. Louis
Spartacus
Casablanca
Gone with the Wind
Rebel Without a Cause

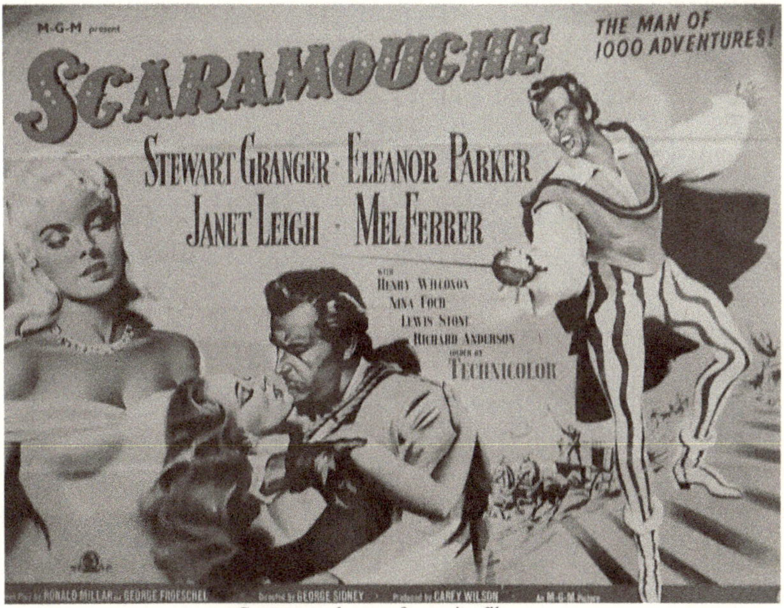

Scaramouche, my favourite film.

ALL-TIME TOP TEN TV SHOWS

The Prisoner (1966-67)
Elvis Presley : The '68 Comeback Special
Elvis Presley : Aloha from Hawaii
Oh Boy!
Boy Meets Girls
Wham!
6.5 Special
That Was The Week That Was
The Big Bang Theory
Whack-O!

SIGNIFICANT MAY 6TH BIRTHDAYS

TOP TEN

Sigmund Freud (1856)
Orson Welles (1915)
Stewart Granger (1913)
Rudolph Valentino (1895)
Max Ophuls (1902)
George Clooney (1961)
Ross Hunter (1920)
Maximilian Robespierre (1758)
Simone C. Sloman (1949)
Anthony B. Sloman (1945)

...1945? Well now, this is surely: -- "Where We Came In"... BCNU, Tony S.

-----END OF REEL NINE-----

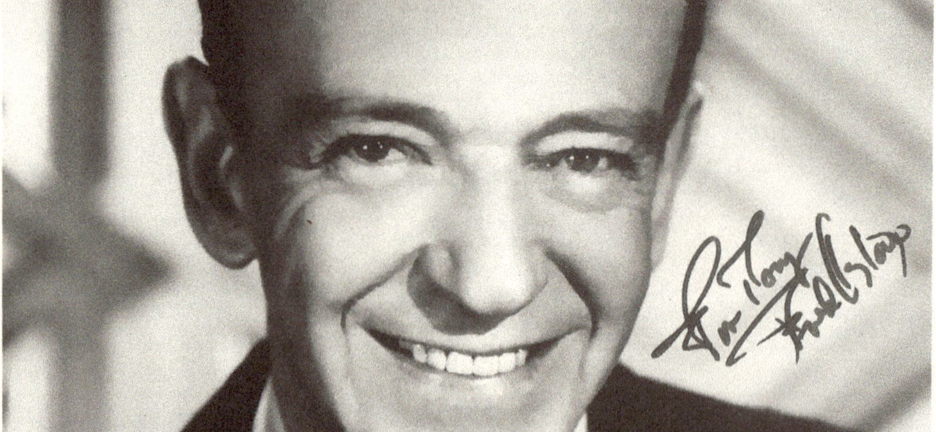

Sometimes, if you're very fortunate, you get to meet your heroes...

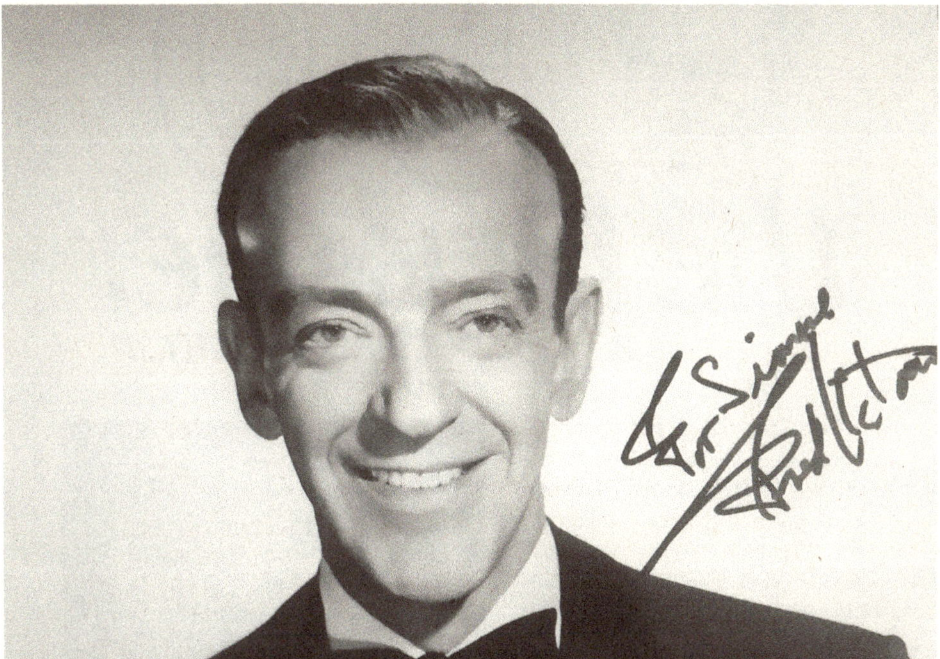

Simone managed to arrange our both meeting the screen's greatest-ever dance star (Gene Kelly duly acknowledged) when she worked at the BBC, after Astaire did an on-stage interview with Michael Parkinson, and Mr.Astaire couldn't have been nicer....